Published by MathsGroundWork
http://www.mathsgroundwork.co.uk

© PD Burnett 2015
This publication is copyright. No reproduction of any part may take place without the written permission of the publisher.

First published 2014
Printed in the United Kingdom
Typeface Frutiger Neue 11pt

The publisher has used its best endeavours to ensure that URL's for external websites referred to in this book are correct and active at the time of going to press. However, we have no responsibility for external or third-party websites referred to in this publication and can make no guarantee that any such content will remain active or that the content will remain accurate and appropriate. The cartoon above, is courtesy of xkcd at http://xkcd.com/

## Physical Constants

| Quantity | Symbol | Value |
|---|---|---|
| speed of light in a vacuum | c | 299792458 m s$^{-1}$ |
| permittivity of free space | $\varepsilon_o$ | 8.854 187 817.. x 10$^{-12}$ F m$^{-1}$ |
| permeability of free space | $\mu_o$ | 4π x 10$^{-7}$ H m$^{-1}$ |
| universal gravitation constant | G | 6.674 x 10$^{-11}$ m$^3$ kg$^{-1}$ s$^{-2}$ |
| Planck's constant | h | 6.626 070 x 10$^{-34}$ J s |
| elementary charge (like electron) | e | 1.602 176 x 10$^{-19}$ C |
| fine structure constant | α | 7.297 352 57 x 10$^{-3}$ |
| Böhr radius |  | 0.529 177 211 x 10$^{-10}$ m |
| electron mass | $m_e$ | 9.109 383 x 10$^{-31}$ kg |
| proton mass | $m_p$ | 1.672 622 x 10$^{-27}$ kg |
| neutron mass | $m_n$ | 1.674 927 x 10$^{-27}$ kg |
| alpha particle mass | $m_\alpha$ | 6.644 657 x 10$^{-27}$ kg |
| atomic mass unit | u | 1.660 5389 x 10$^{-27}$ kg |
| Stefan-Boltzmann constant | σ | 5.670 37 x 10$^{-8}$ W m$^{-2}$ K$^{-4}$ |
| Boltzmann's constant | k | 1.380 650 x 10$^{-23}$ J K$^{-1}$ |
| Avogadro's constant | $N_A$ | 6.022 141 x 10$^{23}$ mol$^{-1}$ |

## Earth, Moon, Sun

| | |
|---|---|
| Earth's Mean Radius | 6372.797 km |
| Earth's Mass | 5.9737 x 10$^{24}$ kg |
| Period of Earth's Orbit (the sidereal year) | 365.25636042 days = 3.155815 x 10$^7$ s |
| Earth's Rotation Period (sidereal day) | 23 hr 56min 04.0905s |
| Radius of Moon (equatorial) | 1737.4 km |
| Mass of Moon | 7.3477 x 10$^{22}$ kg |
| Radius of Sun (equatorial) | 6.955 x 10$^8$ m |
| Mass of Sun | 1.989 x 10$^{30}$ kg |
| Mean Earth-Moon distance | 3.844 x 10$^8$ m |
| Astronomical Unit (A.U.) | 1.49597870696 x 10$^{11}$ m |
| Distance of 1 light-year | 9.4605284 x 10$^{15}$ m |

## Solar System

| Object | Mass (kg) | Mean Distance to Sun (m) | Mean radius (km) | Rotation period (days) | Orbital Period (days) |
|---|---|---|---|---|---|
| Mercury | 3.303 x 10$^{23}$ | 5.791 x 10$^{10}$ | 2439.7 | 58.6462 | 87.97 |
| Venus | 4.869 x 10$^{24}$ | 1.082 x 10$^{11}$ | 6051.8 | -243.0187 | 224.7 |
| Earth | 5.974 x 10$^{24}$ | 1.496 x 10$^{11}$ | 6373 | 0.99727 | 365.26 |
| Mars | 6.419 x 10$^{23}$ | 2.279 x 10$^{11}$ | 3394 | 1.025957 | 686.97 |
| Jupiter | 1.899 x 10$^{27}$ | 7.785 x 10$^{11}$ | 71492 | 0.41354 | 4333 |
| Saturn | 5.688 x 10$^{26}$ | 1.433 x 10$^{12}$ | 60268 | 0.44401 | 10759 |
| Uranus | 8.681 x 10$^{25}$ | 2.877 x 10$^{12}$ | 25559 | -0.71833 | 30799 |
| Neptune | 1.024 x 10$^{26}$ | 4.503 x 10$^{12}$ | 24550 | 0.67125 | 60190 |
| Pluto | 1.303 x 10$^{22}$ | 5.914 x 10$^{12}$ | 1187 | -6.3872 | 89866 |
| Eris | 1.67 x 10$^{22}$ | 1.012 x 10$^{13}$ | 1163 | ≈1 | 204870 |

# Contents page

## Unit 1 Rotational Motion & Astrophysics

1.1   Kinematic relationships   5

1.2   Angular motion   10

1.3   Rotational dynamics   27

1.4   Gravitation   50

1.5   Space and Time   73

1.6   Stellar Physics   85

## Unit 2 Quanta and Waves

2.1   Quantum Theory   97

2.2   Particles from Space   111

2.3   Simple Harmonic Motion   122

2.4   Travelling Waves   131

2.5   Interference   138

2.6   Polarisation   151

## Unit 3 Electromagnetism

3.1a   Electric Fields   156

3.1b   Magnetic Fields   176

3.2a   Capacitors   189

3.2b   Inductors   193

3.3   Electromagnetic Radiation   202

## Equations for Unit 1

$v = \dfrac{ds}{dt}$ $\qquad a = \dfrac{dv}{dt} = \dfrac{d^2s}{dt^2}$ $\qquad v = u + at$ $\qquad s = ut + \dfrac{1}{2}at^2$ $\qquad v^2 = u^2 + 2as$

$\omega = \dfrac{d\theta}{dt}$ $\qquad \alpha = \dfrac{d\omega}{dt} = \dfrac{d^2\theta}{dt^2}$ $\qquad \omega = \omega_o + \alpha t$ $\qquad \theta = \omega_o t + \dfrac{1}{2}\alpha t^2$ $\qquad \omega^2 = \omega_o^2 + 2\alpha\theta$

$s = r\theta$ $\qquad v = r\omega$ $\qquad a_t = r\alpha$ $\qquad a_r = \dfrac{v^2}{r} = r\omega^2$ $\qquad F = \dfrac{mv^2}{r} = mr\omega^2$

$T = rF$ $\qquad T = I\alpha$ $\qquad L = mvr = mr^2\omega$ $\qquad L = I\omega$ $\qquad E_K = \dfrac{1}{2}I\omega^2$

$F = \dfrac{GMm}{r^2}$ $\qquad V = -\dfrac{GM}{r}$ $\qquad v = \sqrt{\dfrac{2GM}{r}}$ $\qquad b = \dfrac{L_{um}}{4\pi r^2}$ $\qquad W = \sigma T^4$

$L_{um} = 4\pi r^2 \sigma T^4$ $\qquad r_{Sch} = \dfrac{2GM}{c^2}$

## Equations for Unit 2

$E = hf$ $\qquad \lambda = \dfrac{h}{p}$ $\qquad mvr = \dfrac{nh}{2\pi}$ $\qquad \Delta x \, \Delta p_x \geq \dfrac{h}{4\pi}$ $\qquad \Delta E \, \Delta t \geq \dfrac{h}{4\pi}$

$F = qvB$ $\qquad \omega = 2\pi f$ $\qquad \phi = \dfrac{2\pi x}{\lambda}$ $\qquad \Delta x = \dfrac{\lambda l}{2d}$ $\qquad d = \dfrac{\lambda}{4n}$

$\Delta x = \dfrac{\lambda D}{d}$ $\qquad n = \tan i_P$ $\qquad y = A\sin\omega t$ $\qquad a = \dfrac{d^2y}{dt^2} = -\omega^2 y$ $\qquad v = \pm\omega\sqrt{(A^2 - y^2)}$

$E_K = \dfrac{1}{2}m\omega^2(A^2 - y^2)$ $\qquad E_P = \dfrac{1}{2}m\omega^2 y^2$ $\qquad y = A\sin 2\pi\left(ft - \dfrac{x}{\lambda}\right)$

## Equations for Unit 3

$F = \dfrac{Q_1 Q_2}{4\pi\varepsilon_o r^2}$ $\qquad E = \dfrac{Q}{4\pi\varepsilon_o r^2}$ $\qquad V = \dfrac{Q}{4\pi\varepsilon_o r}$ $\qquad F = qE$ $\qquad V = Ed$

$F = BIL\sin\theta$ $\qquad B = \dfrac{\mu_o I}{2\pi r}$ $\qquad c = \dfrac{1}{\sqrt{\varepsilon_o \mu_o}}$ $\qquad t = CR$ $\qquad X_C = \dfrac{V}{I} = \dfrac{1}{\omega C} = \dfrac{1}{2\pi fC}$

$V = -L\dfrac{dI}{dt}$ $\qquad E = \dfrac{1}{2}LI^2$ $\qquad X_L = \dfrac{V}{I} = \omega L = 2\pi fL$

# Rotational Motion & Astrophysics

## Section 1.1 Kinematic Relationships

Physics describes the world in terms of physical quantities (like momentum and electric charge), constants (like the speed of light) and the relations between them (like $F = ma$). Studying physics would be a lot simpler if all physical quantities were completely described by real numbers and a unit. Some of them are, like temperature and mass. These are the scalar quantities which you can add and subtract as you did in primary school. One electron has a charge of -1.6 x $10^{-19}$ C, two electrons have a combined charge of -3.2 x $10^{-19}$ C.

Some quantities, like force and momentum, require directions. Called vectors, they need more care in adding and subtracting. Unlike scalars, there are two ways of multiplying vectors. One way, called the Dot Product, gives a scalar for the answer. The other way, called the Cross Product, gives a vector for the answer. Some quantities can't be described by either scalars or vectors. A property of a rotating body known as its Moment of Inertia is handled using matrices. The quantum state of an electron is described by a mathematical object which isn't a scalar or a vector. It's called a spinor and requires the use of not just real numbers, but also complex numbers (square root of -1 stuff).

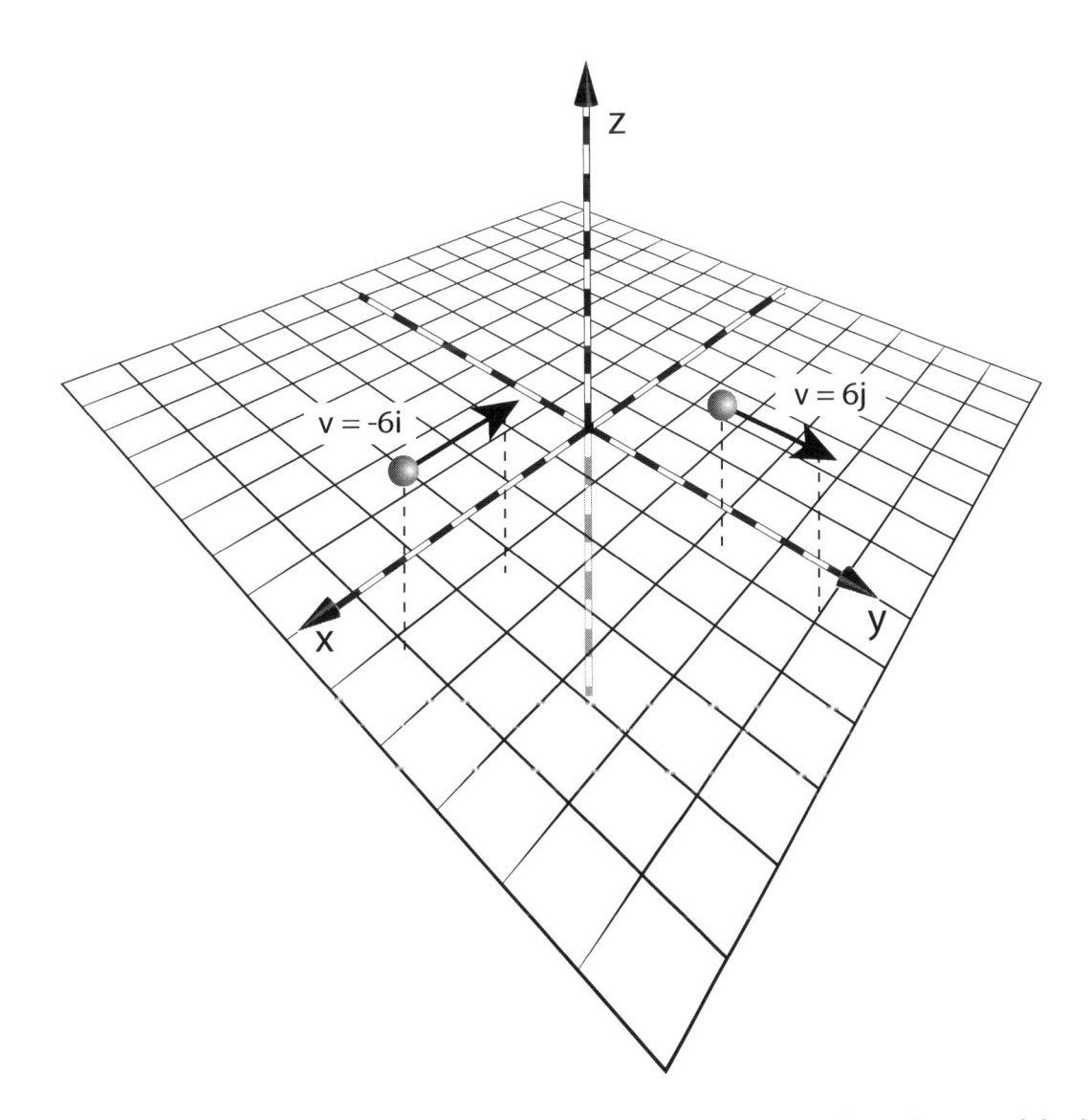

Blame it on the fact that we live in a 3 dimensional space, where we analyse velocity and displacement as in the diagram above using Cartesian coordinates (x,y,z) and unit vectors (i,j,k). If we lived in a 1D space, there would only be an 'x' direction and life would be a lot simpler. In fact, it would be too simple. Like no overtaking in the outside lane, no queue jumping.

So what is Kinematics? What it isn't is a bit of physics; it's just maths. How much money have you got after 10 seconds if you start with £20 in your pocket and £4 is added every second? You'll have £60 in your pocket. That's maths, not physics. Do you need to do an experiment to verify that you have £60? No, you don't. This structure is like accelerating from an initial speed to a final speed in time 't':

£20 → initial speed 'u'    £4 per second → acceleration    £60 → final speed 'v'

The equation behind this is: $v = u + at$ and it may look like physics, but it's maths.

## The Equations of Motion

That equation is one of three you've already learned:

$$v = u + at \qquad s = ut + \frac{1}{2}at^2 \qquad v^2 = u^2 + 2as$$

They're all just maths. I prefer to write the first one in the form: $a = \dfrac{v-u}{t}$ since it reminds me of the simple definition of acceleration; a change of velocity with time. Remember that these equations only work for constant acceleration. They only contain the initial and final velocities with no information about what happens in between; whether its smooth or jerky acceleration.

There is a better way of defining velocity and acceleration using calculus. The beauty of it is that it works for **any** motion, not just for uniform acceleration. To show it in action, we will re-derive the above three equations of motion. Firstly, a reminder about gradients.

The velocity-time graphs you've met so far have been straight lines. This is what constant acceleration gives you. However, suppose the acceleration isn't constant and the velocity-time graph is like the curved one on the right. It's for one dimensional motion in a straight line.

As usual, the slope of the curve is the acceleration, but it changes from point to point and gets steeper as time progresses. The gradient to the curve is shown at time t = 1.5s. You know how to calculate this from your maths class. For a curve given by the equation $y = f(x)$ you differentiate the equation and evaluate the result at the point.

This curve relates 'v' to 't' and is given by the equation: $v = f(t) = 0.8t^2 + 2.4$

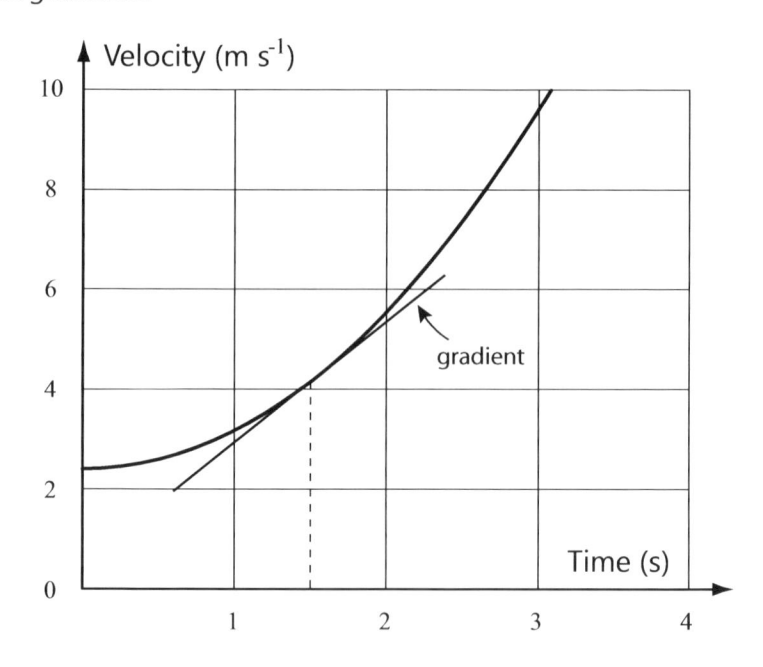

Differentiate the equation to get the acceleration at time 't': $\dfrac{dv}{dt} = 1.6t$

This gives you the gradient of the velocity-time graph for any time 't'. Evaluated at a time of 1.5s it gives a gradient of 1.6 × 1.5 = 2.4 m s$^{-2}$. This differential is our proper definition of acceleration:

$$a = \frac{dv}{dt}$$

This is a better version of our previous definition. Remember that both acceleration and velocity are vectors. Differentiating something with a direction isn't as simple as you might think (see later, page 19, when we consider the acceleration of an object moving in a circle with constant speed).

# Rotational Motion & Astrophysics

The step-up from using equations like $v = u + at$ to their calculus versions was a major advance in physics. Differentials and integrals are the main mathematical tools used in describing our physical world, so try to get comfortable with them and become fluent in their use.

The velocity itself can also be expressed as a differential:

$$v = \frac{ds}{dt}$$

In words, this means that the velocity at any time 't' is the gradient of a displacement - time graph. In your earlier days in physics, you may remember calculating the speed of an object using a timer and meter stick. Measure how much time it takes to travel a certain distance then use the speed equals distance divided by time equation to get the answer. Then your teacher pointed out that this should be called the *average* speed, not just the speed. Measuring the speed as it passed a certain point introduced light gates and rectangular cards. Strictly speaking it wasn't *quite* the speed at a point. It was an average speed over a distance of the card width, but still a vast improvement over hand timers. Using narrower cards with shorter times gets you nearer and nearer to that *speed at a point*, but you never quite get there. Using differentials gets you exactly the speed at a point, not experimentally, but mathematically. Mathematicians would put it this way:

$$v = \lim_{\Delta t \to 0} \frac{\Delta s}{\Delta t} = \frac{ds}{dt}$$

It takes the limit of a narrower and narrower card width Δs with a briefer and briefer time Δt to get the speed when a card of no width would cut the light beam in no time at all! (The Δ symbol is spoken 'delta' and usually denotes a small size). You change from the delta symbol 'Δ' to the 'd' symbol when you take the limit. When it's a delta symbol you still have small but finite sizes, so dividing Δs by Δt makes sense. Once you reduce them to zero, dividing zero (ds) by zero dt isn't allowed. Okay, this is picky and you'll see it done all the time (even by me), but $\frac{ds}{dt}$ shouldn't be separated into two parts as if it was a division. It denotes a single thing.

Here's what the maths looks like in our new definition of acceleration at a point:

$$a = \lim_{u \to v} \frac{(v-u)}{t} = \lim_{\Delta t \to 0} \frac{\Delta v}{\Delta t} = \frac{dv}{dt}$$

The velocity 'v' in this equation can itself be expressed as a differential to relate acceleration with displacement.

$$a = \frac{dv}{dt} = \frac{d}{dt}\left(\frac{ds}{dt}\right) = \frac{d^2 s}{dt^2}$$

The most important equations in physics and engineering are often expressed using these symbols; from Maxwells equations in electromagnetism, to Einstein's equation in General Relativity, to the Diffusion equation in Heat.

# Derivation of the Equations of Motion using Calculus

In Higher Physics you derived the equations of motion from a straight line graph of velocity against time using the slope of the line and the area under the graph:

$$v = u + at \qquad s = ut + \frac{1}{2}at^2 \qquad v^2 = u^2 + 2as$$

Here's how to get the same result using calculus with our new definitions of velocity and acceleration.

7

Taking $\frac{dv}{dt} = a$, and remembering that to find 'v' means "undoing" the derivative, we integrate both sides with respect to 't':

$$dv = adt \quad \Rightarrow \quad \int dv = \int adt = a\int dt$$

$$\int_u^v dv = a\int_0^t dt$$

$$[v]_u^v = a[t]_0^t$$

$$[v-u] = a[t-0]$$

$$\Rightarrow v = u + at$$

When you include the limits on the integral (the 'u' and 'v' on the left integral and the 't' and '0' on the right integral), it's called a definite integral since it has definite limits. If you don't have limits on the integrals, it's called an indefinite integral and you have to add a constant after integration.

Continue in a similar way to derive the displacement:

$$v = \frac{ds}{dt} \quad \Rightarrow \quad ds = vdt$$

$$\int_0^s ds = \int_0^t vdt = \int_0^t (u + at)dt$$

$$[s]_0^s = \left[ut + \tfrac{1}{2}at^2\right]_0^t$$

$$\Rightarrow s = ut + \frac{1}{2}at^2$$

At $t = 0$, the particle is at the origin ($s = 0$) and its initial velocity is 'u'. (If the particle wasn't at the origin at the start of timing, $s = s_o$ at $t = 0$, then the equation would be: $s = s_o + ut + \tfrac{1}{2}at^2$ ).

The third equation of motion is usually derived from the first two with a bit of algebra:

$$t = \frac{(v-u)}{a} \quad \Rightarrow \quad s = ut + \frac{1}{2}at^2 = u\frac{(v-u)}{a} + \frac{1}{2}a\left(\frac{(v-u)}{a}\right)^2$$

$$s = \frac{v^2}{2a} - \frac{u^2}{2a} = \frac{(v^2 - u^2)}{2a} \quad \Rightarrow \quad v^2 = u^2 + 2as$$

Nerds will prefer to derive it using calculus, but scoff at the sloppy maths used along the way (and note that it comes in handy with the Advanced Higher Maths Mechanics syllabus). Like this.......

# Rotational Motion & Astrophysics

Start by decomposing the derivative for acceleration into two parts (putting a *ds* top and bottom):

$$a = \frac{dv}{dt} = \frac{dv}{dt}\frac{ds}{ds} = \frac{dv}{ds}\frac{ds}{dt} = \frac{dv}{ds}v$$

Now 'undo' the derivative: $a\,ds = v\,dv \quad \Rightarrow \quad \int_0^s a\,ds = \int_u^v v\,dv$

$$[as]_0^s = \left[\frac{1}{2}v^2\right]_u^v \quad \Rightarrow \quad as = \frac{1}{2}(v^2 - u^2)$$

$$\Rightarrow \quad v^2 = u^2 + 2as$$

# Using Graphs

Problems can be solved only using equations, but there's something about the way our brains work which makes it easier if we can picture it. Sketch the experimental set-up and / or a graph showing the relationship between two of the quantities. A line drawn on graph paper can give you two things: the area under it down to the x axis, and the slope at a point on the line. The area under it comes from integration and the slope comes from differentiation. Here's an example of non-uniform acceleration.

It's a velocity-time graph of an object whose motion is given by:

$$v = 1.8t^2 - 3t + 5$$

Differentiating the velocity gives the acceleration at any time '*t*':

$$a = \frac{dv}{dt} = 3.6t - 3$$

This is the same as the gradient at any time '*t*'. For example, at 3s the acceleration is 7.8m s$^{-2}$. There is a turning point (zero slope, so no acceleration) at:

$$a = 0 \quad \Rightarrow \quad 3.6t - 3 = 0 \quad \rightarrow \quad t = 0.83s$$

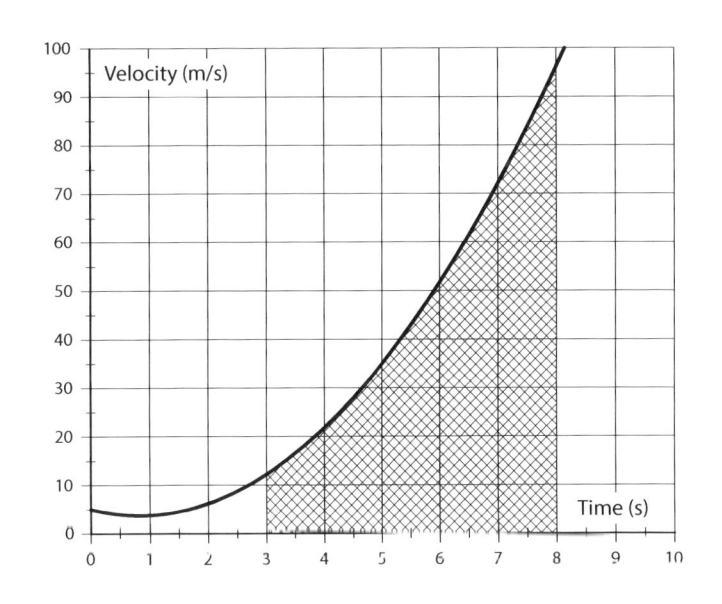

To calculate the displacement, we start from our definition of velocity: $v = \frac{ds}{dt}$, hence $s = \int v\,dt$

For example, to calculate the displacement from a time of 3s to a time of 8s would give:

$$s = \int_3^8 v\,dt = \int_3^8 (1.8t^2 - 3t + 5)\,dt = \left[0.6t^3 - 1.5t^2 + 5t + c\right]_3^8$$

I've put in a constant of integration '*c*', but that's not necessary when you have definite limits like we have (the 3s and the 8s). It cancels out when you put in the limits:

$$s = \left[0.6t^3 - 1.5t^2 + 5t + c\right]_3^8 = (0.6 \times 8^3 - 1.5 \times 8^2 + 5 \times 8 + c) - (0.6 \times 3^3 - 1.5 \times 3^2 + 5 \times 3 + c) = 233.5\,\text{m}$$

## Section 1.2 Angular Motion

Motion in a straight line is relatively simple; changing direction can make things quite complicated. Let's keep things simple and just consider motion in a circle. What quantities do we need to do this? Like straight line motion, we'll have the speed (both initial and final if we change our speed), and the time taken. The radius of the circle will have to be used, and the angle you turn through will be needed. Angles are usually measured in degrees. Students like their angles to be in degrees. So why do physicists like to use another unit, the radian? 'Degrees' is based on history. If we met an extra-terrestrial civilisation, it's unlikely they would have divided a circle into 360 equal parts like the ancient Babylonians did 3000 years ago. The extra-terrestrials would use radians! Radians are special; here's why.

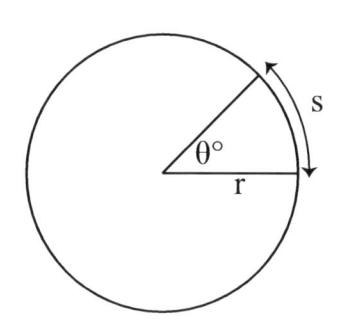

The ratio of the angle 'θ' to the whole circle (360°) is the same as the ratio of the arc length 's' to the circumference (2πr).

$$\frac{\theta°}{360°} = \frac{s}{2\pi r} \Rightarrow s = \frac{2\pi}{360°} r\theta°$$

The physics bit is the 's', 'r' and 'θ°'; these are the things you measure. The bit that's left: $\frac{2\pi}{360°}$, is the clumsy bit and it's there because you're following the Babylonians. Using radians makes that bit disappear! Here's how.

Draw an angle so that the arc length 's' equals the radius 'r'. The angle is shown on the right diagram. That's an angle of one radian. It's big for one unit of angle; a lot bigger than one degree.

The circumference is 2πr (same as 2πs), so 2π lots of 's' gets you the whole way around. By proportion, 2π lots of an angle of one radian must also take you around one complete turn of the circle. In other words, there are 2π of these radians in a whole circle. Here it is again: *there are 2π radians in a whole circle.* Think of 2π (which is 2 x 3.14) as six and a bit.

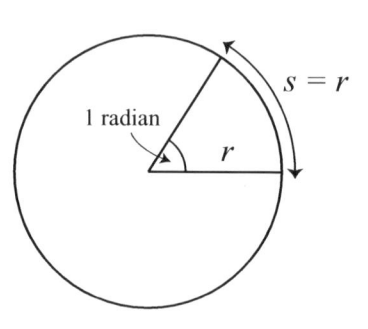

For any angle 'θ' in radians, subtending an arc length 's', our 'by proportion' equation becomes:

$$\frac{\theta}{2\pi} = \frac{s}{2\pi r} \Rightarrow s = r\theta$$

Many problems use nice rounded-off angles like 30° and 45°. When using radians, get used to expressing angles in relation to π. For example, if a whole circle of 360° is the same as 2π radians, then a half circle of 180° will be π radians, and a quarter circle (aka. a right-angle) would be π/2 radians. Get used to thinking of 30° as π/6 radians and 45° as π/4 radians. Here is a table showing some common angles:

| Degrees | 30° | 45° | 60° | 90° | 120° | 135° | 180° | 270° | 360° | 720° |
|---------|-----|-----|-----|-----|------|------|------|------|------|------|
| Radians | π/6 | π/4 | π/3 | π/2 | 2π/3 | 3π/4 | π | 3π/2 | 2π | 4π |

**Example:** Convert 17.8° to radians. 360° is 2π radians so 17.8° is: $2\pi \times \frac{17.8°}{360°} = 0.311 \text{ rad}$

### Units and Dimensions.

A distance can be measured in units of metres, centimetres, miles, nanometres, inches and so on, but they all have something in common; the dimensions of length [L]. Similarly, time can be measured in units of seconds, hours, days, but they all have the dimensions of time [T]. Angles can be measured in units like degrees (360 in a circle), the neglected 'grad' (100 in a right angle) and radians (2π in a circle); but they all have the same dimensions. In this case, no dimensions. You can see this from $s = r\theta$. The dimensions of length from the 's' and 'r' cancel out, leaving nothing for the angle 'θ' (except its units).

**Rotational Motion & Astrophysics**

## Rate of Change of Angle - the Angular Velocity

The equation $s = r\theta$ relates the arc length 's' to the angle 'θ'. If a particle was travelling along the circumference of a circle of radius 'r' at a constant speed 'v', we could calculate its speed using:

$$v = \frac{s}{t} = \frac{r\theta}{t} = r\frac{\theta}{t}$$

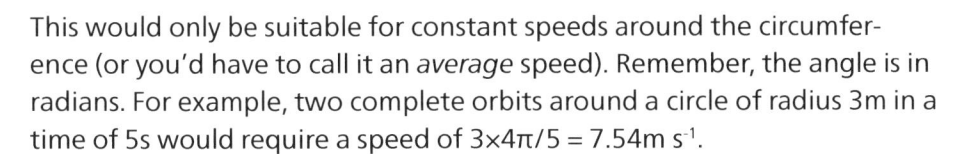

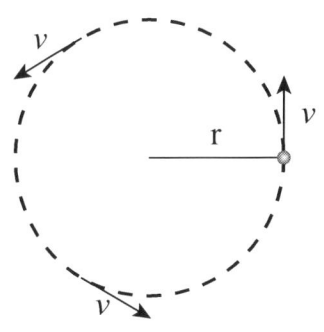

This would only be suitable for constant speeds around the circumference (or you'd have to call it an *average* speed). Remember, the angle is in radians. For example, two complete orbits around a circle of radius 3m in a time of 5s would require a speed of 3×4π/5 = 7.54 m s⁻¹.

The proper name for 'θ' is the **angular displacement** of the particle. Despite its name, it's not a vector (though many people think it is), since it doesn't obey the vector law of addition in 3D space.

For *changing* speeds around the circumference, we have to use our new calculus definition:

$$v = \frac{ds}{dt} = \frac{d(r\theta)}{dt} = r\frac{d\theta}{dt}$$

The radius is constant, doesn't change with time, so doesn't get differentiated. I've grouped the angle and time together (same with the top equation) since that combination is given a special name and symbol. It's called the **angular velocity**, symbol 'ω', (pronounced 'omega') and is measured in radians per second (rad s⁻¹):

$$\omega = \frac{d\theta}{dt}$$

Unlike the angular displacement, the angular velocity is a vector. Later on in the course (page 124), you will see the same 'ω' symbol, but it'll be called the angular frequency (where it's a scalar). In dynamics, it's the 'angular velocity', and it's a vector, but we will only use it in simple situations where its vector properties aren't needed (so we use it like a scalar). Confused?

Using our new symbol, the speed of an object 'v' in metres per second, going around a circle of radius 'r' in metres, at an angular velocity 'ω' in radians per second, is given by:

$$v = \omega r$$

**Example** An object with an angular velocity of 0.73 rad s⁻¹ moving around a circle of radius 40cm would have a speed of: $v = \omega r = 0.73 \times 0.4 = 0.29 \, \text{m s}^{-1}$

Okay, what do radians per second feel like? One complete turn per second is 2π radians per second. Going through a right-angle each second would be π/2 radians per second (and so take 4 seconds for a complete turn).

We can relate the angular velocity 'ω' to the time it takes for one complete turn (remember that's called the Period 'T'). In the example above, an angular velocity 'ω' of π/2 rad s⁻¹ gave a period 'T' of 4s.

$$\omega = \frac{v}{r} = \frac{s/t}{r} \quad \text{and for 1 turn with } s = 2\pi r \text{ and } t = T, \text{ this gives:} \quad \omega = \frac{2\pi r / T}{r} = \frac{2\pi}{T}$$

Bigger 'ω' must be a smaller 'T' so it's an inverse relation. Put in a period of 4s and you'll get π/2 for the angular velocity. It's a surprisingly useful little expression, so try to remember it. Here are two examples using angular velocity.

**Example 1**: Calculate the angular velocity of a turntable spinning vinyl singles at 45rpm.

Firstly convert from rpm (revolutions per minute) into radians per second.

One revolution is 2π radians, so 45 of them will be 90π radians.

This is for one minute, so divide by 60 to get an angular velocity of ω = 90π/60 = 1.5π rad s$^{-1}$.

You could convert this into 4.71 rad s$^{-1}$ but it's usually best keeping the π in place.

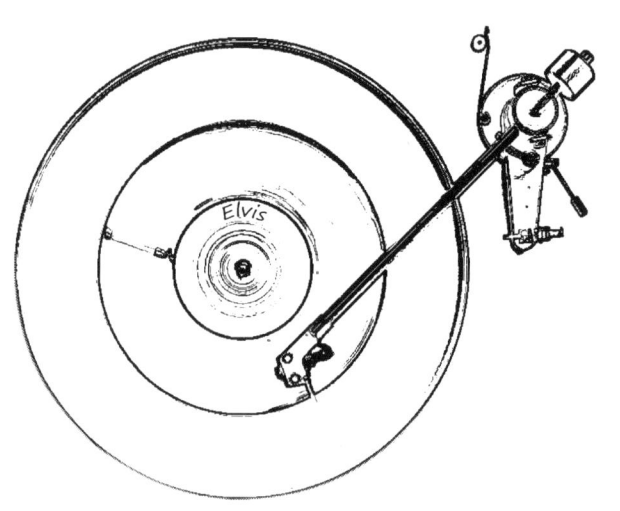

**Example 2**: A particle moves with constant speed in a circle with a period 'T' of 0.2s. Calculate its angular velocity and its frequency.

$$\omega = \frac{2\pi}{T} = \frac{2\pi}{0.2} = 10\pi \text{ rad s}^{-1} \qquad f = \frac{1}{T} = \frac{1}{0.2} = 5 \text{ Hz}$$

I've used the frequency-period relation and this should be familiar to you from Higher Physics. It means you can relate the angular velocity 'ω' (the number of **radians** turned through in a second) to the frequency 'f' (the number of **orbits** in a second):

$$T = \frac{2\pi}{\omega} \qquad T = \frac{1}{f} \quad \Rightarrow \quad \frac{2\pi}{\omega} = \frac{1}{f} \quad \Rightarrow \omega = 2\pi f$$

A period of ⅓ second gives a frequency of 3Hz and an angular velocity of 6π rad s$^{-1}$.

## Changing Angular Velocity - the Angular Acceleration

Here'a a table showing the angular displacement 'θ' with time of an object moving in a circle:

| Angular displacement (°) | 0 | 30 | 60 | 90 | 120 | 150 |
|---|---|---|---|---|---|---|
| Time (s) | 0 | 4 | 8 | 12 | 16 | 20 |

The angle is measured from the start position (usually taken as 3 o'clock) and goes anticlockwise. You can easily picture the motion - it moves around the circle at a slow but constant rate. In this case 30° in 4s, which is ω = 7.5°/s (π/24 rad s$^{-1}$).

How would the object be moving from the table below?

| Angular displacement (°) | 0 | 1.5 | 6 | 54 | 96 | 150 |
|---|---|---|---|---|---|---|
| Time (s) | 0 | 4 | 8 | 12 | 16 | 20 |

The object is speeding-up. How the angles change leads us on to the idea of angular acceleration.

# Rotational Motion & Astrophysics

**Example 1:** An object starts from rest and speeds-up uniformly on its track around a circle. It reaches an instantaneous angular velocity 'ω' of 60° per second after 5s.

Since the motion was uniform, it must have increased its angular velocity by 12° per second each second. This is called an angular acceleration of 12 degrees per second per second.

**Example 2:** An object has an initial angular velocity of $\omega_o = 3\pi$ rad/s then speeds-up uniformly along a circular path with an angular acceleration of $\alpha = \pi/2$ rad/s² for a time of 8s. Calculate its final angular velocity 'ω'.

It gains an angular velocity of π/2 rad/s every second, so must increase by 4π rad/s in 8s. The final angular velocity is 7π rad/s.

This should remind you of initial speeds, final speeds and accelerations from Higher Physics. In that case distances were being changed. In this case, angles are being changed. That's why it's called the angular acceleration. It's the same maths with different symbols. We can use the same equation structure and just change distances to angles (in radians for us).

$$v \rightarrow \omega \qquad u \rightarrow \omega_o \qquad a \rightarrow \alpha \qquad s \rightarrow \theta \qquad t \rightarrow t$$

For example, an initial velocity in metres per second maps to an initial angular velocity $\omega_o$ (called omega nought) in radians per second. The acceleration 'a' in m s⁻² maps to the angular acceleration 'α' in rad s⁻².

This gives us the rotational equations of motion:

$$v = u + at \qquad \Rightarrow \qquad \omega = \omega_o + \alpha t$$

$$s = ut + \frac{1}{2}at^2 \qquad \Rightarrow \qquad \theta = \omega_o t + \frac{1}{2}\alpha t^2$$

$$v^2 = u^2 + 2as \qquad \Rightarrow \qquad \omega^2 = \omega_o^2 + 2\alpha\theta$$

Most problems come down to choosing the correct equation. An equation must only have one unknown for it to have a solution. So if both 'α' and 't' are unknown in a problem, you can't start with the first equation.

**Example 1** Start rotating at two turns per second and increase this uniformly to five turns per second in a time of 12 seconds. Calculate the angular acceleration and the angular displacement.

In symbols: $\omega_o = 4\pi$ rad s⁻¹   $\omega = 10\pi$ rad s⁻¹   $t = 12$ s   $\alpha = ?$   $\theta = ?$

$$\omega = \omega_o + \alpha t \quad \Rightarrow \quad \alpha = \frac{\omega - \omega_o}{t} = \frac{10\pi - 4\pi}{12} = \frac{\pi}{2} \text{ rad s}^{-2}$$

I always prefer doing the problem using words: 'two turns per second to five turns per second is an increase of 6π rad s⁻¹ in 12s, so it's an increase of ½π rad s⁻¹ every second'.

$$\theta = \omega_o t + \frac{1}{2}\alpha t^2 \quad \Rightarrow \quad 4\pi \times 12 + \frac{1}{2} \times \frac{\pi}{2} \times 12^2 = 84\pi \text{ radians}$$

Leaving the 'π' in the answer makes it easy to see that this is 42 complete turns.

**Example 2** This one has negative signs in it. An initial angular velocity of 20 turns per second clockwise is reduced uniformly to a final angular velocity of 4 turns per second anticlockwise having turned through an angular displacement of 250π radians. Deduce all you can about the motion through the use of both equations and graphs.

Firstly, choose a sign convention; I'm using 'clockwise is positive'.

In symbols, initial data is:   $\omega_o = 40\pi$ rad s$^{-1}$   $\omega = -8\pi$ rad s$^{-1}$   $t = ?$   $\alpha = ?$   $\theta = 250\pi$ rad

If possible, start off with a graph; the data gives the straight line graph of 'ω' against 't' below. I've also marked on the numbers on the time axis for later reference, though at present they're unknown.

The time and angular acceleration are unknown, so we can't use the first equation. Use the third equation to calculate the angular acceleration:

$$\omega^2 = \omega_o^2 + 2\alpha\theta$$

$$\Rightarrow \quad \alpha = \frac{\omega^2 - \omega_o^2}{2\theta}$$

$$= \frac{(-8\pi)^2 - (40\pi)^2}{2 \times 250\pi}$$

$$= -3.072\pi \text{ rad s}^{-2}$$

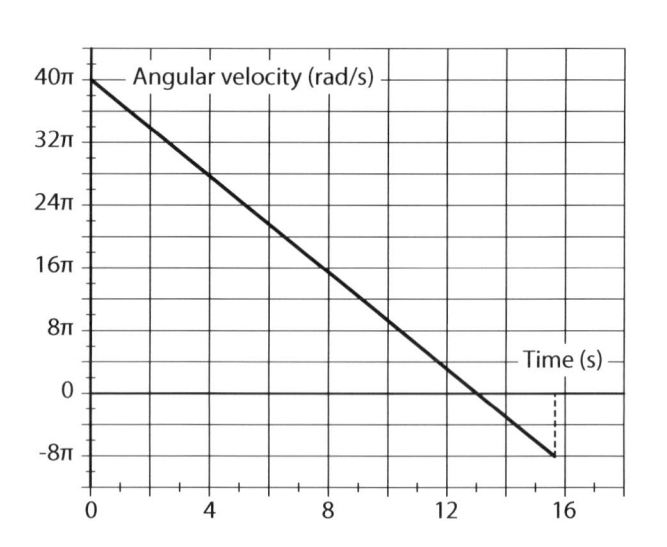

As expected, the angular acceleration is negative (from the slope of the graph). In the question, the angular displacement is given as 250π radians (equal to 125 complete turns). This is the *resultant* angular displacement. From the graph above, we see that it ended below the zero line. This means that it turned 125 more clockwise turns than anticlockwise turns. Using the second equation of motion with our value of angular acceleration allows us to draw the graph of angular displacement against time. The slope of this graph at any point would give the angular velocity 'ω'.

Use the first equation to calculate the time taken:

$$\omega = \omega_o + \alpha t$$

$$\Rightarrow \quad t = \frac{\omega - \omega_o}{\alpha}$$

$$= \frac{-8\pi - 40\pi}{-3.072\pi}$$

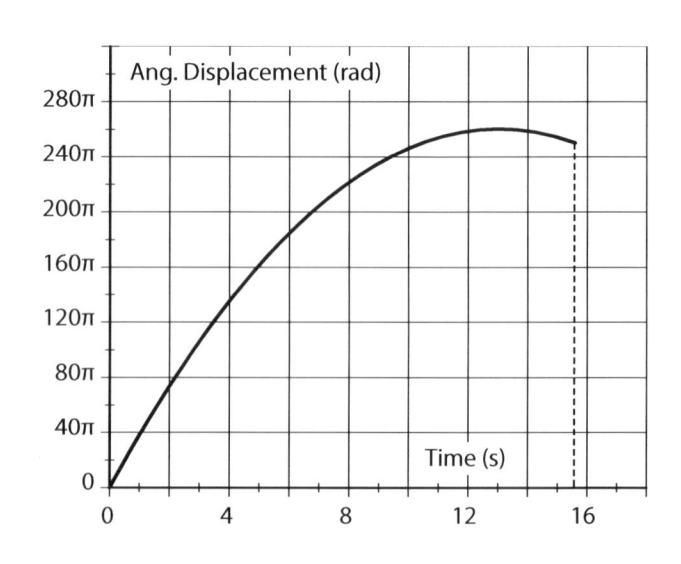

$$= 15.625 \text{ s}$$

This sets the scale for the time axis. Using the equations with the value ω = 0 would give you the time at which the first graph cuts the time axis (when it's angular velocity is zero and it's changing direction), and the maximum angular displacement of the object (how many radians it went through before turning backwards). See if you agree with my answers, 13.02s and 260.4π rad (that's just over 130 turns).

**Rotational Motion & Astrophysics**

## Derivation of the Angular Equations of Motion using Calculus

The previous examples were of uniform circular motion where the angular acceleration was constant. Non-uniform motion can be handled using the same calculus methods as for straight line acceleration. As before, it is a more powerful method. The derivations for constant angular acceleration '$\alpha$' are given below beside the equivalent ones for straight line accelerations; same maths, different symbols.

$$v = \frac{ds}{dt} \qquad a = \frac{dv}{dt} = \frac{d}{dt}\left(\frac{ds}{dt}\right) = \frac{d^2s}{dt^2} \qquad\qquad \omega = \frac{d\theta}{dt} \qquad \alpha = \frac{d\omega}{dt} = \frac{d}{dt}\left(\frac{d\theta}{dt}\right) = \frac{d^2\theta}{dt^2}$$

$$a = \frac{dv}{dt} \qquad\qquad\qquad\qquad\qquad\qquad \alpha = \frac{d\omega}{dt}$$

$$\int_0^t \frac{dv}{dt} dt = \int_0^t a\, dt \qquad\qquad\qquad\qquad \int_0^t \frac{d\omega}{dt} dt = \int_0^t \alpha\, dt$$

$$\int_u^v dv = a \int_0^t dt \qquad\qquad\qquad\qquad \int_{\omega_o}^{\omega} d\omega = \alpha \int_0^t dt$$

$$[v]_u^v = a[t]_0^t \qquad\qquad\qquad\qquad\qquad [\omega]_{\omega_o}^{\omega} = \alpha[t]_0^t$$

$$[v - u] = a[t - 0] \qquad\qquad\qquad\qquad [\omega - \omega_o] = \alpha[t - 0]$$

$$\Rightarrow \boxed{v = u + at} \qquad\qquad\qquad\qquad \Rightarrow \boxed{\omega = \omega_o + \alpha t}$$

$$v = \frac{ds}{dt} \quad \Rightarrow \int_0^t \frac{ds}{dt} dt = \int_0^t v\, dt \qquad\qquad \omega = \frac{d\theta}{dt} \quad \Rightarrow \int_0^t \frac{d\theta}{dt} dt = \int_0^t \omega\, dt$$

$$\int_0^s ds = \int_0^t v\, dt = \int_0^t (u + at)\, dt \qquad\qquad \int_0^\theta d\theta = \int_0^t \omega\, dt = \int_0^t (\omega_o + \alpha t)\, dt$$

$$[s]_0^s = \left[ut + \tfrac{1}{2}at^2\right]_0^t \qquad\qquad\qquad [\theta]_0^\theta = \left[\omega_o t + \tfrac{1}{2}\alpha t^2\right]_0^t$$

$$\Rightarrow \boxed{s = ut + \tfrac{1}{2}at^2} \qquad\qquad\qquad \Rightarrow \boxed{\theta = \omega_o t + \tfrac{1}{2}\alpha t^2}$$

The third equation can be derived as before, or you could use the average angular velocity '$\overline{\omega}$':

$$\overline{\omega} = \frac{\omega + \omega_o}{2} = \frac{\theta}{t} \quad \Rightarrow \quad (\omega + \omega_o) = \frac{2\theta}{t}$$

$$\Rightarrow \quad (\omega + \omega_o)(\omega - \omega_o) = \frac{2\theta}{t} \times \alpha t = 2\alpha\theta$$

$$\omega = \omega_o + \alpha t \quad \Rightarrow \quad (\omega - \omega_o) = \alpha t$$

$$(\omega + \omega_o)(\omega - \omega_o) = 2\alpha\theta \quad \Rightarrow \quad \omega^2 - \omega_o^2 = 2\alpha\theta \quad \Rightarrow \quad \omega^2 = \omega_o^2 + 2\alpha\theta$$

## Measuring Angular Acceleration

This is a standard experiment using simple apparatus. There are variations on the layout, but they all consist of a rigid body in the form of a rotating disc with a constant force applied off-centre. The disc could have a horizontal spin axis (as in a typical windfarm) or a vertical spin axis as shown in the diagram. A cord is wrapped around the perimeter of the disc and runs over a pulley wheel to a weight hanger.

The equations of motion are used to calculate the angular acceleration '$\alpha$'. But, which one to use?

$$\omega = \omega_o + \alpha t$$

$$\theta = \omega_o t + \frac{1}{2}\alpha t^2$$

$$\omega^2 = \omega_o^2 + 2\alpha\theta$$

The first one needs both initial and final angular velocities, plus the time taken. Starting from rest makes the initial angular velocity zero. You can measure the final angular velocity by placing a card on the disc and having it cut a light beam. The card has a speed 'v' as it cuts the beam (calculated from the card width and the time for which the beam was cut). Its angular velocity '$\omega$' is given by $v = \omega r$ where 'r' is the distance from the centre of the disc to the card. Finally use a hand timer to record the time taken from rest until the card was cut.

An alternative uses the second equation. Starting from rest, time how long it takes to make, say, two complete turns. Substitute in the time you measured and use $4\pi$ for the angular displacement.

Using the third equation with a card cutting a light gate after, say, half a turn, would also give the angular acceleration. No hand timers needed.

Don't have a light gate handy? Hand-time how long it takes to go from rest through a full turn. The average angular velocity is $\bar{\omega} = \theta/t$ with $\theta = 2\pi$ for one turn. For uniform acceleration starting from rest, the final angular velocity is twice the average angular velocity. So just double your answer for the average. Then use the first equation of motion to obtain the '$\alpha$'.

Don't have a timer? There are commercially available versions with paper roll wrapped around the perimeter (where the cord is in the diagram). The cord has to be wrapped around the smaller, inner disc, then over the pulley as before. A vibrating arm set to a natural frequency of 5Hz with an ink pen on its end touches against the paper roll and draws out an ever elongating sine wave as the disc accelerates. Count the number of waves and divide by five to get the time in seconds. Very retro.

Most of the above methods require human timing so should be repeated a number of times. Is it best taking an average of each final answer for the angular acceleration, or taking an average of all the times then obtaining only one final answer? Does it make a difference?

These are all low-tech experiments. Nothing is hidden from view. You can understand all aspects of the experiment and gain confidence in planning and carrying out experiments.

# Rotational Motion & Astrophysics

## The Inner Ear - where Physics meets Biology

There's a real, physical, natural world 'out there' and the way we are aware of it is through our senses. Without our sense mechanisms, we couldn't react to changes in our environment. We're all familiar with the sense of sight (our bodies detection and interpretation of light rays), the sense of sound (ditto sound waves), plus those of smell, taste and touch. There is another one which is so much part of our lives that we might not think of it as a sense mechanism.

Lie flat on your back for 5 minutes then stand up quickly, or close your eyes and spin around 20 times. How does it feel? We're not talking alcohol here, this is for people when they're sober. Our bodies have a sense mechanism which can detect body movement and be used to maintain balance.

The bit that does it is called the *vestibular system* (diagram left) and is part of our inner ear. There's a part which detects linear motion of the head (that's velocity and straight line acceleration) and a part which detects rotational movement of the head (angular velocity and angular acceleration).

The rotational detection and response is done by the semi-circular canals. Think of three hollow doughnuts, filled with a liquid which can slosh around inside when your head moves. They are mounted at right angles to each other like an XYZ coordinate system. Being circular makes them sensitive to rotations of the head.

If you stand on a turntable and spin around, the liquid inside the tube mounted horizontally is free to rotate within the tube; but not in the other two tubes since they are mounted at right angles to the motion. At a point inside the tube, there is a gooey bit surrounding some hairs (the *cupola*, diagram right) which gets in the way of the flow of liquid. If it gets deflected to the side, as in the diagram, the nerve endings are stimulated and send a signal to the brain. You interpret this signal as a certain type of motion. Similar story with the other two tubes; tilting your head from one shoulder to the other, or moving your head towards your lap.

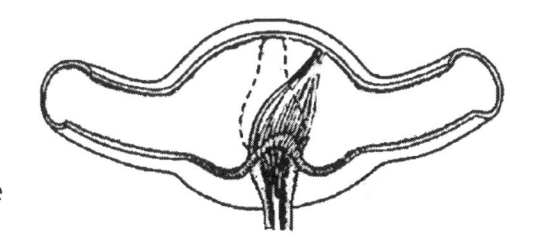

The brain sometimes gets in wrong and misinterprets the information. What happens if the signal to your brain tells you that you are rotating but your eyes tell you that you are stationary? You reach for the sickbag. Search YouTube with 'Barany Chair' for an eye-opener.

The head rotates and the tube rotates in step with it, but the liquid inside lags behind. If you've been rotating and come to a sudden stop, the liquid comes to rest in about half a second, but the cupola only slowly unbends back to its upright position over about one minute (see the two time constants mentioned below). It's this mismatch between the nerve signals from your eyes and your ears which makes you dizzy and puke-up the diced carrots and green huey.

You can mathematically model the angular movement of the cupola. It's treated as an upside down bendy pendulum with the forces coming from angular displacement (stiffness of the goo; think restoring force), and the angular velocity (from friction with the liquid). The solution is: $\theta = A\left(e^{-bt} + e^{-ct}\right)$. The two constants 'b' and 'c' (actually frequencies) are very different in size and give rise to two different time scales; hence the different reactions to different stimuli. Fascinating area of study!

## Acceleration and its Adjectives

For circular motion, you will see the word 'acceleration' with different adjectives before it: angular, tangential, centripetal, radial, centrifugal. Two of these, centripetal and radial, mean much the same thing (see top of page 20 for the difference). We're down to four: angular, tangential, centripetal, centrifugal.

You're in a car going around a bend to the left. The force responsible for this (the centripetal force), is pointing to the left. But your body is a loyal follower of Newton's First Law and wants to go straight on. Relative to the car seat, your body moves rightwards, and your brain throws a thought into your cranial mailbox; 'something pushed you to the right'. The popular name for this 'thought' is the centrifugal force. As with Quantum Mechanics and Relativity, your commonsense has let you down.

We're down to three adjectives: angular, tangential, centripetal. These are the ones we use. The last two (tangential and centripetal acceleration) are actually the components of a single vector; the '**a**' that's in Newton's Second Law **F** = m**a**. It's (they are) measured in metres per second squared (m s$^{-2}$).

The angular acceleration is measured in radians per second squared (rad s$^{-2}$). The diagrams below show the time lapse motion of two identical spheres moving in circles of the same radius:

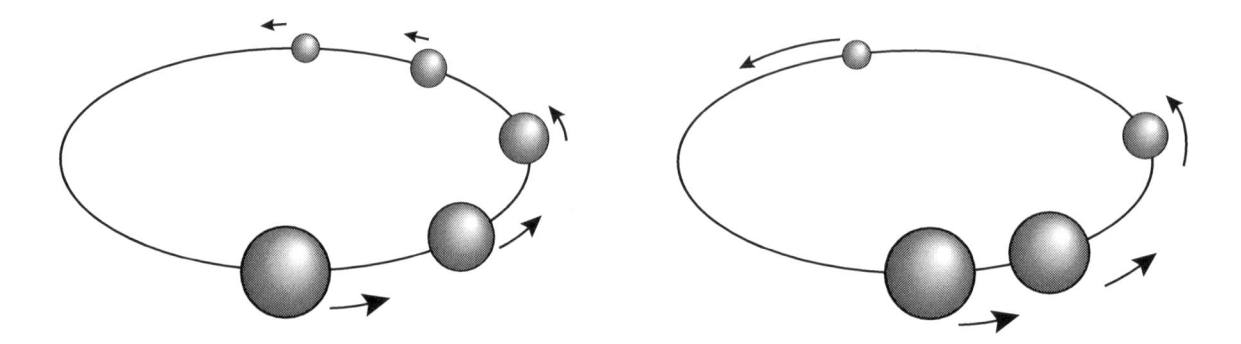

The sphere on the left is moving at a constant angular rate. If the positions were taken at one second intervals, its angular velocity would be 180° in 4 seconds ($\omega = \pi/4$ rad s$^{-1}$). The angular velocity is constant all the way around: we describe this as having no angular acceleration ($\alpha = 0$). The sphere on the right is getting faster; its angular velocity is changing (increasing). It has a non zero angular acceleration ($\alpha \neq 0$).

Given the speed of the sphere at an instant (in m/s) and the radius of the orbit, we've already seen on page 11 how to relate this to the angular velocity:

$$v = \frac{ds}{dt} = \frac{d(r\theta)}{dt} = r\frac{d\theta}{dt} = r\omega$$

Differentiate again with respect to time:

$$\frac{dv}{dt} = \frac{d(r\omega)}{dt} = r\frac{d\omega}{dt} = r\alpha$$

The left hand side describes how the speed changes. At any instant, the velocity points along the tangent to the circle at that point, so the left hand side is called the tangential acceleration '$a_T$' in m s$^{-2}$. It's the same thing we've been discussing above, the component of the objects acceleration along the tangent to the circle:

$$a_T = r\alpha$$

The subscript '*T*' reminds us it's a component. The equation applies to *any* circular motion.

**Rotational Motion & Astrophysics**

**Example** A particle accelerates uniformly along a circular track of radius 75cm from rest to an angular velocity of 5 rad s$^{-1}$ in a time of 20s. Calculate the tangential component of its acceleration, and its final speed.

First calculate its angular acceleration:

$$\alpha = \frac{(\omega - \omega_o)}{t} = \frac{(5-0)}{20} = 0.25 \text{ rad s}^{-2}$$

Then use our new equation to calculate the tangential component of the acceleration:

$$a_T = r\alpha = 0.75 \text{ m} \times 0.25 \text{ rad s}^{-2} = 0.1875 \text{ m s}^{-2}$$

To calculate the final speed, we just use our equations of motion from Higher Physics (it's uniform motion and although it's travelling in a circle, the numbers still increase as if it was moving in a straight line).

$$v = u + a_T t = 0 + 0.1875 \times 20 = 3.75 \text{ m s}^{-1}$$

Use the equations of motion to show that it travelled a distance of 37.5m through an angular displacement of 50 rad (almost 8 orbits).

## Accelerating at Constant Speed

Let's go back to the simplest case of an object moving in a circle at constant speed. There is no angular acceleration, so there is no tangential component of the acceleration. We have only the centripetal component. This is in units of m s$^{-2}$ and points towards the centre of the circle. We already have an expression for the tangential component of the acceleration $a_T = r\alpha$. We also need an expression for the centripetal component of the acceleration. The smart thing to do is to start from the definition of acceleration as the rate of change of velocity:

$$\underline{a} = \frac{d\underline{v}}{dt} = \lim_{\Delta t \to 0} \frac{(\underline{v}-\underline{u})}{\Delta t}$$

Moving from an initial velocity of '**u**' to a final velocity of '**v**' takes us through an angle of 'Δθ' (see diagram above) in a time of 'Δt'. The initial and final velocities have different directions but the same magnitude 'v' (the 'speed'). The top line of the definition has a difference of two vectors. Apply the usual technique of adding the negative (diagram on the right):

$$\underline{v} - \underline{u} = \underline{v} + (-\underline{u})$$

The result points inwards but also slightly downwards. As the limit is taken and Δθ gets smaller and smaller, this resultant vector will point towards the centre of the circle. It's an isosceles triangle with the long sides equal to the speed 'v'. We need to calculate the length of the short side. The length of an arc of a circle was calculated using $s = r\theta$ where 's' is the arc length and the angle 'θ' is in radians. Our triangle is a bit like that; but its got a straight base rather than a curvy arc. Would it make any difference in the limit Δθ→0 ?

19

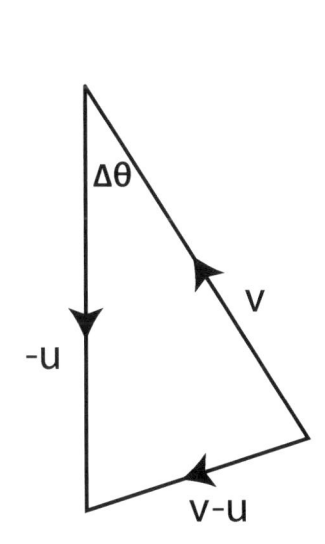

It doesn't! So the length of the resultant vector is:

$$|\underline{v}-\underline{u}|=|\underline{v}|\Delta\theta$$

Substitute this in the definition of acceleration:

$$\underline{a} = \frac{dv}{dt} = \lim_{\Delta t \to 0} \frac{(\underline{v}-\underline{u})}{\Delta t} = \lim_{\Delta t \to 0} \frac{|\underline{v}|\Delta\theta}{\Delta t} = |\underline{v}| \lim_{\Delta t \to 0} \frac{\Delta\theta}{\Delta t} = |\underline{v}|\omega$$

We drop the magnitude braces around the velocity '$\underline{v}$' and just call it the speed '$v$'. Strictly speaking, the phrase 'radial acceleration' takes the positive direction as out from the centre, so the radial acceleration of an object moving in a circle is: $a_r = -\omega v$ with subscript 'r' for 'radial' acceleration and a minus sign to show it's towards the centre. If asked for the centripetal acceleration, you would use the same expression without the minus sign. Both are measured in m s$^{-2}$.

We already have $v = \omega r$ and this gives us two alternative forms for the radial acceleration:

$$a_r = -\omega v = -\omega \times \omega r = -\omega^2 r \qquad\qquad a_r = -\omega v = -\frac{v}{r} \times v = -\frac{v^2}{r}$$

The subscript 'r' and the sign are usually omitted if it's obvious we're talking about centripetal acceleration. These are the two most useful forms in answering questions.

**Example 1**  Calculate the centripetal acceleration of an object travelling along the arc of a circle of radius 6.5m with a speed of 2.4m s$^{-1}$.

$$a = \frac{v^2}{r} = \frac{2.4^2}{6.5} = 0.886 \text{ m s}^{-2}$$

(towards the centre)

**Example 2**  During training in a human centrifuge, an astronaut experiences a centripetal acceleration of 9.8 m s$^{-2}$. At what tangential speed must he be travelling if the centrifuge has a radius of 5.7m.

$$a = \frac{v^2}{r} \quad\Rightarrow\quad v = \sqrt{ar} = \sqrt{9.8 \times 5.7} = 7.47 \text{ m s}^{-1}$$

Without doing a calculation, what would be the effect on the centripetal acceleration if the speed doubled?

$$a \propto v^2 \qquad v \to 2v \quad\Rightarrow\quad a \to 4a$$

**Example 3**  A car is driven around a bend of constant radius 82m on a horizontal road. Calculate the angular velocity and speed of the car if the driver experiences a centripetal acceleration of 0.5g.

$$a = \omega^2 r \quad\Rightarrow\quad \omega = \sqrt{\frac{a}{r}} = \sqrt{\frac{0.5 \times 9.8}{82}} = 0.244 \text{ rad s}^{-1}$$

$$v = \omega r = 0.244 \times 82 = 20 \text{ m s}^{-1} \quad (\approx 45\text{mph})$$

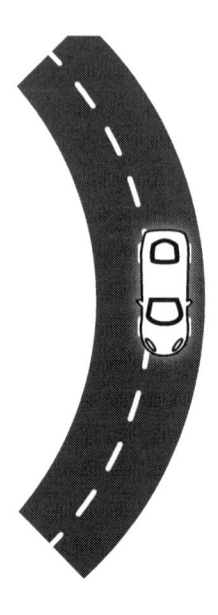

# Centripetal Force.

Newton's 2nd Law, $F=ma$ states that a resultant force will produce a non-zero acceleration. The simplest example of centripetal acceleration is moving in a circle at a constant speed. How can we apply a force to an object and keep it moving at constant speed? The answer is to apply the force 'sideways', that is, at right-angles to the velocity of the object. There is no component of the force in the direction of the velocity, so we don't speed it up or slow it down; we just change its direction. This means the force points towards the centre of the circle, so it's called a centripetal ('centre seeking') force.

In problem solving, it's just a question of identifying which force is responsible. Common forces are gravitational, electrostatic, magnetic, tension, normal reaction, friction etc. You do not add centripetal force to that list! The centripetal force required in a problem will **come from** that list.

Two important examples are the motion of the planets about the sun, where gravity supplies the centripetal force (see top of page 68), and the Bohr model of the atom where the electrostatic force supplies the centripetal force (see page 102).

The next section illustrates its use with 7 examples. In each case, we use Newton's 2nd Law to get the centripetal force from the centripetal acceleration.

### Example 1    Remaining Attached to your Planet

Planet Earth spins on its axis once every 24hrs. It takes you with it. You move in a big circle once every 24 hrs so your body must have a centripetal acceleration. There must be a force on your body directed towards the centre of the planet. It's actually a resultant force; the force of gravity pulling you towards the centre and the Normal reaction of the ground pushing up on your feet. Take the case of standing on the equator. Your body has mass 'm' and requires a centripetal force of:

$$F = ma = m\frac{v^2}{r}$$

Your speed at the equator will be:

$$v = \frac{s}{t} = \frac{2\pi r}{T} = \frac{2\pi \times 6.378 \times 10^6}{24 \times 60 \times 60} = 464 \text{m s}^{-1}$$

Giving a centripetal acceleration of:

$$a = \frac{v^2}{r} = \frac{464^2}{6.378 \times 10^6} = 0.034 \text{m s}^{-2}$$

For a person of mass 60kg, this requires a centripetal force of:

$$F = ma = 60 \times 0.034 \approx 2\text{N}$$

to keep you attached to the equator. The force of gravity on your body: $W = mg = 60 \times 9.8 = 588\text{N}$ is more than enough to supply this. Of that 588N, only 2N is required to keep you following the curve of the Earth. The other 586N will press down on the bathroom scales under your feet. The Normal Reaction is the scales pushing back with 586N (which is the reading on the scales).

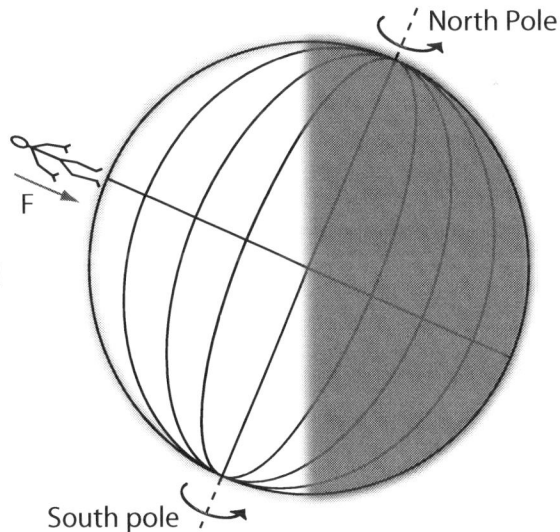

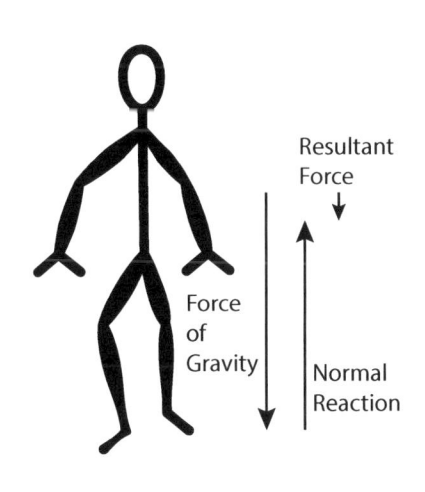

Suppose the Earth rotated a bit quicker? As you get faster, the centripetal acceleration of your body will increase. That 2N we calculated will increase, and the bathroom scales will have a smaller reading. How short would the 'day' have to become such that gravity was just enough to supply the centripetal force required to keep your feet on the equator?

$$F_{gravity} = F_{centripetal} \quad \Rightarrow \quad mg = m\omega^2 r \quad \Rightarrow \quad g = \omega^2 r$$

$$\omega^2 = \left(\frac{2\pi}{T}\right)^2 = \frac{g}{r} \quad \Rightarrow \quad T = 2\pi\sqrt{\frac{r}{g}} = 2\pi\sqrt{\frac{6.378 \times 10^6}{9.8}} = 5069\text{s}$$

This is about 84 minutes! On the spring and autumn equinoxes (21st March and 21st Sept.), you would have 42 minutes daylight and 42 minutes night. If you stood on the equator, the bathroom scales would read zero! You would regain some weight if you walked away from the equator; only regaining your full weight when you reached the poles! And suppose the Earth rotated even faster……?

### Example 2  Car on a bend in the road

If you've been in a car in the winter time when the roads were covered in 'black ice', you'll appreciate the importance of friction. Try to turn a corner and you would just go straight on (Newton's 1st Law). A car needs friction to follow the curve of the bend; it requires a centripetal force 'F' and that force is enabled by friction! A car of mass 1400kg on a bend of radius 20m doing a speed of 15m s$^{-1}$ would require a centripetal force of:

$$F = ma = m\frac{v^2}{r} = 1400 \times \frac{15^2}{20} = 15750\text{N}$$

Formula 1 racing cars increase friction through aerodynamic downforce (it increases the normal force 'N', which is related to the force of friction between the road and the tyres: $F \leq \mu N$ ). At 100mph, this force is about equal to its weight.

### Example 3  Whirling cork

This is a standard experiment which you will perform during the course. It's used to investigate the centripetal force formula. Take the simplest approximation with the string horizontal. The centripetal force 'F' is supplied by the tension in the cord.

If the top of the glass tube is friction-free, the force 'F' will equal the weight on the other end of the cord. You would choose the $F = m\omega^2 r$ version of the formula since you measure the period of rotation. Typically, you keep the radius constant by keeping a mark on the string just below the glass tube, and you keep the mass 'm' constant by leaving the cork unchanged. This is testing the relationship: $F \propto \omega^2$. Measure the time for 10 turns, increase the weight, and repeat. Plot the weight (on the x-axis since this is the independent variable) against $1/T^2$ and hope for a straight line.

A non-zero intercept is an indication that there is friction at the mouth of the tube.

**Rotational Motion & Astrophysics**

In reality, the weight of the cork tilts the string down at an angle as shown. Assuming no friction, the weight $W=Mg$, provides the tension 'F' in the string. The tension acts along the string, but the centripetal force acts along the radius, so we have to take the horizontal component of the string tension for the centripetal force:

$$m\omega^2 r = W \cos\theta$$

Measuring the radius 'r' is tricky, so measure the length 'L'. Change the variable using: $r = L\cos\theta$

The equation becomes:

$$m\omega^2 r = m\omega^2 L \cos\theta = W \cos\theta \quad \Rightarrow \quad m\omega^2 L = W$$

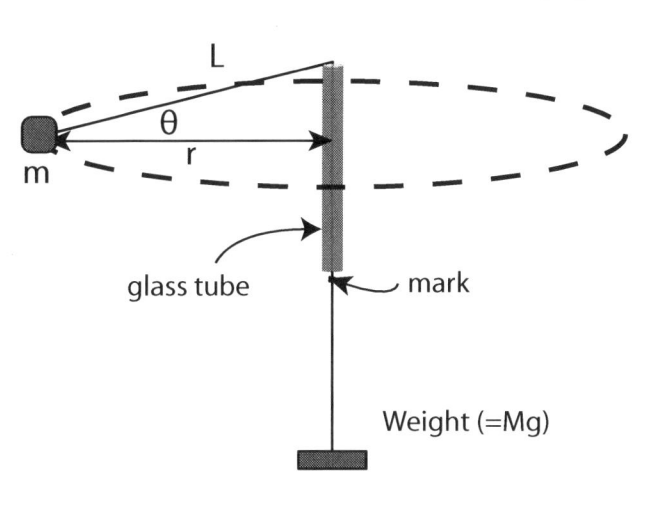

Keeping the string horizontal gave a similar result (just measure the 'L' instead of the 'r'). Remember to wear eye protection. It may seem unnecessary, but it's actually a good idea.

### Example 4  Turning aircraft

An aircraft can easily change direction vertically; just throttle back and you start to descend. How does it change direction 'sideways'? It needs a centripetal force, but where does it come from? As the air moves over the plane, the shape of the wings provides a lift force at right angles to the wings (the 'Wing Force' in the diagram). Tilt the plane so that one wing goes down and the other goes up. The lift force will also tilt over; it is the horizontal component of this tilted lift force which supplies the centripetal force.

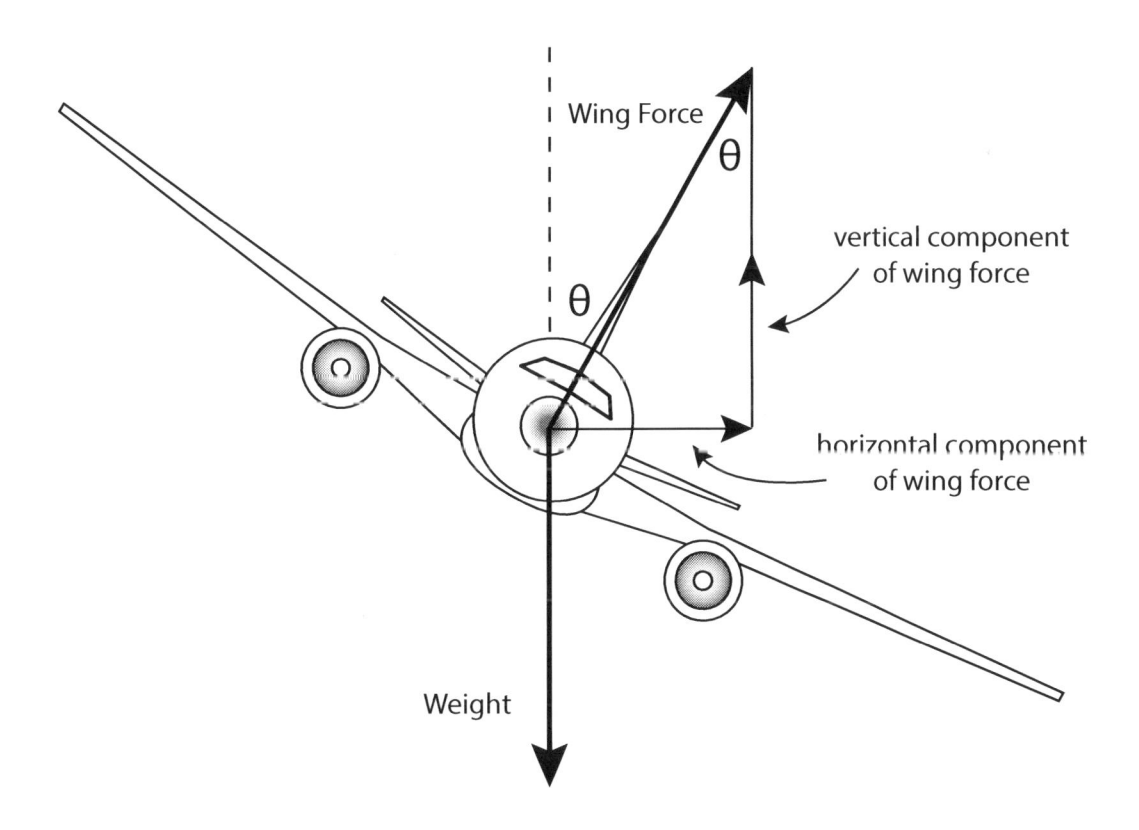

The vertical component of the wing force must be equal in size but opposite in direction to the weight, otherwise the plane would change altitude.

23

The plane has banked though an angle 'θ' to the vertical. Notice the wing force must increase during this manoeuvre to maintain altitude; achieved by going faster or employing flaps. For constant altitude, the right angled triangle gives:

Horizontal component of force: $\dfrac{mv^2}{r}$

Vertical component: $mg$

Use the tangent to relate them: $\dfrac{mv^2}{r} = mg \tan\theta \quad \Rightarrow \quad r = \dfrac{v^2}{g \tan\theta}$

Notice how this is independent of the mass of the plane. As an example, an aircraft with a speed of 560mph (250m s$^{-1}$) wishing to execute a turn of radius 16km, would require to bank at an angle of:

$$\tan\theta = \dfrac{v^2}{gr} = \dfrac{250^2}{9.8 \times 16000} = 0.4 \quad \Rightarrow \quad \theta = 21.7°$$

This seems like a wide turn, but it would still tip your IRN-BRU into the aisle.

## Example 5    Car on a banked track

The car drives around in a circle on a track tilted at an angle 'θ'. We take the simplest case of no friction between the tyres and the road! The car keeps the same height on the track as it moves in the circle.

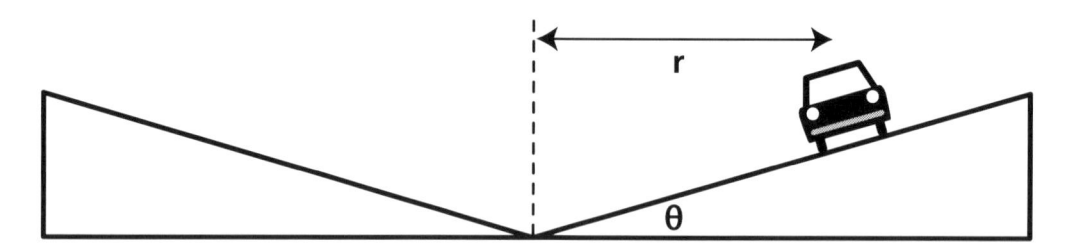

The car moves in a circle so there must be a centripetal force. This centripetal force is provided by the horizontal component 'H' of the normal reaction (diagram below). The normal reaction is at 90° to the surface; this is the direction the molecules of the road push back. The car keeps the same height on the track, so the weight of the car must be balanced by the vertical component 'V' of the normal reaction.

$\dfrac{H}{V} = \tan\theta \quad \Rightarrow \quad H = V\tan\theta = mg\tan\theta$

This provides the centripetal force:

$H = mg\tan\theta = m\dfrac{v^2}{r} \quad \Rightarrow \quad \tan\theta = \dfrac{v^2}{gr}$

Once again, independent of the mass of the car!

As an example, what speed does a car have to travel at on a track banked at 15° in a circle of radius 20m?

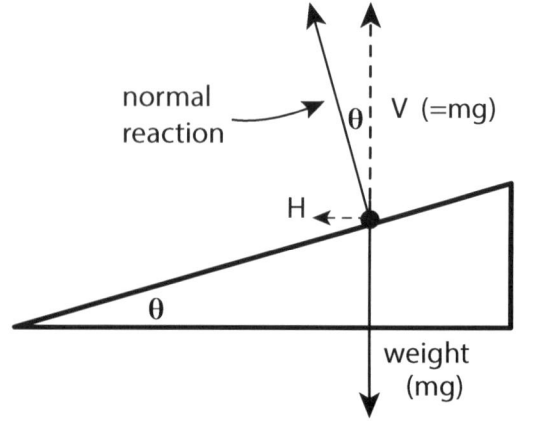

$$\tan\theta = \dfrac{v^2}{gr} \quad \Rightarrow \quad v^2 = gr\tan\theta \quad \Rightarrow \quad v = \sqrt{gr\tan\theta} = \sqrt{9.8 \times 20 \times \tan 15°} = 7.25 \text{m s}^{-1}$$

## Example 6    Vertical whirling cork

The cork moves in a perfect circle (in a vertical plane) so there must be a centripetal force of constant magnitude. It is provided by a combination of string tension and gravity. They combine as vectors to give a result of constant magnitude which always points towards the centre. The simplest positions to analyse are at the top (A) and bottom (B) of the circle.

At the **Top** (A): string tension 'T' and weight 'W' both point downwards

T ↓  +  W ↓  =  Centripetal Force ↓

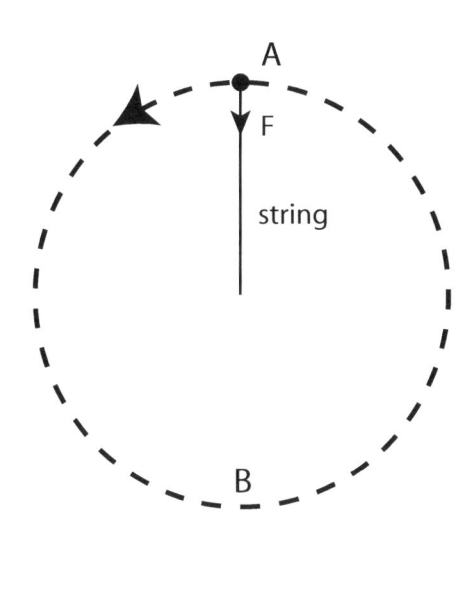

If the cork was moving faster, the string would be tighter and the tension vector in the last diagram would be longer. If the cork is moving more slowly, the tension in the string reduces and if you went slow enough, the string would go slack. For this special speed the centripetal force is provided solely by the weight of the cork:

$$m\frac{v^2}{r} = mg \quad \Rightarrow \quad v^2 = gr \quad \Rightarrow \quad v = \sqrt{gr}$$

Notice, once again, how the speed is independent of the mass of the cork.

**Example**   A steel sphere of mass 300g swinging vertically on the end of a light string moving in a vertical circle of radius 0.75m would require a minimum speed of $v = \sqrt{gr} = \sqrt{9.8 \times 0.75} = 2.7\,\text{m s}^{-1}$ at the top.

At the **Bottom** (B): string tension points upwards and gravity points downwards

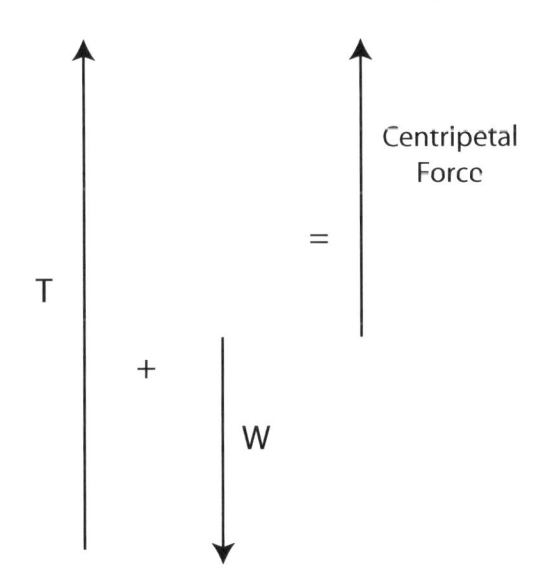

T ↑  +  W ↓  =  Centripetal Force ↑

Compare the lengths of the vectors with the previous force diagram. The weight must stay the same (magnitude and direction), but see how much bigger the tension has become. If you've ever swung a mass like this, you'll remember how much different it feels at the bottom of the circle. The result of the weight and tension gives a centripetal force of the same magnitude as before and still pointing towards the centre (in this case, upwards).

If the cork is at an intermediate position, the tension and weight combine to provide the centripetal force (constant in magnitude as before) and a force acting in the direction of the tangent. This tangential force gives the mass its tangential acceleration (in m/s²) and speeds-up or slows-down the particle in its orbit. At the 9 o'clock and 3 o'clock positions, the force along the tangent comes from the weight, and the centripetal force equals the tension in the string.

Examples are often solved by considering the kinetic and potential energy rather than forces.

The 'hamster wheel' is closely related to the whirling cork. In this case, there is no string. The centripetal force comes from a combination of gravity and the normal reaction of the molecules under your feet.

Apart from that, the analysis is the same as the string. To pass the high point without falling down requires a certain minimum speed. At that speed the normal reaction will reduce to zero and your weight will provide the centripetal force. As before:

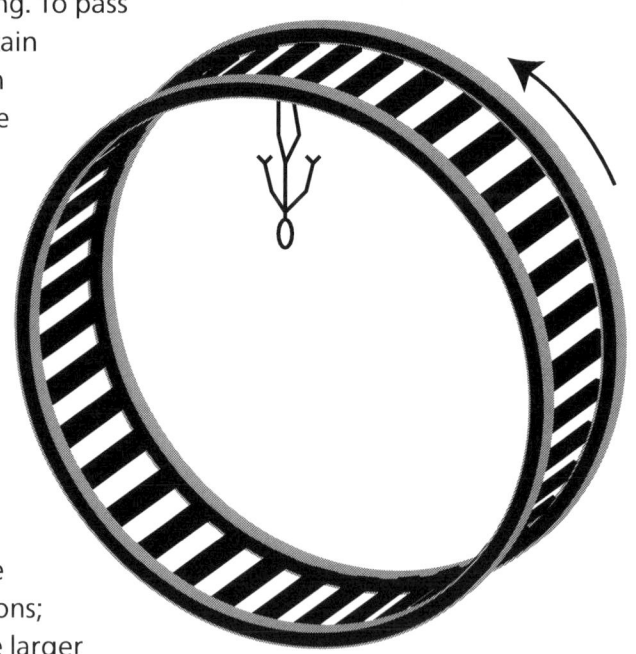

$$v_{at\ top} = \sqrt{gr}$$

With no normal reaction at this special speed at the top, there is no push against your feet from the floor and you would feel 'weightless'. For example, a wheel of radius 5m would require a minimum angular velocity of 1.4 rad s⁻¹.

At the bottom, the normal reaction will produce a force which your legs don't often experience. The normal reaction and weight are in opposite directions; the normal reaction points upwards so must be the larger force.

### Example 7     The Conical Pendulum

The pendulum mass goes in a horizontal circle instead of back and forwards. The forces in the problem are string tension and gravity. It is the horizontal component of the string tension which supplies the centripetal force. The mass keeps the same vertical height, so the gravitational force is equal in size and opposite in direction to the vertical component of the string tension. As before:

$$\frac{H}{V} = \tan\theta \quad \Rightarrow \quad H = V\tan\theta = mg\tan\theta$$

Experiments with conical pendulums measure the time for one rotation (the Period 'T'), so we use the most appropriate form for the centripetal force:

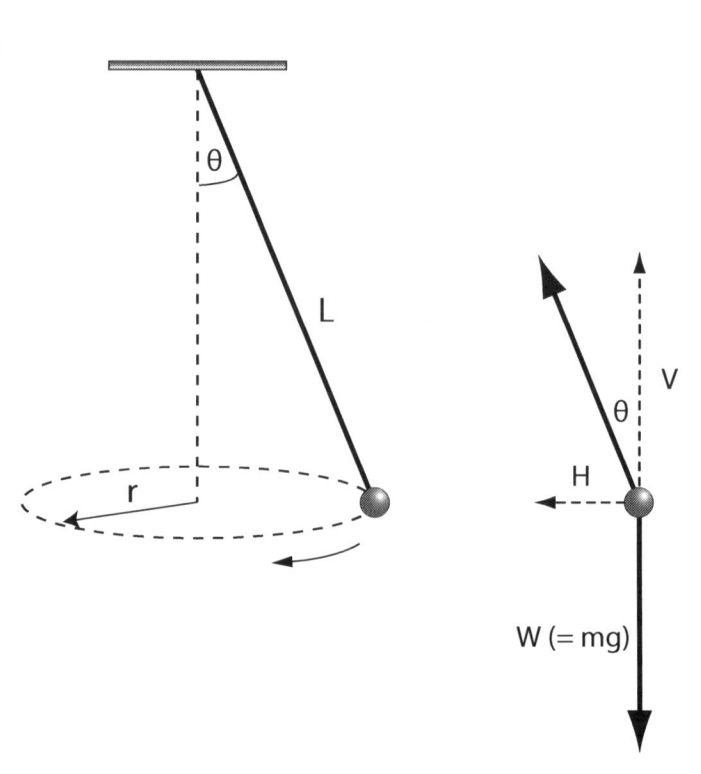

$$F = m\omega^2 r$$

$$m\omega^2 r = mg\tan\theta \quad \Rightarrow \quad \omega^2 = \frac{g\tan\theta}{r}$$

With: $\omega = \frac{2\pi}{T}$ and $r = L\sin\theta$ we get:

$$\omega^2 = \frac{g\tan\theta}{r} \quad \Rightarrow \quad \left(\frac{2\pi}{T}\right)^2 = \frac{g\tan\theta}{L\sin\theta} = \frac{g}{L\cos\theta}$$

This gives a period of:

$$T = 2\pi\sqrt{\frac{L\cos\theta}{g}}$$

# Section 1.3 Rotational Dynamics

The previous examples of centripetal force introduced masses and forces into our kinematic formulas. In each case, the mass was treated as a point, whether it was a person or a car. None of the formulas contained the object's dimensions. In the hamster wheel example, the centre of mass of the person is nearer the centre of the wheel. The radius of the orbit is thus shorter than the radius of the wheel. If you have a problem with forces but don't want the complication of size and shape, you would direct the force along a line through the centre of mass of the object. This ensures that the thing doesn't rotate; energy doesn't go into rotating the object. In this section, we learn how to handle masses which have size and shape (called 'extended' objects).

Our approach is to treat an extended object as a collection of points (a typical physics technique), and only consider *rigid* objects (so no wishy-washy stuff like jelly or liquids).

If you spin a rigid object like the disc on the right, every single particle of the shape will take the same time to make one complete turn. Read that sentence one more time. If it was a squishy object like a jelly, different parts of it would react differently to an angular acceleration. A neat way of expressing this is to say that all the parts of a rigid object have the same period (T) of rotation. Since $\omega = \dfrac{2\pi}{T}$, you could also say that all parts of a rigid body spin with the same angular velocity '$\omega$'. Parts further away from the spin axis (like point 'A' in the diagram) will have a faster speed than parts closer to the spin axis (like 'B' and 'C'), but they all have the same period and angular velocity. They all sweep out the same angle each second.

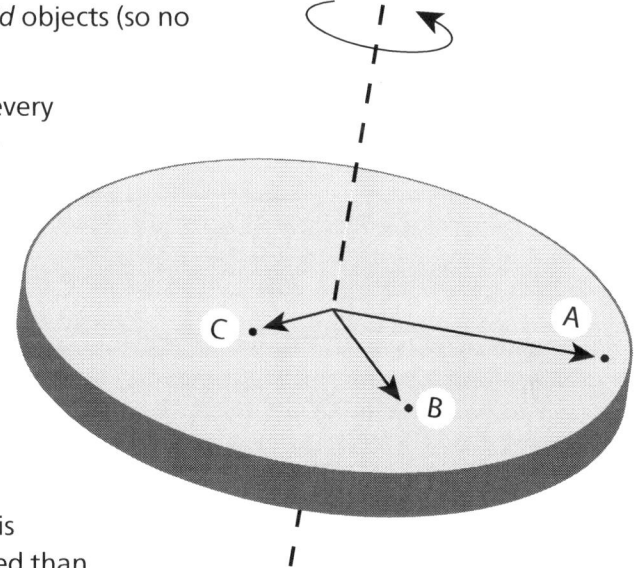

## Kinetic Energy of Rotation

When a rigid body rotates, all of the little parts of it move in circles. Each part (each molecule, if you like), has its own distance (r) from the spin axis and its own speed (v). The distance (r) is always the line perpendicular to the spin axis (as in the diagram on the disc above) since this is the radius of the circle around which the part moves.

Each little bit has mass '$m$' and kinetic energy $E_K = \dfrac{1}{2}mv^2$. The total kinetic energy of rotation of the rigid body is the sum of all those little kinetic energies. We can add them like this since kinetic energy is a scalar. We don't even bother with the signs since kinetic energy is always a positive number.

A typical everyday object consists of about $10^{28}$ molecules, so to get the total, we have to add up a very long series of numbers!! Here's how it starts:

$$E_K(total) = \tfrac{1}{2}m_1v_1^2 + \tfrac{1}{2}m_2v_2^2 + \tfrac{1}{2}m_3v_3^2 + \tfrac{1}{2}m_4v_4^2 + \tfrac{1}{2}m_5v_5^2 + \tfrac{1}{2}m_6v_6^2 + \tfrac{1}{2}m_7v_7^2 + \tfrac{1}{2}m_8v_8^2 + \ldots$$

Writing out all $10^{28}$ terms would take a stack of A4 paper beyond our galaxy (that's not end to end, that's stacked, and it's printing on both sides with a 12pt font!). To save ink, a shorthand notation was invented. It's a capital sigma '$\sum$', and stands for 'sum of'. The total kinetic energy is now written:

$$E_K(total) = \sum_{all\ i} \left(\tfrac{1}{2}m_i v_i^2\right)$$

The subscript 'i' starts at 1 and stops at $10^{28}$. The bit below the '$\Sigma$' tells you how many terms to take; in this case all of them.

This total contains a constant (the ½), and two variables, the mass of each little bit and its speed. The constant of ½ can be taken out of the sum. It's just like taking out the constant and forming a bracket:

$$E_K(total) = \frac{1}{2}\sum_{all\ i}\left(m_i v_i^2\right)$$

Remember that for a rigid body, each particle has a different speed but they all have the same angular velocity. So substitute for 'v' using: $v = \omega r$ to get:

$$E_K(total) = \frac{1}{2}\sum_{all\ i}m_i \omega^2 r_i^2 = \frac{1}{2}\left[\sum_{all\ i}m_i r_i^2\right]\omega^2$$

There's no subscript 'i' with the 'ω' since it's the same for all particles. That means you can take it outside the bracket (I've put it to the right of the bracket; you'll see why below).

Now compare with the original formula for the kinetic energy $E_K = \frac{1}{2}mv^2$ of a body moving in a straight line. There's the ½ in both cases. We have the angular velocity 'ω' in place of the linear velocity 'v', but we already knew about that replacement from the rotational equations of motion. The interesting bit is what you replace the total mass 'M' of a point object with; the bit in the brackets. For the rotational motion of a rigid body, the role of the mass is replaced by:

$$M \Rightarrow \left[\sum_{all\ i}m_i r_i^2\right]$$

This is called the *Moment of Inertia*; the symbol is a capital 'I'. Its units are kg m² (since it's a mass multiplied by a distance squared). So a body of total mass 'M' rotating with an angular velocity of 'ω' has a (rotational) kinetic energy given by:

$$E_k = \frac{1}{2}I\omega^2 \qquad \text{where:} \qquad I = \sum_{all\ i}m_i r_i^2 \quad \text{and} \quad M = \sum_{all\ i}m_i$$

Just as mass tells you how difficult it is to accelerate a body in a straight line, the moment of inertia tells you how difficult it is to give a body an angular acceleration.

**Example 1** Calculate the kinetic energy of a body which is rotating with an angular velocity of 6π rad s⁻¹ if its moment of inertia is 4.8 kg m².

$$E_k = \frac{1}{2}I\omega^2 = \frac{1}{2}\times 4.8 \times (6\pi)^2 = 853\ J$$

**Example 2** A spacecraft of mass 1250kg and moment of inertia 6000kg m² is moving in a straight line with a speed of 450m s⁻¹. It also rotates with an angular velocity of 3 rad s⁻¹. Calculate its **total** kinetic energy.

$$E_k = \frac{1}{2}mv^2 + \frac{1}{2}I\omega^2 = \frac{1}{2}\times 1250 \times 450^2 + \frac{1}{2}\times 6000 \times 3^2 = 126,562,500 + 27000 = 1.27\times 10^8\ J$$

Straight line motion is called 'translational' motion. In the last example, the translational kinetic energy is much larger than the rotational kinetic energy.

**Rotational Motion & Astrophysics**

## The Moment of Inertia of Simple Shapes

You get a 'feel' for what mass is by shaking it about a bit ('shaking' not 'lifting', since the latter indicates the weight). You get a 'feel' for what moment of inertia is like by making an object spin.

Take two balls, one big ball, one little ball joined by a thin rod, all of the same material (diagram below). Your experience tells you it's easier to spin-up the right hand object. There's less of it far away, and far away things are harder to spin. The moment of inertia '$I$', gives this 'feel' a number. The bigger the number for the moment of inertia, the harder it is to spin-up (to change its angular velocity). A bit like straight-line mechanics; the bigger the mass, the harder it is to accelerate.

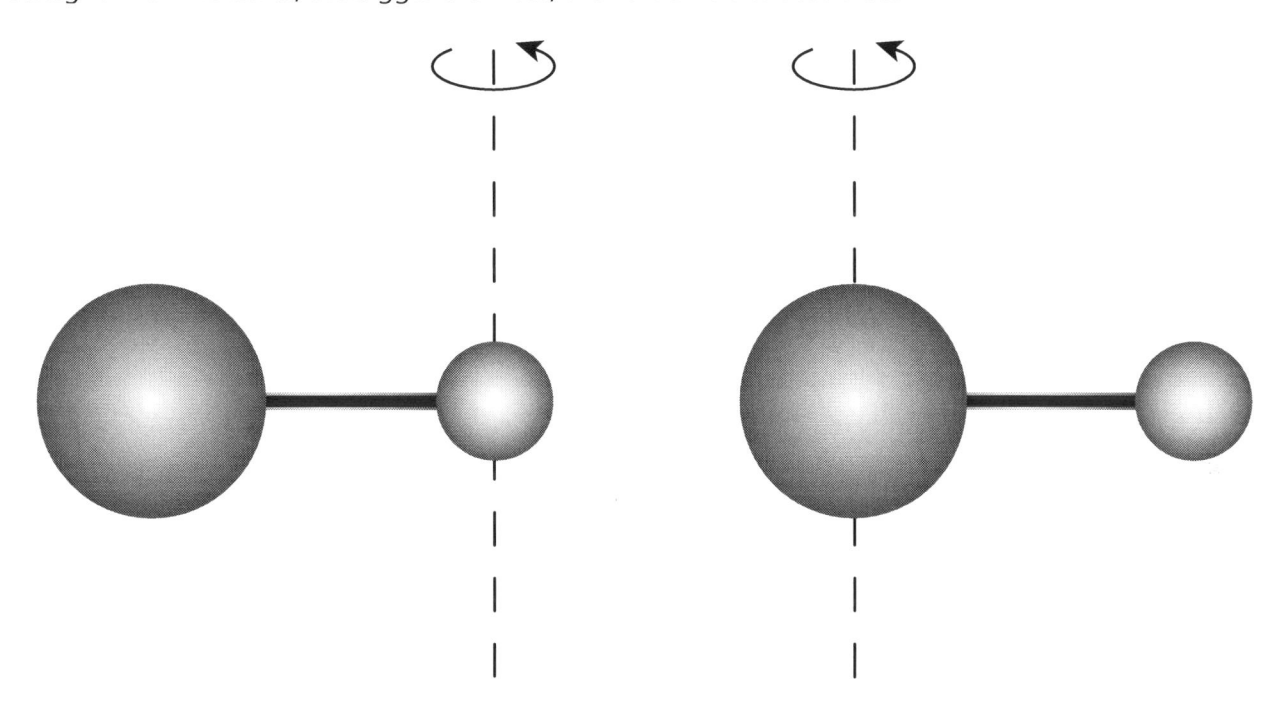

The moment of inertia has units of kg m² (that's m², not m⁻²). One unit of this would be the moment of inertia of a 1kg point mass swung around on a 1m long cord. Take a moment to imagine it.

The moment of inertia of an object depends upon **where you put the spin axis**. You can position the spin axis for any object in an infinite number of ways, and each one will give a different moment of inertia for the object. You can even place the spin axis outside the object. We will now calculate the moment of inertia of some common shapes.

### 1   Point Mass

It doesn't come any simpler than a point mass. There is just one mass at a fixed distance from the spin axis so we don't have to add up lots of bits!

$$I = \sum_{all\ i} m_i r_i^2 = mr^2$$

Remember that the distance '$r$' is always at 90° to the spin axis.

**Example:**   Calculate the moment of inertia of a 2.75kg point mass moving in a circle of radius 82cm.

$$I = mr^2 = 2.75 \times 0.82^2 = 1.85 \text{ kg m}^2$$

Let's now consider a collection of point masses and do some addings-up.

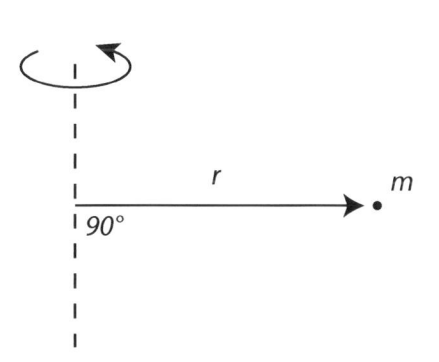

## 2  Hoop

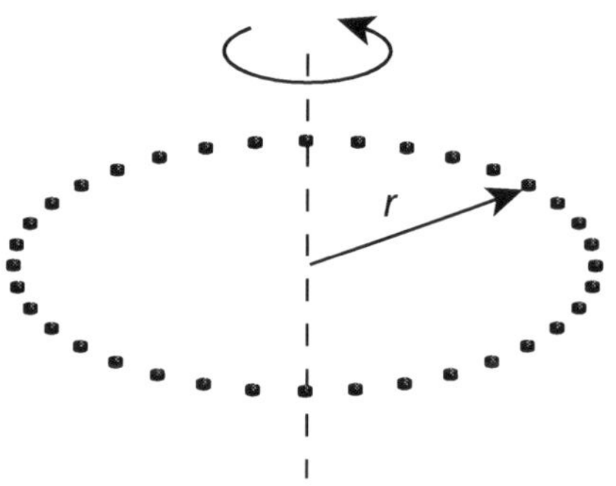

Imagine the hoop consists of many small bits of mass. The diagram on the right shows just 36 of them. If you position the spin axis through the centre, then all these little masses are at the same distance from the spin axis. So the sum for the moment of inertia has 36 terms:

$$I = \sum_{\text{all } i} m_i r_i^2 = m_1 r_1^2 + m_2 r_2^2 + m_3 r_3^2 + \ldots\ldots m_{36} r_{36}^2$$

All the r's are the same, so take them outside the sum:

$$I = r^2 \left( m_1 + m_2 + m_3 + \ldots\ldots m_{36} \right)$$

The bit in brackets is just the total mass of the hoop, which we write as a capital 'M', so: $I = Mr^2$

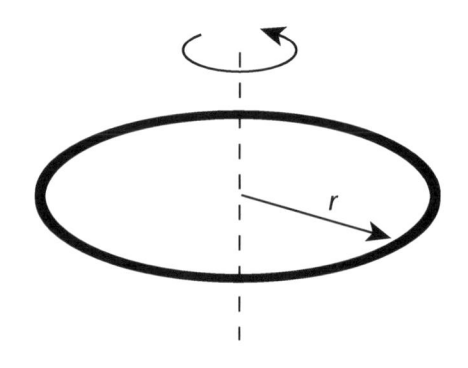

Notice that the little masses $m_1$, $m_2$ .... don't even need to be the same. Taking a greater number of smaller and smaller masses would eventually make a solid hoop like the one on the right. The answer is still the same. It's the same answer as a single point mass and you always get this for any object where all the parts are equidistant from the spin axis. Another example would be a hollow cylinder spun as shown (like a tin of beans with the ends taken off and the beans eaten). Each particle of the can is at the same perpendicular distance to the spin axis.

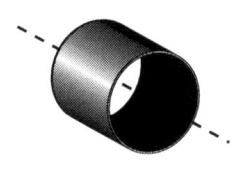

**Example:**   Calculate the moment of inertia of a thin hoop of mass 420g and radius 30cm.

$$I = mr^2 = 0.42 \times 0.3^2 = 0.0378 \,\text{kg m}^2$$

## 3  Flat Disc

The particles of the disc aren't all at the same distance from the centre; they are spread out evenly to make a solid surface. This means that the moment of inertia must be less than MR² because MR² is what you get if all of the mass is at distance 'R'. There are two ways to get the result. The second method uses integration. This first method uses an approximation, so won't give us the exact answer.

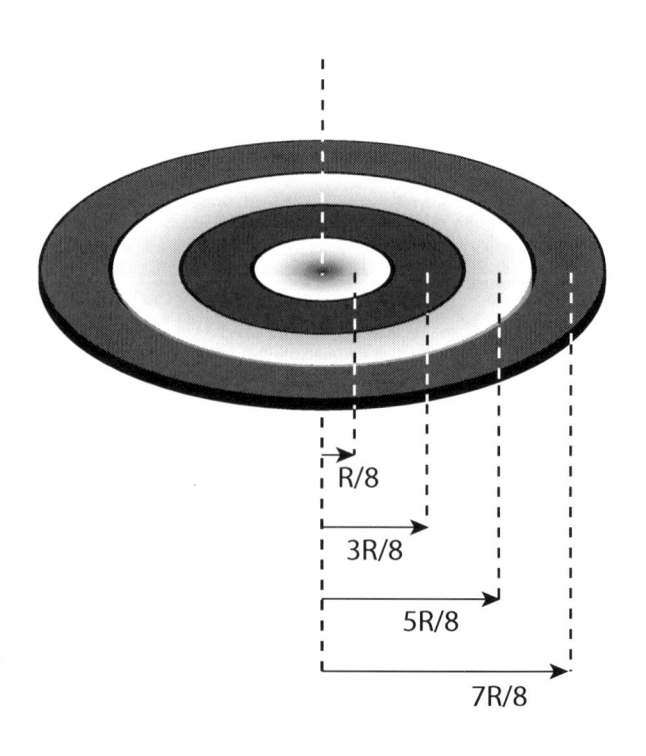

Divide the disc into 4 areas, shown on the diagram at right. The outer area is like a wide hoop. Treat this as a thin hoop with the mass concentrated along its centre line at a distance of 7R/8 from the centre of the disc. Repeat for the other three areas.

Our strategy is to calculate the moment of inertia of each 'hoop' then add to get the total for the whole disc. Firstly, we have to calculate the mass of each section.

## Rotational Motion & Astrophysics

The mass of the whole disc has symbol capital 'M' and for a disc of uniform composition, the mass will be proportional to its area. The first column shows the inner and outer radii for each hoop. The second column is the difference of the two areas obtained using the inner and outer radii. The last column shows the fraction of the whole disc, and hence the fraction of the whole mass 'M'.

$1^{st}$ Hoop: $\quad 0$ to $\dfrac{R}{4} \quad\quad$ Area: $\pi\left(\dfrac{R}{4}\right)^2 - \pi(0)^2 = \dfrac{1}{16}\pi R^2 \quad\Rightarrow \dfrac{1}{16}M$

$2^{nd}$ Hoop: $\quad \dfrac{R}{4}$ to $\dfrac{2R}{4} \quad\quad$ Area: $\pi\left(\dfrac{2R}{4}\right)^2 - \pi\left(\dfrac{R}{4}\right)^2 = \dfrac{3}{16}\pi R^2 \quad\Rightarrow \dfrac{3}{16}M$

$3^{rd}$ Hoop: $\quad \dfrac{2R}{4}$ to $\dfrac{3R}{4} \quad\quad$ Area: $\pi\left(\dfrac{3R}{4}\right)^2 - \pi\left(\dfrac{2R}{4}\right)^2 = \dfrac{5}{16}\pi R^2 \quad\Rightarrow \dfrac{5}{16}M$

$4^{th}$ Hoop: $\quad \dfrac{3R}{4}$ to $R \quad\quad$ Area: $\pi(R)^2 - \pi\left(\dfrac{3R}{4}\right)^2 = \dfrac{7}{16}\pi R^2 \quad\Rightarrow \dfrac{7}{16}M$

Match up these masses with the correct radii. Calculate the moment of inertia of each 'hoop', then sum to get the total:

$$I = \sum_{i=1}^{4} m_i r_i^2 = \dfrac{1}{16}M\left(\dfrac{R}{8}\right)^2 + \dfrac{3}{16}M\left(\dfrac{3R}{8}\right)^2 + \dfrac{5}{16}M\left(\dfrac{5R}{8}\right)^2 + \dfrac{7}{16}M\left(\dfrac{7R}{8}\right)^2$$

Take out the common factors of R² and the 'M':

$$I = \sum_{i=1}^{4} m_i r_i^2 = \dfrac{1}{16\times 8^2}MR^2\left[1\times 1^2 + 3\times 3^2 + 5\times 5^2 + 7\times 7^2\right] = \dfrac{496}{1024}MR^2 = \dfrac{31}{64}MR^2 = 0.484 MR^2$$

The correct answer is 0.5MR², so our approximation is quite accurate. This method is a good example of how physicists approach problems. Sometimes you can't get the exact answer from calculus and have to use approximations. Two examples of this, are in weather forecasting where the atmosphere is divided into boxes (with each box having uniform weather), and in particle physics where gluon interactions are modelled in discrete spacetime steps (the University of Glasgow has a group specialising in this). That's why I've written the calculation out in detail. Try eight hoops, or better still, spot a pattern and predict the series for any number of sections. You should get even closer to a coefficient of 0.5. Remember that this answer is for a disc spun about its centre.

This leads on to the second method; using calculus. You work out the contribution from a small area (shaded in the diagram opposite), then widen it out to 'integrate' over the whole disc. Start with the grey shaded area as shown. Extend the angle Δθ from zero to 2π to make it into a hoop then extend the distance Δr along the radius from zero to 'R'. This widens the hoop to cover the whole disc. The 'integration' process is the adding together of an infinite number of infinitesimally small masses.

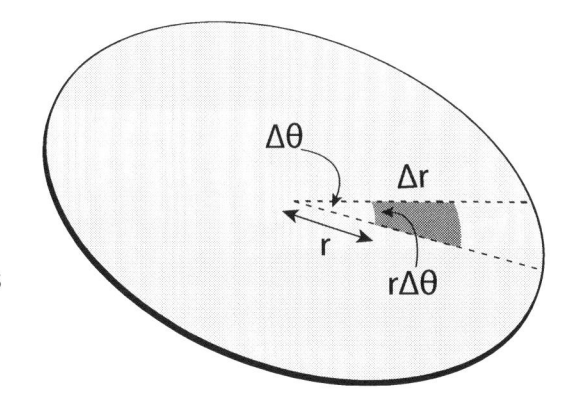

For the moment of inertia calculation, we treat the shaded area as a point mass. We require its mass and its distance from the spin axis at the centre of the disc. For a uniform disc, the mass of the grey area is proportional to its area. For very small Δθ, the shaded area is like a rectangle of length Δr and width rΔθ giving an area of rΔrΔθ. By proportion, the ratio of the mass of the shaded part to the mass of the whole disc, must equal the ratio of the area of the shaded section to the area of the whole disc:

$$\frac{\Delta m}{M} = \frac{r\Delta\theta\,\Delta r}{\pi R^2} \quad \Rightarrow \quad \Delta m = \frac{M}{\pi R^2} r\Delta\theta\,\Delta r$$

This gives us the mass of the shaded area. When going from a finite number of terms to an infinite number of terms, the expression for the moment of inertia is changed from a sigma sign to an integral sign. The delta symbol 'Δ' denoting a small but finite quantity, changes to a differential 'd', a quantity with no size (blame the mathematicians):

$$I = \sum_{all\ i} \Delta m_i r_i^2 \quad \Rightarrow \quad \int r^2 dm$$

$$\sum_{all\ i} \frac{M}{\pi R^2} r_i \Delta\theta\,\Delta r_i\ r_i^2 \quad \Rightarrow \quad \int_0^{2\pi}\int_0^R r \frac{M}{\pi R^2} r^2 d\theta\,dr$$

$$= \frac{M}{\pi R^2}\int_0^{2\pi} d\theta \int_0^R r^3\,dr \;=\; \frac{M}{\pi R^2}[2\pi]\left[\frac{1}{4}R^4\right] \;=\; \frac{1}{2}MR^2$$

When we calculated the moment of inertia of the hoop, we could use the same expression for a hollow cylinder. Same here, same reason. Think of a solid cylinder as a stack of thin discs. The expression for the moment of inertia of a thin disc is identical to the one for a solid cylinder.

**Example 1:** A 30cm diameter (aka 12 inch) vinyl record of the 'audiophile' variety has a mass of 180g. Calculate its moment of inertia.

$$I = \frac{1}{2}mr^2 = \frac{1}{2}\times 0.18\times 0.15^2 = 2\times 10^{-3}\ \text{kg m}^2$$

**Example 2:** A uniform solid cylinder has a mass of 29kg. Calculate its diameter if its moment of inertia is 0.37 kg m².

$$I = \frac{1}{2}mr^2 \quad \Rightarrow \quad r = \sqrt{\frac{2I}{m}} = \sqrt{\frac{2\times 0.37}{29}} = 0.16\,\text{m} \quad \Rightarrow \quad d = 0.32\,\text{m}$$

## 4  Thin straight rod

Where do you put the spin axis? The common place is through the centre at right angles to the length of the rod (diagram below). Another common position is at one end (also at 90° to the rod's length). You get different moments of inertia. Taking it through the centre, we can calculate the moment of inertia by splitting it into sections or by calculus. Sections first.

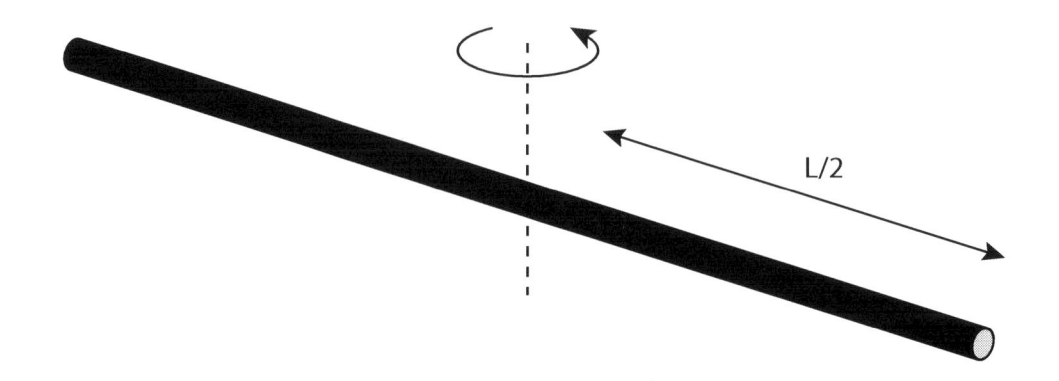

**Rotational Motion & Astrophysics**

The horizontal dotted line represents the whole length 'L' of the rod. Divide the rod into two equal parts and replace each part by a point mass at its centre (diagram below).

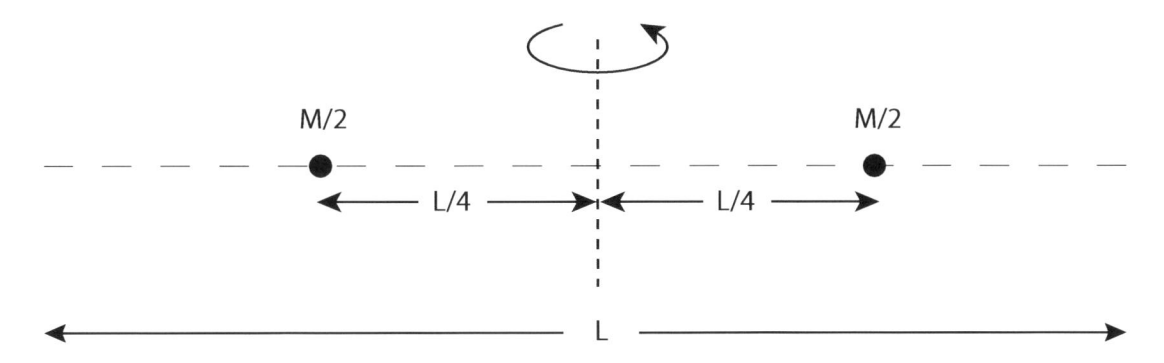

Calculate the moment of inertia of a point mass M/2 at distance L/4, then double it:

$$I = 2 \times \frac{M}{2}\left(\frac{L}{4}\right)^2 = \frac{1}{16}ML^2 = 0.0625\,ML^2$$

This answer seems small. It's partly due to expressing the answer in terms of the whole length (unlike the solid disc where we use the radius instead of the diameter), and also the fact that most of the mass isn't at the ends of the rod. Dividing the rod into two parts is a rough approximation. The obvious thing to try next is to divide the rod into four equal sections:

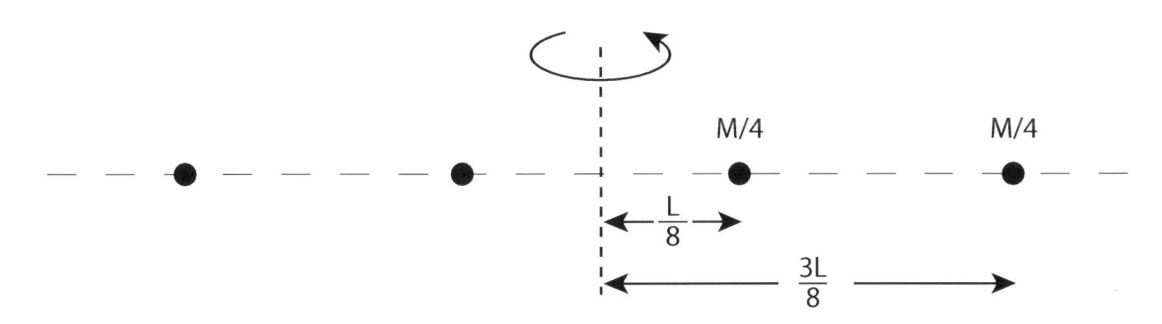

I've only shown the symbols on the right side to keep the diagram simple, but we include all four parts in the total. The masses are still placed at the centre of each section; check for yourself that the distances are as shown. The total moment of inertia for this better approximation is:

$$I = 2 \times \left[\frac{M}{4}\left(\frac{L}{8}\right)^2 + \frac{M}{4}\left(\frac{3L}{8}\right)^2\right] = 2 \times \frac{1}{4 \times 8^2}ML^2\left[1^2 + 3^2\right] = \frac{20}{256}ML^2 = 0.078125\,ML^2$$

The '2' at the front of the bracket takes care of the masses on both sides. Notice the bracket in the middle of the line above. Expressed this way, you will see a pattern emerging when dividing the rod into more parts. Taking eight equal parts gives the following result (it's a useful exercise to draw the diagram and work through the calculation yourself):

$$I = 2 \times \left[\frac{M}{8}\left(\frac{L}{16}\right)^2 + \frac{M}{8}\left(\frac{3L}{16}\right)^2 + \frac{M}{8}\left(\frac{5L}{16}\right)^2 + \frac{M}{8}\left(\frac{7L}{16}\right)^2\right]$$

$$= 2 \times \frac{1}{8 \times 16^2}ML^2\left[1^2 + 3^2 + 5^2 + 7^2\right] = \frac{84}{1024}ML^2 = 0.0820\,ML^2$$

This answer will be quite accurate. If you can spot the pattern emerging, try sixteen parts and see if you can get a coefficient of 0.08301.

The other method uses calculus. It's easier than the solid disc since you just integrate along one dimension. Consider a small part of the rod of mass Δm and length Δr:

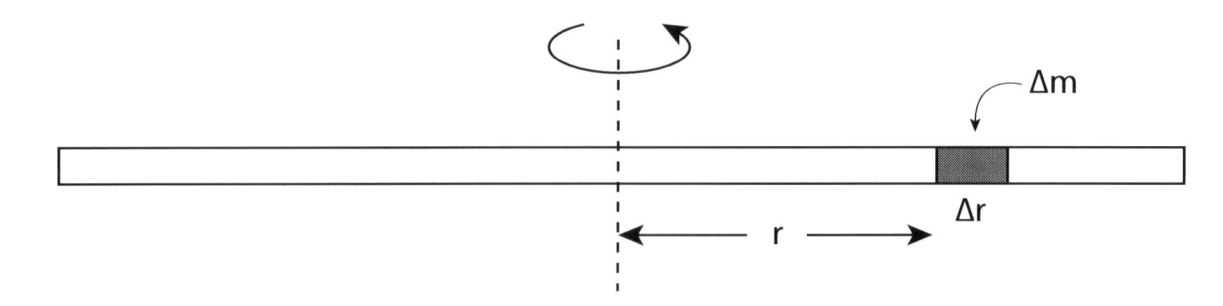

If the rod is uniform we can use proportion. The ratio of the mass of the shaded part to the whole mass is equal to the ratio of the length of the shaded part to the whole length:

$$\frac{\Delta m}{M} = \frac{\Delta r}{L} \quad \Rightarrow \quad \Delta m = \frac{M}{L}\Delta r$$

Using the sigma notation then reducing the size of the shaded area to zero by integration gives:

$$I = \sum_{\text{all } i} \Delta m_i r_i^2 \quad \Rightarrow \quad \int r^2 dm$$

$$\sum_{\text{all } i} \frac{M}{L} \Delta r_i \, r_i^2 \quad \Rightarrow \quad 2\int_0^{L/2} \frac{M}{L} r^2 dr$$

Notice the limits on the integration; from zero to L/2 rather than -L/2 to +L/2. Taking the latter limits would give an answer of zero for the moment of inertia when you performed the integration. The integral 'thinks' that the moment of inertia can take negative values, whereas we have to force it to have positive values. Left and right halves are identical, hence the '2' outside the integral. Evaluating:

$$I = 2 \times \frac{M}{L} \int_0^{L/2} r^2 dr = 2 \times \frac{M}{L}\left[\frac{1}{3}r^3\right]_0^{L/2} = \frac{2M}{3L}\left[\left(\frac{L}{2}\right)^3 - (0)^3\right] = \frac{1}{12}ML^2 = 0.08\dot{3}ML^2$$

Our previous approximation gave a coefficient of 0.08301 for sixteen parts. You can see how close this was to the correct answer of 0.08333. This concludes our derivation of the moments of inertia of simple shapes.

**Example**  A barbell consists of a long thin rod with masses on each end as shown. Calculate the total moment of inertia of the system. Treat the small spheres on the ends as point masses.

$$I = m_1\left(\frac{L}{2}\right)^2 + \frac{1}{12}m_2L^2 + m_1\left(\frac{L}{2}\right)^2$$

$$= 15 \times 0.4^2 + \frac{1}{12} \times 2 \times 0.8^2 + 15 \times 0.4^2$$

$$= 2.4 + 0.107 + 2.4 = 4.91 \text{ kg m}^2$$

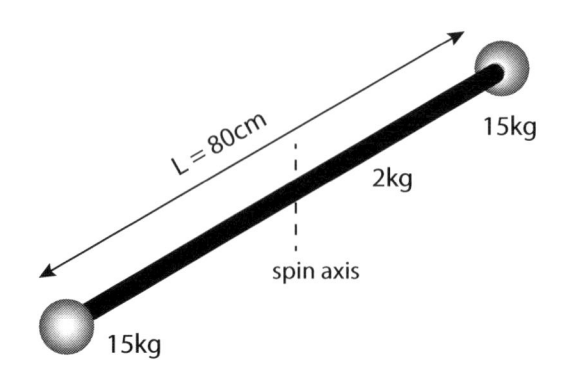

# Rotational Motion & Astrophysics

## Moments' of Inertia of Common Shapes

**Thin Rod** 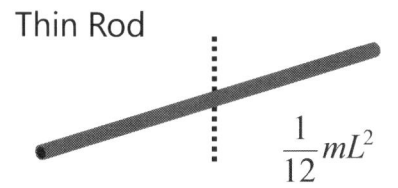
$$\frac{1}{12}mL^2$$

**Thin Rod** 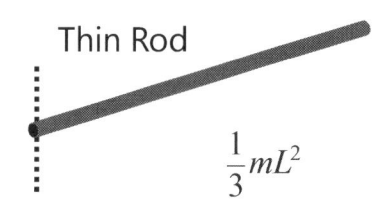
$$\frac{1}{3}mL^2$$

**Solid Cylinder** 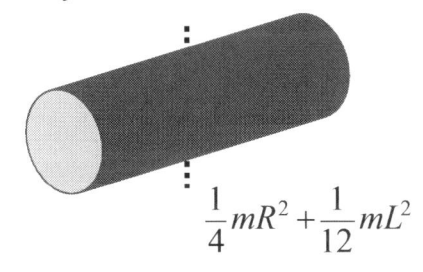
$$\frac{1}{4}mR^2 + \frac{1}{12}mL^2$$

**Solid Cylinder** 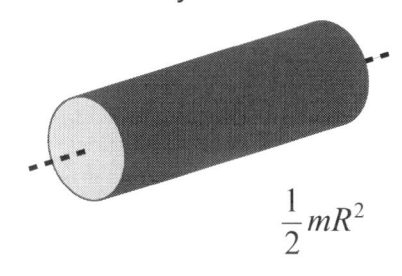
$$\frac{1}{2}mR^2$$

**Hoop** 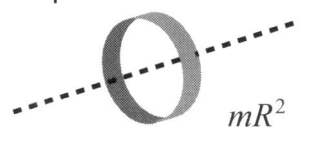
$$mR^2$$

**Hoop** 
$$\frac{1}{2}mR^2$$

**Solid Sphere** 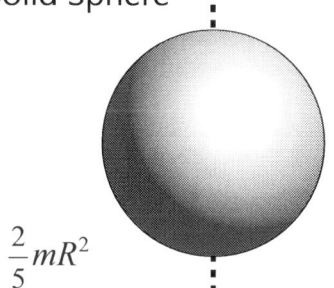
$$\frac{2}{5}mR^2$$

**Thick Walled Cylinder** 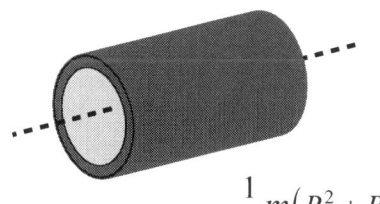
$$\frac{1}{2}m(R_1^2 + R_2^2)$$

# Torque

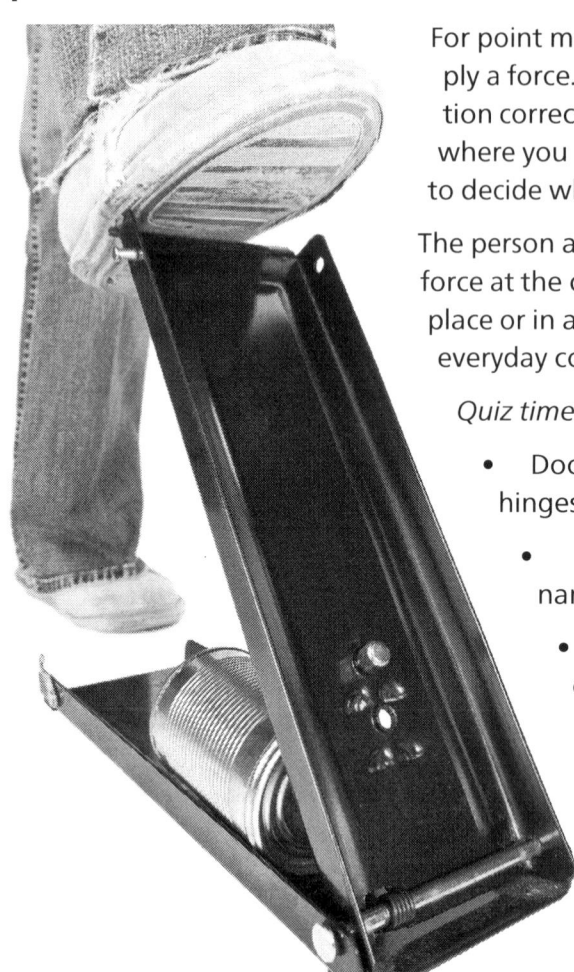

For point masses, you don't have to think about where to apply a force. Anywhere will do, you just have to get the direction correct. You can change the direction of the force, but not where you apply it. If the object has a size, then you also have to decide which part to aim at, because it makes a difference.

The person about to crush the can in the image has applied the force at the correct place. Applying the same force to a different place or in a different direction gives a different result. This is everyday commonsense.

*Quiz time*. True or false?

- Door handles are placed on the opposite side from the hinges because they look better.
- Spanners are made longer so the company can fit its name along the shaft.
- Snooker players aim for the side of the ball because they are pissed.
- A screwdriver is used to lift the lid off the top of a paint tin to keep your hands clean.

I hope you got 4 out of 4 (or at least 3).

There are three things to consider; the force, where you apply it, and in what direction. You can apply a small force far out on a lever and get a 'good' result. Or a large force at a small distance and get the same result. The name for this effect is *Torque*. A stubborn nut on a rusty bolt requires a large torque to remove it. You can achieve this torque by applying a huge force with your fingers, or by a moderate force using a spanner. It produces the same effect on the nut (unless you push the spanner inwards rather than sideways). Torque requires the force 'F', the distance to the spin axis 'r' and the direction in which you apply the force. This is the definition:

$$Torque\ (T) = rF\sin\theta$$

The unit is Newtons x Metres (Nm). Notice the symbol is '*T*'; the same symbol as the period and the temperature! An alternative symbol is τ ('tau'). You have to be careful with the angle. It's taken as the angle between the direction of the force and the outward pointing direction from the spin axis.

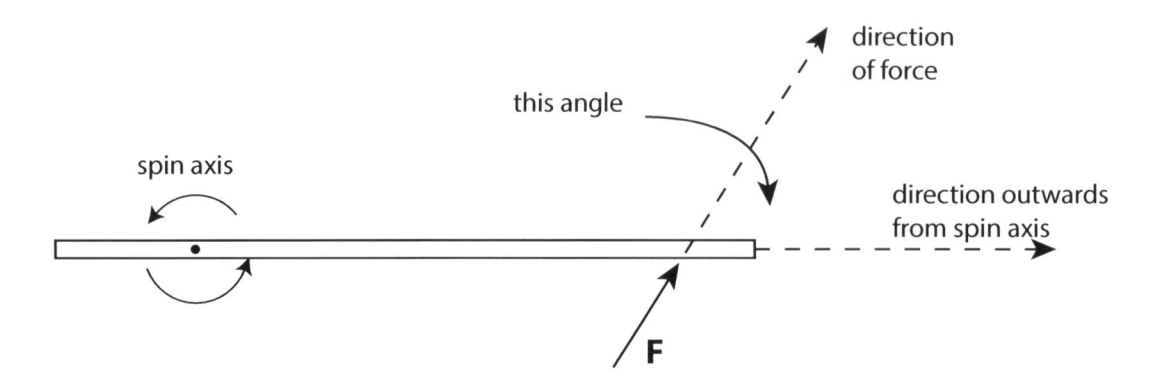

36

# Rotational Motion & Astrophysics

The greatest effect is when $\sin\theta = 1$, that is $\theta = 90°$, when the force and distance are at right angles. No torque is applied when $\sin\theta = 0$, that is $\theta = 0°$ or $180°$ and corresponds to the force pointing directly away from or towards the spin axis. This is common sense.

*Nerdy Note*: There is only one way of multiplying two real numbers together and it's the one taught from primary school. However, force and distance are both vectors (actually displacement, not distance), and there are two ways of multiplying vectors. One way gives a scalar for the answer and the other way gives a vector for the answer. You've already come across the first way; that was the dot product $\underline{A}.\underline{B}$. The dependence on the angle enters with the cosine of the angle between the two vectors $\underline{A}.\underline{B}=|A||B|\cos\theta$. The result is just a number and a unit. The dot product of force and displacement is the Work Done in joules.

The other way of multiplying two vectors is called the cross product. It has a 'cross' symbol between them, $\underline{A}\times\underline{B}$ and it's spoken as 'A cross B'. (You also see the notation $\underline{A}\wedge\underline{B}$ ). This time, the angle enters with the sine. The result of the cross product is a vector of magnitude $|A||B|\sin\theta$. You get maximum effect when they are at right angles (unlike the dot product where maximum effect occurs when the two vectors are parallel). The direction of the cross product is the tricky bit; it's at right angles to both the 'A' and the 'B' !! The full definition of torque uses the cross product: $\underline{T} = \underline{r}\times\underline{F}$. This is largely avoided at Advanced Higher level since the direction of the torque vector can seem a bit odd. Sometimes the torque points the same way as the spin axis; when it doesn't, the fun begins. See page 49.

**Example 1**   Calculate the torque applied to each object below:

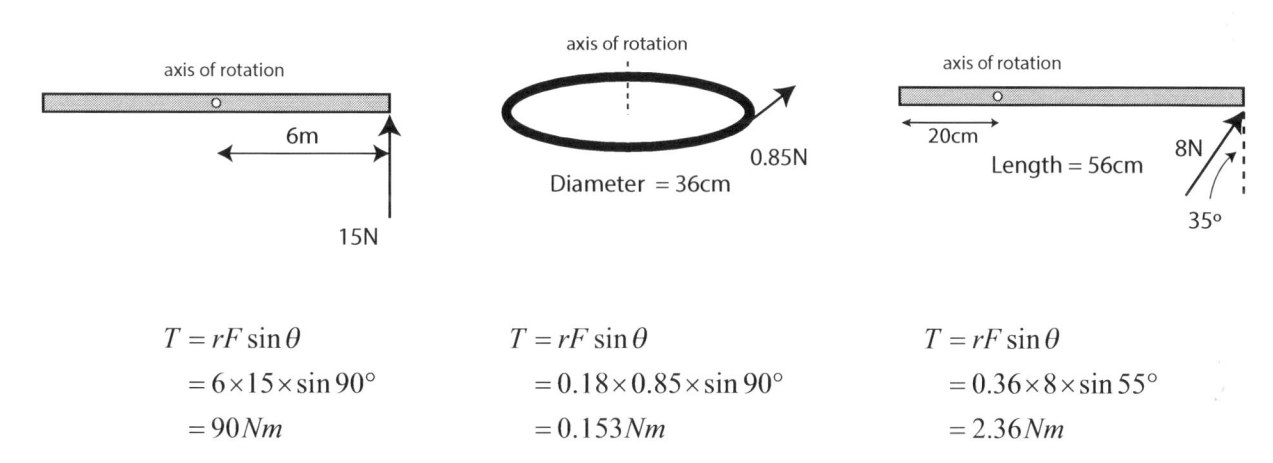

$T = rF\sin\theta$
$= 6\times 15\times\sin 90°$
$= 90\,Nm$

$T = rF\sin\theta$
$= 0.18\times 0.85\times\sin 90°$
$= 0.153\,Nm$

$T = rF\sin\theta$
$= 0.36\times 8\times\sin 55°$
$= 2.36\,Nm$

**Example 2**   The thin rod below is at rest. What force 'F' is required to keep it that way?

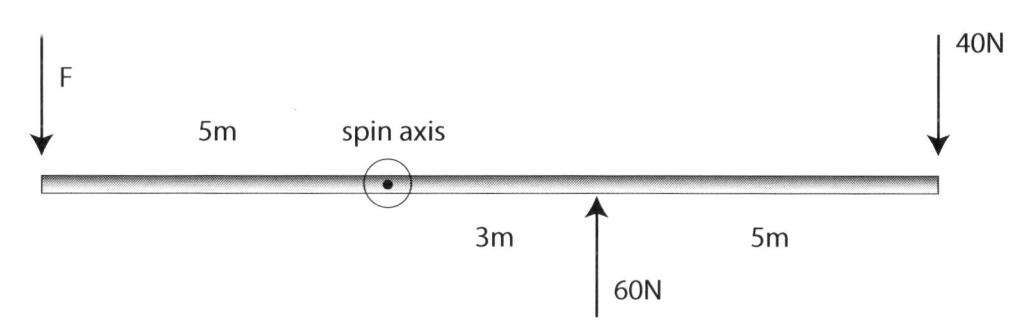

The torque comes from three places. If we add up the torques it should give a result of zero. Taking anticlockwise as the positive direction, and with the forces applied at an angle of 90°, in each case:

$$5\times F + 3\times 60 - 8\times 40 = 0 \quad\Rightarrow\quad 5F = 140 \quad\Rightarrow\quad F = +28\,\text{N}$$

# Bringing it Together...Torque and Moment of Inertia

**Questions** on Newton's 2nd Law *F=ma* can be quite easy; like this one:

A car engine provides a forward force of 3900N to the right. The forces due to friction on the car are 1500N. Calculate the acceleration of the car if its mass is 1200kg.

Usual procedure: pick the single body to which Newton's Law is to apply (the car), calculate the result of all the forces on the single body (3900N - 1500N = 2400N to the right), then work out the acceleration:

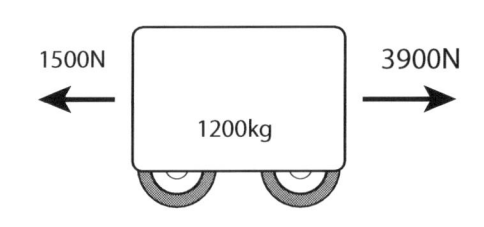

$$a = \frac{F}{m} = \frac{2400}{1200} = 2\,\text{m s}^{-2}$$

**Questions** in rotational dynamics are similar. We use moment of inertia instead of mass. We use torque instead of force. We get the answer for the angular acceleration rather than the linear acceleration. So instead of *F=ma* we use the equation:

$$T = I\alpha$$

Think of moment of inertia as a measure of the resistance to changes in the speed of rotation, and torque as a bit of rotational 'welly'.

**Example 1** A solid cylinder of mass 15kg has radius 0.12m. It is subject to a driving torque of 6Nm. The shaft produces a frictional torque of 2Nm. Calculate the angular acceleration of the cylinder.

Work out the result of the torques: (6 - 2) = 4Nm (in the same direction as the driving torque).

Calculate the moment of inertia of the cylinder:

$$I = \frac{1}{2}mr^2 = \frac{1}{2} \times 15 \times 0.12^2 = 0.108\,\text{kg m}^2$$

Pop it in the equation:

$$\alpha = \frac{T}{I} = \frac{4}{0.108} = 37\,\text{rad s}^{-2}$$

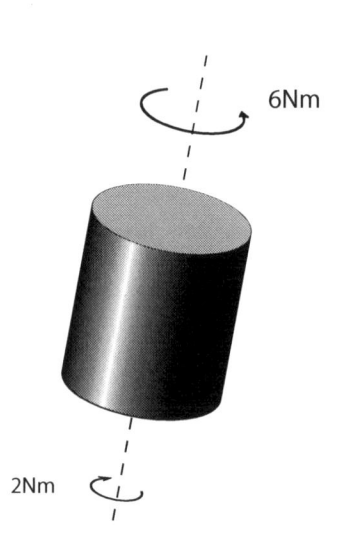

Basically, that's it. We could make it a bit harder by:

- getting you to work out the torques applied to the cylinder rather than just being given it. You would have to use:
  $$T = rF\sin\theta$$

- giving you an object with two parts to it so that you have to work out the moment of inertia of each part then add them to get the total.

- really trying to vex you. We could give you the dimensions of the cylinder with its density. You then have to calculate the mass using:
  $$\rho = M/V$$

- camouflaging it with a story about a pair of denims in a spin dryer.

These are all little details, don't lose sight of the overall simplicity.

**Example 2** A propeller / rotor system is modelled as a long thin rod attached at its centre to a solid cylinder (diagram below). The whole system rotates about the dotted axis. The data for the components are as follows:

Rod length: 2.4m

Rod mass: 98kg

Rotor radius: 0.5m

Rotor depth: 0.2m

Rotor density: 7800kg m$^{-3}$

(a) Calculate the mass of the rotor:

$$\rho = M/V$$

$$M = \rho V$$

$$= 7800 \times \pi r^2 h$$

$$= 7800 \times \pi \times 0.5^2 \times 0.2 = 1225 \text{kg}$$

(b) Calculate the total Moment of Inertia:

$$I = \frac{1}{12}ml^2 + \frac{1}{2}mr^2$$

$$= \frac{1}{12} \times 98 \times 2.4^2 + \frac{1}{2} \times 1225 \times 0.5^2 = 47 + 153 = 200 \text{kg m}^2$$

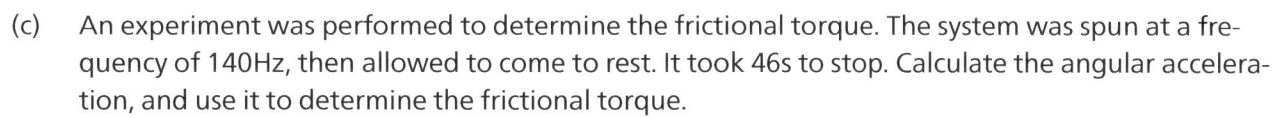

(c) An experiment was performed to determine the frictional torque. The system was spun at a frequency of 140Hz, then allowed to come to rest. It took 46s to stop. Calculate the angular acceleration, and use it to determine the frictional torque.

$$\alpha = \frac{(\omega - \omega_o)}{t} = \frac{(0 - 140 \times 2\pi)}{46} = -19.12 \text{rad s}^{-2}$$

use $T = I\alpha$ with 'T' the frictional torque:

$$T_{Frictional} = I\alpha = 200 \times (-19.12) = -3825 \text{Nm}$$

(d) A force of 17000N is applied tangentially to the rim of the rotor. Calculate the angular acceleration of the system. Firstly, work out the driving torque:

$$T_{Driving} = rF\sin\theta = 0.5 \times 17000 \times \sin 90° = 8500 \text{Nm}$$

Then the result of the driving and frictional torques:

$$T_{Result} = T_{Driving} + T_{Frictional} = 8500 + (-3825) = 4675 \text{Nm}$$

Finally calculate the angular acceleration: $T = I\alpha \Rightarrow \alpha = \frac{T}{I} = \frac{4675}{200} = 23.4 \text{rad s}^{-2}$

## Pulley & Weight

This looks like a straightforward example but it can catch out the unwary.

A free pulley wheel has a light cord wrapped around it with a weight attached to the other end, as shown. The pulley has mass 'M' and radius 'R'. The weight on the end of the cord has mass 'm' and we ignore the mass of the cord. I'm using the symbol 'T' for the tension in the cord; do not confuse this with the torque (symbol '$\tau$').

On the diagram, notice that the cord has 'T' for tension in two places. The bottom one labelled 'T' is part of the force diagram for the small mass 'm'. The top one labelled 'T' is used to calculate the torque on the rim of the pulley. The cord is in tension, and as far as the small mass is concerned, it experiences an upwards force due to this tension (otherwise the small mass would just accelerate at 'g').

*You could easily have made a mistake here and just put all the torque on the rim due to the small weight 'mg'. The torque is due to the tension in the cord.*

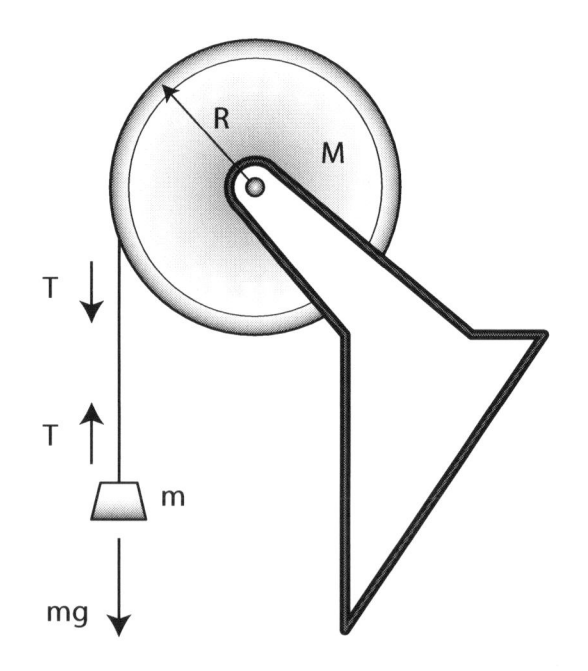

The small mass accelerates downwards, so there is an unbalanced force on it. Using Newton's 2nd Law on the small mass:

$$mg - T = ma$$

The torque on the rim produces an angular acceleration:

$$\text{Torque } \tau = I\alpha \quad \Rightarrow \quad RT = \frac{1}{2}MR^2\alpha \quad \Rightarrow \quad T = \frac{1}{2}MR\alpha$$

The tangential acceleration '$a_t$' of the rim is the same as the acceleration 'a' of the small mass, so use the expression $a_t = R\alpha$ to get: $T = \frac{Ma}{2}$. Substitute into the equation for the small mass to get:

$$mg - T = ma \quad \Rightarrow \quad mg - \frac{Ma}{2} = ma \quad \Rightarrow \quad a = \left(\frac{2m}{M+2m}\right)g$$

Analysing the behaviour of an equation is something a physicist should be good at. The equation above for the acceleration is an example. The two things you can change are the masses 'm' and 'M'. If you divide top and bottom by 'M', you can rewrite the equation in terms of the mass ratio m/M:

$$a = \left(\frac{2m}{M+2m}\right)g \quad \Rightarrow \quad a = \left(\frac{2\frac{m}{M}}{1+2\frac{m}{M}}\right)g$$

This is an equation in one variable, the ratio m/M. It's graph is plotted on the next page. You'll notice that it has a funny scale; it's called four cycle log-linear. It's a way of plotting a wide range of values without getting the left side all squashed-up. Ask your Maths teacher about the horizontal scale.

# Rotational Motion & Astrophysics

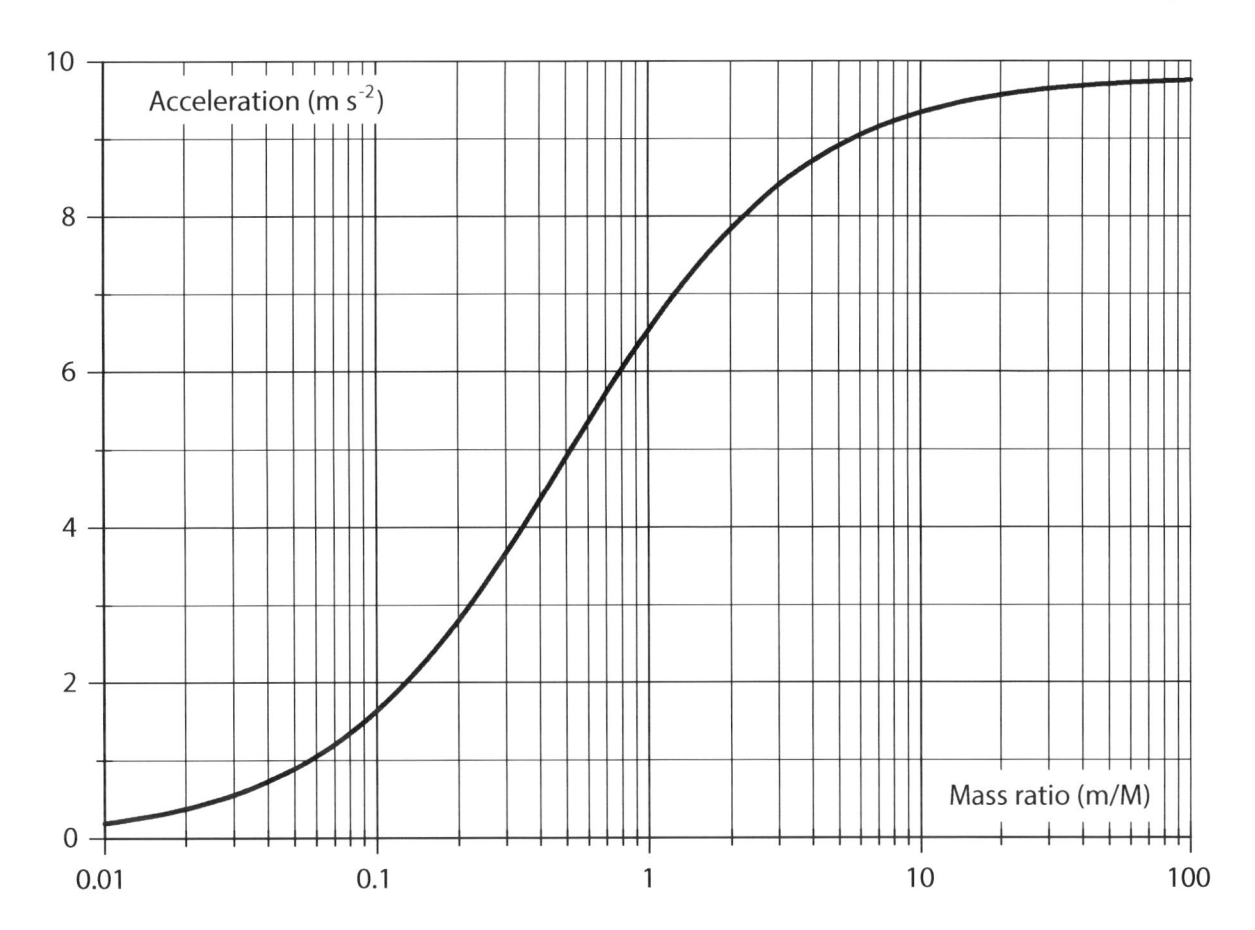

[Graph: Acceleration (m s⁻²) vs Mass ratio (m/M) on a logarithmic x-axis from 0.01 to 100, showing an S-shaped curve rising from near 0 to approximately 9.8 m s⁻².]

From the graph:

$\dfrac{m}{M} \ll 1$   The small mass is much less than the mass of the pulley and the acceleration is very small. This agrees with your common sense.

$\dfrac{m}{M} = 1$   When the small mass is the same as the mass of the pulley we get:

$$a = \left(\dfrac{2M}{M+2M}\right)g = \dfrac{2}{3}g = 6.5\,\text{m s}^{-2}$$

$\dfrac{m}{M} \gg 1$   When the weight is much heavier than the pulley, the acceleration tends towards 9.8 m s⁻².

You can also solve for the tension 'T' giving: $T = \left(\dfrac{Mm}{M+2m}\right)g$. If the mass of the pulley 'M' is much greater than the small mass 'm', this reduces to $T = mg$ (the bottom line tends to 'M' and you can cancel 'M' top and bottom). So the force on the rim is given by the weight of the small mass only when the pulley is much heavier $M \gg m$. If the small mass 'm' is much heavier than the pulley, the tension tends towards $T = \dfrac{1}{2}Mg$ which is half the weight of the pulley.

Investigating all of this would make a good project. You could bring in the frictional torque of the pulley, pulleys with holes in them, cords which aren't lightweight. . . . . . . .

## Angular Momentum

The momentum 'p' of a body moving in a straight line is $p = mv$. Isaac Newton considered momentum as more than just a product of two numbers. To him it was a stand-alone single item; he called it the 'quantity of motion'. We usually write his 2nd Law as:

$$F = ma = m\frac{dv}{dt}$$

Newton kept the mass and velocity terms together and wrote it like this:

$$F = \frac{d(mv)}{dt} = \frac{dp}{dt} \quad \text{....'force equals rate of change of momentum'...}$$

This is a better definition of the 2nd Law than we had before. For a start, it means we can handle situations where the mass changes:

$$F = \frac{d(mv)}{dt} = m\frac{dv}{dt} + v\frac{dm}{dt}$$

The second term arises since we differentiated a product. You would have to use this with the launch of a spacerocket where the mass of the rocket decreases as fuel is burned.

This better definition also leads us straight to what we want in rotational motion. We just make the usual substitutions: torque for force, moment of inertia for mass and angular velocity for velocity.

$$F = \frac{d(mv)}{dt} \quad \Rightarrow \quad T = \frac{d(I\omega)}{dt} \quad \text{....'torque equals rate of change of angular momentum'}$$

Just as linear momentum has its own symbol 'p', the angular momentum has its own symbol 'L':

$$p = mv \quad \Rightarrow \quad L = I\omega$$

And just as linear momentum is conserved, angular momentum is conserved (with the usual add-ons):

*'linear momentum is conserved if there are no external forces acting on the system'*

*'angular momentum is conserved if there are no external torques acting on the system'*

You get a 'feel' for linear momentum when someone throws a medicine ball at you. But what does angular momentum 'feel' like? Ask a carpenter. He'll have used an electric planar and an angle grinder. Hold the planar in your hand, switch it on, press the trigger for full power. And then turn around. The planar doesn't want to go with you. It tries to keep the direction of the angular momentum constant. There's nothing in nature like it (lack of high speed rotations there), so it feels odd.

Should you ever find yourself tightening a nut with a spanner on the outside of a spaceship, you'll find it difficult. Unless you've something to hold down your feet, you will just turn around. Magnetic boots might help if the spaceship is made of steel, but this is unlikely due to its weight. Solutions?

**Units**: the units of angular momentum come from $L = I\omega$. There's kg m² from the moment of inertia, and rad s⁻¹ from the angular velocity. Using radians for the angle means no additional constant in the formula and by convention, you don't include it in the unit. This gives: kg m² s⁻¹.

# Rotational Motion & Astrophysics

## Example

Calculate the angular momentum for each case below:

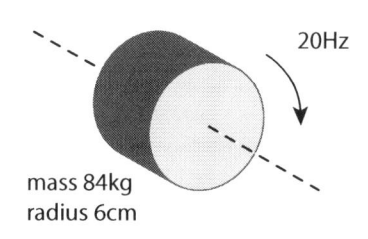

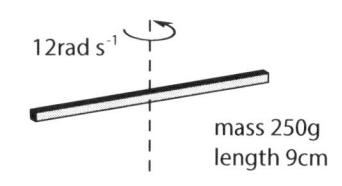

**Solid Cylinder:** mass 84kg, radius 6cm, 20Hz

**Thin Rod:** 12 rad s$^{-1}$, mass 250g, length 9cm

**Hoop:** 30rpm, mass 5kg, diameter 4cm

$$L = I\omega = \frac{1}{2}MR^2\omega$$

$$= \frac{1}{2} \times 84 \times 0.06^2 \times 20 \times 2\pi$$

$$= 19 \text{ kg m}^2 \text{ s}^{-1}$$

$$L = I\omega = \frac{1}{12}ML^2\omega$$

$$= \frac{1}{12} \times 0.25 \times 0.09^2 \times 12$$

$$= 0.002 \text{ kg m}^2 \text{ s}^{-1}$$

$$L = I\omega = MR^2\omega$$

$$= 5 \times 0.02^2 \times 30 \times 2\pi / 60$$

$$= 0.0063 \text{ kg m}^2 \text{ s}^{-1}$$

Earlier on, we derived an expression for the kinetic energy of the object due to its rotation:

$$E_K(Rot.) = \frac{1}{2}\left[\sum_{all\ i} m_i r_i^2\right]\omega^2 = \frac{1}{2}I\omega^2$$

For the three examples above, this would be:

The Solid Cylinder: $\quad E_K(Rot.) = \frac{1}{2}I\omega^2 = \frac{1}{2} \times \left(\frac{1}{2} \times 84 \times 0.06^2\right) \times (20 \times 2\pi)^2 = 1194$ Joules

The Thin Rod: $\quad E_K(Rot.) = \frac{1}{2}I\omega^2 = \frac{1}{2} \times \left(\frac{1}{12} \times 0.25 \times 0.09^2\right) \times 12^2 = 0.012$ Joules

The Hoop: $\quad E_K(Rot.) = \frac{1}{2}I\omega^2 = \frac{1}{2} \times \left(5 \times 0.02^2\right) \times (30 \times 2\pi / 60)^2 = 0.00987$ Joules

*Nerdy note*: Rotational motion is much more complicated than I've let-on. The problem is that many of these quantities are vectors. I've written the simplest scalar versions of these. Here are the proper vector definitions:

$$\underline{v} = \underline{\omega} \wedge \underline{r} \qquad \underline{T} = \underline{r} \wedge \underline{F} \qquad \underline{T} = \frac{d\underline{L}}{dt} \qquad \underline{L} = \underline{r} \wedge \underline{p}$$

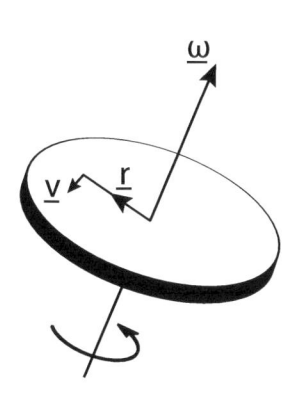

They involve vector cross products, and the direction of a cross product is at right angles to the plane formed by the other two. The diagram shows the direction of the angular velocity vector '$\underline{\omega}$' for a rotating disc. The position vector '$\underline{r}$', instantaneous velocity '$\underline{v}$' of a point of the disc and the angular velocity are all at right angles to each other.

We will encounter an example later in this unit (page 47) where the vector nature of these quantities is important: that's the precession of the direction of the spin axis of planet Earth.

## Conservation of Angular Momentum

The one system I haven't mentioned yet, is the angular momentum of a point particle. It uses the same formula as before $L = I\omega$, but it's easy to take the wrong numbers; this example shows the correct way.

The diagram shows a solid disc of radius 'R' and mass 'M'. The disc is at rest and is free to rotate about its centre without any frictional torque acting from the bearings. A point particle of mass 'm' is moving in a straight line with velocity 'v' directed towards a small cup on the rim of the disc. The point mass will be caught in the cup and start the solid disc rotating.

Conservation of angular momentum is used to predict the final angular velocity '$\omega$' of the disc:

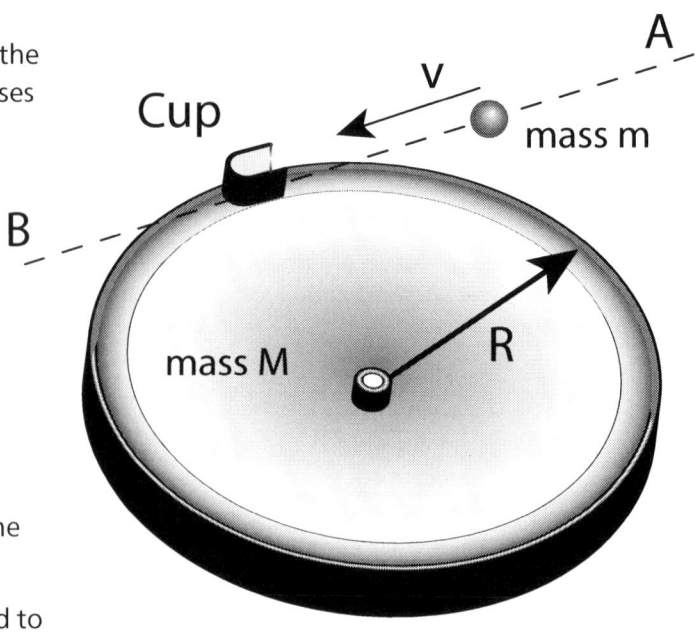

*Total angular momentum before collision equals total angular momentum after collision.*

The friction free bearings ensure that there are no external torques applied. The initial angular momentum is due to the point particle. This will seem strange as it isn't rotating. All that means is that it has no angular momentum with respect to an axis through its own centre, but it does have an angular momentum with respect to an outside axis, like the one through the centre of the solid disc. This makes angular momentum (like potential energy and like velocity), depend on what you measure it with respect to. For this system, we take it with respect to the axis of spin about the centre of the solid disc. We can start from $L = I\omega$ and apply it to a point particle to get:

$$L = I\omega = \left(mr^2\right)\omega = mr(r\omega) = mvr$$

The question is what you take for the 'r'. The small mass travels along the direction AB in the diagram. The distance 'r' is the shortest distance from the line AB to the axis of spin (sometimes called the 'moment arm'). For our experiment, the cup is on the rim, so 'r' is the radius of the disc. (The proper definition of the angular momentum of a point particle is the cross product $\underline{L} = \underline{x} \times \underline{p} = xp\sin\theta = mvx\sin\theta$ where 'x' is the distance from the particle to the axis of spin. The moment arm is $x\sin\theta$).

The final angular momentum is due to the total from the solid disc and the small mass stuck in the cup:

$$L = I\omega_{disc} + I\omega_{mass\,in\,cup} = \frac{1}{2}MR^2\omega_{final} + mR^2\omega_{final}$$

Apply conservation of angular momentum before and after impact, (where $mvr \rightarrow mvR$):

$$mvR = \frac{1}{2}MR^2\omega_{final} + mR^2\omega_{final} \qquad \text{Rearrange to get: } \omega_{final} = \frac{v}{R}\left(\frac{2m}{M+2m}\right)$$

You can catch a glimpse of one of our earliest equations $\omega = \frac{v}{r}$ with a constant $\left(\frac{2m}{M+2m}\right)$. This is always a good sign; it shows you've got the variables correct. Also, the direction of the spin axes before and after collision was the same, so it's okay to treat the problem using scalars.

# Rotational Motion & Astrophysics

## Ice Skater in a Spin

Figure skating on ice is a good example of the Law of Conservation of Angular Momentum. Remember it is only exactly true if there are no external torques applied. In the case of the figure skater, there is contact between the ice skate and the ice. This applies a frictional torque to the skater which resists the motion. The International Space Station is the ideal venue to demonstrate the Conservation Law and there are short video clips available on the internet. Here is one: http://www.our-space.org/materials/states-of-matter/angular-momentum (this site has a downloadable video clip for PC or Mac).

The skater starts spinning slowly with both arms straight out. She then brings her arms into the tuck position against her body. As she does so, her angular velocity increases. The Conservation Law states that:

$$L_{before} = L_{after} \quad \Rightarrow \quad I_{before}\omega_{before} = I_{after}\omega_{after}$$

Bringing her arms in decreases her moment of inertia. The Law demands that her angular velocity increases. Here is a rough calculation using typical values.

Model the human body as a solid cylinder, with two rods for arms. The typical skater has a mass of about 50kg with each arm accounting for about 6.5% of the total. The body core has a radius of about 15cm. The moment of inertia for a rod spinning about one end has a coefficient of one third, and the solid cylinder has a coefficient of one half.

Moment of inertia with arms out ('before'):

$$I_{before} = 2 \times \frac{1}{3} m_{arm} l_{arm}^2 + \frac{1}{2} m_{body} r_{body}^2$$

$$= 2 \times \frac{1}{3} \times 3.5 \times 0.75^2 + \frac{1}{2} \times 43 \times 0.15^2$$

$$= 1.31 + 0.48 = 1.79 \, \text{kg m}^2$$

Moment of inertia with arms in ('after'):

$$I_{after} = \frac{1}{2} m_{body} r_{body}^2 = \frac{1}{2} \times 50 \times 0.15^2 = 0.56 \, \text{kg m}^2$$

The ratio of angular velocities is:

$$I_{before}\omega_{before} = I_{after}\omega_{after} \quad \Rightarrow \quad \frac{\omega_{after}}{\omega_{before}} = \frac{I_{before}}{I_{after}} = \frac{1.79}{0.56} = 3.2$$

Start with one leg out and it'll be even larger!

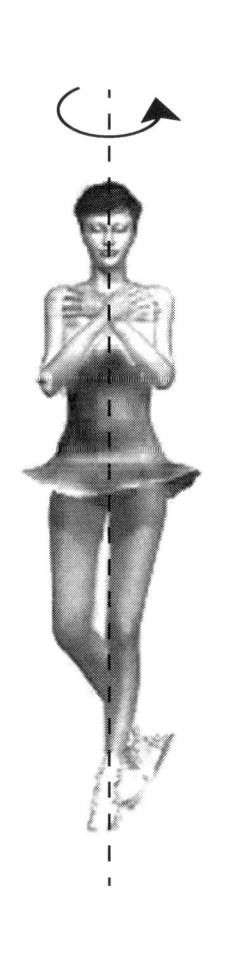

## The Rolling Cylinder

This is the standard example of energy conservation in a rotating system. A solid cylinder rolls down a slope without slipping. The object is to derive an expression for the speed of the cylinder at the bottom of the slope as a function of its starting height.

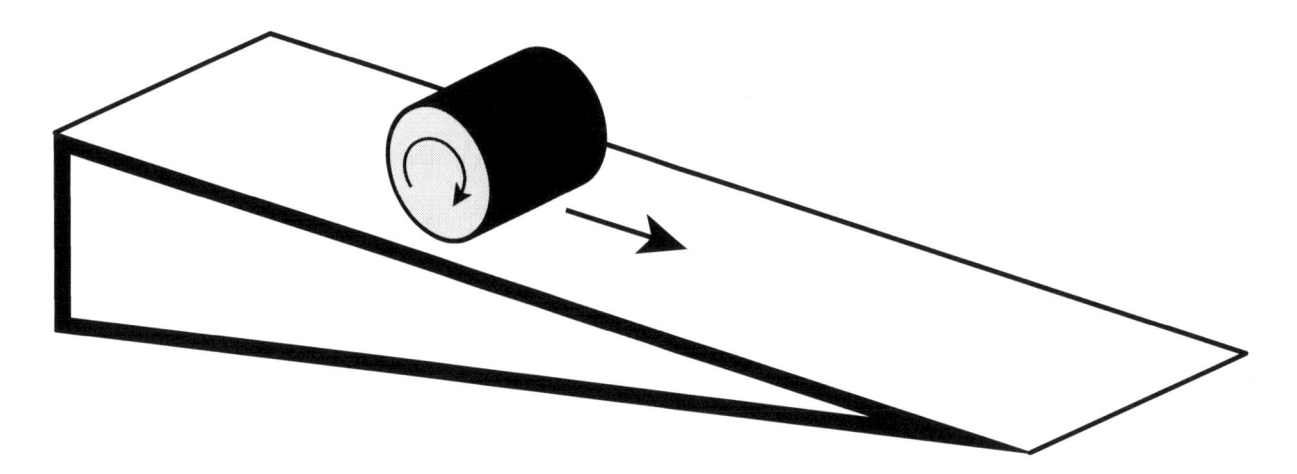

We ignore friction to keep the problem simple. Unfortunately we require friction between the cylinder and the slope to make the cylinder turn. This goes under the name of 'rolling without slipping' and it's a contradiction; no question about it. Mathematicians will be slightly annoyed by this manoeuvre but physicists will shrug their shoulders and get cracking. Lets assume there's enough friction to make the cylinder turn, but the conversion to heat energy has a negligible effect on the answer!

The gravitational potential energy at the top is converted into kinetic energy of motion. Assume that the total kinetic energy is just the sum of the rotational kinetic energy and the kinetic energy of translation (see bottom of page 49 for a nerdy proof):

$$mgh = \frac{1}{2}I\omega^2 + \frac{1}{2}mv^2$$

We use $I = \frac{1}{2}mr^2$ for the moment of inertia of the cylinder and $v = \omega r$ for the speed of a point on the rim of the cylinder. If the cylinder doesn't slip on the slope, the speed of a point on the rim of the cylinder will be the same as the speed of the (centre of mass of the) cylinder down the slope. Many people have trouble with this bit. Think of the cylinder making a full turn and the centre of mass moving a distance of 2πr down the slope. Putting it together:

$$mgh = \frac{1}{2}\left(\frac{1}{2}mr^2\right)\left(\frac{v}{r}\right)^2 + \frac{1}{2}mv^2 = \frac{1}{4}mv^2 + \frac{1}{2}mv^2 = \frac{3}{4}mv^2$$

Can you spot that the translational kinetic energy is always twice the rotational kinetic energy?

Rearrange as a function of the starting height 'h':

$$v^2 = \frac{4}{3}gh \quad \Rightarrow \quad v = \sqrt{\frac{4}{3}gh}$$

As usual, the mass cancels out, so it doesn't matter about the mass of the cylinder. There's no radius in the result either, so it can also be a small or big cylinder. The only things which count are the starting height and gravitational field strength. Compare the result with a mass dropped vertically $v = \sqrt{2gh}$. Four-thirds is less than two, so rolling down a slope makes you slower at the bottom, as expected.

# Rotational Motion & Astrophysics

## Torquing of Planet Earth.........Precession

Our Solar System could have been a lot simpler. The planets could be perfect spheres instead of being a bit flattened. They could go around the Sun in perfect circles instead of being ellipses. Their north-south poles could stick straight up the way instead of being tilted. Being flattened and moving in elliptical orbits with tilted axes drops a whole host of complications on astronomers; in addition to things like the seasons and long term climatic patterns.

Here's one of them; the result of the Earth having a bulge at the equator. The diagram shows planet Earth with a greatly exaggerrated bulge at the equator (in reality it's about ⅓% greater). Both the Sun and the Moon contribute to the effect with the Moon about twice as important.

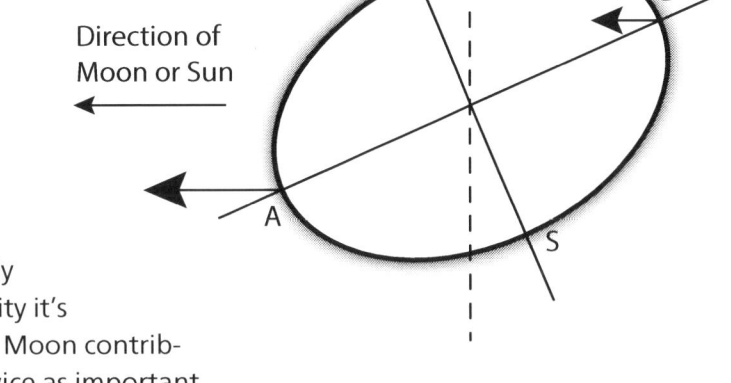

The Earth spins on its axis once a day at an angle of 23½° to the dotted vertical line. It has an angular velocity of:

$$\omega = \frac{2\pi}{T} = \frac{2\pi}{24 \times 60 \times 60} = 7.27 \times 10^{-5} \text{ rad s}^{-1}$$

This gives the Earth an angular momentum of:

$$L = I\omega = 8 \times 10^{37} \times 7.27 \times 10^{-5} = 5.8 \times 10^{33} \text{ kg m}^2\text{s}^{-1}$$

Angular momentum 'L' is a vector and points along the north south spin axis as shown on the diagram.

Look at the vertical dotted line. Half of the planet's mass is on each side of the line. The half on the left nearest the Moon (I'll use the Moon since it's the dominant force) has more mass on its bottom part. The centre of mass for this left half is below the horizontal midway line. The right side has its centre of mass above the midway line. Both halves get pulled gravitationally to the left, but the left half is nearer the Moon so gets a slightly stronger pull. This results in a clockwise torque on the planet.

This is where your commonsense gets in the way. Torque is also a vector and for the system in the diagram, it points **into** the page. Torque is the rate of change of angular momentum:

$$T = \frac{dL}{dt} \quad \Rightarrow \quad \Delta L = T \Delta t$$

These are vectors and the torque 'T' acting over a small time 'Δt' produces a small change in the angular momentum 'ΔL'. The torque and *change* in angular momentum point in the same direction (into the page). This makes the angular momentum vector follow the dotted circular path; a cone of angle 23½°.

What does this mean for Earthlings like us? Virtually nothing, since it takes 25,800 years for our north south axis to make one complete circuit of the dotted line. At present, it points very near to the star named Polaris, which is handy for navigation since it's quite bright.

The effect is known as the Precession of the Equinoxes. The diagram above shows the Earth with its north pole tilted towards the Sun. There are two positions in its orbit around the Sun where it is neither tilted towards nor away from the Sun (the sun would pass directly overhead if you were on the equator). The Spring and Autumn equinoxes are the positions of the Sun against the starry background at these two times. This position shifts in step with the polar axis, hence Precession of the Equinoxes.

47

# Satellite Stability & Control

Since its launch in 1990, the Hubble Space Telescope has provided some of the most detailed images of the universe. Above Earth's protective atmosphere, it sees deep into space and far back in time with images of the early universe like the Extreme Deep Field in the constellation of Fornax, or stunning images of star nurseries like the Pillars of Creation in the Eagle Nebula.

The instrument is a 2.4m diameter reflector. During image recording, it must be kept very steady, pointing in a constant direction. We're talking about a serious amount of 'steady' here. Over a 24hr period, it can't deviate more than an angle of 2 millionths of a degree. That's the thickness of a human hair at a distance of one mile. How steady is that! From a Scottish perspective, it's like keeping a laser beam from Glasgow trained on a shirt button at the phoney milepost at John o'Groats.

The engineering requires a system to detect changes in position and a system to make the corrections required if it changes position. The detection system consists of six gyroscopes contained in three paired units. Gyroscopes can malfunction and the satellite requires at least three of these to be in working order for full control of the system. Each gyroscope spins with a frequency of 320Hz and friction is kept very low through the use of air bearings. Electronics within the gyro detect very small movements of the spin axis and communicate this information to the onboard computer.

Satellites are lifted into orbit by sitting on top of powerful main-stage rockets, then released when high above most of the atmosphere. Just like rifle bullets, a rocket will travel along a smoother trajectory if it's spinning. The faster the spin, the better, but once released the satellite has to reduce its spin to a lower rate. This is achieved through conservation of angular momentum. Think back to the ice skater bringing her arms in to increase her angular velocity. The satellite does the opposite. It's called YoYo despin. This YouTube video shows an animation of a rocket launch, separation of the satellite, then de-spinning:

http://www.youtube.com/watch?v=ULTKCAINe5A

It illustrated the simple system shown in the diagram. Two equal masses on elastic cords are released from the core of the spaceship. They move outwards, and in doing so, increase the spaceships moment of inertia. By the Law of Conservation of Angular Momentum, the angular velocity of the whole assembly must decrease. Typically, the masses are a few kilograms and the cords are about 10 metres long. Once the operation is completed, the masses and cords are often dumped overboard to become space debris. In 2009, the astronauts in the International Space Station had to take refuge in their Soyez capsule when a piece of junk, thought to be from de-spinning, came close to hitting them at 22,000mph. It missed.

The Hubble Space Telescope is unusual in that the whole spaceship doesn't spin. If it did spin, it would produce images of curving star trails. Doh!

# Rotational Motion & Astrophysics

## Moving the Axis of Rotation

This demonstrates the vector nature of rotational motion and the strange things that happen when you change the direction of the spin axis.

Take something like a bikewheel and load it with weights along the rim to increase its moment of inertia. Stand on a platform which is free to rotate (usually based on a car axle plus wood). Ask an assistant to spin-up the wheel and pass it to you on the platform with the spin axis in the vertical position as shown. The axis of rotation of the platform and the wheel should both point vertically. Tilt the top of the wheel axle away from you and bring the bottom of the axle towards you. You will start rotating on the platform!

It's the universe obeying its own law of conservation of angular momentum. The total angular momentum of the system in the absence of external torques (that is, mechanically isolating you and the turntable) must remain constant. When the axis of spin of the wheel is tilted, the vertical component of the angular momentum is decreased. Angular momentum is conserved by transferring that change in angular momentum to the rest of the system, making you spin about a vertical axis. The torque produced is the rate of change of angular momentum so the quicker you tilt the wheel, the greater the torque (for a shorter time). If angular momentum was a scalar, it wouldn't work. Experiment by tilting the wheel axle horizontally or through 180°. It's all outside your comfort zone.

*Nerdy Note:* Finally, something for the purists. One thing a good physicist should always do is to take nothing for granted.
The assumption made in the rolling cylinder experiment was that the total kinetic energy was the sum of the rotational and translational contributions. This seems reasonable enough, but it should be proved. Here's how. Velocity is a vector, so we should write the expression for the kinetic energy in its vector form (a dot product):

$$E_K = \sum_{all\ i} \left(\frac{1}{2} m_i v_i^2\right) \quad \rightarrow \quad \sum_{all\ i} \left(\frac{1}{2} m_i \left(\mathbf{v_i} \cdot \mathbf{v_i}\right)\right)$$

The substitution: $\mathbf{v_i} \rightarrow \mathbf{v_i} - \mathbf{V}$ makes the whole object move sideways with velocity V, giving us:

$$E_K = \sum_{all\ i} \left(\frac{1}{2} m_i \left(\mathbf{v_i} \cdot \mathbf{v_i}\right)\right) \quad \rightarrow \quad \sum_{all\ i} \left(\frac{1}{2} m_i \left(\mathbf{v_i} - \mathbf{V}\right) \cdot \left(\mathbf{v_i} - \mathbf{V}\right)\right) = \sum_{all\ i} \left(\frac{1}{2} m_i \left(\mathbf{v_i} \cdot \mathbf{v_i} - 2\mathbf{v_i} \cdot \mathbf{V} + \mathbf{V} \cdot \mathbf{V}\right)\right)$$

$$E_K = \sum_{all\ i} \left(\frac{1}{2} m_i \left(v_i^2 - 2\mathbf{v_i} \cdot \mathbf{V} + V^2\right)\right) = \sum_{all\ i} \left(\frac{1}{2} m_i v_i^2\right) - \mathbf{V} \cdot \sum_{all\ i} \left(m_i \mathbf{v_i}\right) + \sum_{all\ i} \left(\frac{1}{2} m_i V^2\right)$$

The first term is the rotational kinetic energy and the last term is the translational kinetic energy. The middle term is zero since it contains the vector sum of the momenta of the particles of a rotating object in its centre of mass frame (opposite pairs cancel). QED.

# Section 1.4 Gravitation

The Moon goes around the Earth in an elliptical orbit at an average distance of 385000km. It does this because the Earth exerts a gravitational force on the Moon. Nothing unusual there, you might say. But, how about the fact that there's nothing between the Earth and the Moon; it's just space. A big load of zero. You might then begin to wonder how gravity works. We will return to this question on page 78.

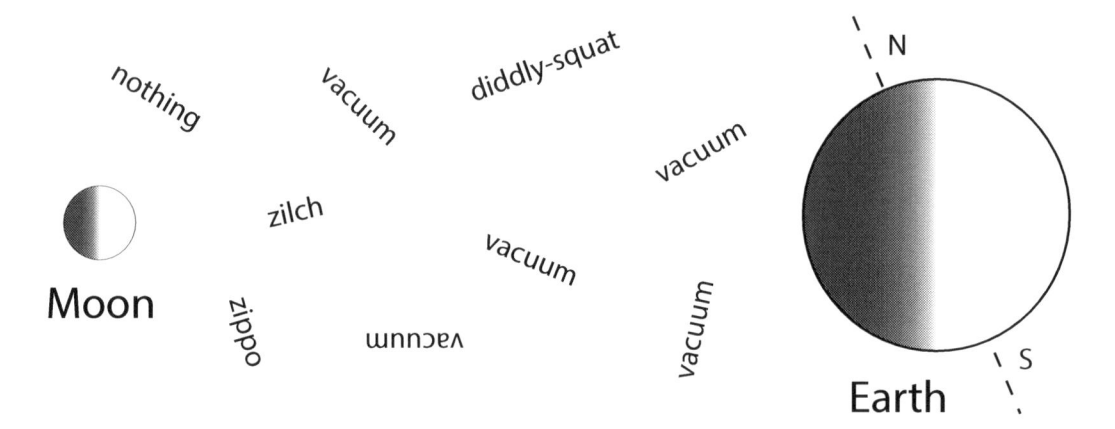

One idea though, is that the Earth and the Moon are surrounded by their own gravitational fields and interact through them. With that as your starting point, you go on to investigate the motion of objects in a gravitational field. But before the field concept was introduced, Copernicus (1500), proposed his life threatening idea that the Sun was at the centre of things. Galileo and Kepler (early 1600's), accepted this sun-centred view. Kepler produced a law relating the period of a planet to its distance from the Sun. It was based on accurate observations rather than a theory; he wasn't interested in how it might work. They didn't know what was 'out there'. How could they? It might have been air 'all the way up' as far as they were concerned. The idea of a force between the planet and the sun came with Newton in 1665, but that thorny question of how it might work was set aside for future generations of scientists. And it's still a mystery. The 'solution' of a gravitational field just begs the question.

## The Inverse-Square Law of Gravity

A gravitational field is produced by a mass 'M' and it fills the space around it, getting weaker as you go further away. Another mass 'm', positioned within the field produced by the first mass, will feel an attractive force towards it. This is how you know the field is there. A passing asteroid like the one in the obviously fake diagram opposite, will feel a force of attraction as it shoots passed the earth. This will make it follow a curved path.

The equation for the force of attraction of one mass on another came from Newton in 1665:

$$F = \frac{GMm}{r^2}$$

It is an example of an inverse square law; double the distance 'r' and you quarter the force of attraction 'F'. I've written it in its scalar form with no directions, but it's understood that the force between the masses is attractive. The two masses 'M' and 'm' attract each other with the same force 'F'. This equation isn't a definition (unlike $F=ma$), and requires to be experimentally tested.

# Rotational Motion & Astrophysics

If you study the subject at university, they will remind you that force is a vector and present you with the vector form of the equation. This comes in two versions. The position vector is $\underline{r} = r\hat{\underline{r}}$ where the one with the 'hat' above it is the unit vector (that is, 1 unit long and pointing outwards from 'M', the source of the gravitational field). When an object is at a distance of 50metres, the little italic '$r$' part is the 50m. Multiplying this by the unit vector gives the position (displacement) vector for the object.

You can express the force of 'M' on 'm' in terms of the unit position vector:

$$\underline{F} = -|F|\hat{\underline{r}} = -\frac{GMm}{r^2}\hat{\underline{r}}$$

Taking the scalar parts gives us the equation we will use. An alternative form uses the position vector:

$$\underline{F} = -\frac{GMm}{r^3}\underline{r}$$

Notice the cube of the distance in this one (since the position vector contains the distance '$r$'). The minus sign shows that the force is in the opposite direction from the outward pointing position vector (ie. 'm' is attracted towards 'M').

## The Universal Constant of Gravitation 'G'

The universal constant of gravitation (known as 'big G') sets the scale of the force. It's on the top line so the bigger it is, the bigger the force between the masses. Why do we need a constant? Newton had already used the equation $F=ma$ to define the unit of force and he wanted to use newtons for gravitational force. If you take two masses, each of 1kg, and placed them 1metre apart, the number for big 'G' is the same as the number for the force of attraction:

$$F = \frac{GMm}{r^2} \quad \Rightarrow \quad F = \frac{G \times 1 \times 1}{1^2}$$

If the gravitational force of attraction between them was exactly 1Newton, then big 'G' would be one and we wouldn't need a constant. In fact, the force of attraction is a lot less than one newton, it's about $6.674 \times 10^{-11}$N. This number is the size of 'big G'. To obtain its units, rearrange the force equation:

$$F = \frac{GMm}{r^2} \quad \Rightarrow \quad G = \frac{Fr^2}{Mm} \quad \Rightarrow \quad \frac{\text{Nm}^2}{\text{kg}^2} \quad \Rightarrow \quad \frac{(\text{kg m s}^{-2})\text{m}^2}{\text{kg}^2} = \text{m}^3\,\text{s}^{-2}\,\text{kg}^{-1}$$

Big 'G' has to be determined by experiment. It is the least well known of the important constants; the value given above ($6.674 \times 10^{-11}$ m$^3$ s$^{-2}$ kg$^{-1}$), is the most up to date measurement. Currently, experiments are being performed to determine whether 'G' is actually constant and if the inverse square law is accurate. Recent measurements using torsional pendulums have confirmed this law to be reliable down to separations of the two masses of at least 25μm.

Is big 'G' constant? If big 'G' changes by as much as 1 part in $10^{13}$ in a year, it will be detectable using Lunar Laser Ranging. During the Apollo Moon flights in the 1970's, the astronauts left reflectors on the surface. The picture on the right shows the one left behind by the Apollo 14 crew on the Fra Mauro region of the Moon. The reflector consists of about 100 corner cubes, mounted in a square aluminium panel resting on the lunar surface, pointed in such a way that it faces toward the Earth. The McDonald Observatory in Texas sends a laser beam through an optical telescope to hit one of the reflectors, and the corner cubes reflect the beam directly back toward the point of origin.

The reflector makes a very small target, so even when the beam is correctly aligned in the telescope, actually hitting a lunar reflector is quite challenging. Laser pulses are sent out from Earth at a rate of 20Hz. The round-trip is timed and with knowledge of the speed of light, the distance can be calculated.

The numbers are impressive! The laser pulse of wavelength 532nm is about 3cm long and contains $3.1 \times 10^{17}$ photons. When the beam reaches the moon it is about 2km in diameter. The beam returns to Earth spread over 15km. Each pulse only returns about one to ten photons to the telescope! By comparison, the faintest stars the human eye can detect will put about 500 photons per second into each eye pupil. The time taken for the round trip is measured to within a few picoseconds and gives a distance to the moon accurate to about 1mm!!!!

This technique has determined that the Moon is receding from the Earth at a rate of 3.8cm per year and that big 'G' is constant to a very high degree.

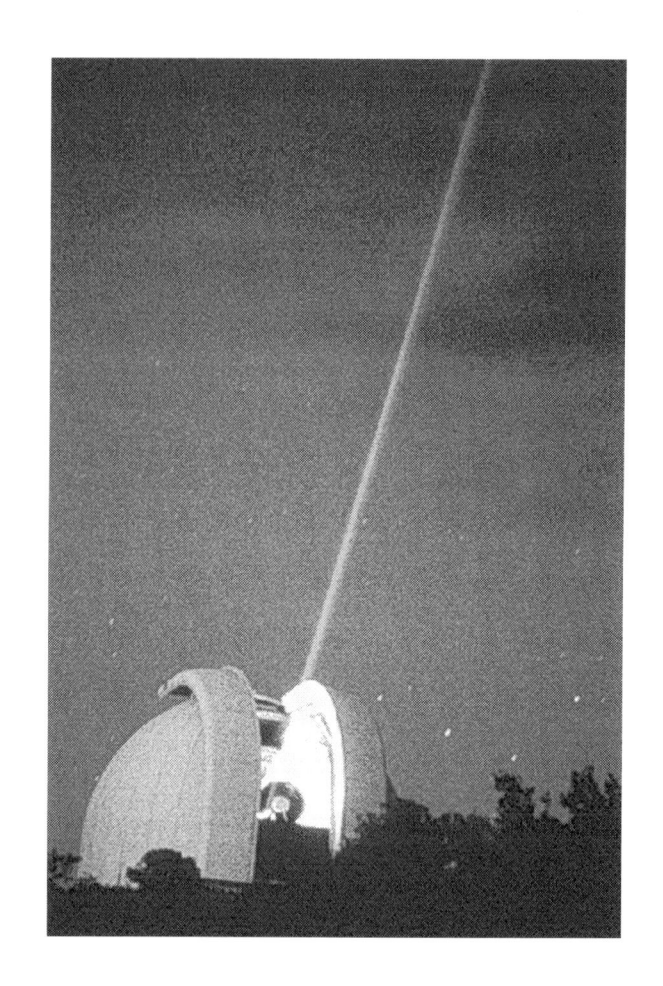

## Measuring 'G' – the Michell – Cavendish Experiment

Henry Cavendish (late 1700's), didn't invent this apparatus; he gives the credit to John Michell;

> *Many years ago, the late Rev. John Michell of this Society, contrived a method of determining the density of the Earth, by rendering sensible the attraction of small quantities of matter; but, as he was engaged in other pursuits, he did not complete the apparatus till a short time before his death, and did not live to make any experiments with it. After his death, the apparatus came to the Rev. Francis John Hyde Wollaston, Jacksonian professor at Cambridge, who, not having conveniences for making experiments with it, in the manner he could wish, was so good as to give it to me.*

In addition, Cavendish didn't use it to measure big 'G'! He used it to measure the average density (strictly, the specific gravity) of planet Earth. The diagram on the right is a modern version of Michell's original. His version suspended the two small masses (m) with a wire over 1m long and a piece of wood almost 2m in length. The small masses were lead spheres 5cm in diameter (about ¾kg) and the large masses (M) were lead spheres 8cm in diameter (about 3kg). The motion of the arm was observed using a telescope. During observations, in his own words, "he had to defend it from the wind".

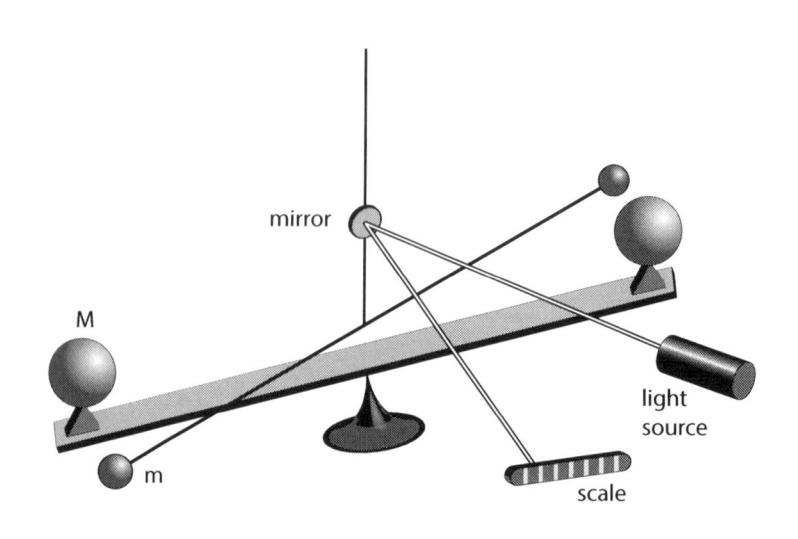

# Rotational Motion & Astrophysics

Briefly, here's how it works ( it's called a torsional pendulum). Two small spheres on the ends of a fine arm are suspended by a thin wire. If you twist the wire by rotating the fine arm, the wire will try to restore itself to its original untwisted state (you'll know about this if you've ever coiled up a hawser-laid rope). This is a restoring torque and it's proportional to the angle: $T = -k\theta$. You have to perform a preliminary experiment to measure the constant 'k'. This is done by giving the arm a gentle swing and timing the period of oscillation. The apparatus is allowed to settle, then the two large spheres 'M' are introduced as shown on the diagram. The gravitational attraction between the small and large spheres produces a torque. The fine arm slowly adjusts and overshoots, finally coming to a stop after about a day's worth of slow oscillations. At this position, the restoring torque is balanced by the torque due to the gravitational attraction:

$$T_{restore} = k\theta \qquad T_{grav} = \frac{L}{2} F \sin 90 + \frac{L}{2} F \sin 90 \qquad \Rightarrow \qquad k\theta = LF$$

where 'L' is the length of the fine arm. Substitute for the gravitational force of attraction:

$$k\theta = L \times \frac{GMm}{r^2}$$

All the quantities are known except 'G'. If Cavendish's raw data had been used to calculate 'G', his answer would be about 1% too small ( a very notable achievement).

## Drawing / Illustrating a Gravitational Field

Illustrating gravitational fields using shading (like the field around the Earth on page 50), is quite difficult to draw, so an alternative system using lines was invented. The lines themselves aren't real; they are just a quick way of illustrating the strength and direction of the field. Later, on page 162, I'll show you one of the pitfalls of taking them too seriously,

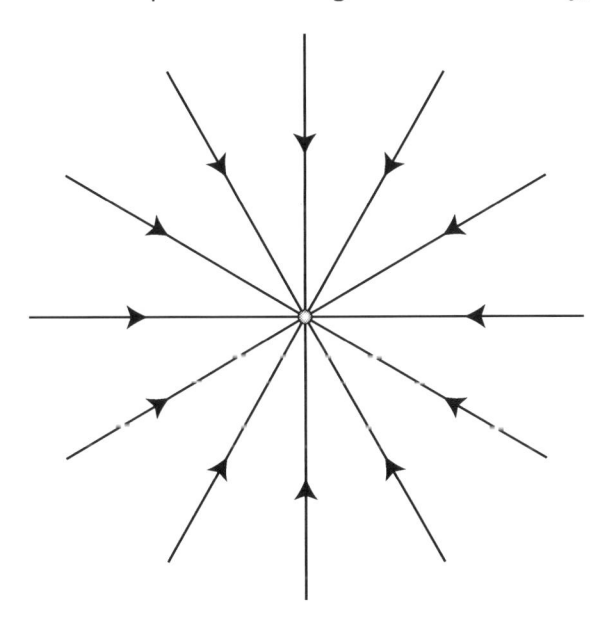

The field around a point mass must have spherical symmetry and the only system of lines you can draw with this symmetry is a radial pattern. The field lines will radiate in 3 dimensions; the diagram shows a 2D slice taken through it.

Arrows are needed on field lines like the gravitational and electromagnetic fields. The direction of the arrow shows the direction of the force on what's called a test mass. Real masses placed in a radial gravitational field would produce their own field and distort the nice radial pattern opposite. A 'test' mass is one where you ignore its own field. The test mass is *attracted* to the mass producing the radial field so the arrows point inwards. If there was such a thing as 'negative mass', you'd have field lines pointing outwards. Electric fields can cause attraction or repulsion of a test electric charge (by convention always taken to be positive), so needs arrows to distinguish between the fields of negative charges and the fields of positive charges. The gravitational and electromagnetic fields are examples of vector fields. Each point in the space of a gravitational field is represented by a number with a direction. The diagram above is a shorthand summary of that situation.

Nature also produces scalar fields. The recently discovered Higgs field of particle physics pervades the whole universe and is an example of a scalar field. It gives most other particles a mass when they interact with it. Scalar fields are just represented by numbers for every point in space. No little arrows.

## Rules for Drawing Field Lines

- direction of the arrow is always in towards the mass for the attractive force of gravity
- lines must not cross (since the force on the test mass must only be in one direction)
- lines must end on a mass (not in mid-air)
- gravitational field lines must start at spatial infinity (what can they emerge from?)

Using these rules (and by symmetry), this is the pattern for two equal masses.

The dotted lines are lines of symmetry, so if you calculate the direction and strength of the field at one point, you've pretty well done it for four points. The diagram shows two masses separated by a certain distance. If you viewed the field along the horizontal line of symmetry either from the left or the right, you would see a radial pattern. If you receded a very long distance back from your current view, the two masses would look like one mass and the pattern at that distance would appear radial.

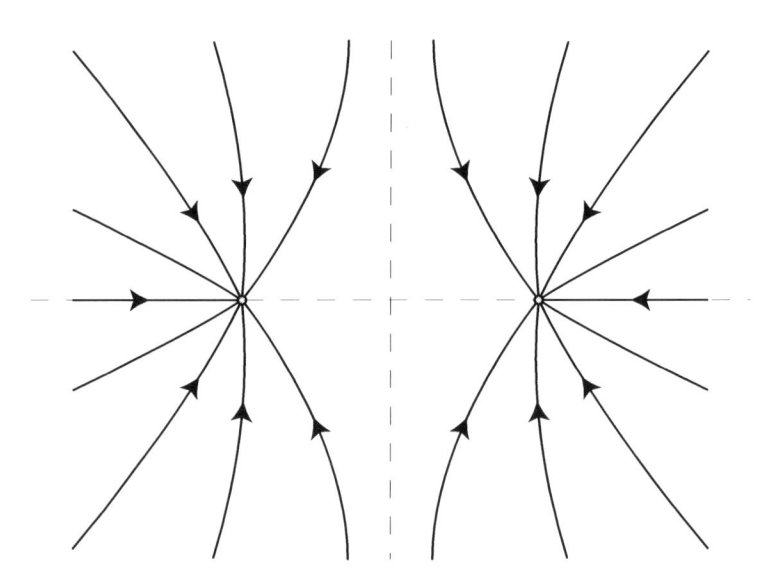

## Examples of Gravitational Force

1. Planet Earth is exerting a gravitational force on you at this moment, it's popularly called your 'weight'. This word causes confusion; it can have two meanings. The one I use is the gravitational force of attraction $W=mg$. As such it doesn't depend upon how you are moving and it points downwards. The other meaning is the force required to bring you to rest in a gravitational field; this one points upwards. On page 21, I discussed the centripetal force on a person standing on the equator. The figure of 588N is what I call the weight, and the figure of 586N is what the bathroom scales push upwards on you to bring you to rest (giving the other meaning of 'weight'). With my meaning, an astronaut in orbit above the Earth isn't 'weightless'; he still has a weight calculated by $W=mg$ with the appropriate 'g' value. The other meaning would describe the astronaut as 'weightless', since it requires no upward force to keep him in position. Equating your weight at the surface of the Earth to the gravitational force of attraction:

$$mg = \frac{GM_E m}{R_E^2}$$ cancel out your mass to get: $$g = \frac{GM_E}{R_E^2} \; \left(=9.8\,\text{N}\,\text{kg}^{-1}\right)$$ vector form $$\underline{g} = -\frac{GM_E}{R_E^2}\hat{\underline{r}}$$

The gravitational field strength 'g' is a vector pointing towards the centre of the Earth.

2. Earth – Moon System: $$F = \frac{GMm}{r^2} = \frac{6.674\times10^{-11} \times 5.97\times10^{24} \times 7.35\times10^{22}}{\left(3.84\times10^8\right)^2} \approx 2\times10^{20}\,\text{N}$$

3. Electron – Proton in H atom: $$F = \frac{GMm}{r^2} = \frac{6.674\times10^{-11} \times 1.673\times10^{-27} \times 9.11\times10^{-31}}{\left(5.29\times10^{-11}\right)^2} \approx 3.6\times10^{-47}\,\text{N}$$

The electrostatic force between the electron and proton in the same hydrogen atom is about $2 \times 10^{39}$ times greater.

**Rotational Motion & Astrophysics**

4. Astronaut on 1km Asteroid: $F = \dfrac{GMm}{r^2}$ $\quad \rho = \dfrac{M}{V} \quad V = \dfrac{4}{3}\pi r^3 \quad \Rightarrow \quad F = \dfrac{4}{3}\pi \rho G m r$

For a 1km diameter spherical rocky asteroid of density 5000kg m⁻³:

$$F = \dfrac{4}{3}\pi \rho G m r = m\left(7 \times 10^{-4}\right)$$

Writing it this way gives a direct comparison with: $W = mg$. It's a 'g' value of $7 \times 10^{-4}$ N kg⁻¹. You would be very 'light' in weight and have problems walking!

## Variation of 'g' with height above Earth's surface

The acceleration due to gravity is a bit less at your head than it is at your feet. Not that you'd notice a bit of stretching during a parachute drop, but it's there. Small 'g' gets less and less as you gain altitude in the atmosphere, and for an ideal Earth of radius $R_E$ it is given by the equation:

$$g = \dfrac{GM_E}{r^2} = \dfrac{GM_E}{(R_E + h)^2}$$

Small 'r' is the distance from the Earth's centre to the point where 'g' is calculated, and 'h' is the height above the idealised surface. Here's the graph showing the fall-off in 'g':

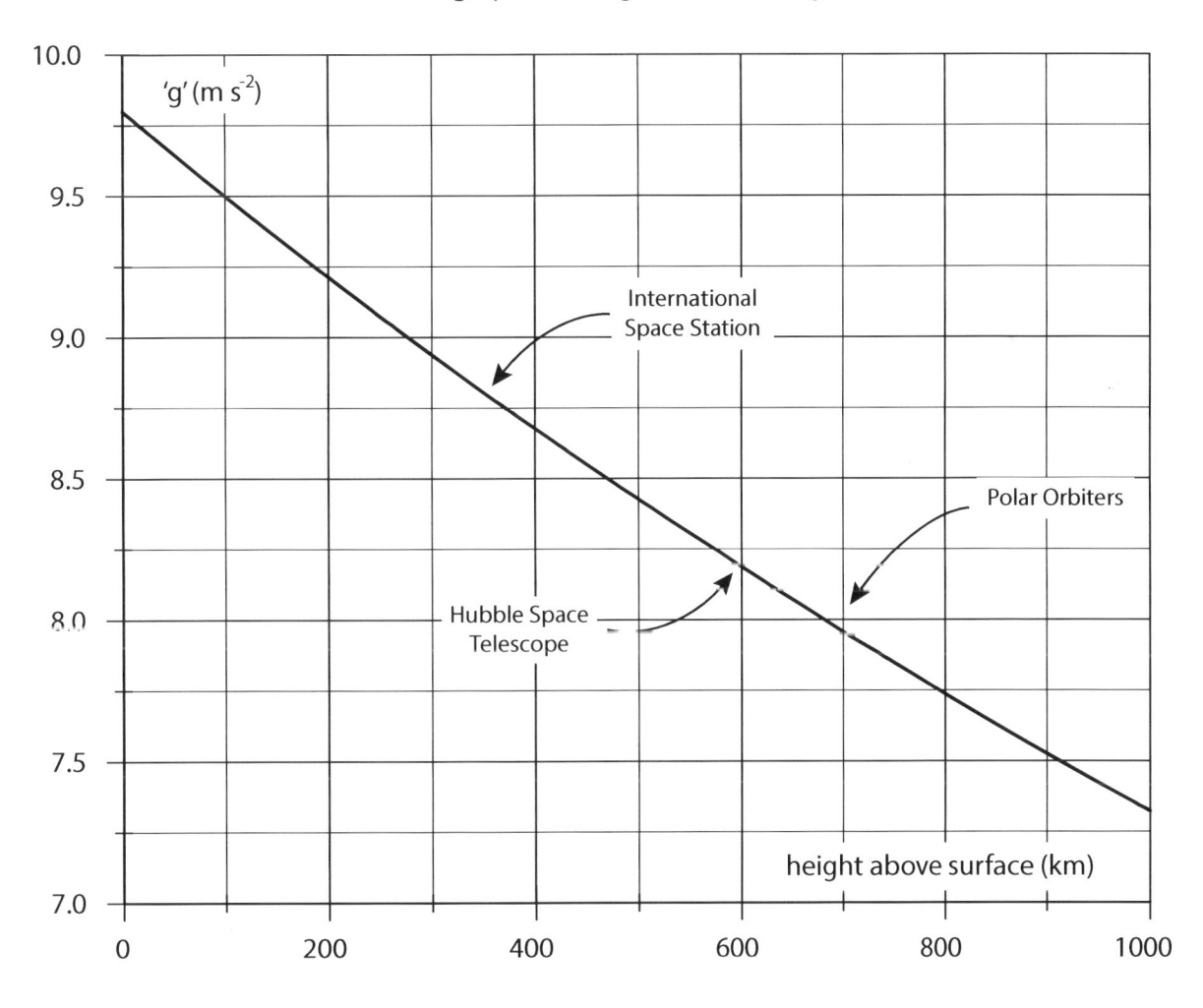

The shape is only slightly curved. A straight line approximation like 'it drops by 0.02 m s⁻² with 6.5km gain in altitude, so it drops by 0.04 m s⁻² with 13km gain in altitude' is very accurate for most purposes on the surface. But not for everyone. Some investigators need ultrahigh accuracy..........

55

## Gravity Mapping

The Earth's surface is lumpy and bumpy. Walk up a hill and the gravitational field strength will decrease. There's nothing weird going on under your boots; you're just going further away from the planet. But, suppose there *was* something weird going on under your boots? Could a very dense, iron rich meteorite have landed there 10 million years ago? It would increase the gravitational field strength in the area due to its increased mass relative to the lower density rocks.

Geologists have wandered all over the UK measuring the gravitational field strength to high accuracy. The land west and north west of a line from Durham to Bristol has higher than average values, and east of this (and out over the North Sea) has lower values. They don't express the result like 9.81374 m s$^{-2}$. The results are given in terms of how far away the measured value is from a standard value for 'g' of 9.80665 m s$^{-2}$.

The geophysicists invented a unit for expressing tiny variations in gravity called the Gal (in honour of Galileo), where 1Gal equals 0.01m s$^{-2}$. Subunits are milliGal (mGal) and microGal (µGal). For example, at Ibrox Park, Glasgow the variation from the standard value is +1586mGal and at Celtic Park, Glasgow it's at +1580mGal. Deduce from that what you will.

The ability to measure the local 'g' value to such high accuracy has opened up many avenues of research in oil exploration, geology and oceanography. These can be carried out on the ground, or by satellite. The latter method accesses areas which are difficult to reach but at a lower resolution (being hundreds of kilometers above the ground). One such satellite is the GRACE project.

## Gravity Recovery and Climate Experiment (GRACE)

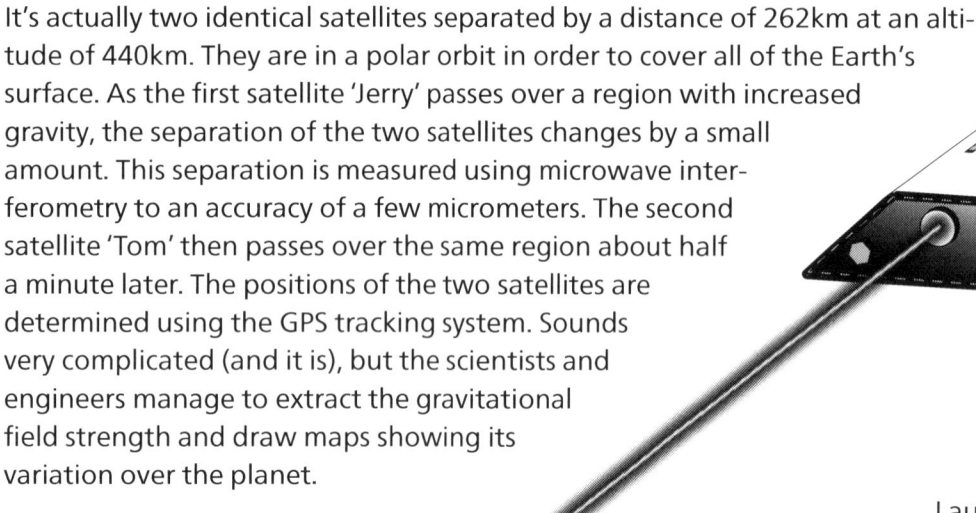

It's actually two identical satellites separated by a distance of 262km at an altitude of 440km. They are in a polar orbit in order to cover all of the Earth's surface. As the first satellite 'Jerry' passes over a region with increased gravity, the separation of the two satellites changes by a small amount. This separation is measured using microwave interferometry to an accuracy of a few micrometers. The second satellite 'Tom' then passes over the same region about half a minute later. The positions of the two satellites are determined using the GPS tracking system. Sounds very complicated (and it is), but the scientists and engineers manage to extract the gravitational field strength and draw maps showing its variation over the planet.

The data is used to measure the thinning of the Arctic icesheet, the cur-

MISSION DATA:
Launched: March 2002
Mass: 2 × 432kg
Orbit: polar
Altitude: 440km
Period: 90 min
Separation: 262km
Power: battery/solar cell
End mission: ≈ 2015

rents in the Oceans, and provide hydrology information in arid regions of the world. One unexpected discovery was of a 300km diameter crater under the ice of Antarctica possibly due to a 30km wide asteroid striking the surface about 250 million years ago. Would we be here if it hadn't happened?

# Rotational Motion & Astrophysics

## Energy in Gravitational Fields

*The concepts of force and energy are the two main methods for solving problems in dynamics. The energy method is often simpler since it involves scalars. In advanced courses in dynamics, the methods used are all energy based.*

I'm going to approach this topic 'back to front'. I start with the result and work back to the principles. This way, we don't get lost in the details and forget the big picture. The question is this. How much energy does it take to move a spaceship from one place to another in a gravitational field? Here's the answer.

**Step 1** take the number for the start position 'A' eg. 400

**Step 2** take the number for the finish position 'B' eg. 700

**Step 3** subtract them: this gives 300

**Step 4** multiply by the mass of the spaceship eg. 6kg : this gives 6 x 300 = 1800J

**Step 5** there's no step five

That's the big picture; don't lose sight of its simplicity. Here are a few details.

- the numbers for positions 'A' and 'B' have units of joules per kilogram  J kg$^{-1}$

- these numbers should be negative, so it's  -400J kg$^{-1}$ and -700J kg$^{-1}$

- these numbers are called the 'gravitational potentials' at 'A' and 'B'

- the symbol is V so :  $V_A$ = -400J kg$^{-1}$ and $V_B$ = -400J kg$^{-1}$

- you calculate the gravitational potential using: $V = -\dfrac{GM}{r}$    ('r' on bottom, not $r^2$)

  where 'M' is the mass producing the field and 'r' is the distance from the centre of 'M' to the spaceship.

**Example** putting it all together:

A spaceship of mass 15250kg is at rest at a distance of 9000 km from the centre of planet Earth. How much energy is required to move it out to a distance of 20000 km at rest?

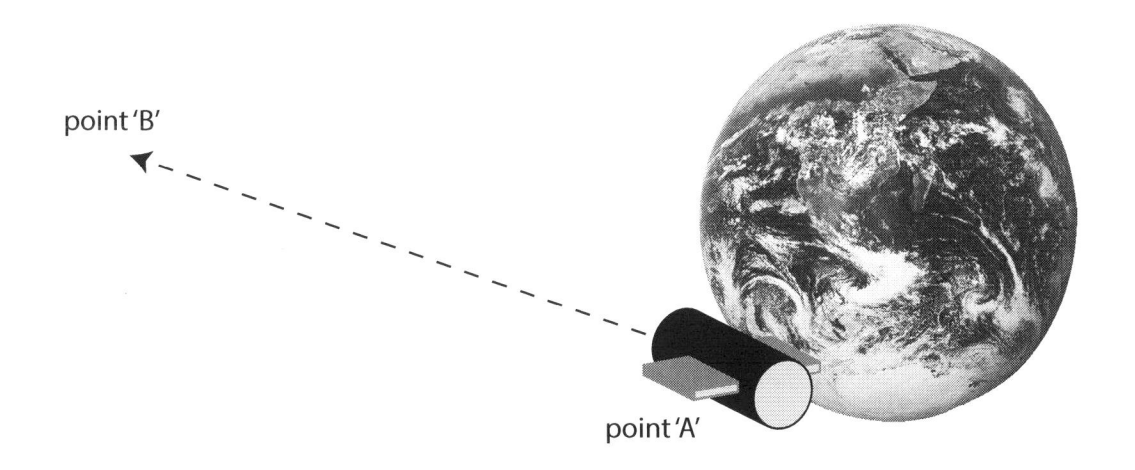

point 'B'

point 'A'

57

**Step 1** calculate the gravitational potential at point 'A':

$$V_A = -\frac{GM}{r} = -\frac{6.674\times10^{-11}\times5.97\times10^{24}}{9\times10^6} = -4.43\times10^7 \text{ J kg}^{-1}$$

**Step 2** calculate the gravitational potential at point 'B':

$$V_B = -\frac{GM}{r} = -\frac{6.674\times10^{-11}\times5.97\times10^{24}}{20\times10^6} = -1.99\times10^7 \text{ J kg}^{-1}$$

**Step 3** subtract (to calculate a difference in physics you always take final – initial)

$$V = (V_B - V_A) = -1.99\times10^7 - (-4.43\times10^7) = 2.44\times10^7 \text{ J kg}^{-1}$$

**Step 4** multiply by the mass moved

Work Done in moving from 'A' to 'B' = 15250kg × 2.44×10$^7$ J kg$^{-1}$ = 3.72×10$^{11}$ Joules

The calculation happens *so quickly* that you might miss a few important points:

- the formula $V_A = -\frac{GM}{r}$ doesn't say exactly where 'A' is located. Since it contains an 'r' it could be anywhere on the surface of a sphere of that radius centred on the Earth.
- if your spaceship travels from one point on that surface to another point on that surface, that is points 'A' and 'B' have the same 'r' value, then it takes no energy to make the trip.
- the *path* you take to go from 'A' to 'B' doesn't matter; you don't have to go straight there, it's only the start and end points which count. Fields which let you do this are special and given the name '*conservative*' fields.
- surfaces where the gravitational potential is the same at every point are called '*equipotential* surfaces' For the ideal spherical Earth they are the surface of a sphere. No work is done against the field in moving along them.
- if you start at an infinite distance from the Earth, $r = \infty$ substituted in the formula $V_A = -\frac{GM}{r}$ will give zero. Infinity is like a reference point, it is where the gravitational potential is zero.

## Derivation of Gravitational Potential

We've been working backwards all the time and now we reach the start! This is how you obtain the formula $V = -\frac{GM}{r}$. Gravitational potential has a definition:

***the gravitational potential at a point is the work done per unit mass by external forces in moving a unit mass from infinity to that point***

The gravitational field is created by mass 'M'. Mass 'm' is moved by external forces (that's you) from infinity to a point a distance 'r' from the centre of 'M'. One thing the books don't mention is that the mass 'm' can't go flying past the point. It must be brought to rest at the point. Gravity is an attractive force and you could otherwise just give the mass 'm' a tiny nudge at infinity, sit back, and watch it fly past the point. To bring it to rest, you have to apply a force pointing outwards from mass 'M', the same direction as the position vector whose origin is at the centre of 'M'. This is important for the sign of the answer.

# Rotational Motion & Astrophysics

The diagram shows the mass 'M' which produces the gravitational field, and the mass 'm' which you are moving from infinity to point 'A'. The two masses attract one another, so you have to apply an external force *to the left* to bring the mass to rest at point 'A'.

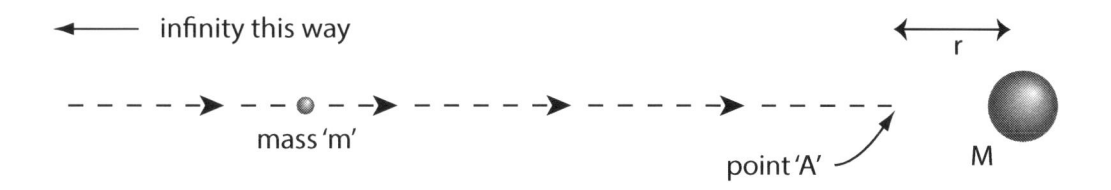

⟵ infinity this way

- - - → - - ○ - -→ - - - - -→ - - - - → - - - -
mass 'm'                                    point 'A'    M

⟷ r

The work done by the external force in moving the mass a distance of 1 metre will be small when it's far away and big when it's close in to mass 'M'. This is because the field gets stronger. It means we have to use calculus to obtain the total work done in reaching point 'A'. Basically, you split the path into little sections of length '$\Delta x$', assume the force is constant for each short section, then calculate the work done using; Work Done = force times distance = $F\Delta x$. Add them all up to get a total. The calculus method takes an infinite number of infinitesimally small sections:

$$\text{Work Done} = \int F dx = \int_{\infty}^{r} F \, dr \qquad \text{with} \quad |F| = G\frac{Mm}{r^2}$$

the little 'm' is the mass moved and the 'F' is the external force pointing outwards from 'M'.

$$\text{Work Done} = \int_{\infty}^{r} G\frac{Mm}{r^2} dr = GMm \int_{\infty}^{r} \frac{1}{r^2} dr = GMm\left[-\frac{1}{r}\right]_{\infty}^{r} = -GMm\left[\frac{1}{r} - \frac{1}{\infty}\right] = -\frac{GMm}{r}$$

With the little 'm' still in the formula, this gives you the work done in joules in moving mass 'm' from infinity to point 'A'. This is called the gravitational potential energy $E_p$ of mass 'm' at point 'A'. You'll recognise the symbol for it, $E_p$, from your earlier days in physics. This isn't the same as the gravitational potential 'V'. The word 'energy' is there. The gravitational potential is the work done **per unit mass** so we just divide the gravitational potential energy by little 'm':

$$V = -\frac{GM}{r}$$

So where did your old formula for the potential energy $E_p = mgh$ come from? This formula assumes a constant gravitational field, unlike the inverse square law we've been using. So you can still use it as long as the distances (the '$h$') are short compared with the radius of the Earth. It also answers the old problem of where you take the zero of potential energy. You might have had one of those teachers who asked an awkward question like 'how much potential energy has it got?' After you gave the correct answer as demanded by the formula, the smartass then asks you if the height '$h$' is measured from the floor or from the ground or from sea level. Now you know the answer. The '$mgh$' is (approximately) the difference in gravitational potential energy between your start height and your finish height. In other words:

$$\Delta E_p = -\frac{GMm}{r_B} - \left(-\frac{GMm}{r_A}\right)$$

This should reduce to '$mgh$' where the height gained $h = (r_B - r_A)$ in going from your start position (A) to your finish position (B) is small. It takes a few lines of maths:

$$-\frac{GMm}{r_B} - \left(-\frac{GMm}{r_A}\right) = GMm\left(\frac{1}{r_A} - \frac{1}{r_B}\right) = GMm\left(\frac{r_B - r_A}{r_A r_B}\right)$$

The top of the bracket is just the height 'h' and when the height is small, the bottom of the bracket is approximately $r^2$. Remembering that $g = \dfrac{GM}{r^2}$, we get:

$$GMm \times \dfrac{h}{r^2} = \dfrac{GM}{r^2} \times mh = mgh$$

## How Accurate is E_p = mgh?

The gravitational field strength due to the Earth at a distance 'r' from its centre is: $g = \dfrac{GM_E}{r^2}$. If you increase 'r' by a small amount $\Delta r$, what would be the decrease in 'g', the $\Delta g$? When $\Delta r$ and $\Delta g$ are very small, you can manipulate them like the differentials $dr$ and $dg$. This gives:

$$\dfrac{\Delta g}{\Delta r} \approx \dfrac{dg}{dr} = \dfrac{d}{dr}\left(\dfrac{GM_E}{r^2}\right) = -2GM_E\left(\dfrac{1}{r^3}\right)$$

Separate the $\Delta g$ and the $\Delta r$ then divide both sides by 'g':

$$\Delta g = -2GM_E\left(\dfrac{1}{r^3}\right)\Delta r \quad \Rightarrow \quad \dfrac{\Delta g}{g} = -2\dfrac{\Delta r}{r}$$

On the surface of the Earth ($r = 6.37 \times 10^6$ m), if you move upwards by $\Delta r = 3.2$ m, the gravitational field strength will decrease by about one part per million. Most school physics experiments are in this height range. The story at the surface of a neutron star is a bit different. The 'g' value is:

$$g = \dfrac{GM}{r^2} \approx \dfrac{6.674 \times 10^{-11} \times 1.2 \times 10^{31}}{\left(5 \times 10^3\right)^2} = 3 \times 10^{13} \text{ N kg}^{-1}$$

The difference between your head and toes would be $2 \times 10^{10}$ N kg$^{-1}$. Bit of a stretch.

## Equipotential Surfaces

Gravitational potential 'V' is a scalar. If you have more than one mass producing a gravitational field you simply add the contribution from each one to get the total gravitational potential at a point. No directions, just numbers! If you do this for two equal masses, the equipotential surfaces are like distorted balloons. This diagram shows a 2D slice through the middle:

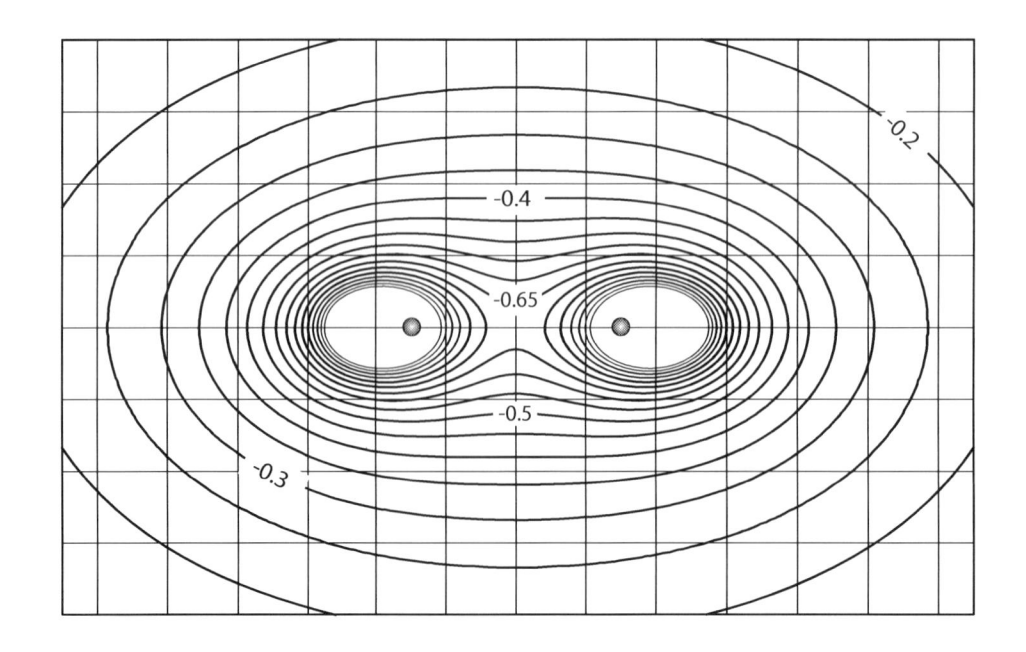

**Rotational Motion & Astrophysics**

The numbers are in units of J kg$^{-1}$. The gravitational field only provides an attractive force, so the potentials are always negative. The idea is that you have to do work on the system (put in energy) to escape from it to reach a state of zero mechanical energy (where the sum of kinetic and potential energies is zero). You've escaped the field, and where there is no field, there is no potential energy.

As you head towards each mass, you become more trapped and the potentials get more negative. It would take a bigger effort to escape from its clutches. Using the previous method, you can easily work out how much energy is required to move a small mass from one point on an equipotential surface to another point on a different equipotential surface.

If you plot the gravitational potential values on a z-axis rather than marking them on the 2D diagram, you get the diagram below.

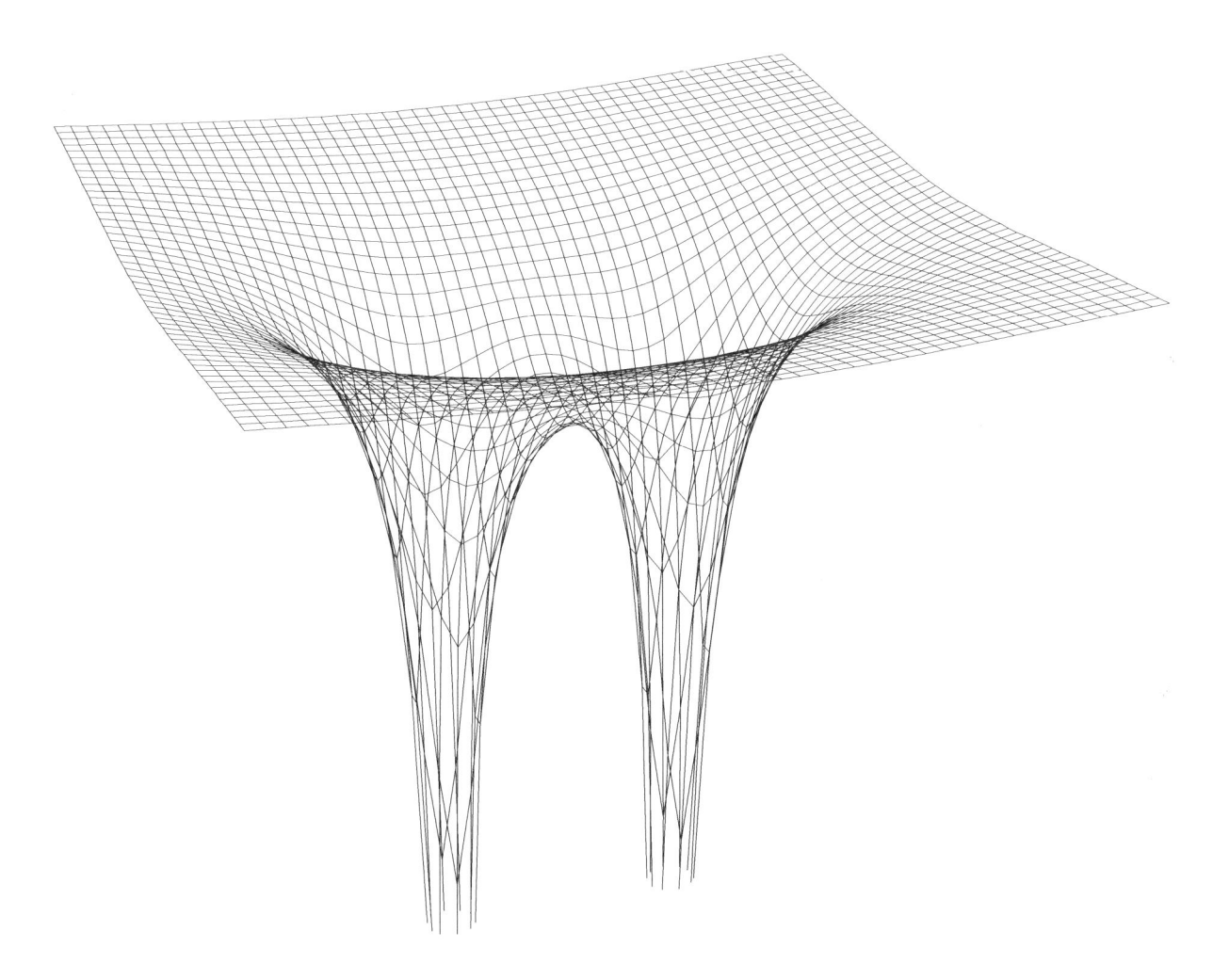

The top surface is smoothly heading off towards a plane approaching zero gravitational potential. That's freedom from the field. Take flat horizontal slices through the above diagram and you get the contours on the previous page. The 'threads' of the net above aren't the equipotential contours. They are just my way of showing the shape of the surface. The equipotential contours are where horizontal slices cut the net surface (constant z-axis value).

The diagram is a vivid depiction of how you can be trapped by a gravitational potential. The two 'sticky out' things are called Potential Wells. Standing on the surface of a planet, you would be deep down one of them. In terms of energy, escaping your planet is like climbing out of the well. A spacecraft launched from Earth's surface and placed in an orbit at an altitude of 400km has just used up lots of chemical energy to move slightly higher up the Well.

## Journey to the Moon

The mass of the Earth is about 81 times the mass of the Moon, so the Potential Well at the Earth's surface is bigger than that of the Moon. It's a big energy climb to escape the Earth but a lot easier to leave the Moon. The diagram below shows the gravitational equipotential lines between the Earth (not shown on the diagram, it's about half a metre off to the left) and the Moon. The distance scales up the left side and along the bottom are 1 unit for every 100,000km. The diagram covers an area of 100000km by 100000km. The bottom scale is the distance from the centre of the Earth. The Moon is 385000km from Earth, so is at 3.85units. The equipotential contours are in units of megajoules per kilogram (MJkg$^{-1}$). Near the Moon, I haven't drawn in the contours; they are almost circular. The Moon is drawn to scale, and I've ignored the Sun (though I shouldn't).

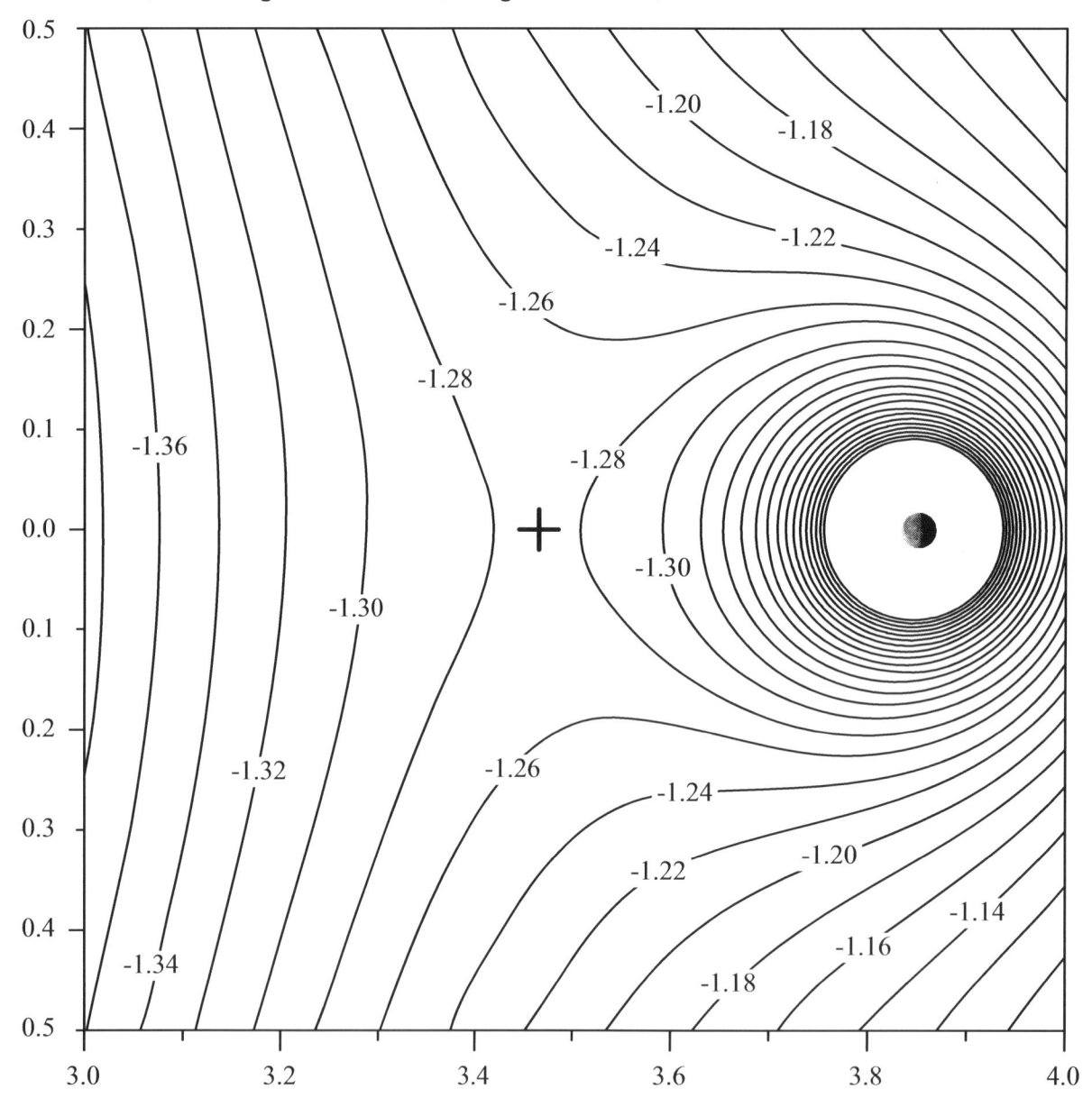

The 3D net contour diagram would be similar to the one on the previous page, but with one Potential Well bigger than the other. A spaceship travelling from the Earth to the Moon has to get itself up the Earth's Well to the 'neck' between the two Wells, then down to the Moon. The 'neck' is marked by a cross on the diagram above and it's called a 'saddle point' (just like in Maths).

The saddle point is at a higher potential than the surface of the Moon, so you need more energy to reach it. You regain some of that energy on the way down to the Moon. The trouble is that the energy you gain isn't useable. Once you pass the saddle point, the Moon's gravity speeds up the spaceship and you have to expend more chemical energy to slow down for a safe landing.

The saddle point is the turning point in the gravitational potential. You calculate its position just as in the Maths class - differentiate the function and put it equal to zero. The gravitational potential 'V' as a function of 'x' measured from Earth's centre, is the scalar sum of the contributions from the Earth and the Moon:

$$V(x) = -\frac{GM_E}{x} + \left(-\frac{GM_M}{(d-x)}\right)$$

Refer to the diagram below for the meanings of the symbols.

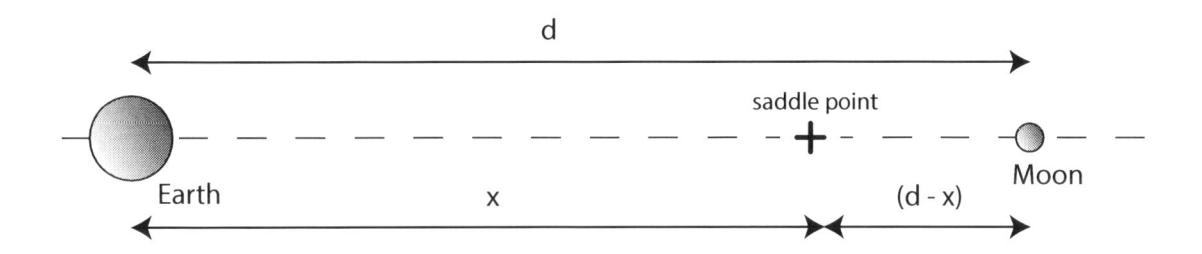

Differentiate and put equal to zero:

$$\frac{dV}{dx} = \frac{d}{dx}\left(-\frac{GM_E}{x}\right) + \frac{d}{dx}\left(-\frac{GM_M}{(d-x)}\right) = \frac{GM_E}{x^2} - \frac{GM_M}{(d-x)^2} = 0$$

$$\frac{GM_E}{x^2} = \frac{GM_M}{(d-x)^2} \quad \Rightarrow \quad \left(\frac{d-x}{x}\right)^2 = \frac{M_M}{M_E} \quad \Rightarrow \quad \left(\frac{d-x}{x}\right) = \sqrt{\frac{M_M}{M_E}}$$

Solve to obtain:

$$x = \frac{d}{\left(1+\sqrt{\frac{M_M}{M_E}}\right)} = \frac{3.844 \times 10^8}{\left(1+\sqrt{\frac{7.348 \times 10^{22}}{5.974 \times 10^{24}}}\right)} = 346000 \text{ km}$$

This is the distance of the saddle from Earth; a long way up, then a short way down to the Moon!

## Escape Velocity

When you throw an object up in the air, it returns after a few seconds, even if you're an Olympic standard javelin thrower. What speed is needed so that it escapes the Earth and never returns? By 'escapes the Earth', a physicist means: reaches infinity. They also ignore practical problems like air resistance, low flying jets, rain, (midges if you're reading this in Skye) and planets.

Suppose a cricket ball was thrown up and just reached infinity 'running on empty' ie. with no speed left. Its total energy at infinity is the scalar sum of the kinetic energy (zero since its at rest) and the potential energy (zero from our definition). Grand total at infinity is zero joules. By energy conservation it must be the same total when it was released on the surface ie. zero. So the total energy is:

$$E_K + E_P = \frac{1}{2}mv^2 + \left(-\frac{GM_E m}{R_E}\right) = 0$$

$$\frac{1}{2}mv^2 = \frac{GM_E m}{R_E} \quad \Rightarrow \quad v = \sqrt{\frac{2GM_E}{R_E}} = \sqrt{\frac{2 \times 6.674 \times 10^{-11} \times 5.97 \times 10^{24}}{6.373 \times 10^6}} = 11200 \text{ m s}^{-1}$$

That's why the cricket ball always comes back. At the speed you need to throw it, you could cross from Glasgow to Edinburgh in about 6 seconds. The calculation assumed that the Earth was the only mass in the Universe. In our solar system it's not just the Earth's gravity you escape from, it's the Sun's gravity. The gravitational potential at the orbit of the Earth due to the Sun is:

$$V_{Sun} = -\frac{GM_{sun}}{r} = -\frac{6.674\times10^{-11}\times1.989\times10^{30}}{1.496\times10^{11}} = -8.87\times10^8 \text{ J kg}^{-1}$$

This is 14 times stronger than the contribution due to the Earth, so if you chucked your cricket ball at a speed of 11200 m s$^{-1}$ it would end up in the Sun. Throwing it during the night would take a little longer. Starting from the Earth's surface, escape from our Sun's solar system requires a speed of about:

$$v = \sqrt{\frac{2GM_{sun}}{r}} = \sqrt{\frac{2\times6.674\times10^{-11}\times1.989\times10^{30}}{1.496\times10^{11}}} \approx 42000 \text{ m s}^{-1}$$

Escaping from the Moon to infinity is usually considered relatively easy. Assuming the Moon is the only body in the Universe you get:

$$v = \sqrt{\frac{2GM_{moon}}{R_{moon}}} = v = \sqrt{\frac{2\times6.674\times10^{-11}\times7.35\times10^{22}}{1.737\times10^6}} = 2380 \text{ m s}^{-1}$$

Including the correction due to the Earth gives 2780 m s$^{-1}$. Adding in the Sun gives 42000 m s$^{-1}$.

## Escape Speeds – Large and Small

How small would a planet have to be before you could jump off it? And not come back. The escape velocity formula has two variables '$M$' and '$r$', which both change when you reduce the radius. Far better to have just one variable. You can do this by using the density:

$$M = \rho V = \frac{4}{3}\pi\rho r^3 \qquad v = \sqrt{\frac{2GM}{r}} \qquad \Rightarrow \qquad v = \left(\frac{8\pi\rho G}{3}\right)^{\frac{1}{2}} r$$

"Je n'ai pas besoin de cette hypothèse"

For constant density, the escape speed is proportional to the radius. A typical rocky planet has a density of about 5500 kg m$^{-3}$. Using this gives: $v_{escape}=0.00175r$. If you can launch yourself at about 1 m s$^{-1}$, you could wave goodbye to an asteroid of radius less than 570 m. The asteroid wouldn't make a good prison and its citizens could claim they didn't have a litter problem (since the litter ends on the Sun).

The idea that even light might not escape from a massive body like the Sun goes back to our old friend, the Rev. John Michell, in 1783. The Frenchman, Marquis de Laplace also thought of it independently in 1795 and is often given the credit. We start with the present day Sun and shrink its radius until the escape speed is the speed of light. Re-arrange the formula:

$$v = \sqrt{\frac{2GM_{Sun}}{r}} \quad \Rightarrow \quad r = \frac{2GM}{c^2} = \frac{2\times6.674\times10^{-11}\times1.989\times10^{30}}{(3\times10^8)^2} = 2950\text{m}$$

A beam of light emitted from the surface of the shrunken Sun would not escape. Contrary to popular opinion, it doesn't zoom up and turn around like a cricket ball. It doesn't even make the first millimetre above the surface. A beam of light emitted from just *outside* the surface would reach infinity, reddened.

64

# Rotational Motion & Astrophysics

## Planetary Motion

The progress of humankind from superstition to rationality is no better illustrated than in the history of astronomy. The idea that the Earth is at the centre of the Universe reigned supreme, with one little blip, until Nicolaus Copernicus (1473 – 1543). That one little blip was the Greek thinker Aristarchus of Samos (310 - 230BC). His achievements were remarkable; he was 2000 years ahead of his time and deserves great credit. From measurements of Lunar eclipses, he related the distances to the Sun and Moon to the radius of the Earth (he already knew the Earth was a sphere). Realising that the Sun was much bigger than the Earth, this led him to put the Sun at the centre of the world.

Why did the old Earth-centred Ptolemaic view last so long? Isn't it obvious! If the Sun was at the centre then everything would fall towards it, whereas things fall to the Earth. To make the heavens turn once a day, the Earth would have to rotate and it obviously doesn't. If you threw a stone up in the air it would be deflected sideways and it isn't (actually, it is). And humans live on it.

Copernicus' famous book 'De Revolutionibus' (1543), contains a diagram (shown on the right) representing one of the crowning achievements in the history of science; the planets in orbit around the Sun. The planets extend to Saturn, with the outer circle being the 'stellarium', the sphere of the fixed stars.

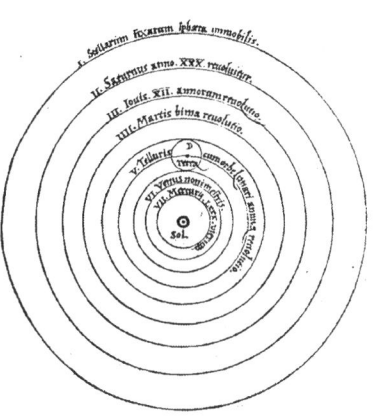

**Galileo Galilei** heard about the invention of an instrument in 1609 by a Dutch lens grinder, which could give the appearance of magnifying things. One month later, Galileo had built one for himself with a magnifying power of 9 times. Being of great use to a maritime nation, this brought Galileo a better job and more money. By years-end, he'd built another one with a magnifying power of 30 times and trained it on the night sky. Discoveries followed in quick succession: the Moon isn't smooth, it's mountainous; the Milky Way is made of numerous stars, not 'painted on'; Jupiter has four satellites; the discovery of the rings of Saturn; and most crucially of all, the phases of the planet Venus. The diagram below shows the predictions for the sunlit areas of Venus as viewed from the Earth. The wrong Ptolemaic model is on the left and the correct Copernican model is on the right.

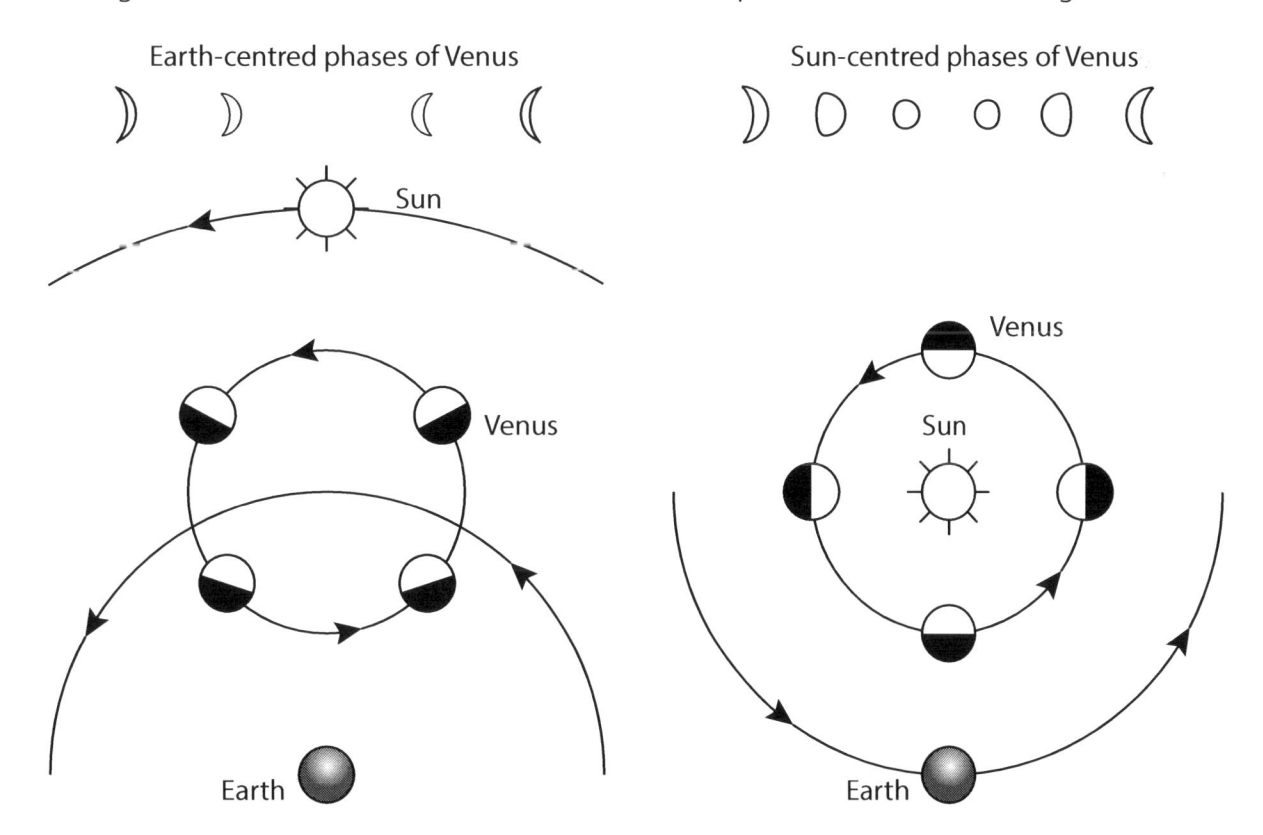

In the world of Ptolemy, the Earth is at the centre of the universe and the Sun orbits around it. Venus also orbits around us, but in addition goes around in smaller circles ('epicycles'). If this was correct, Galileo would have seen the phases of Venus (the shape of the sunlit part) as a series of thin crescents. With the Sun at the centre, and everything else orbiting around it, you get the phases on the right. This is what Galileo saw through his telescope.

## Tycho Brahe & Johannes Kepler

These two lived about the same period as Galileo though Brahe didn't live long enough to see through the telescope. Brahe was a colourful character. He'd lost the end off his nose in a duel in 1566 after a quarrel with a relative over the correctness of a mathematical formula. The sketch on the right shows the brass one made up to fill the gap. His passion was astronomy and he managed to find a rich patron, Frederick II of Denmark, to finance it. Later, Tycho modestly said that it had cost Frederick 'more than a tun of gold' to finance his activities.

His observations of the positions of the stars and planets were ten times more accurate than anything before it; the result of being the first person to incorporate systematic and random errors (the scourge of the Advanced Higher student) into his results. For example, he realised that refraction of starlight by the atmosphere gave a false position for a star, and that his instrument would bend out of shape when tilted. He published a catalogue of 777 stars measured to an accuracy of one fiftieth of a degree. After his patron died, to be replaced by a less generous monarch, he moved to Prague in 1597. However, his stay was short-lived. Attending a banquet in 1601, etiquette at the time demanded that one doesn't leave the table whatever the state of ones urinary requirements. Just before he died two weeks later (of a burst bladder), he showed better judgment by employing Johannes Kepler to analyse the huge pile of data related to planet Mars, accumulated over 20 years.

Kepler was 25 years younger than Brahe. He was a kind of prototype hippy; 'into' harmony and the discovery of God's great plan of the creation of the universe. At University, Kepler was a bit of a rebel. He would listen patiently to his teacher on the Ptolemaic system while secretly believing the Copernican system:

> *"I followed attentively the instruction of the famous Maestlin, and already perceived how clumsy in many respects is the customary notion of the structure of the universe. I was so very delighted by Copernicus that I repeatedly advocated his views in disputations"*

In Brahe's employ, he set to work on the observations of the orbit of Mars. Being 'into' harmony, he assumed a circular orbit for Mars. Brahe's accurate observations ruled out this possibility. He then tried 'egg shaped' orbits with the Sun at the centre; better, but still outside Brahe's observation uncertainties. Then came the idea of ellipses, and placing the Sun at one of the foci.

Kepler had discovered a crucial fact about the orbits of the planets, but he had no physical explanation for it. It turned out to be one of the key discoveries for a proper understanding of the law of gravity, but it had to await the genius of Isaac Newton before its full significance was appreciated.

You might think that Galileo would have found a strong ally in Kepler, but he was wary of him in two respects. Kepler was so 'into' harmony that he came across as a bit of a 'nut' (he speculated on all sorts of whacky areas). A serious scientist doesn't want to be associated with a 'nut'. Secondly, Galileo himself suffered from the Aristotelian disease of perfection being found only in straight lines and circles. Kepler wanted ellipses and these were intellectually repugnant to Galileo; something of an unexamined prejudice on Galileo's part.

# Rotational Motion & Astrophysics

## Kepler's Three Laws

*....the planetary orbits are ellipses with the Sun at one focus....*

To draw an ellipse, place a sheet of paper over a board, hammer two nails into the board 5cm apart, then place a 14cm loop of string loosely over the nails. Put your pencil in the loop, pull tight and draw.

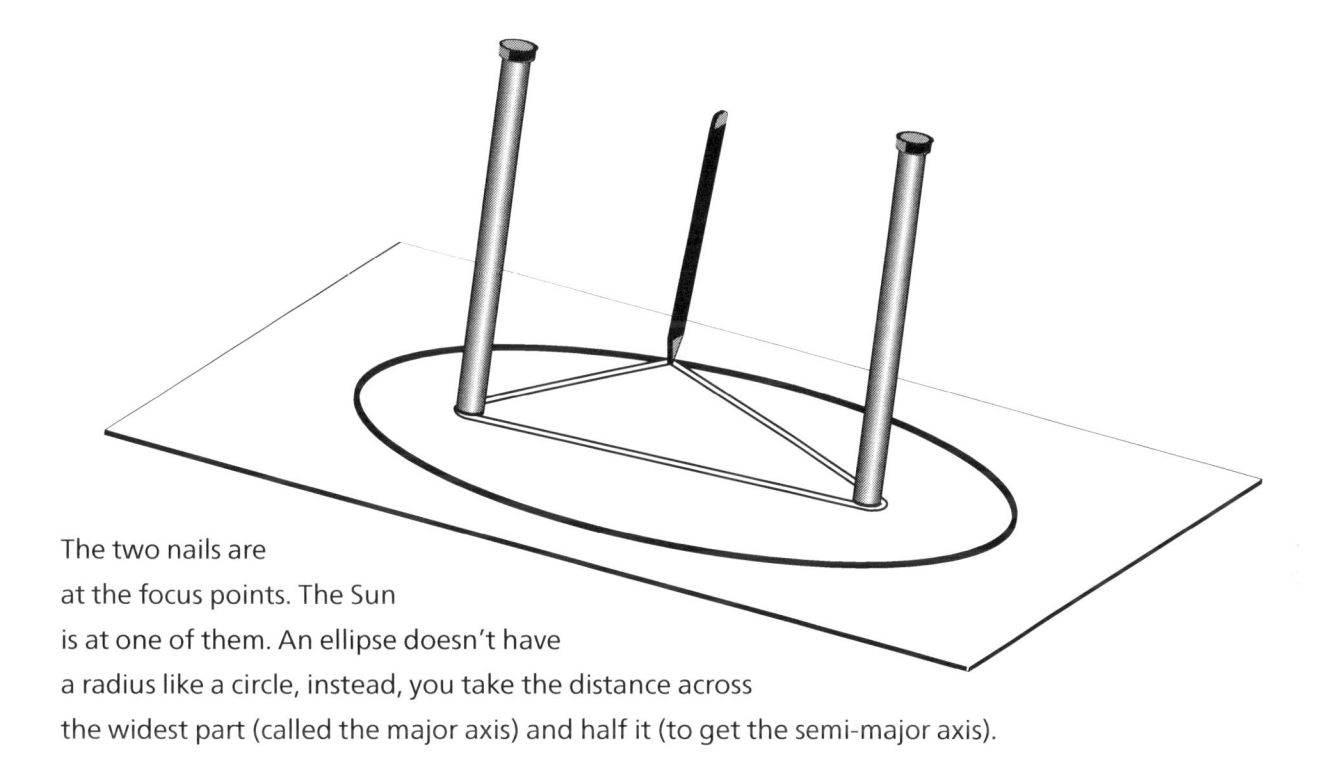

The two nails are at the focus points. The Sun is at one of them. An ellipse doesn't have a radius like a circle, instead, you take the distance across the widest part (called the major axis) and half it (to get the semi-major axis).

*...equal areas are swept out by the line from the Sun to the planet in equal times...*

Refer to the diagram on the right. The time taken for a planet to go from 'A' to 'B' on its elliptical orbit is the same as from 'C' to 'D'. The areas swept out by the planet are shaded grey. This means that the planet moves faster from 'A' to 'B'; achieving its greatest speed at closest approach to the Sun (called perihelion) and its slowest speed at its greatest distance from the Sun (called aphelion).

Kepler's 2ND Law is a consequence of conservation of angular momentum. Consider one of the grey areas:

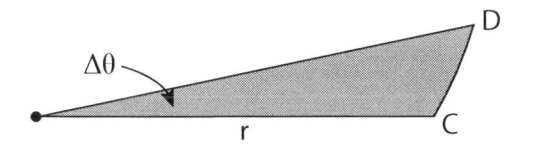

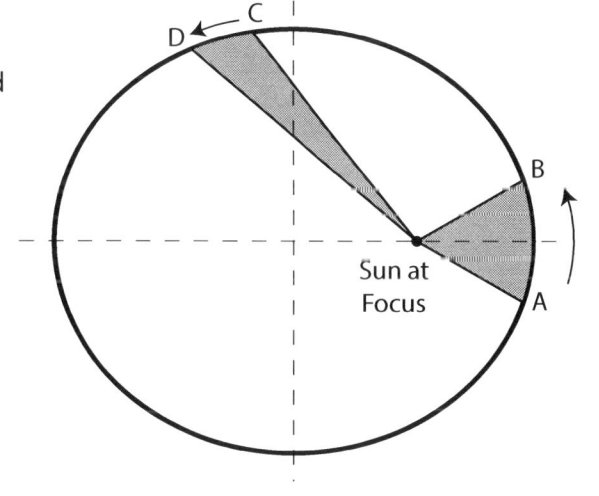

For $\Delta\theta$ very small, it's like a rectangle cut in half along a diagonal. The shaded area is then half the base (r) times the height CD, which is the arc length (r$\Delta\theta$):  area $\Rightarrow \frac{1}{2}r^2\Delta\theta$. The time taken to sweep out this area is $\Delta t$. The change of area with time is: $\frac{1}{2}r^2\Delta\theta \div \Delta t = \frac{1}{2}r^2\omega$. This is proportional to the angular momentum $L=mr^2\omega$, so equal areas in equal times is equivalent to conservation of angular momentum.

## ...the square of the period of the orbit is proportional to the cube of the semi-major axis...

Newton started from this Law and deduced that the force between two masses is of the inverse square type. In exams, you're usually asked to start from the inverse square law and derive Kepler's 3rd Law for a circular orbit. Here it is:

$$F_{centripetal} = F_{gravity} \Rightarrow m\frac{v^2}{r} = m\omega^2 r = \frac{GMm}{r^2} \qquad \omega^2 = \left(\frac{2\pi}{T}\right)^2 = \frac{GM}{r^3} \Rightarrow T^2 = \left(\frac{4\pi^2}{GM}\right) r^3$$

For a circular orbit, 'r' is the radius and for an elliptical orbit, 'r' is the semi-major axis. If you're being really picky, the mass on the bottom line should be the total mass of the Sun and the planet.

### The Mass of the Sun

You can use Kepler's 3rd Law to calculate the mass of the Sun. The big 'M' in the formula is the thing at the centre (the Sun in this case). The 'T' and 'r' refer to the body in orbit around the big 'M'. This could be any of the planets; we will take the Earth. $T$ = 1 year = $3.156 \times 10^7$ s, $r$ = 1 A.U. = $1.496 \times 10^{11}$ m.

$$T = 3.156 \times 10^7 \text{ s} \quad r = 1.496 \times 10^{11} \text{ m} \Rightarrow M_{Sun} = \frac{4\pi^2 r^3}{GT^2} = \frac{4\pi^2 (1.496 \times 10^{11})^3}{6.674 \times 10^{-11} (3.156 \times 10^7)^2} = 1.99 \times 10^{30} \text{ kg}$$

### The Mass of the Earth

The 'M' in Kepler's 3rd Law is the central body producing the gravitational field. The 'T' and the 'r' refer to the smaller body in orbit around it. So if you have a planet with a satellite around it, you can obtain the mass of the planet. This time, we take the Earth as the big 'M'. Earth has a lot of stuff in orbit about it; artificial satellites and one natural satellite, the Moon. Using the Moon:

$$T = 2.361 \times 10^6 \text{ s} \quad r = 3.844 \times 10^8 \text{ m} \rightarrow M_E = \frac{4\pi^2 r^3}{GT^2} = \frac{4\pi^2 (3.844 \times 10^8)^3}{6.674 \times 10^{-11} (2.361 \times 10^6)^2} = 6.0 \times 10^{24} \text{ kg}$$

### The Mass of Pluto

Being furthest from the Sun, it was difficult to obtain data on 'planet' Pluto. Its mass was estimated from its brightness, together with assumptions about how much light it reflected (its albedo), and its density. Answers varied from 0.9 down to 0.002 of the Earth's mass. Then in 1978, the photograph on the right was taken, showing a 'bump', which suggested that Pluto might have a satellite in orbit around it. It was named 'Charon', and the 'bump' in the photograph suggested it wasn't all that small compared to Pluto.

If its distance from Pluto and period around Pluto could be measured, you could use Kepler's 3RD Law to obtain the mass of Pluto. You'd have to use the modified version of the Law since Charon's mass can't be ignored.

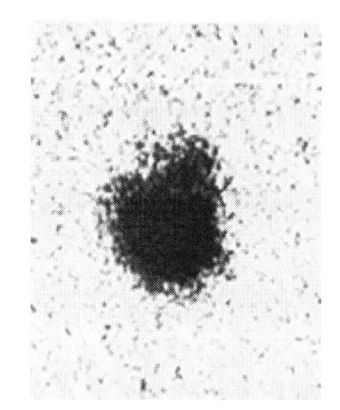

$$T^2 = \left(\frac{4\pi^2}{GM}\right) r^3 \Rightarrow T^2 = \frac{4\pi^2}{G(M_{pl} + M_{Ch})} r^3$$

The period of Charon is 6.39 days with an orbital radius of 19570 km. These give a combined mass for the system of $1.45 \times 10^{22}$ kg (about 0.0024 $M_E$). The Hubble Space Telescope has revealed a total of 5 satellites (image on the left), the smallest discovered in 2012 and no bigger than about 20km in diameter. On 14th July 2015, the New Horizons spacecraft took high resolution images of Pluto. Check them out!

# Rotational Motion & Astrophysics

## Satellite Motion

Since 1957, there have been thousands of satellites launched into orbit about the Earth. Some of these satellites have crashed back into the atmosphere, others have escaped Earth orbit and are flying off into the Solar System. But most are still orbiting the Earth. At present (2014), there are about 600 operational satellites, and about ten times that number knackered.

Of the ones in Earth orbit, they have different altitudes above the surface (prevents pile-ups) and different inclinations (orbiting above the equator, or over the poles, or tilted in between). What they all have in common is that the plane of the orbit passes through the centre of the Earth. Best position to launch from is on the equator and to head eastwards. You get a head-start of about 460 m/s from the Earth's rotation. An equatorial satellite passes over the same ground on every orbit. If you launch from further north or south of the equator, the orbit will be tilted (remember the plane of the orbit must pass through the centre of the Earth). The satellite in a tilted orbit will 'see' a wider area of ground under it on each orbit. Polar orbiting satellites can cover the entire Earth's surface over successive orbits (useful for mapping).

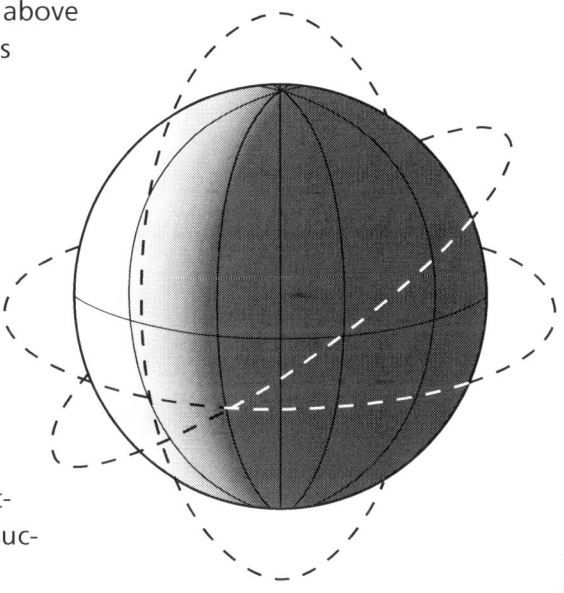

## Orbital Dynamics

Chemical rocket motors lift the satellite above the Earth's atmosphere. The main rocket motors are then switched off (called burnout) and fall back to Earth. Failure to lift the satellite above the atmosphere will result in a decaying orbit. The vehicle must reach at least 120 to 160 km above the surface, or atmospheric drag will bring it down in a few days, with disintegration at an altitude of about 80km. Above approximately 600 km, drag is so weak that orbits usually last more than 10 years - beyond a satellite's operational lifetime. Between 500km and 800km altitude, the density of the atmosphere is extremely low but can vary by a factor of 100 between solar maximum and solar minimum activity.

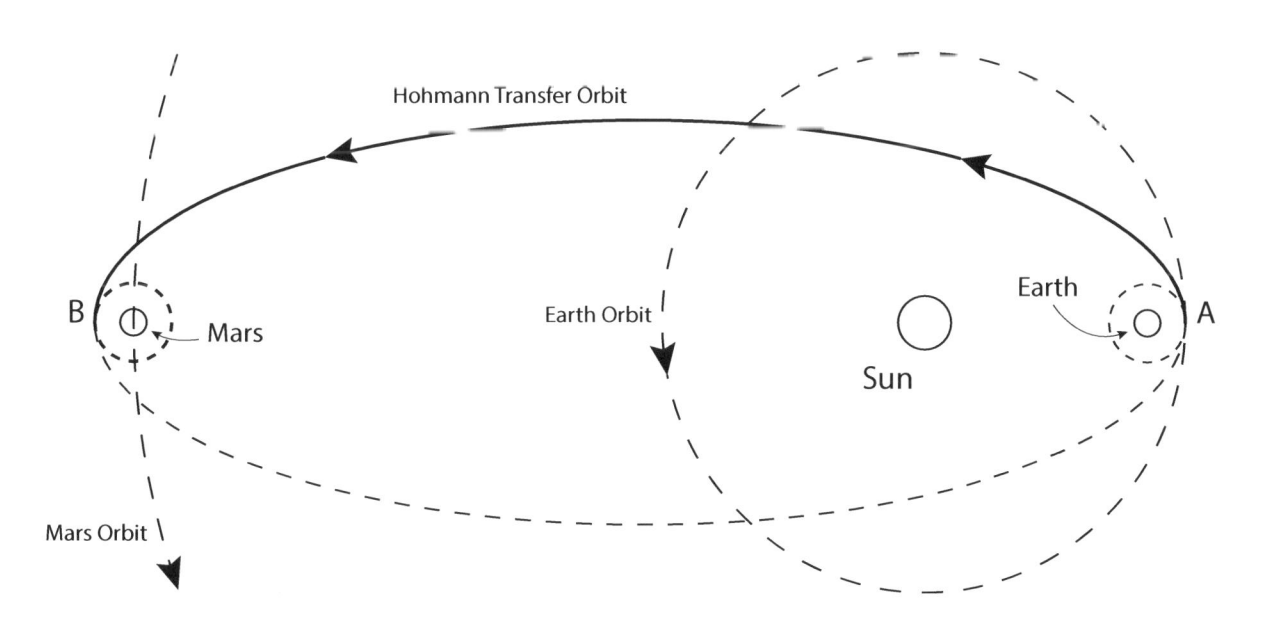

Some satellites orbit our planet day after day bringing multitudes of TV channels. Others are heading for distant planets and require special trajectories called Hohmann Transfer Orbits. You just don't have enough fuel to point your ship at its destination and give it a bit of 'welly' like Flash Gordon. Every drop of fuel means more mass to carry, which means more fuel. The satellite starts off in orbit around the Earth, so is also following Earth's orbit around the Sun (see diagram page 69). The idea is to speed up the satellite at point 'A' to change this circular Earth orbit into an elliptical one which just reaches out to the destination planet. Slow down at point 'B' so that the spacecraft is captured and goes into a circular orbit around the planet. You have to get the timing and the velocity changes just right.

**Gravity Assist**

The Hohmann Transfer Orbit is one method of minimising fuel usage on a mission between planets. There is another method, one which takes energy from an intermediate planet and gives it to the spacecraft, thereby increasing the spacecraft's kinetic energy.

If you throw a ball vertically into the air at a certain speed, it will return with the same speed. The initial vertical and final vertical components will have the same magnitude (though different sign). Suppose a sideways force was also acting during the flight? It will return with the same final vertical component as before, but also have a horizontal component of speed. The resultant final speed (by vector addition) is a hypotenuse of greater magnitude than the launch speed. This is how gravity assist works; the 'sideways' force is due to the gravitational field of the intermediate planet.

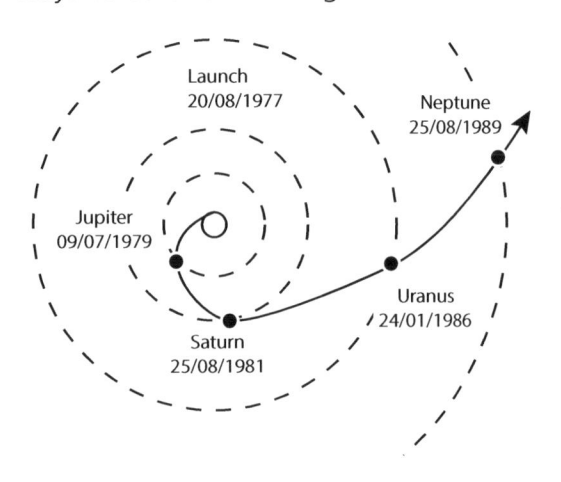

The boldest example of gravity assist was the launch of the two Voyager probes in 1979. They took advantage of an unusual alignment of the planets (one which won't occur again until the 22$^{ND}$ century) to put together a Grand Tour of the gas giants of our solar system. For Voyager 2, this involved successive 'slingshots' past Jupiter, then past Saturn, then onto Uranus and finally Neptune. They all had to be in the right place at the right time! At each stage, the spacecraft was injected into a Hohmann Transfer Orbit ending on the next target planet. The left diagram shows the timings of each encounter, and the diagram below shows the speed changes of Voyager 2 on its long journey through the Solar System.

The dotted line shows the escape velocity from the gravitational pull of the Sun. The gravity assist at Jupiter lifted the spacecraft's speed above that escape velocity and ensured its voyage would continue into interstellar space. The encounter at Neptune was designed to bring the spacecraft near to the satellite Triton rather than give it extra speed.

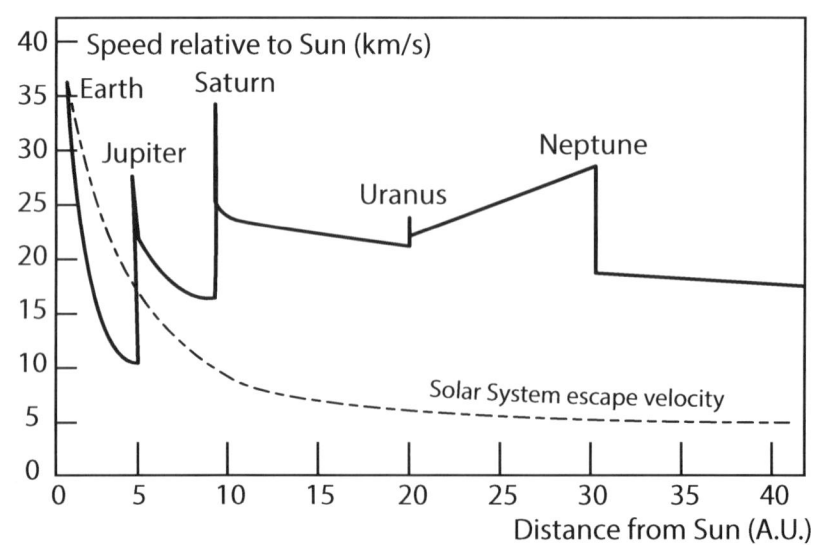

Both Voyagers are heading outside the solar system in search of the heliopause, the region where the Sun's influence gives way to interstellar space. The Voyagers have enough electrical power to operate at least until 2020. Eventually, they will pass other stars. In about 40,000 years, Voyager 1 will be within 1.6 light years of AC+79 3888, a star in the constellation of Camelopardalis. In 296,000 years, Voyager 2 will pass 4.3 light years from Sirius, the brightest star in the sky. As seen in the night sky from Earth, Voyager 2 is presently within the bounds of the constellation Telescopium in the far southern night sky. Perhaps alien beings will detect these probes in the distant future and find the 12" gold plated discs compiled by Carl Sagan with some sights and sounds of our homeworld.

# Rotational Motion & Astrophysics

## The Kinetic and Potential Energy of a Satellite

The total energy of an object in a circular orbit above a planet is the sum of the kinetic and potential energies:

$$E_{Total} = E_{Kin} + E_{Pot} = \frac{1}{2}mv^2 + \left(-\frac{GMm}{r}\right) = \frac{1}{2}mv^2 - \frac{GMm}{r}$$

This is also true whether it's in orbit around the planet or 'just passing through', like these asteroids that whiz past us. There is no relation between the speed 'v' and the distance 'r'. If the object (a satellite) is in a circular orbit around the planet, then you impose a constraint on it (that the centripetal force is supplied by gravity). This relates the speed 'v' to the distance 'r'.

$$\frac{mv^2}{r} = \frac{GMm}{r^2}$$

We can now relate the kinetic and potential energies. Cancel an 'r' from the equation above, then substitute for 'mv²':

$$E_{Total} = \frac{1}{2}mv^2 - \frac{GMm}{r} = \frac{1}{2}\frac{GMm}{r} - \frac{GMm}{r}$$

Interesting result! The kinetic energy is half the size of the potential energy (and opposite sign). If you took a one kilogram satellite and put it in orbit around planet Earth, its kinetic, potential and total energies would be given in the graph below; just select the orbit radius and read off the energy values. The kinetic energy of the satellite is always positive, but the satellite is trapped by the gravitational field, so its total energy is always negative.

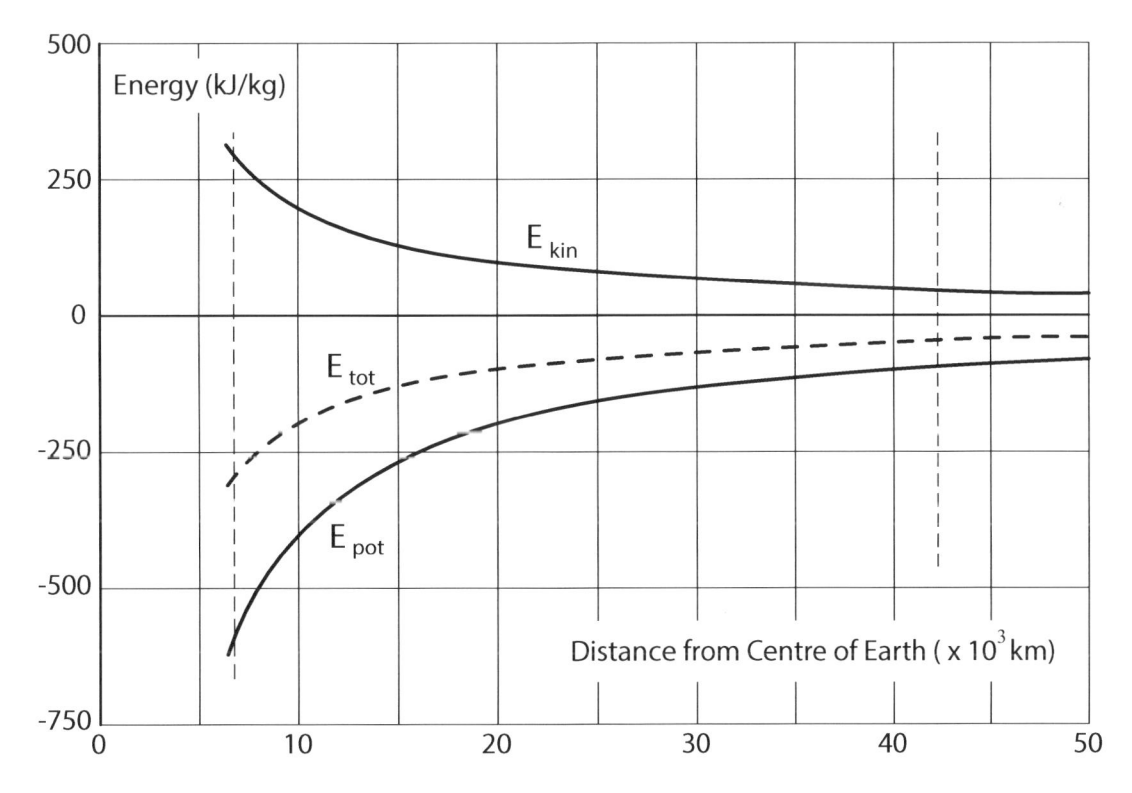

There are two narrow straight dotted lines on the graph. If you placed your kilogram of satellite at the left-hand dotted line, it would be in the same orbit as the International Space Station. The ISS now has a mass of over 450000kg, so multiply the left scale by 450000 to get its energy values. The right-hand dotted line is for a kilogram in geostationary orbit. To calculate the energy required to lift each kilogram from one orbit to another, just read off the two values of the total energy and subtract.

**Example**  A satellite of mass 4780kg is in a circular orbit around planet Mars at an altitude of 700km above its surface. Calculate its total energy in this orbit, and also the energy required to move it to a higher orbit at an altitude of 1150km. Diameter of Mars is 6788km.

At 700Km: $\quad E_P = -\dfrac{GMm}{r} = -\dfrac{6.67 \times 10^{-11} \times 6.42 \times 10^{23} \times 4780}{(3394000 + 700000)} = -5.0 \times 10^{10}$ J

Kinetic energy is half this and positive in sign: $E_K = 2.5 \times 10^{10}$ J

So total energy is: $E_{Tot} = E_K + E_P = 2.5 \times 10^{10}$ J $+ (-5.0 \times 10^{10}$ J$) = -2.5 \times 10^{10}$ J

At 1150Km: $\quad E_P = -\dfrac{GMm}{r} = -\dfrac{6.67 \times 10^{-11} \times 6.42 \times 10^{23} \times 4780}{(3394000 + 1150000)} = -4.5 \times 10^{10}$ J

Kinetic energy is half this and positive in sign: $E_K = 2.25 \times 10^{10}$ J

So total energy is: $E_{Tot} = E_K + E_P = 2.25 \times 10^{10}$ J $+ (-4.50 \times 10^{10}$ J$) = -2.25 \times 10^{10}$ J

Change in total energy = $\Delta E_{Tot} = (-2.25 \times 10^{10}$ J$) - (-2.50 \times 10^{10}$ J$) = 2.5 \times 10^{9}$ J

That's about 70 litres of petrol.

The period of the satellite at the new altitude is obtained by:

$$T^2 = \dfrac{4\pi^2}{GM} r^3 = \dfrac{4\pi^2 \times (1.15 \times 10^6)^3}{6.67 \times 10^{-11} \times 6.42 \times 10^{23}} \quad \Rightarrow \quad T = 1184 \text{s}$$

## Parking your Satellite without a Handbrake - the Lagrange Points

Objects in space find it hard to stand still. The force of gravity has an infinite range and it pulls on them from all directions. Are there places where a satellite could remain in a relatively stable position? The gravitational fields of the Sun, Earth and Moon would have to add-up and 'balance out'. Ignore the Moon. The satellite will be at a fixed distance from the Earth so must have a circular orbit around the Sun. The forces from the Sun and Earth must supply the centripetal force on the satellite. There are five places where this is possible, known as the Lagrange Points.

The diagram on page 62 of the gravitational potential between the Moon and the Earth had a saddle point. The Lagrange points L1, L2 and L3 are like that. It's uphill along one direction and downhill along the other. A satellite placed at these points would drift away and require small corrections every month. L4 and L5 are on 'the top of a hill'. Their locations make an equilateral triangle with the Sun and Earth and a satellite would be trapped there. Whenever they drift 'downhill', they get a sideways force which makes them orbit the Lagrange Point. The Solar Observatory satellite SOHO, is at L1 and is ideal for observing the Sun. The WMAP satellite is at L2 measuring the cosmic microwave background. L2 is about 1.5 million km from Earth. When the Hubble Space Telescope is replaced (about 2018), its successor will be placed at L2.

# Rotational Motion & Astrophysics

# Section 1.5 Space & Time

*"Common sense is the collection of prejudices acquired by age eighteen"...Albert Einstein*

Common sense is no longer a secure guide to the discovery of the inner workings of the universe. Understanding Quantum Mechanics, Special and General Relativity requires profound changes in our thinking; about Determinism and about the nature of Space and Time. What we have is a new set of rules which govern the behaviour of all objects in the universe.

We all carry the old Newtonian assumptions with us between our ears. From birth, we interact with everyday objects, the behaviour of which embeds and confirms our understanding of the physical world on a minute by minute basis. Deepest down, and hardest to shift, are our unshakeable beliefs about time and about space. This unit will put a very long crowbar under your Newtonian head and apply a very big force to the end of it. You have to rebuild your head from the neck up.

## Special Relativity

Equations like $F = ma$ make up a part of Physics which has been tested many times over, not only by engineers and scientists, but by everybody. Cars, bridges and aircraft are testimony to its effectiveness, but that doesn't mean that it's correct for absolutely everything. All it means is that it works for cars, bridges, aircraft, bikes, cement mixers, windmills, cd players, trebuchets ........ Scientists like to test theories over a wider and wider range of experiments just to see how good they are. So you might imagine the surprise they received when they did experiments where it didn't work.

It doesn't work in two particular realms; the world of the atom (where Newton's Laws are replaced by Quantum Mechanics) and the world of the very fast/large (where it is replaced by Special and General Relativity).

Newton's Laws have no built-in limiting speed. You can put your foot on the gas right past 11 on the dial all the way to Ludicrous Speed. Einstein's Theory has a universal limiting speed, the speed of light in a vacuum $3 \times 10^8$ m s$^{-1}$. Only a few special things (like photons and gravitons) can travel at that speed but everything else must go slower. This is the only difference between Einstein's Special Relativity and Newton's Mechanics. It may not sound to you like such a big deal, but the consequences create complete mayhem with your common sense. Try simple addition of speeds.

One observer goes left at the speed of light and another observer goes right at the speed of light.

How fast are they speeding apart?

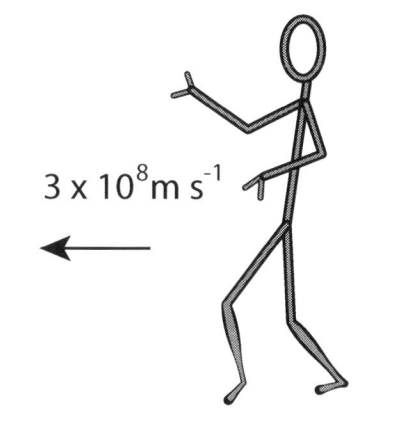

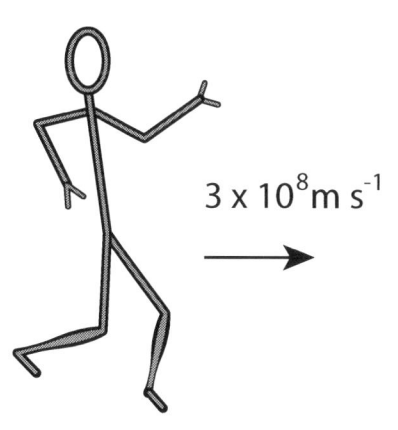

$3 \times 10^8$ m s$^{-1}$ ←    → $3 \times 10^8$ m s$^{-1}$

According to Newton and also common sense, it would be twice the speed of light, $6 \times 10^8$ m s$^{-1}$. It would make things a lot simpler if we lived in a universe like that, but the fact is that we don't! In the universe that we've been born into, each observer measures the other receding at $3 \times 10^8$ m s$^{-1}$. Yuck! You now have a choice. Either shut your eyes, pull the quilt over your head and pretend it doesn't happen, or accept reality and face up to the challenge.

What it means is that time isn't what we, or Isaac Newton, thought it was. Two observers can be timing the same event and get different times; and it's not due to experimental error. It only happens if one observer is moving relative to the other; if they were both at rest or both moving with the same velocity, they would record the same results. This is the basic feature of Special Relativity; an observer moving with a constant velocity relative to another observer will record different results. By results, we mean measurements of time intervals and position co-ordinates in space. Both observers will use their results to deduce the Laws of Physics. The first observer will discover the same laws of electromagnetism (we call them Maxwell's Equations) as the second observer. Some things would be the same to both observers, like the electric charge (this is called an invariant). But the equations which correctly describe the behaviour of the experiment will have a form such that both observers can input their own measurements and obtain the same prediction.

## Frames of Reference

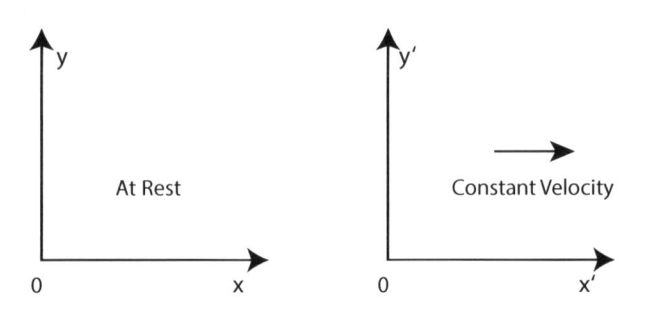

The core idea is the inertial reference frame. You can think of an observer in a reference frame as someone with a pair of binoculars, a metre stick and a stopwatch. It sets an origin in space and time and allows you to make measurements of position (x, y, z) and time (t) relative to that origin. An *inertial* reference frame is one travelling with a constant velocity (zero or non-zero). Two inertial frames are shown on the right. Their 'x' axes are aligned and each one has an observer going along with it. They both observe an event, the explosion of a bomb. The observer at rest locates the point where the bomb exploded with co-ordinates (x,y) and the constant velocity observer records the same event with co-ordinates (x',y'). They might also time when the explosion happened. Being sensible scientists, they zeroed their clocks when the origins of their two axes lined up. The observers recorded the time of the explosion as t and t'. By common sense and by the laws of Newtonian mechanics, the two times are the same eg. the explosion happened at t = 8s according to the observer at rest and at t' = 8s according to the moving observer. The x-value of the observer at rest will be different from the x'-value of the moving observer since the explosion was at different distances from them, but the y-values will be the same and the times will be the same.

*This is no longer true once Einstein demanded that the speed of light be the same for all observers.*

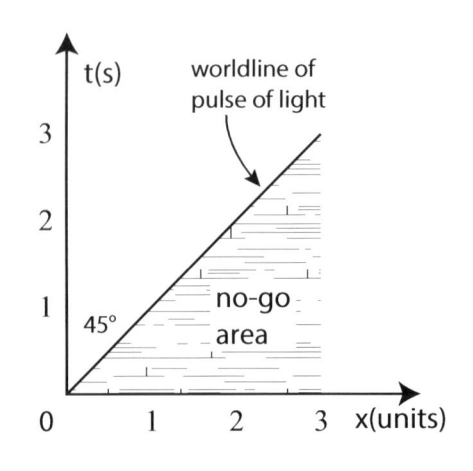

We will see the implications of this later with the twin paradox. The point about Newtonian mechanics is that it keeps space separate from time; the two are not connected in any way. In Relativity Theory, the three dimensions of space and the one dimension of time are considered to be a single four dimensional arena known as SpaceTime (one word). Drawing axes showing both space co-ordinates and the time co-ordinate is the essential tool in tackling problems in Relativity. Since we can't draw four axes (x,y,z,t) all at right angles to each other, we must content ourselves with graphs showing only the time and 'x' axes. This is the spacetime diagram on the right. The observer whose reference frame this is, will plot points on it showing the motion of the object under investigation (where it is (x) at what time (t)). The line on the graph shows the recorded space 'x' and time 't' readings by the observer for a pulse of light.

The time axis is marked in seconds. The 'x' axis isn't in metres. If we had used metres for our unit, the pulse would be at x = 300,000,000metres when t = 1second. If you're reading this facing south, you would need to extend the graph to New York to plot the point. For convenience, one unit of distance is how far light travels in 1 second. This is 300,000,000 metres (a distance of 1 light-second).

Using our new system (seconds and light-seconds), the pulse travels one unit of distance in one second; so it makes an angle of 45º with the time axis. Objects which travel slower than light would trace out a steeper line (eg. taking 2s to travel one unit of distance). Demanding that the speed of light is a limiting speed means that you can't plot points between the line of the light pulse and the x-axis. There are no-go areas on spacetime graphs, unlike Newton where you can go anywhere you like on his graphs.

In defining Newtonian Mechanics and Special Relativity, Newton and Einstein made an assumption called the Principle of Relativity:

*The laws of physics have the same form in all inertial reference frames.*

You might have noticed this if you've ever drunk a cup of coffee in an aeroplane at 600mph. If you accidentally spilled the coffee, it still ended up on your trousers; not on your chest, as Aristotle might have hoped. Remember, that when you performed the standard *F = ma* experiment at school, the laboratory was on a planet travelling at 15 miles per second. Newton's 2nd Law *F = ma*, is based on acceleration, which is the *change* in velocity rather than the actual velocity. Speeding up from 10m s$^{-1}$ to 15m s$^{-1}$ in 2s is the same acceleration as speeding up from 1000m s$^{-1}$ to 1005m s$^{-1}$ in 2s.

Where Einstein departs from Newton is his second postulate:

*The speed of light is finite and is an invariant for all inertial observers.*

The word 'invariant' is an important one to learn; it means 'is the same'. Physical quantities which have the same value for all inertial observers are the 'gold nuggets' of a theory. Examples of invariants in Special Relativity are electric charge and mass (yes, that's right; relativistic mass is a bad idea). Measurements of position and time form an invariant in the following combination (which we usually reduce to 2 dimensions for simplicity):

$$c^2t^2 - (x^2 + y^2 + z^2) \rightarrow c^2t^2 - x^2$$

Suppose an object moves a certain distance in a certain time and is observed by two scientists. One observer records the distance moved and time taken as (x, t). Another observer using a different coordinate system records his readings (x', t'). If they both calculate that special combination above, they will find that:

$$c^2t^2 - x^2 = c^2t'^2 - x'^2$$

That minus sign is the most important thing in Special Relativity. If it was a plus sign, it would be just like Pythagoras Theorem extended to 4 dimensions. In the early days of Relativity, Minkowski replaced real time with imaginary time *t → it* so that when you squared it you got the same sign as the x$^2$. This still lingers on with amateur enthusiasts who've just uncovered the secrets of time, but is now considered a dead-end since it removes Special Relativity's most important feature.

There is a similar invariant combination in dynamics. Time is replaced by energy *ct → E* , and position is replaced by momentum *x → pc* . (Notice scalar goes with scalar and vector with vector!) This gives the invariant:

$$E^2 - p^2c^2$$

All inertial observers will get the same answer for that combination:

$$E^2 - p^2c^2 = E'^2 - p'^2c^2$$

We can easily work out what that answer is; just apply it to the special case of an inertial observer travelling along with the same velocity as the object. For that observer, his readings are: observed momentum $p=0$ and observed energy equals the rest energy $E \to E_o = m_o c^2$.

$$E^2 - p^2c^2 \quad \to \quad E_o^2 - 0^2 c^2 = \left(m_o c^2\right)^2 = m_o^2 c^4$$

So, the correct expression for the energy (variously called 'relativistic energy', 'total energy', 'total relativistic energy') is:

$$E^2 - p^2c^2 = m_o^2 c^4 \quad \Rightarrow \quad E^2 = p^2c^2 + m_o^2 c^4$$

The dependence of the total energy on the speed is expressed through the momentum. However, in the mind of the public, the most famous equation in physics is $E = mc^2$. Written this way, the dependence of the total energy on the speed is expressed through the mass. You should resist this piece of 'pop culture' since it hides the most important asset in Special Relativity, the idea of an invariant. It also tempts the unwary into wrong physics. You often see it used to calculate the mass of a photon:

$$E = hf = mc^2 \quad \Rightarrow \quad m_{photon} = hf/c^2 \qquad \textbf{(health warning: wrong physics)}$$

Applied to particles with no mass (the photon is the best example) the proper equation reduces to:

$$E^2 = p^2c^2 + m_o^2 c^4 \quad \Rightarrow \quad E^2 = p^2c^2 \quad \Rightarrow \quad E = pc \qquad \textbf{(correct physics)}$$

So, it should read: $\quad E = hf = pc \quad \Rightarrow \quad p = hf/c = h/\lambda \qquad \textbf{(correct physics)}$

## The Twin Paradox

If Humankind is to explore beyond the Solar System, the first problem to overcome is the vast distances involved. For the last 30000 years, the nearest star beyond the Sun has been part of a triple system called alpha centauri, presently at a distance of 4.24 lightyears. Even at the speed of light, the return trip would take eight and a half years. However, not all stars have suitable planetary systems. Over the last decade, we have discovered that many stars have planets which are gas giants like Jupiter, or even bigger. At present, rocky planets are still too small to detect (though this could change with the discovery of KOI-172.02, with an Earth size planet). The alternative is to select a nearby star similar to the Sun, be of about the same age (about 5 billion years), and hope it has a solar system like ours.

Rather than travel to the stars , we could wait until they come closer. At present, a star with half the mass of the Sun, called Gliese 710, is at a distance of 50 ly. One million years from now, its distance will be one lightyear, close enough to gravitationally disrupt the Oort Cloud and send comets our way.

For those without the patience to wait around, you could investigate the brightest star in the northern sky, Sirius, at a distance of only 8.58 ly. However, it is part of a triple star system and any planet would be in a weird orbit and experience large temperature extremes. You can also rule out other close stars like Barnard's Star (5.96 ly) and Wolf 359 (7.78 ly) since they are too small.

Below the constellation of Orion, and so not visible from the Northern Sky, is the constellation of Eridanus (the River). Within its boundary lies a star named 82 Eridani at a distance of 19.8 lightyears. This is very similar to our Sun but about twice the age (about 10billion years). If life is common throughout the galaxy, civilisations may have come and gone many times on such an old star. At the speed of light, it would take our spaceship almost 40 years to make the round trip.

# Rotational Motion & Astrophysics

This is where the twin paradox arises. Suppose there were twins, Homer and Wanderer, both aged 20 years. Wanderer wishes to travel to explore 82 Eridani while Homer prefers to stay on Earth. When Wanderer returns from his journey and greets Homer on the tarmac, he notices that Homer looks much older than he does. Wanderer recognises this as the 'time effect' of high speeds in Special Relativity. Homer thinks for a minute, then protests that due to relative motion, you could consider that Wanderer was at rest and Homer had receded in the opposite direction then returned, so he should look younger! Isn't that what 'relative motion' means? Who's correct?

Start with a spacetime diagram for the whole journey. Homer's spacetime diagram for his own trip (going nowhere in space, but sometime in time) would be a vertical line up the time axis. This diagram shows Homers log of Wanderer's journey. He sees him heading out at 0.9c and returning at 0.9c.

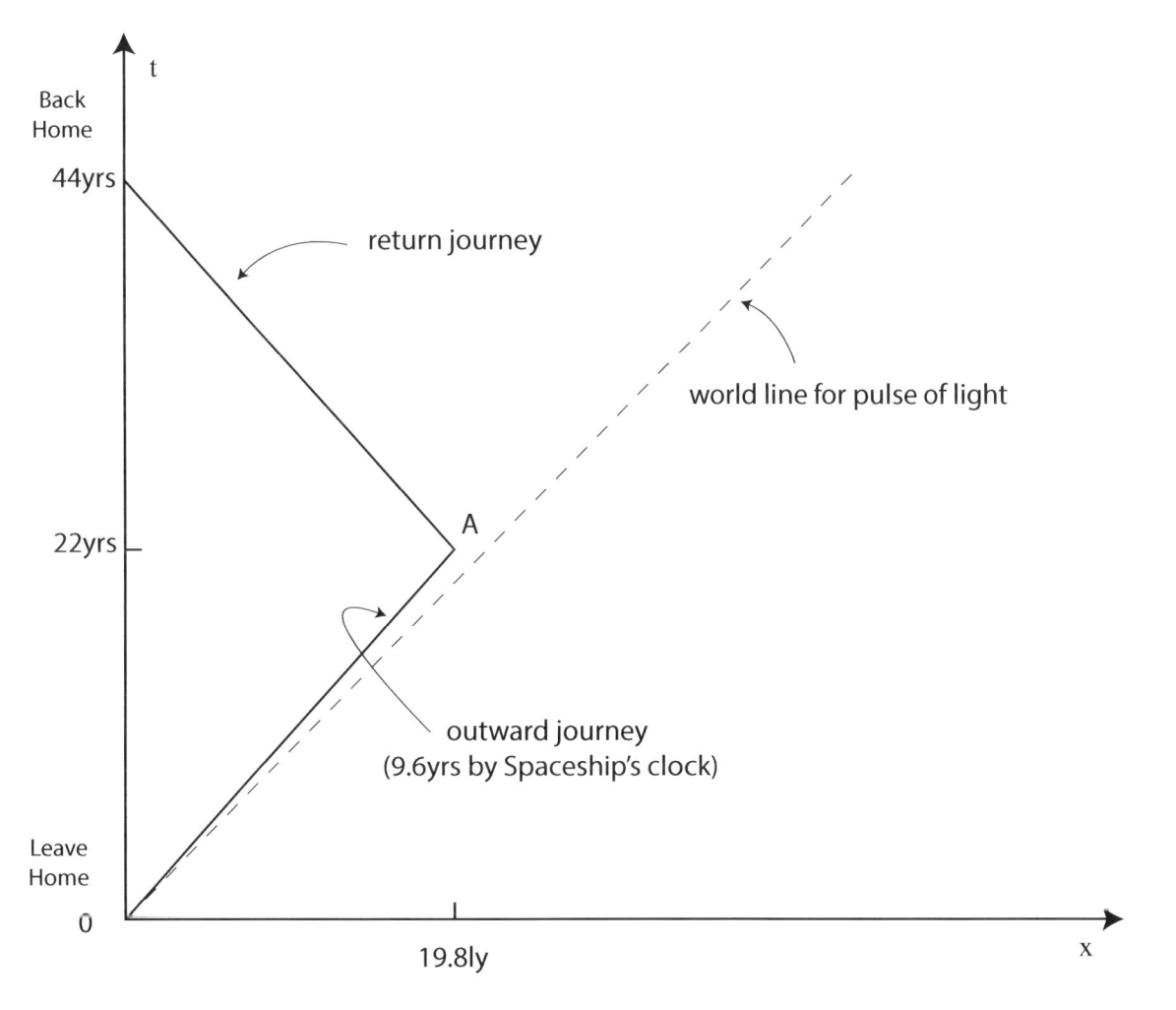

The units are years for time and lightyears for distance. The speed of light is 1 lightyear per year, in other words c = 1. In this system, the speed of the rocket, $2.7 \times 10^8$ m s$^{-1}$ is v = 0.9c. The target star is 19.8 ly from Earth and at a speed of 0.9c, the spaceship will reach it in 22 yrs. The spacetime diagram was drawn by Homer back on Earth, so that's 22 yrs of his time spent observing the spaceship on the way out and another 22 yrs watching it come back. Homer will be 44 yrs older when Wanderer returns from his trip.

I've mentioned the importance of invariants in a theory. One of them was: $c^2t^2 - x^2$. In our system of units with c = 1, this becomes: $t^2 - x^2$. On the outward trip from Earth to the star (at point 'A' above), both Homer and Wanderer will make measurements of the spacetime displacement of the spaceship, but they must get the same answer for the invariant $t^2 - x^2$.

Homer's readings outward trip: $\quad t = 22\,yrs \quad\quad x = 19.8\,ly \quad \Rightarrow \quad t^2 - x^2 = 22^2 - 19.8^2 = 91.96$

77

Wanderer's time on his clock is $t'$ and his position reading is $x' = 0$ (since he is on the spaceship), so:

Wanderer's readings outward trip:  $\quad t'^2 - x'^2 = t'^2 - 0^2 = t'^2 = 91.96 \quad \Rightarrow \quad t' = 9.6\,yrs$

The return journey is similar, giving a total elapsed time measured by Wanderer of 2 × 9.6 = 19.2 yrs. Setting out at age 20, Wanderer will be 39.2 yrs old when he returns. Homer will be 64yrs old. You often come across 'explanations' for the twin paradox as being outside Special Relativity, and that 'accelerations' are involved, so that makes it General Relativity. Don't believe that garbage.

The whole thing probably still doesn't feel right. Blame it on experience. But if you make a hypothesis (constancy of the speed of light for all observers), test it and find it to be true, what else can you do but accept the consequences? That's what I call Science. What do you call it?

## General Relativity

After formulating Special Relativity, Einstein was keenly aware that his theory had nothing to say about gravity. Isaac Newton had used the idea of mass in two different contexts. One was his 2ND Law $F = ma$ where mass is the constant of proportionality between the force on a body and its resultant acceleration. In this context it's called the *inertial* mass, suggesting a reluctance to a change in motion. The other one was his Law of Gravitation expressing the gravitational force between two masses separated by a certain distance $F = GMm/r^2$. In this context, the 'M' and 'm' are called *gravitational* masses. Everyone studying Physics at school learns that it's all the same thing. It's just mass. Einstein was fascinated but troubled by this simple equivalence of inertial and gravitational mass. There would still be inertial mass in a world without gravity. Bodies would still be reluctant to move when a force is applied to them.

He also noted Galileo's alleged experiment at the Leaning Tower of Pisa where big and small cannon-balls were released at the same time and hit the ground at the same time. He thought that a person in freefall would feel 'weightless'. Parachutes weren't in use in his day, and only came to public attention with leaps off the Eiffel Tower from 1911, and the death of the Austrian Franz Reichelt in 1912. So Einstein didn't have the experience of weightlessness that so many of us have today. In 1908, he heard of a painter who'd fallen off a roof. Asking the painter what it felt like to fall, he received the reply ' no weight at all'. Einstein described this as the greatest idea of his life.

For dropped objects in freefall:

$$m_I a = \frac{GMm_G}{r^2} \quad \Rightarrow \quad a = \frac{GMm_G}{r^2 m_I} \quad \Rightarrow \quad a = g = \frac{GM}{r^2}$$

The equality and cancellation of the inertial mass '$m_I$' and gravitational mass '$m_G$' of the object is done without much thought, especially when it doesn't have the subscripts. To Einstein this revealed a profound insight into the nature of gravity; something which his Special Theory had lacked.

Inertial mass is related to acceleration. Gravitational mass is related to gravity. Einstein speculated that you couldn't distinguish between standing on the surface of the Earth where the gravitational field strength is 9.8 N/kg, and being accelerated at 9.8 m/s² in a region without any masses. He went further. It wasn't just that you couldn't tell them apart, **they were the same thing!** This is known as the **Principle of Equivalence**. What we experience as the force of gravity is just 'us' being accelerated through space. Einstein believed that inertial and gravitational 'forces' weren't just equivalent; they were identical! To Einstein, gravity isn't a force! It's a property of space. The same 'space' we mentioned on page 50 when asking how the Earth attracts the Moon. Let's now investigate that load of nothing called space.

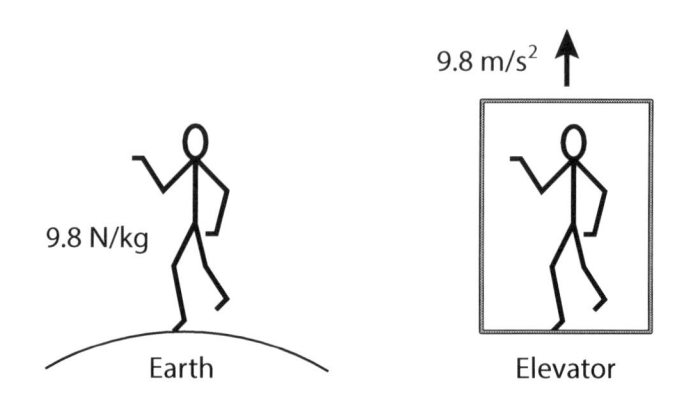

# Rotational Motion & Astrophysics

## Curved SpaceTime

From Higher Physics we learned that an object undergoing uniform acceleration obeys the equation $s = ut + \frac{1}{2}at^2$. To measure the acceleration of the object, you could record the position 's' at time 't' over a number of positions, then fit the data to a quadratic equation. The coefficient with the time squared term would be half the acceleration. For uniform or non-uniform motion you could use the definition from calculus: $a = \dfrac{d^2 s}{dt^2}$. The important point is that acceleration is related to measurements of position and time made by an observer. This might seem straightforward, but we make a number of assumptions which are so obvious that we don't even think about them.

Suppose the Earth was a perfectly smooth sphere. No mountains, no valleys, no ridges. Our object moves over the surface and we wish to measure its acceleration. As before, we would record its position at various times then fit the graph to a quadratic function. How would you measure its position? Easy, use a co-ordinate system with an origin. What would this co-ordinate system 'look' like? Easy, big bit of graph paper. What happens if you wrap a tennis ball in a sheet of A4 paper? Tricky, the paper gets crumpled. The table-top flat graph paper you're used to in school is a grid of lines which are all 'parallel' and are the shortest distance between two points. You can't use a table-top flat co-ordinate system here; you have to draw one on the surface of the sphere. The grid lines would be made of lines of latitude and longitude. Just like your ordinary graph paper, the line from 'A' to 'B' on the diagram is the *shortest* line from 'A' to 'B'.

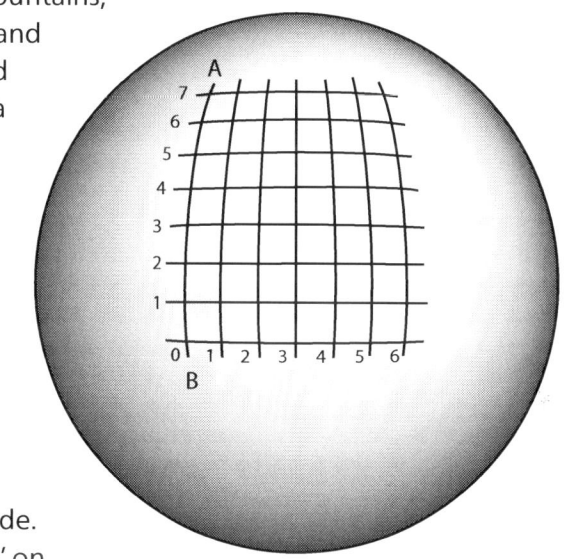

The grid spacing along the 'x' direction is closer at the top than it is at the bottom. Yet the experimental physicist who drew the grid on the ground followed the rules; a grid of 'straight' lines all cutting each other at 90°. What would this grid do to your calculation for the acceleration?

Of course, you can always tell if something is 'straight' by just looking along it. Right? 'Looking' involves rays of light, and you were taught that they travel in straight lines. Suppose our universe was made in such a way that rays of light might not travel in straight lines in a vacuum? Suppose that 'mass' distorts spacetime so that rays of light follow paths which 'look' straight but are curved. A ray of light emitted from 'A' in the above diagram in a curved spacetime would follow the path to 'B'. Standing at 'A', you would see a ray of light heading off in a 'straight' line. You would swear to it in a court of law.

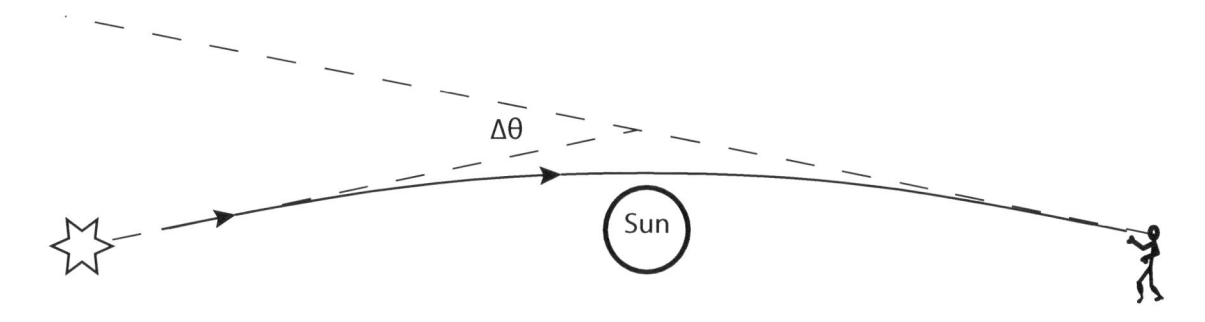

This happens when rays of light pass near objects with mass; like stars and black holes. The Sun's mass distorts spacetime around it. A ray of light from a distant star just grazing past the surface of the Sun is predicted to be deflected by an angle $\Delta\theta = 1.75$ arc seconds. You can't see stars in the sky during daylight, so to test this prediction, an expedition was mounted in May 1919 to measure the deflection angle during a total solar eclipse. The track of the eclipse started in Brazil, went across the Atlantic Ocean and onto Africa. A budget of £1000 for the expedition and £100 for instruments was set and Sir Arthur Eddington and Co. set off for Sobral in Brazil and the Isle of Principe in the Atlantic Ocean. The results were consistent with Einstein's prediction but not super-accurate. This had to wait until the 1970s when radio waves were used instead of light waves. Using several large radio telescopes separated by 35km allowed the use of long baseline interferometry to achieve great precision in locating the radio stars as the Sun passed nearby. The results confirmed Einstein's Theory. Remember, the photon isn't deflected because it has mass (which it hasn't) or that it has energy (which it has). It isn't 'deflected' in curved spacetime at all. It's moving along its version of 'straight'.

## Gravity as a Lens

This bending of light should remind you of the physics of optics, where light rays are refracted by glass to produce a different view of what's really there. Microscopes and telescopes make things look smaller and bigger, and spectacle lenses sharpen up an otherwise blurry image on your retina. We've just discovered that masses also change the path of light rays, a sort of gravity-based optics, but you need very heavy masses to make it obvious and the place to look is in the night sky.

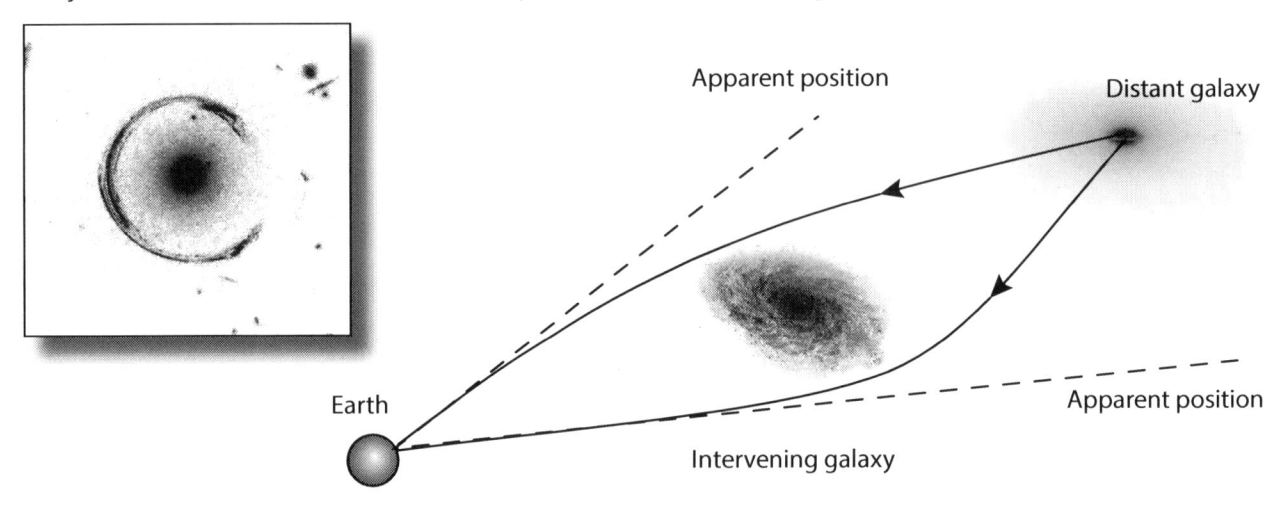

The diagram above shows the bending of two light rays from a very distant galaxy. This galaxy, and the other closer one, happen to line-up with the Earth. It wouldn't just be two rays reaching Earth; it's a cone of rays, and the Earth just happens to be at the tip of the cone. On Earth, we project back along straight lines (the tangent to the light ray entering the telescope) and see a ring around the closer galaxy. This is called an Einstein Ring, and several have been discovered. The inset image shows the ring-light from a galaxy with a redshift of 2.4. This light has been travelling for about 10 billion years. The intervening galaxy LRG 3-757, is unusually massive (about ×10 our own galaxy), and is in almost perfect alignment between us and the distant galaxy. The ring has an angular diameter of 12 arc seconds.

## SpaceTime Diagrams

Imposing a speed limit on the universe means that you can't get to some places fast enough. You can go anywhere you like, but not anywhere at anytime (see diagram page 74). You can contact a star 4 lightyears away in a time of 4 years but not in a time of 3 years. SpaceTime diagrams plot position 'x' against time 't', with the time 'up' the way. The distance scale on the following diagram is shown in 'natural units' where the speed of light is taken as 1 unit. So a ray of light will make an angle of 45° (dotted lines on diagram). Due to the speed limit, the regions of spacetime which are inaccessible to a space traveller at the origin are shown shaded. Newtonian Space Time diagrams don't have forbidden areas; you can go anywhere at anytime in his theory.

Two trips are shown on the spacetime diagram. Trip 'A' is at a constant speed of about 0.2c. Trip 'B' starts off near the speed of light then slows down. These are called '*World Lines*'. You are making a world line in spacetime at the moment. An observer standing beside you could draw a spacetime diagram of your motion. You are at rest with respect to the observer, so your world line would go up the time axis.

# Rotational Motion & Astrophysics

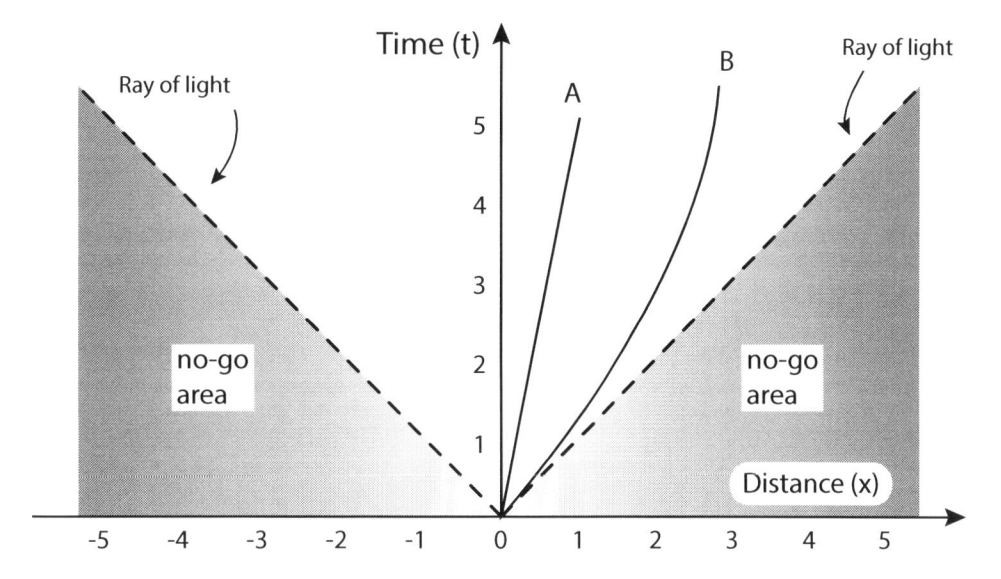

There is a special type of world line called a 'Geodesic'. This is the spacetime history of an object in free-fall. 'Freefall' used to mean no forces other than gravity. In General Relativity it means no forces. It's Newton's 1$^{ST}$ Law updated to include gravity, and with a new interpretation of 'straight'.

A satellite in orbit about the Earth isn't going in a circle because the Earth is exerting a force on it. The Earth's mass has distorted the otherwise flat spacetime around it (á la Newton) and the satellite is following a 'straight' line (ie. the shortest spacetime interval) in that curved spacetime. The satellite's world line is a geodesic. As are the world lines of the 'weightless' astronauts in freefall inside. The high orbital speed of the satellite prevents the geodesic from intersecting with the hard ground of planet Earth down below. Back at ground level, the seat you're sitting on prevents *you* from going into freefall and following a geodesic path. Another example of a geodesic is of a comet going around the back of the Sun. The Sun's mass distorts the spacetime around it and the comet is in a freefall elliptical orbit. No force of gravity!

One last point. The axes on the diagram above can be extended to infinity / eternity in Special Relativity Theory where spacetime is flat. In General Relativity you can't extend Newtonian straight line axes out into curved spacetime, so these diagrams should be as small as possible. 'Local' is the term.

## Testing General Relativity

It would be wise to test a wacky theory like Einsteins pretty thoroughly before jumping from the good-ship 'commonsense'. In the century since its 'discovery', General Relativity has been asked many questions by the experimenters and come out on top every time! One such test is the prediction of the orbit of planet Mercury about the Sun.

Like the other planets, Mercury follows an elliptical orbit about the Sun. The major axis of the ellipse (show by a dotted line in the diagram) doesn't stay in the same place pointing at the same distant star background. It moves around by a very small angle each orbit to the other dotted line, an effect called the **Precession of the Orbit of Mercury**. It's been measured very accurately over many years and it's about 1½° during a period of a century. This is 5599.74 arc-seconds per century.

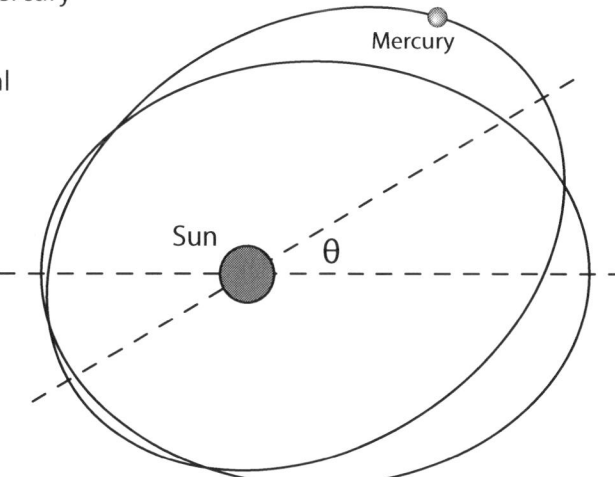

81

Most of this is due to changes in the motion of the Earth, from where we are observing. So we have to subtract that from the observed value. It leaves 574 arc-seconds per century. Most of this (532 arc-seconds per century) comes from Newtonian / Kepler torques from the other planets. The remaining 42 arc-seconds per century comes from Einstein's General Relativity. The Sun's mass has a curved space-time around it and it is this difference from a flat spacetime which produces the small difference. Mercury is nearest the Sun so has the biggest precession of its orbit.

A more severe test of Einstein's theory is a **Binary Pulsar** system. A pulsar is the dense remnant of a supernova explosion made up of neutrons packed closely together. The explosion sends out material radially and so the angular momentum remains largely unchanged. Just like a skater's arms coming in (page 45), the angular velocity of the star increases as it collapses. If it's not too massive, the collapse stops when the neutrons get close, only stopping when commanded by the rules of quantum mechanics. They are also highly magnetic with north and south magnetic poles. These poles send out radiation of various wavelengths, some in the visible region. The magnetic poles don't line-up with the spin axis, and sweep around in a cone shape which points towards Earth every rotation (hence the flash). The numbers are impressive. A 10km diameter sphere of the mass of the Sun rotating at a frequency of tens of Hertz. This produces a decent curvature on the surrounding spacetime.

The *binary* pulsar system has two neutron stars orbiting a common centre of mass. Either one star pulses and the other one doesn't, or more rarely, they both pulse. PSR J0737-3039 discovered in 2003 in the southern sky is about 2000 ly away and is the only known example of the latter. The pair are of similar mass ($\approx 1.3$ M$_{Sun}$), have a separation of only 100000Km, and rotate about a common centre in a period of 2.4 hrs. The more 'flashy' one rotates at 44Hz. The precession of the orbit due to General Relativity is 17° per year. The rotation frequency of a pulsar is one of the most accurately measured quantites in physics eg. 16.940539303Hz for the most famous one discovered in 1974 called PSR B1913+16.

### Gravitational Redshift

The diagram on the next page uses the Principle of Equivalence. No experiment can distinguish between being in a constant gravitational field of gravitational field strength 9.8 N/kg, and uniformly accelerating in a mass-free region at 9.8 m/s². The experiment being performed inside the building and inside the lift will have identical results.

It shows a pulse of light being emitted from the ceiling and received at the floor. In the lift, the observer notes that the pulse takes a time 't' to travel from the emitter on the ceiling to the detector on the floor. During this time, the lift has accelerated upwards from rest to a speed 'v' when the pulse is detected: $v = at = |g|t$. The acceleration and the gravitational field strength are in the opposite direction so the modulus of 'g' is used. To the observer inside the lift, the pulse has travelled a distance 'h' in time 't', so $t = h/c$. Eliminate 't' to obtain:

$$v = |g|t = |g|\frac{h}{c}$$

The frequency of the pulse will be Doppler shifted due to the speed 'v' of the approaching detector:

$$f' = f\left(1 + \frac{v}{c}\right)$$

**Rotational Motion & Astrophysics**

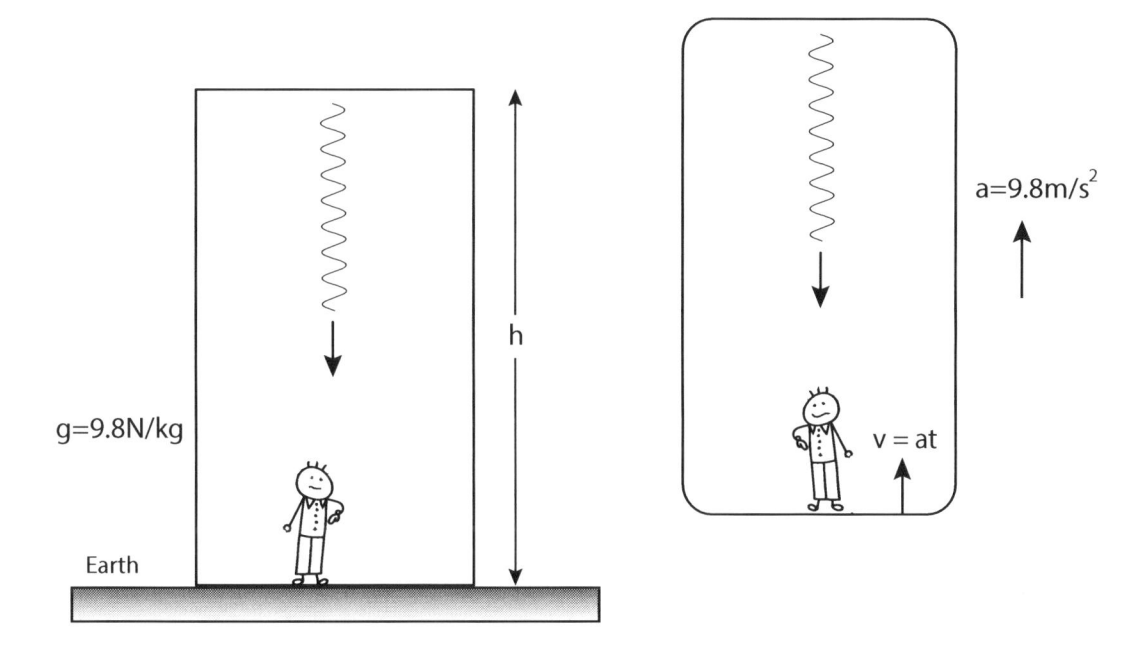

Substitute for the speed 'v' at the instant the pulse is detected:

$$f' = f\left(1+\frac{v}{c}\right) = f\left(1+\frac{|g|h}{c^2}\right)$$

The height 'h' and the gravitational field strength 'g' produce a difference in gravitational potential. The symbol we've used for this previously is a capital 'V' but we'll use phi 'φ' to avoid confusion with the speed 'v'. A difference in a value is always taken as the final minus the initial value. The initial position at the ceiling is distance $r_2$ from the centre of the Earth, and the final position at the detector is $r_1$ from the centre of the Earth. The difference in gravitational potential Δφ between the top and bottom of the lift due to the Earth is:

$$\Delta\varphi = \left(-\frac{GM}{r_1}\right) - \left(-\frac{GM}{r_2}\right)$$

$$= -GM\left(\frac{r_2 - r_1}{r_1 r_2}\right) = -GM\frac{h}{r^2}$$

The height of the lift is much smaller than the distance to the centre of the Earth so $r_1 \approx r_2 = r$. The combination of G, M and $r^2$ should remind you of:

$$m|g| = \frac{GMm}{r^2} \quad \Rightarrow \quad |g| = \frac{GM}{r^2} \quad \Rightarrow \quad \Delta\varphi = -|g|h \quad \Rightarrow \quad |g| = -\frac{\Delta\varphi}{h}$$

Substitution into the Doppler expression gives:

$$f' = f\left(1 - \frac{\Delta\varphi}{c^2}\right)$$

The change in gravitational potential Δφ is negative for the lift example above since the pulse goes 'deeper into the gravitational well' of the Earth. This means that the observed frequency 'f′' will be greater than 'f' and hence be 'blueshifted'. A beam of light moving outwards from the Earth would be redshifted to a longer wavelength.

The above derivation has a few dodgy bits in it (like assuming the Doppler formula works for an accelerating detector), but it's correct to first order (ignores squares, cubes etc).

## The Global Positioning System

Originally designed for the US Military, this has become an indispensible aid for people who can't read maps. It nominally consists of 24 satellites at a distance of 20,000km above the ground, orbiting with a period of 12hours. Four satellites are used to locate the position on the ground of a receiver. Three of them use a carrier frequency of 1575MHz to record the times for a signal to travel between the receiver on the ground and each satellite. Travelling at the speed of light, these three times define three spheres, the intersection of which locates the receiver in latitude, longitude and altitude. The accuracy depends upon the precision of the timing; at present it's better than 10metres. The fourth satellite is used to check and correct the timing of cheap handheld receivers. In theory, its possible to achieve a timing accuracy of 14ns, though most receivers will push this back to 100ns.

This accuracy requires corrections from various sources, of which Special and General Relativity play a part. From Special Relativity, the clocks run slower compared to the ground due to the speed of the satellite by 7μs/day. From General Relativity, the stronger gravitational potential makes the clocks run slower on the ground by 45μs/day. These two effects add-up to make the satellite clocks run faster by 38μs/day.

China, Russia and the European Space Agency are also building their own satellite navigation systems. The US actually has 31 GPS satellites in space that are operational, with 36 planned and 4 in reserve. Sounds crowded up there!

## Black Holes - the Physics of the Extreme

Hardcore sci-fi fans like Black Holes. Things get sucked in and don't come back. They're big and nasty. So, wow!; what would happen if you replaced our Sun with a Black Hole of the same mass? Actually, not much, apart from the lower temperatures and lack of light. Planets would still orbit as before; Mercury wouldn't 'get sucked in'. And neither would you.

The name Karl Schwarzschild (pronounced something like 'Swort-shilt') is closely associated with Black Holes. Despite his 1916 solution to Einstein's field equation for a static, spherical mass clearly indicating that something dodgy was going on (see the spacetime interval below), he himself didn't believe they existed. Since then, we've accumulated very good evidence that black holes do exist.

The spacetime interval 'ds' of the flat space of Special Relativity is given in Cartesian co-ordinates by:

$$(ds)^2 = -c^2(dt)^2 + (dx)^2 + (dy)^2 + (dz)^2$$

The spacetime interval in the neighbourhood of a spherical, uncharged, non-rotating mass is:

$$(ds)^2 = -\left(1 - \frac{2GM}{c^2 r}\right)c^2(dt)^2 + \left(1 - \frac{2GM}{c^2 r}\right)^{-1}(dr)^2 + r^2\left((d\theta)^2 + \sin^2\theta(d\phi)^2\right)$$

Cartesian co-ordinates make tough algebra when you have spherical symmetry, so the interval above is expressed in spherical co-ordinates (r,θ,φ).

Consider the coefficient outside the radial part: $\left(1 - \frac{2GM}{c^2 r}\right)^{-1}$

It gives infinity when: $2GM = c^2 r \Rightarrow r = \frac{2GM}{c^2}$

This radius is called the Schwarzschild Radius. For our Sun it's 2.96km. For the Universe, it's the radius of the Universe (so it's not just dense things). This distance is the point of no return, the point beyond which you get 'sucked in', the place you pick up your one-way ticket to nowhere. A beam of light emitted from just outside the Schwarzschild Radius would reach infinity highly red-shifted. A photon produced inside this radius won't make it to the outside. Sad.

# Section 1.6 Stellar Physics

In the beginning there was the Big Bang. *You* came much later, by about 13.82 billion years, and apart from your mum and dad, the most essential step in your arrival was the formation of stars. Everything else derives from it. This chapter is their story.

The clock starts at time zero. Funny things happened for a brief time after that. Until $10^{-34}$ s, the universe consisted of a simple scalar field (not Higgs bosons, but think Higgs bosons) and was happily expanding at the speed of light to a radius of about $3 \times 10^{-26}$ m, when something upset it. It decided to increase its expansion rate exponentially: $r \propto e^{t/T}$. This kept going until $t \approx 100T$ giving an expansion by a factor of $e^{100} \approx 10^{43}$. It increased the size of the universe from $3 \times 10^{-26}$ m at a time of $10^{-34}$ s to about $3 \times 10^{17}$ m at a time of $10^{-32}$ s. 'Normal' expansion then resumed. This makes the radius of the universe at the present day about $3 \times 10^{42}$ m. The observed radius of the universe is 'only' about $10^{26}$ m so there's a lot more 'out there' that we can't see and can't access. This inflationary expansion left the universe looking the same in all directions (Google 'horizon problem' for details).

Lots of cooling down and exotic particle physics took place with rivalry between matter and radiation; first one dominating, then the other. Fast forward to a minute or two after the Big Bang. The photons were 'cooling' and becoming less energetic. Until five minutes after the Big Bang, the protons and neutrons would try to combine and make deuterium nuclei, but the photons would slam into them and break them up. At five minutes, the photons didn't have enough energy to do this anymore, so the protons and neutrons could get to work and produce deuterium nuclei. At that time, the nucleons were greatly outnumbered by the photons and there were about eight times as many protons as neutrons.

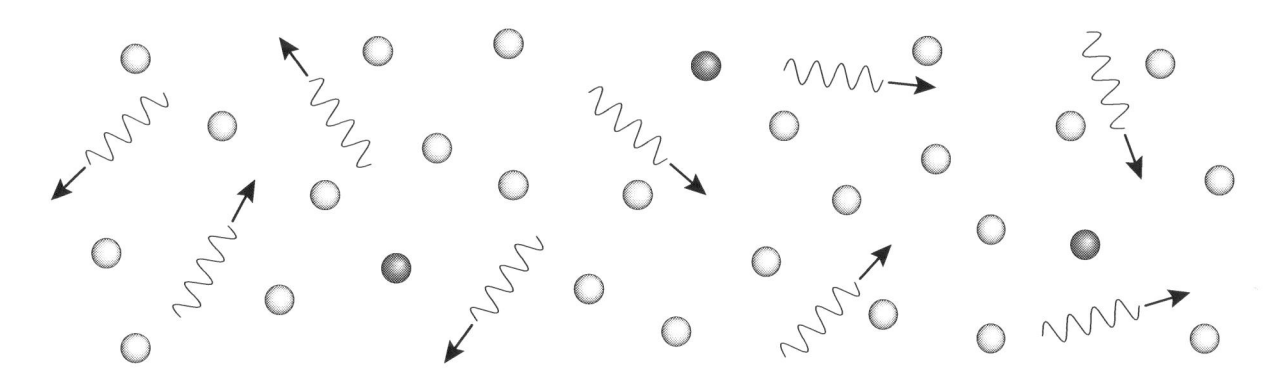

The reactions taking place are shown in the box below. Once deuterium is produced, other reactions become possible and the very stable helium-4 nuclei comes into existence. In terms of numbers, two of these neutrons and two of the protons were needed to make one helium-4 nucleus. For every four of these particles tied up as a helium nucleus, there would be fifteen or sixteen spare protons. In terms of mass, it's about four times the mass of protons as helium nuclei (16:4). This is the present day observed mass ratio of hydrogen to helium, averaged over the whole universe, and these nuclei constitute the basic building blocks of stars.

$$p + n \rightarrow {}_1^2H + \gamma \qquad p + {}_1^2H \rightarrow {}_2^3He + \gamma$$

$$n + {}_1^2H \rightarrow {}_1^3H + \gamma \qquad p + {}_1^3H \rightarrow {}_2^4He + \gamma$$

$$n + {}_2^3He \rightarrow {}_2^4He + \gamma \qquad {}_1^2H + {}_1^2H \rightarrow {}_2^4He + \gamma$$

$$ {}_1^3He + {}_1^3He \rightarrow {}_2^4He + 2p$$

Time passed, the universe cooled and the photons became even less energetic. At 380,000 yrs, the nuclei could attract electrons to make atoms, without the photons breaking them apart again. The first atoms were produced. Photons couldn't cause any more disruption and were free to head off by themselves. After 13.82 billion years of expansion, these photons now constitute the cosmic microwave background. Studying this microwave background can give us information about the state of the universe when it was 380,000 years old, but no further back in time. A similar thing happened with neutrinos when the universe was only about 1second old. They stopped reacting with the neutrons and protons at that time and became free to travel unhindered. In theory this 'cosmic neutrino background' could give us information on the early universe back to 1s, but they are so hard to detect that it's unlikely to happen for decades into the future. When photons were set free, the universe was a uniform 'soup' without structure. We continue the story of the universe over the next few hundred million years when gravity became strong enough to exert its influence over matter and give it some large scale structure.

**The First Stars**

The uniformity of the cosmic microwave background radiation indicates that matter was distributed uniformly at that time. There were no large luminous objects to disturb this primordial soup, so it must have remained smooth and featureless for millions of years afterward. As the cosmos expanded, the background radiation redshifted to longer wavelengths and the universe grew increasingly cold and dark. This is known as the cosmic Dark Ages.

However, through the force of gravity, small differences in the distribution of matter would coalesce into larger regions from about 100 million to 250 million years after the Big Bang. At about 100 light-years in size, these regions, known as protogalaxies, are much smaller than those of 'today'. They would be made from a mixture of the hydrogen and helium discussed above, plus other mysterious particles which also made it through the tumult of the first few minutes of the Big Bang (known as dark matter). The theory of protogalaxy formation comes from computer simulations of large aggregates of matter containing small irregularities. These models should be treated as a good working hypothesis rather than an unchanging fact. The 'Dark Ages' are actually less well known than the eras before and after.

When gravity takes its attractive grip on matter, it makes it smaller. The gravitational potential energy of two masses depends on their separation. The closer they are, the greater the potential energy of the system. The total energy of the system is constant. The gravitational potential energy is negative (getting more negative as the masses get closer), and the energy balance is maintained by its constituents gaining kinetic energy (that is, getting hotter). This is the Kelvin-Helmholtz mechanism, wrongly proposed in the Victorian era as the source of the Sun's energy, but correct as the mechanism for heating cold interstellar gases by gravitational contraction.

The models suggest that the first stars may have been much more massive than todays stars; somewhere about 300 to 1000 times more massive than our Sun. Their surface temperatures were also higher, about 100,000K compared with about one-tenth of that for todays stars. This higher temperature produces photons of shorter wavelength, beyond the visible and into the ultraviolet region. The early stars would have been powerhouses of ultraviolet radiation beaming into the surrounding regions and ionising the cold hydrogen atoms.

But their lives were short, perhaps typically one million years, ending in massive supernovae explosions. Lucky for us, because these explosions produced the first heavier elements, and these elements went into the mix when the next batch of stars started clumping-up. These heavier elements also prevent the gravitational collapse from making the stars so hot. Instead of ultraviolet radiation, it was warm friendly visible light which was emitted. The era of the Dark Ages was over.

We've reached the time to which modern telescopes can probe, back to about 12 billion years ago, and can glimpse the tail end of these early processes. Astronomers don't usually express their results in times and distances for their observations; they use the redshift 'z' of the object. It's related to the 'size' of the universe with this equation:

$$1 + z = \frac{a_{Now}}{a_{Then}}$$

The right hand side is the ratio of the size '$a_{Now}$' of the universe we observe, to the size '$a_{Then}$' of the universe when the object emitted its light. For example, the largest redshift measured of z = 10.3 from an object imaged by the Hubble Telescope Ultra Deep Field project gives:

$$1 + z = \frac{a_{Now}}{a_{Then}} \quad \Rightarrow \quad a_{Then} = \frac{a_{Now}}{(1+z)} = \frac{1}{11.3} \times a_{Now}$$

The universe was less than 10% of its present observed size and less than 10% of its present age. Using the redshift measure, the furthest quasar is about z = 7, the furthest Gamma Ray burst z = 9.4, and our earliest stars beyond z = 20. The cosmic microwave background has been around for even longer of course, and has a redshift of z = 1089 (corresponding to an age of 380,000yrs).

## Stellar Nuclear Reactions

Our Sun is a good example of an ordinary sort of star. Not too big, not too small, not too hot, not too cold. Being nearby, it's ideal for scientific study, and with the increase in satellite / electronic communication it's also important to know if it can throw anything at us.

It's almost a perfect sphere of radius 696,000km. From Earth it subtends an angle of about ½° across its width. The surface we can see is called the Photosphere and sunspots appear to drift slowly across it from time to time, taking about a fortnight to cross the disc.

Our Sun started its 'life' about 4,600 million years ago in the outer arm of an ordinary galaxy as a patch of cold gas. As before, the gas was pulled together by gravity and started heating-up. The difference from the early post Big Bang gravitational collapse of the gas, was that this gas already contained heavier elements from older supernovae explosions. This limited the temperature reached by the heating, reduced the mass of the Sun and prolonged its lifespan. At present, our Sun is in middle age.

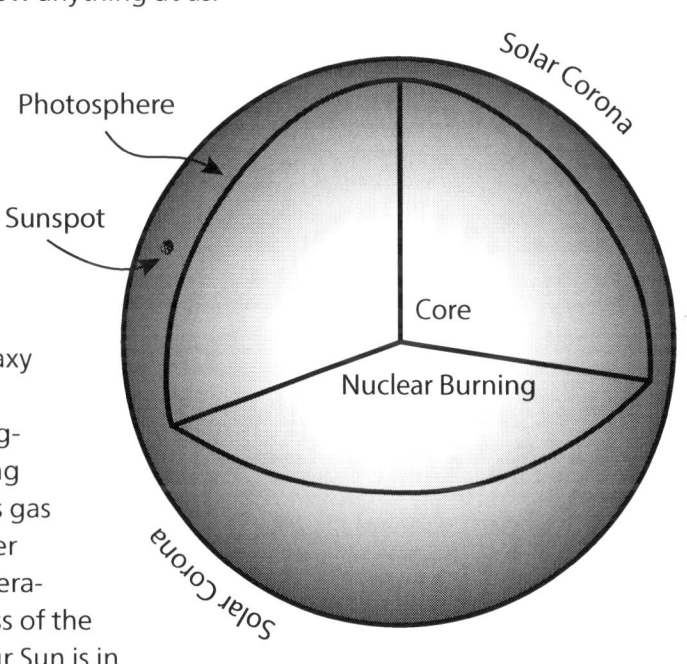

The photon of visible light which strikes your skin on a sunny day came from the Photosphere. Underneath this is a turbulent, seething mass of ions and plasma, churned-up by convective heating and magnetic fields. The surface is at the temperature of yellowish/white heat, about 5500K to 6000K. The really hot stuff is deep down towards the centre. This is where the nuclear reactions take place at a temperature of over 10million Kelvin. There aren't any atoms down there, it's all plasma. Everything except neutrons and neutrinos is electrically charged and needs lots of kinetic energy to give the short range nuclear forces a chance to bind the charged particles together. There is a sequence of nuclear reactions starting with protons making deuterium nuclei (it's called a deuteron):

$$^1_1H + ^1_1H \rightarrow ^2_1H + e^+ + v_e$$

The positron quickly annihilates with an electron to produce a gamma ray. This single gamma ray undergoes many collisions and has a tortuous life inside the Sun. What started as a single high energy photon reaches the surface as many lower energy photons, taking over 10,000yrs in the process. The neutrino zooms off into space in a couple of seconds. The deuteron can also be produced by the much less likely 'pep' reaction:

$$^1_1H + ^1_1H + e^- \rightarrow ^2_1H + v_e$$

Both reactions produce deuterium which can then react with another proton to produce helium-3:

$$^2_1H + ^1_1H \rightarrow ^3_2He + \gamma$$

What we have so far can be used to build the ultra-stable helium-4 nucleus. There are three main routes. This one contributes 85% of the helium-4:

$$^3_2He + ^3_2He \rightarrow ^4_2He + ^1_1H + ^1_1H$$

This route provides 15% of the helium-4:

$$^3_2He + ^4_2He \rightarrow ^7_4Be + \gamma$$

$$^7_4Be + e^- \rightarrow ^7_3Li + v_e$$

$$^7_3Li + ^1_1H \rightarrow ^4_2He + ^4_2He$$

The third route only makes 0.01% of the helium-4:

$$^3_2He + ^4_2He \rightarrow ^7_4Be + \gamma$$

$$^7_4Be + ^1_1H \rightarrow ^8_5B + \gamma$$

$$^8_5B \rightarrow ^8_4Be + e^+ + v_e$$

$$^8_4Be \rightarrow 2\,^4_2He$$

The Sun produces 99% of its helium-4 by this method. The neutrinos are all of the electron type and each reaction produces neutrinos of different energy. In three body decays (like the reaction at the top of the page), the energy is distributed statistically between the three products with the neutrino getting a maximum of 0.41MeV. The two decay products in the 'pep' reaction have definite energies with the neutrino always taking 1.44MeV. In principle, this gives experimenters on Earth a way of checking the theory with measured flux rates. Not easy, but it can be done with very large detectors, shielding the detectors, and waiting a long time to gather the data. We'll return to neutrinos later.

So far, we have nuclei as heavy as helium-4. How can we make heavier elements? These elements have more protons in them and hence more electric charge, which makes them harder to bang together. The beryllium-8 produced in the last reaction is extremely unstable (it splits in less than $10^{-16}$ s under normal conditions on Earth) due to its manic desire to split into a pair of ultrastable helium-4's. The helium-4 nucleus is very exclusive and doesn't like company unless really forced. Increase the temperature though, and a helium-4 nucleus will get close enough to the beryllium-8 nucleus **before** the latter has time to split. At 100million Kelvin, this reaction starts to happen:

$$^{8}_{4}Be + ^{4}_{2}He \rightarrow ^{12}_{6}C$$

For some people this reaction is proof of the existence of God. It would normally be extremely unlikely to occur. By a bit of good luck, there is a state of the carbon-12 nucleus which matches the beryllium-helium combination for energy. There's a quantum mechanics rule which states that the probabliity of a reaction taking place is related to the energy difference between initial and final states. The closer they are, the more likely it is to happen. As with music, there's a sort of overtone of the carbon-12 nucleus that hits the sweet-spot. Lucky for us, 'cause without it, we 'carbon based lifeforms' wouldn't be here. Hence the God angle.

The Carbon-12 nucleus has always been difficult for nuclear physicists to model. How can two joined helium-4 nuclei be so unstable, yet three joined helium-4 nuclei be so stable? It's involved in yet another way of making helium-4. This is called the CNO cycle (for carbon, nitrogen, oxygen).

$$^{12}_{6}C + ^{1}_{1}H \rightarrow ^{13}_{7}N + \gamma$$

$$^{13}_{7}N \rightarrow ^{13}_{6}C + e^{+} + v_{e}$$

$$^{13}_{6}C + ^{1}_{1}H \rightarrow ^{14}_{7}N + \gamma$$

$$^{14}_{7}N + ^{1}_{1}H \rightarrow ^{15}_{8}O + \gamma$$

$$^{15}_{8}O \rightarrow ^{15}_{7}N + e^{+} + v_{e}$$

$$^{15}_{7}N + ^{1}_{1}H \rightarrow ^{12}_{6}C + ^{4}_{2}He$$

The Sun produces less than 1% of its helium-4 by the CNO cycle. This method is more common in hotter, higher mass stars. Over several billion years, the Sun's nuclear reactions have built-up more helium-4 than it started with. It's now about 60% helium-4 in the core. Most of the heat inside the core escapes by radiation so the material doesn't get mixed with the outer layers (mixing happens in higher mass stars through convection). The composition of the photosphere hasn't changed much since the early days; it's still about 75% hydrogen by mass.

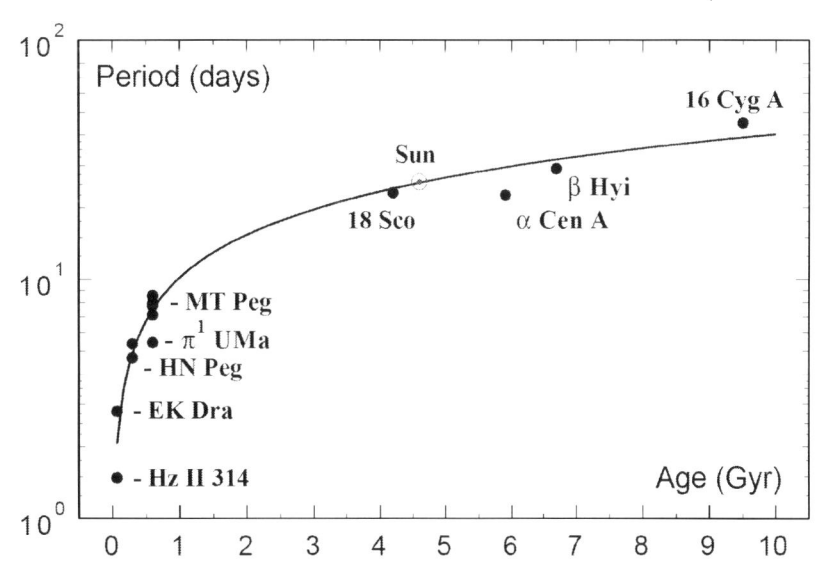

There are many interesting aspects to the Sun. The graph on the right shows the period of rotation for stars like the Sun plotted as a function of their age. Fast spinning stars make strong magnetic fields and throw out a greater intensity of high energy particles ('solar wind'). During the early stages of life on our planet, the Sun's magnetic field must have been stronger and the Solar Wind more intense. Today, the Sun's energy reaches the Earth with an average intensity ('irradiance') of 1370 Wm$^{-2}$ (it varies from 1410 Wm$^{-2}$ in winter, to 1320 Wm$^{-2}$ in summer due to the Earth's orbit). At the centre of the Sun, it's produced at a rate of 270 Wm$^{-3}$. This is surprisingly low since it's not that different to the power of a human body. There's just lots more of it.

## Earth's Future

The graph below shows the Sun's luminosity 'L', temperature 'T' and radius 'R' in the past and in the future. When life began on our planet over 3 billion years ago, the Sun's luminosity was only about ¾ of today's value. This wouldn't have been enough to sustain liquid water. Either life doesn't need water, or the atmospheric composition was different and the greenhouse effect increased the temperature.

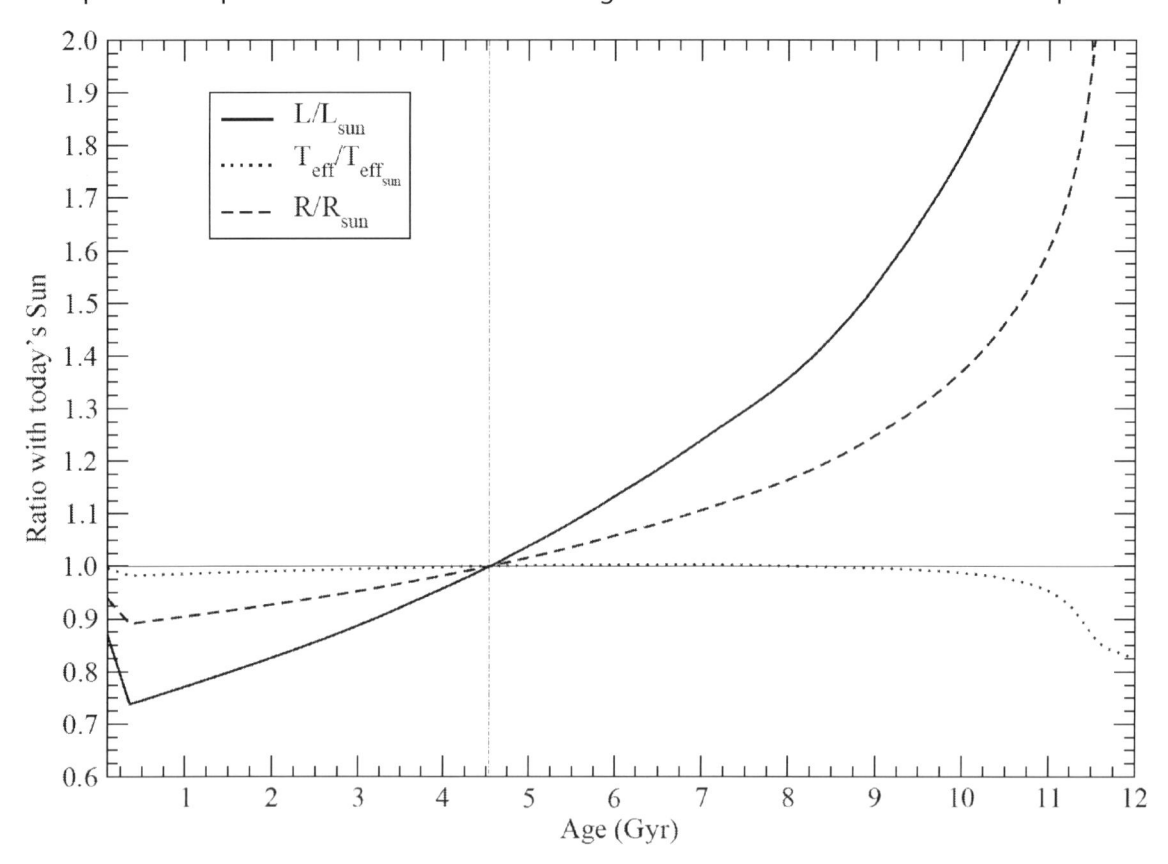

What about the Sun's future? The timescale on the graph is in gigayears so it's largely of academic interest, but it's getting bigger and brighter. During the next 1.2 billion years its luminosity will increase by 10% and its surface will be 150°C hotter. How would Earth's ecosystem respond? There have been large swings in the past with at least two 'snowball Earth' episodes before life emerged on land. There have also been warmer periods when forests covered the poles, and we're currently engaged in a large scale experiment with $CO_2$ in the atmosphere. Regardless of what humans do, the planet will enter a devastating runaway greenhouse phase in the next billion years. It will be a baked, barren dry desert. Over 6 billion years from now, the Sun will be 2.7 times its present luminosity and 2.3 times its present diameter. Venus and Earth will be sulphurous, Mars a desert, Jupiter's satellites will be near thawing. And that's the good news.

The Sun then enters its red-giant phase; that's the bad news. By losing some of its mass, the orbits of the planets will move further out so that Earth will be about where Mars is, and Venus will take our place. By that time, the Sun has expanded to about the present day orbit of Earth and its core is hot enough to ignite the CNO cycle. The Sun uses this new source of energy and contracts, with its luminosity *dropping* by a factor of about 100. Should the Earth still be intact (and the best calculations think 'probably'), we'll be toast; a hard rocky fused silicate surface at a temperature of 600°C.

Helium-4 gets used-up and the Sun's core becomes a white dwarf of carbon and oxygen. The outer layers puff-up and the Sun enters its second red-giant stage. Once again, the Earth's in trouble. This time

# Rotational Motion & Astrophysics

its from 'Helium flashes' of periodic high energy output lasting 10,000 yrs at a time. Our planet could be engulfed by one of these episodes and be completely destroyed. Soon after (that's 100 million years of soon after), the Sun throws off its outer regions leaving a very hot, very small white dwarf. It then cools slowly over the next few hundred billion years, witnessing the gradual dimming of the night sky as the galaxies zoom off into the distance. All that remains is the merger of our Galaxy with the Andromeda Galaxy (and its very massive BlackHole).

## Solar Neutrinos

The Sun produces about $2 \times 10^{38}$ neutrinos every second from the proton helium cycle on page 88. If you stand facing the direction of the Sun (it doesn't matter if it's day or night), about $3 \times 10^{14}$ neutrinos will pass through your body every second. Can't feel them? That's because they don't do anything!

Things like lumps of steel might feel solid from our perspective, but when you get down to the quantum level, there is no 'solid'. There's nothing solid to bump into. It's just force fields. Neutrinos don't have an electric charge so just zip past any electric charges; they don't 'see' the electromagnetic field. They are also blind to the strong interactions from gluons. The only force they 'see' is the very short-range weak interaction force.

Neutrinos travel at the speed of light, spectacularly confirmed with the supernova explosion SN1987A. At a distance of 160,000 lightyears, the neutrinos arrived on Earth 3 hours before the photons (the delay was due to the photons fighting their way out of the blast material while the neutrinos didn't hang around).

A neutrino detector would almost be an oxymoron, but not quite. They have been built, but they're very big and the experimenters have to be very patient. The Sudbury Neutrino Observatory outside Ontario in Canada operated from 1999 until 2006. It's 2km underground in a nickel mine. Starting in 1901, the miners dug out a very big hole, part of which the physicists used for their equipment. The setup consists of 1000 tons of ultra-pure water, not the ordinary type which we drink, but the type with an extra neutron beside the proton in the hydrogen nuclei (called 'heavy water', $D_2O$). It's all contained by an acrylic sphere 12 m in diameter. Around the outside is ultra-pure ordinary water followed by 9456 20cm photodetectors, all contained in a barrel shaped vessel 34m high and 22m in diameter. The photodetectors (photomultiplier tubes with light concentrators) are held in place by a 17.8m diameter stainless steel geodesic structure. Flashes of light from Cerenkov Radiation are produced in the neutrino reactions within the heavy water, each one giving about 500 photons spread over roughly 50 tubes.

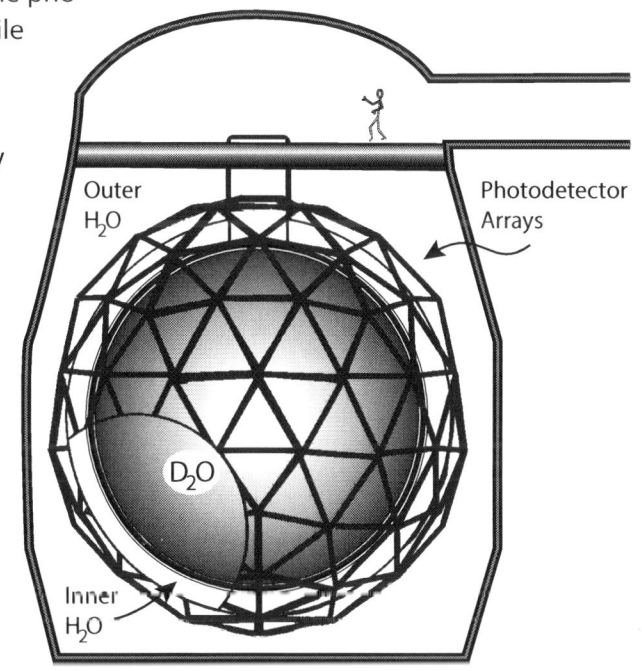

The neutrinos can be detected from three possible reactions.

Charged Current (CC): $\quad v_e + {}_1^2H \rightarrow {}_1^1H + {}_1^1H + e^-$

Neutral Current (NC): $\quad v_{any} + {}_1^2H \rightarrow {}_1^1H + n + v_{any}$

Elastic Scattering (ES): $\quad v_{any} + e^- \rightarrow v_{any} + e^-$

Remember from Higher Physics that neutrinos come in three different types (three 'flavours'): the electron-type neutrino, the muon-type neutrino and the tau-type neutrino. The nuclear reactions within the Sun only produce the electron-type neutrinos. You need higher energy reactions than those found in the Sun, to make the other two types. The first reaction (CC) within the Sudbury heavy water detector is only possible if its an electron-type neutrino. Any of the three flavours of neutrino will trigger the other reactions (NC and ES).

Only electron-type neutrinos are emitted from the Sun, so if nothing happens to them en-route to the Earth, all three reactions are possible and a certain proportion of the total will come from each one. This was the assumption back in the 1960's. But that's not what happens. From a data run lasting 240 days, the experimenters recorded over 355 million events, of which all but 1169 were rejected (being derived from other sources, or having the wrong energy signature). These 1169 events were enough to show that the second and third reactions were getting contributions from the muon and tau-type neutrinos, and that the first reaction had only 35% of the expected value.

The reason is that neutrinos change from one flavour into another between the Sun and the Earth! It's called neutrino oscillations. The neutrinos don't just change once and that's it; they continually change between the three types, one into another.

Three flavours means the proportions of each get quite complicated over time. A process which started with an electron-type neutrino of about 10MeV energy but could only change back and forth into a muon-type neutrino would give the graph below. A probability of 1.0 means it's definitely a muon-type

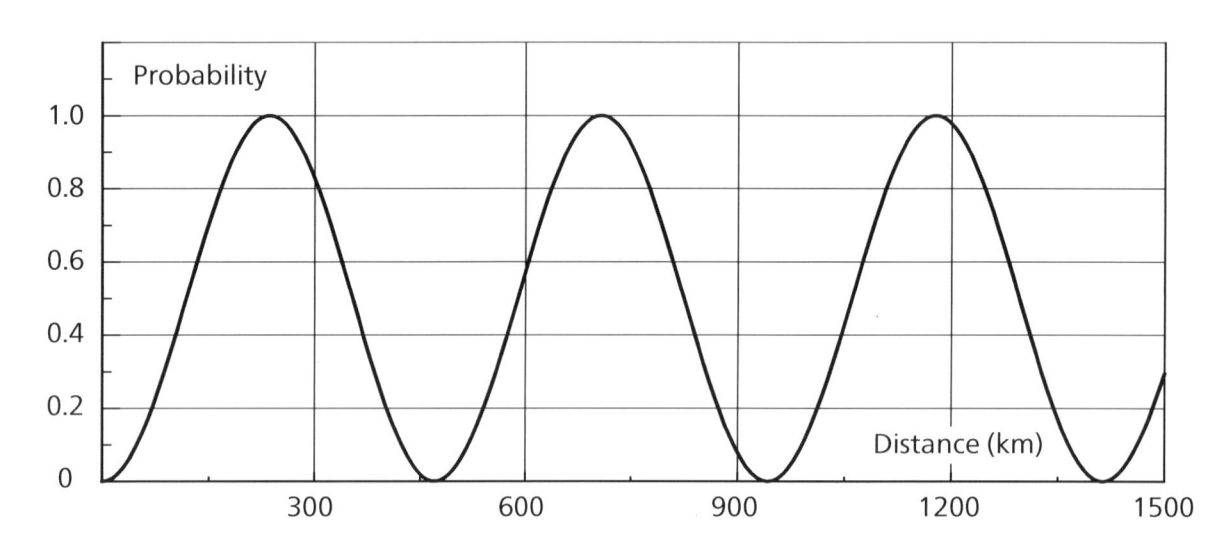

neutrino and a probability of 0.0 means it's definitely an electron-type neutrino. The distance scale won't be exactly accurate since it depends on the neutrino masses and at present, they are only known approximately. Evidence for neutrino oscillations is our first sign of physics beyond the Standard Model (known as BSM physics). Neutrinos may be like photons; they might be their own antiparticle, so that the electron neutrino and electron antineutrino are the same. This would be a violation of the Law of Conservation of Lepton Number (Google it). Spin-½ weirdos like this are called Majorana particles.

## Properties of Stars - Luminosity, Brightness, Magnitude

Get yourself out of town. Look up at the sky on a clear Moonless night and you'll see about 6000 stars. All of different brightnesses and all at different distances from Earth. The first step in understanding stars is to classify them according to their **true** brightness ('brightness' isn't quite the correct word; the screen of a small telly has the same brightness as the screen of a large telly, but I'll use it anyway). You do this by asking what they would look like if they were all at a standard distance from Earth. That distance is 10 parsecs. The average distance from the Earth to the Sun is called an Astronomical Unit (A.U.), about $1.5 \times 10^{11}$m. One arc-second is an angle of one-sixtieth of one-sixtieth of a degree. Combine these two and you have the parsec. One parsec is the distance whereby one A.U. subtends an angle

# Rotational Motion & Astrophysics

of one arcsecond. It's a distance of 206,265 A.U. which is about 3.26 light-years. We need a number to quantify the brightness (once again, 'brightness' isn't the correct word; it's a subjective human attribute and is a qualitative description, but on we go). Brightnesses range from full Sun on a glorious summer's day to distant galaxies barely glimpsed by the Hubble Space Telescope. That's too wide a range for a linear scale, so a logarithmic scale was chosen. It's all completely arbitrary, so they defined the brightness of the star Vega as magnitude zero. Changing by 5 magnitudes changes its brightness by a factor of 100, and just to be different, getting brighter is more negative (so 0 to -1 to -2 to -3 to -4 to -5 is 100 times brighter, and magnitude +5 is 100 times less bright than Vega). Magnitude 6 is about the faintest star the average human can see in a decent sky. The table below gives you some idea of the range of values. Supernova SN 1006 was the brightest extra-solar system object seen in recorded history.

Let $\Delta x$ be the brightness ratio when the magnitude changes by one. Changing by five magnitudes must give:

$$\Delta x \times \Delta x \times \Delta x \times \Delta x \times \Delta x = 100 \quad \Rightarrow \quad (\Delta x)^5 = 100$$

$$5 \log_{10} \Delta x = \log_{10} 100 = 2 \quad \Rightarrow \quad \log_{10} \Delta x = 0.4$$

$$\Delta x \approx 2.512$$

A star of magnitude +3 will be 2.512 times brighter than a star of magnitude +4.

The **Apparent Magnitude** is the 'brightness' of a star (or any other object like a planet) as seen from where you're standing, and the **Absolute Magnitude** is its 'brightness' from a distance of 10 parsecs. From Earth, we can measure its apparent magnitude, and its distance (for the closer stars) using a parallax method.

| Object | Apparent Magnitude |
|---|---|
| Sun | -26.7 |
| Sun viewed from Pluto | -18.2 |
| Full Moon | -12.7 |
| Supernova SN 1006 | -7.5 |
| Venus max. brightness | -4.8 |
| Mars max. brightness | -2.9 |
| Brightest star, Sirius | -1.47 |
| Alpha centauri | -0.27 |
| Supernova SN 1987A | +3 |
| Faintest star seen in big city | +3 |
| Neptune | +7.8 |
| Brightest quasar | +12.91 |
| Pluto | +13.65 |
| Limit for 8m Earth telescope | +27 |
| Faintest seen by HST | +31.5 |

The constellation of Ursa Major has the well known star grouping called the Plough (or Big Dipper). The two right-most stars point (from *Merak* to *Dubhe*) towards the celestial north pole; the point in the sky about which all the stars revolve once every day. The star diagram below shows the apparent magnitude (above each star), the absolute magnitude (below each star in italic), the distance in lightyears, and the common names. Mizar is seen in binoculars to be a double star, and by very large telescopes as a 6-star complex with the two main components about 1ly apart. Unusually for arbitrary, archaic star groupings, the Big Dipper stars are loosely associated.

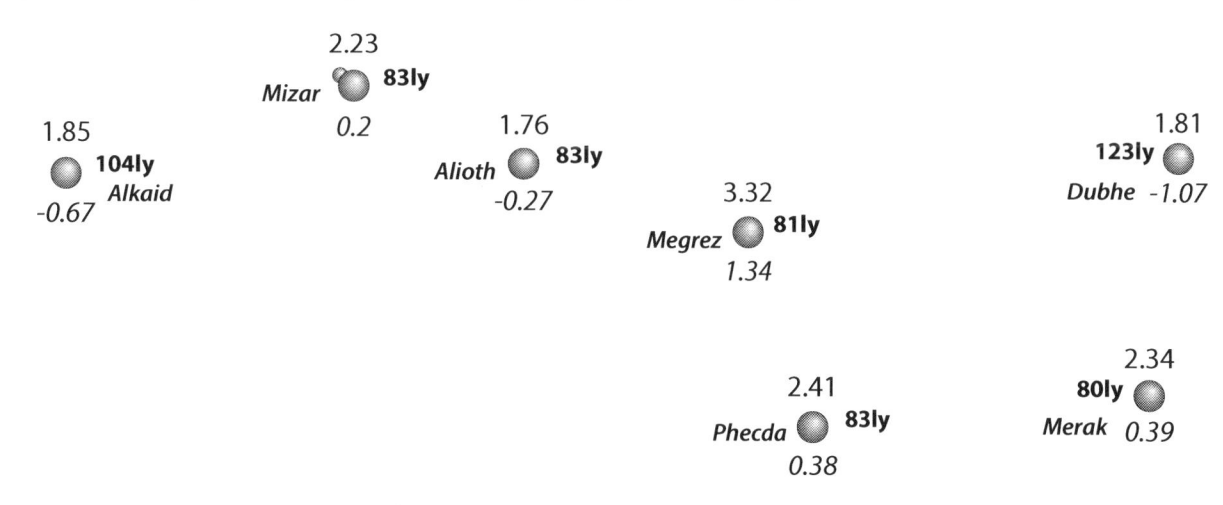

                        2.23

           *Mizar*  83ly

1.85            *0.2*      1.76                                   1.81

   104ly         *Alioth*  83ly                         123ly

   *Alkaid*                            3.32            *Dubhe*  *-1.07*

-0.67                   *-0.27*                 81ly

                              *Megrez*

                             *1.34*

                                                      2.34

                       2.41                  80ly

              *Phecda*  83ly      *Merak*  *0.39*

                     *0.38*

Some stars aren't hot enough to emit visible light. To an observer on Earth, they would have an apparent magnitude of +∞, have 'no brightness', and be invisible to any speedy spaceships relying on optical detectors. But they are still emitting energy in the microwave and infrared wavelength range. The word 'brightness' usually refers to what humans eyes detect. The word 'luminosity' is used to include all wavelengths and this is what we will use to quantify the power output of a star.

The Stefan-Boltzmann Law allows us to calculate the energy emitted from a black-body (a perfect absorber and radiator of all wavelengths of the electromagnetic spectrum). The number of joules of energy emitted every second by one square metre of black-body surface is $\sigma T^4$. This is called the radiant emittance 'W' (and even the ghastly 'radiant exitance'), but not many people use that. The constant 'sigma' has a value of 5.67 × 10$^{-8}$ Js$^{-1}$m$^{-2}$K$^{-4}$ and the temperature of the black-body is in Kelvin. One joule per second is a power of one watt, so the expression gives us the power emitted by one square metre of surface. Multiply this by the total surface area of the star and you have the total power emitted by the star from all wavelengths. This is the star's **Luminosity** 'L'.

All star's rotate and this means thay won't be perfect spheres. Some are pretty good (our Sun is only 0.001% bigger across the equator than the poles) and some aren't (the equatorial radius of the star Vega is 18% larger than its polar radius, and from Earth we see it at its widest since we are looking down on one of its poles). For a perfect sphere the surface area is $4\pi R^2$, so the Luminosity is:

$$L = 4\pi R^2 \times \sigma T^4$$

**Example**   The Sun has a surface temperature of 5800K and a radius of 696,000km. This gives a luminosity of:

$$L = 4\pi R^2 \times \sigma T^4 = 4\pi \times (6.96 \times 10^8)^2 \times 5.67 \times 10^{-8} \times 5800^4 = 3.9 \times 10^{26} \text{ Watts}$$

At the distance of the Earth we receive about 1380Watts per square metre on top of the atmosphere (and this calculation is actually done in reverse to obtain the temperature of the Sun's surface starting from the measured 1380Wm$^{-2}$).

The Luminosity 'L' is an intrinsic property of a star. Alien astronomers on a planet orbiting the star Tau Ceti would also get the answer L = 3.9 × 10$^{26}$ Watts for our Sun. But very little of our Sun's energy would reach them. Certainly not the 1380Wm$^{-2}$ that we get on Earth. The syllabus has a quantity called the **'apparent brightness'**, symbol 'b', which calculates what the Tau Cetians would receive from our Sun. They are at a distance 'r' of 11.9 lightyears (= 1.13 × 10$^{17}$ m) so to them, the Sun's output would be spread over the surface of a sphere of that radius. The answer is tiny. They might get a tan from their own sun, but not from our Sun:

$$b = \frac{L}{4\pi r^2} = \frac{3.9 \times 10^{26}}{4\pi \times (1.13 \times 10^{17})^2} = 2.4 \times 10^{-9} \text{ Wm}^{-2}$$

From the equation $L = 4\pi R^2 \times \sigma T^4$ we can compare Tau ceti with our own Sun:

$$\frac{L_{TC}}{L_{Sun}} = \left(\frac{R_{TC}}{R_{Sun}}\right)^2 \times \left(\frac{T_{TC}}{T_{Sun}}\right)^4 \Rightarrow 0.49 = \left(\frac{R_{TC}}{R_{Sun}}\right)^2 \times \left(\frac{5350}{5800}\right)^4 \Rightarrow \frac{R_{TC}}{R_{Sun}} = 0.82$$

The numbers are the latest measurements on Tau ceti. The answer for the radius of 0.82 R$_{Sun}$ compares well with the radius measured from interferometry of 0.793 R$_{Sun}$ (see page 149).

Remember that the 'apparent brightness' is the power received per square metre from **all** wavelengths of the electromagnetic spectrum. The word 'brightness' can lead to confusion over its common usage meaning of how bright something is to the human eye. A star could have a large 'apparent brightness' and be invisible to the human eye (emitting entirely in the infrared/microwave regions).

# Rotational Motion & Astrophysics

## Properties of Stars - Size and Mass

Measurements of stars are often compared to the Sun, like masses 4$M_\odot$ or radii 1.7$R_\odot$. For conversion to SI units: $M_\odot$ = 1.99 x 10$^{30}$kg , $R_\odot$ = 6.96 x 10$^8$m. The table below shows some values ranging from the smallest to the largest stars. Objects less massive than about 0.08 $M_\odot$ will not ignite nuclear burning. Objects more massive than about 300 $M_\odot$ can't hold themselves together. I've included a column showing a strong correlation between the star's mass and its lifetime. Massive stars have short lives, and they often have very big and very noisy going-away parties. The least massive stars will just cool slowly and live on. Objects below a mass of about 0.08 $M_\odot$ are called Brown Dwarfs and invite comparison with big Jupiters rather than small Suns. Sci-Fi fans will recognise Wolf-359 from Star Trek, as the scene of the battle in AD2367 between the Federation and the Borg. It's a Red Dwarf star about 7.8 ly from Earth so would be a short hop at Warp 9.

| Star name | Radius ($R_\odot$) | Mass ($M_\odot$) | Lifetime (yr) |
|---|---|---|---|
| Denis-P J104814.7 | ? | < 0.1 | > 10$^{13}$ |
| Wolf 359 | 0.16 | 0.09 | 10$^{13}$ |
| Tau Ceti | 0.87 | 0.85 | 20 × 10$^9$ |
| Sun | 1 | 1 | 10 × 10$^9$ |
| Sirius | 2.3 | 2.6 | 500 × 10$^6$ |
| Arcturus | 26 | 1.1 | 900 × 10$^6$ |
| Rigel | 74 | 18 | 10 × 10$^6$ |
| Betelgeuse | ≈1000 | ≈10 | 20 × 10$^6$ |
| VY Canis Majoris | 1420 | 18 | 10 × 10$^6$ |
| R Doradus | 370 | 1.2 | 4 × 10$^9$ |
| V1489 Cygni | 1650 | ≈30 | 5 × 10$^6$ |
| R136a1 | 35 | 265 | ≈ 10$^6$ |

## Properties of Stars - Lifecycle

The Hertzsprung-Russell diagram plots luminosity against temperature over a large sample of stars within our galaxy. The plot shows that stars are not evenly distributed across the diagram, but that the majority fall along a gently curving diagonal called the Main Sequence. The scales are logarithmic so anything roughly straight implies a power law. Any very hot object emitting thermal radiation has a luminosity proportional to its radius squared and its temperature to the fourth power (see opposite page):

$$L \propto R^2 T^4$$

The HR diagram roughly corresponds to these relations, but its more of a qualitative diagram, following the changes that take place as a star evolves. The traditional diagram didn't have a numerical scale along the bottom axis; it denoted the 'spectral type', a method of classification according to a star's visible spectrum (basically, its colour).

It's also something of a lesson in sample statistics. To be of any value, it should include *all* stars within a large sample volume. Not just the brightest stars visible from Earth since that would preferentially skew the data towards the larger stars.

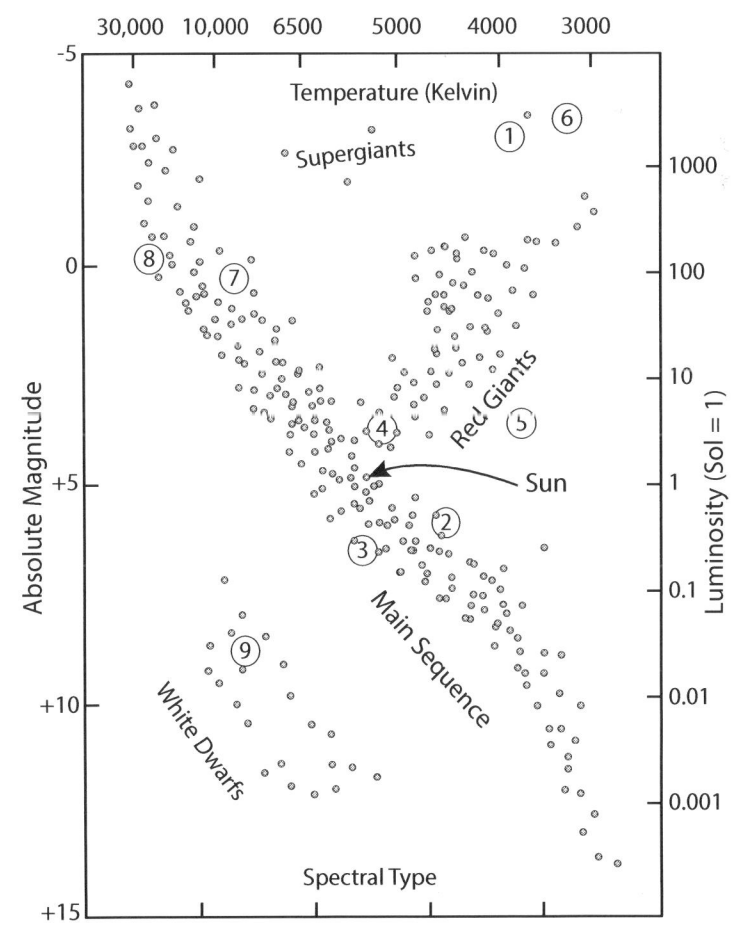

95

The table below shows the stages 1 - 9 in a typical star's lifecycle (numbers annotated on HR diagram

| Nº. | Stage | Age (yrs) | Radius (R$_\odot$) | Temp. core | Temp. surface | Energy source |
|---|---|---|---|---|---|---|
| 1 | Protostar | 1-3 | ≈ 50 | 150,000K | 3,500K | Gravity |
| 2 | Pre-Main Seq. | $10 \times 10^6$ | ≈1⅓ | $10 \times 10^6$K | 4,500K | P-P chain start |
| 3 | Zero Age Main | $27 \times 10^6$ | 1 | $15 \times 10^6$K | 6,000K | P-P chain in core |
| 4 | End Main Seq. | $10 \times 10^9$ | | | | P-P chain around core |
| 5 | Post Main Seq. | Stage 4 + $1 \times 10^9$ | 2.6 | | 4,500K | P-P chain + Grav. contract |
| 6 | Red Giant | Stage 5 + $100 \times 10^6$ | 200 | $200 \times 10^6$K | 3,500K | Ignition of Triple Alpha |
| 7 | Helium Burn Main | Stage 6 + 10,000 | | $200 \times 10^6$K | 9,000 | Triple Alpha |
| 8 | Planetary Nebula | | | | | |
| 9 | White dwarf | | < 0.01 | | 10,000K | Cooling down |

## Supernovae

Gravity is always with us. Nuclear reactions only burn until the fuel's used-up. In its youth and in middle age, the nuclear reactions inside a star hold off the inwards force of gravity. But gravity wins out in the end, and that end depends upon the mass of the star which remains when nuclear burning is defeated. The exact details are still uncertain, but core collapse sends out a non-spherical shockwave at a speed of v ≈ ¼c which meets material still being pulled in by gravity. Under some conditions the shockwave stalls, under other conditions it continues and produces a supernova. Spin-½ particles like electrons resist being forced together (it's not electrostatic repulsion, its a quantum effect) and core collapse will cease below a stellar mass of 1.44 M$_\odot$ to end as a white dwarf. Cores with greater mass overpower the electron pressure and continue until spin-½ neutrons try the same trick. This results in a core density of about $8 \times 10^{17}$ kg m$^{-3}$ and a neutron star is formed. A remnant core of mass greater than 3-4 M$_\odot$ will continue shrinking to form a black hole.

Supernovae create the heavier elements then spread them around (luckily for us), and should occur in our own galaxy at least once a century. Estimates show that a supernova will explode close enough to produce damaging effects on Earth about once every billion years. Of the five mass extinctions on Earth, there is much speculation that at least one of them was triggered by a supernova explosion. Geologists have found deposits of the isotope Iron-60 in sediments 2.8 million years old. This is only formed in supernovae and is strong evidence of a blast about 100ly distant in relatively recent times. As to the future, in your lifetime you probably won't see any extra-galactic supernova as bright as SN-1006, or a possible future candidate from nearer home like IK-Pegasi (only 150ly away). But who knows, astronomy is full of surprises!

# Quanta & Waves

## Section 2.1 Quantum Theory

Quantum Physics is cool. The Age of Cool began during the 1890's, not from an exciting, trendy experiment, but the persistence of big brains on a decades-old problem. The story begins with the humble son of a Bavarian glazier, one Joseph Fraunhofer. He was 'into' glass in a big way; for the manufacture of lenses in surveying and for military purposes. His curiosity brought the dark absortion bands in the solar spectrum to his attention. To help him investigate, he invented a new instrument by placing a theodolite on its side and adding a telescope. We now call it a spectrometer. He started measuring the wavelengths of the dark lines using a diffraction grating invented by Thomas Young. The rest is history.

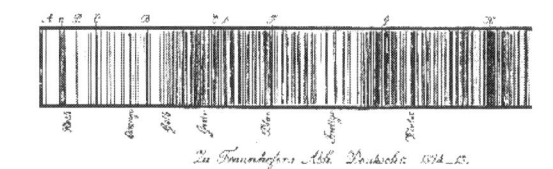

These dark lines were fodder for the theoreticians; how could they explain their origin and spacing? What were hot bodies up to? In 1859, Kirchhoff formulated a law regarding the emission and absorption of radiation, ending with the idea of *black-body radiation*. A *black-body* is an object which will absorb all the radiation falling on its surfaces (so no reflections). It's also a perfect emitter. At a given temperature and wavelength, it emits the most radiation an object can manage under those conditions. The intensity of the radiation emitted depends upon the wavelength. Experimenters strove to measure the radiation at different wavelengths and draw the graph (solid lines in graph below). Theoreticians tried to explain it using what they knew (classical physics).

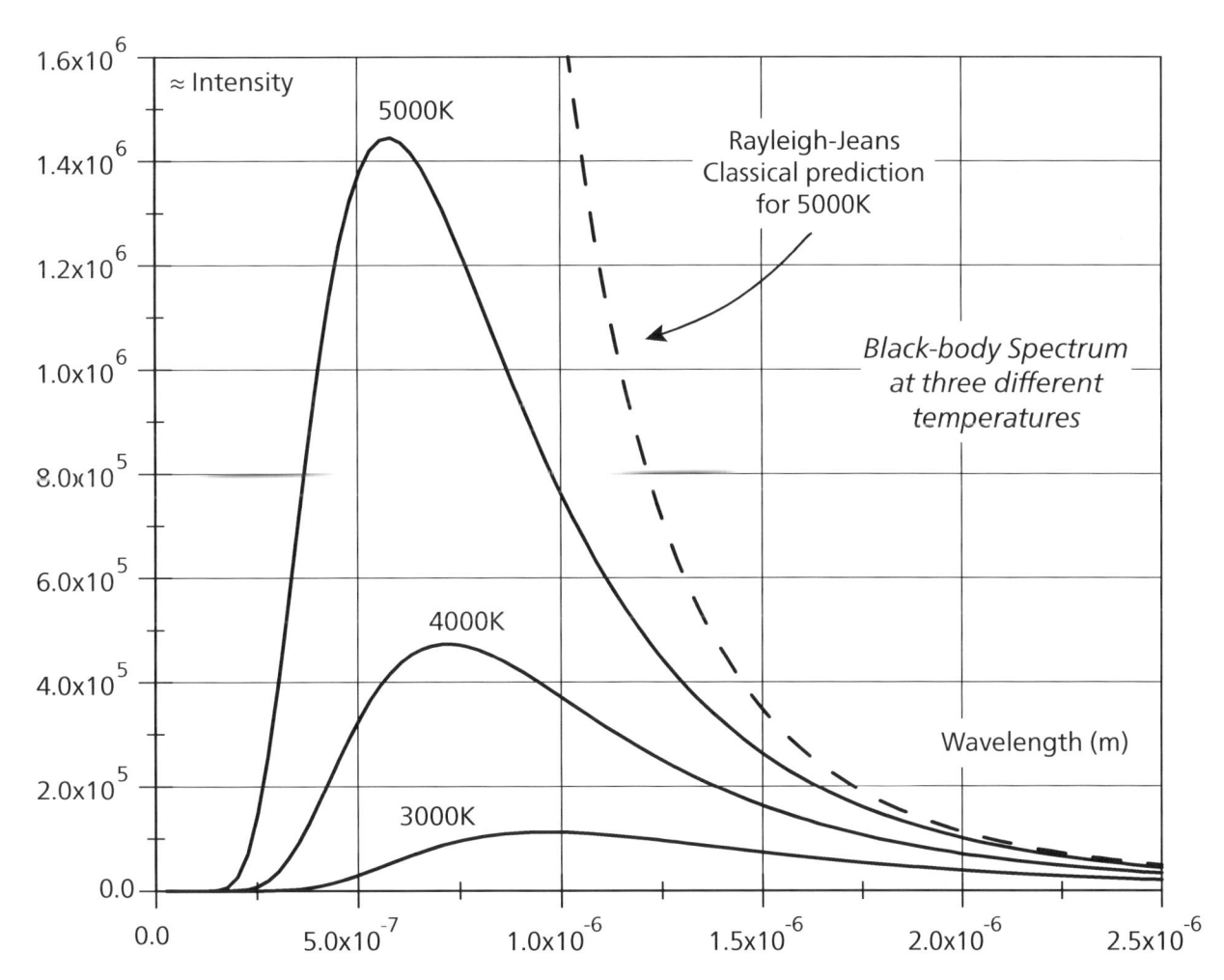

Wilhelm Wien and the 3$^{RD}$ Baron Rayleigh tried separately, and with some success. Wien got the short wavelength part correct, and Rayleigh the long wavelength part. Rayleigh's prediction from classical physics for a black-body at a temperature of 5000K is shown by the dotted line below. The experimentally measured spectrum is the solid line beside it. Not enough for a Nobel Prize, though he did get one in 1904 for other things. The black-body spectrum is shown for three different temperatures: 3000K, 4000K and 5000K. The vertical scale is a bit tricky. Start with the energy emitted per square metre of black-body surface each second (the intensity), then factor in that it's the energy emitted **between** a range of wavelengths. If it had been measured between wavelengths of $5 \times 10^{-7}$m and $6 \times 10^{-7}$m, that would be 'per $1 \times 10^{-7}$m', and you would multiply your answer by $10^7$ to get 'per metre' (that's why the numbers on the scale are so big). The units on the vertical scale are W m$^{-3}$. In addition to emitting more radiation as the object gets to a higher temperature, notice that the peak also shifts (gets 'displaced') towards shorter wavelengths. This is why objects get redder then whiter as you heat them up, and is embodied in Wien's Displacement Law relating the temperature to the wavelength at which the maximum radiation is emitted: $\lambda_{Max}T = 2.9 \times 10^{-3}$ m K. Stefan (experimentally in 1879), and Boltzmann (theoretically in 1884) established an expression for the power emitted per square metre by a black-body: $I = \sigma T^4$ where the constant σ = $5.67 \times 10^{-8}$ Wm$^{-2}$K$^{-4}$. The power of four, makes the emission very temperature dependent eg a doubling in the Kelvin temperature giving sixteen times the output.

Rayleigh's erroneous prediction for the emission from a black-body at short wavelengths was a crisis for the physics at that time. The graph covers wavelengths from the infrared through visible ($5 \times 10^{-7}$ m is greenish-blue) and onto the ultraviolet region. The UV region was the problem for Rayleigh and it was known as the '*ultraviolet catastrophe*'. But difficult times require exceptional people and out stepped two of them; Max Planck and Albert Einstein. Planck has a good claim to be the person who initiated the quantum revolution. Here's what he thought of his lecturers when he was a student:

> *I must confess that the lectures of these men netted me no perceptible gain. It was obvious that Helmholtz never prepared his lectures properly........Kirchhoff was the very opposite......but it would sound like a memorised text, dry and monotonous.*

No coincidence that one so critical of the establishment should be the instigator of a revolution?

Radiation is all about photons flying around. They have different wavelengths and energies. Any hot body (ie. above 0 Kelvin) emits and absorbs photons. The basic process of emission or absorption is an electric charge being accelerated. It's how a TV aerial works. A vibrating electric charge is accelerating, and the atoms in solids and liquids which vibrate back and forwards due to their thermal energy, contain negatively charged electrons. So the problem boils down to calculating the distribution of energy from the emission of a large collection of oscillating charges.

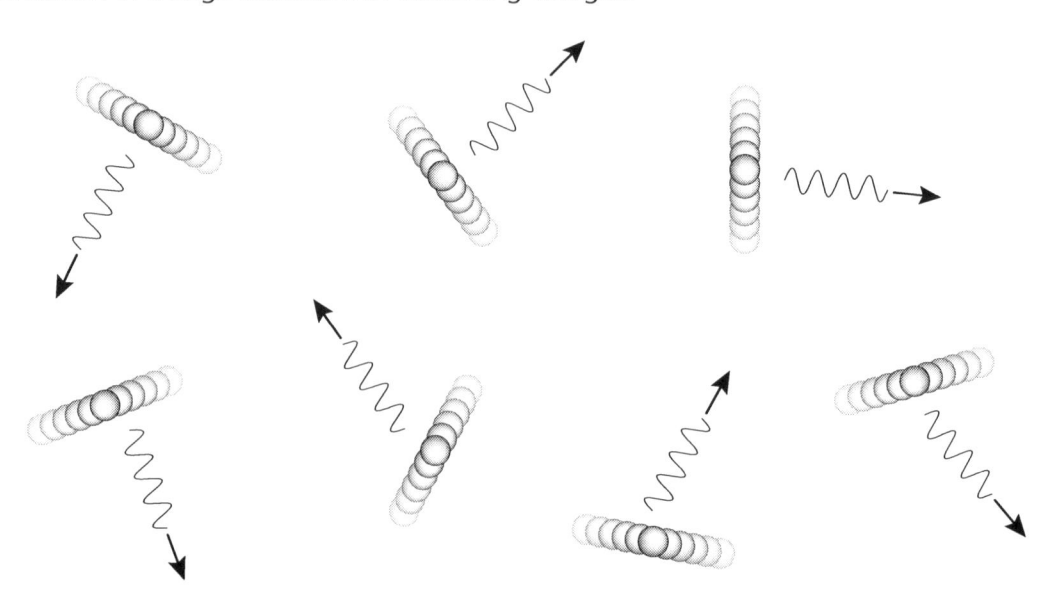

Planck had a prejudice in favour of entropy always increasing (disorder), in all circumstances and in all processes. It was only when he considered Boltzmann's new statistical theory (where disorder was favoured statistically), that he discovered the quantum nature of the oscillators. To obtain the correct black-body curve, the energy of each oscillator had to be in multiples (so not just any old value), and it

# Quanta & Waves

had to be proportional to the frequency of the radiation emitted. Like this:

$$E = hf \text{ or } 2hf \text{ or } 3hf \text{ or } 4hf \text{ or } 5hf \ldots\ldots\ldots$$

Where '$h$' is the constant of proportionality, called by Planck the 'Quantum of Action'. An oscillator of frequency '$f$' could not have an energy of E = 2.6$hf$. If Planck had been a true classical man, his next step would have been E → 0 to reach the classical continuum limit. But he wanted the right answer (as he later admitted), no matter what it took. Planck tried to incorporate his new constant into classical physics but failed; '$h$' heralded new physics and had no place in the old regime. And so the revolution began on the 14th December 1900. It didn't fall 'dead from the presses' like one of David Hume's books; more like 'disbelief' by the establishment who couldn't understand its significance. What kept it 'alive' over the next two decades was the recently discovered fact that electric charge also came in multiples (of $1.6 \times 10^{-19}$C), but more importantly, the emergence of the virtuosity of Albert Einstein.

## The Photoelectric Effect

Max Planck quantised the energy of the oscillators, but was of the firm belief that the radiation emitted was wave-like in nature. The battle between 'light is a wave' and 'light is a particle' had recently thought to have been won decisively in favour of the wave interpretation. It was a bold physicist who said that light was 'corpuscular' (as Newton put it). But that's exactly what Einstein claimed in the third of his three ground-breaking papers during 1905. He was almost alone in this belief until 1923.

You just can't overestimate Einstein's contribution to physics. The first paper was on Brownian Motion and finally convinced the sceptics who didn't believe that matter consisted of atoms (sounds odd, but it was still controversial since it meant that people are also made of atoms). The second paper was on the Special Theory of Relativity, which heralded a revolution on the nature of space and time. The third paper on the photoelectric effect challenged the sceptics on the quantum nature of radiation. Not bad for a year's work. Any of the three would have won him the Nobel Prize; it happened to be the third paper.

Ultraviolet light shines onto a fresh zinc surface as shown in the diagram. The ultraviolet photons act like particles and knock out electrons from the zinc surface. The energy of each photon $E = hf$, is used to remove an electron from the metal (requiring a minimum amount of energy known as the *Work Function W*). Any surplus energy appears as kinetic energy of the electron. By conservation of energy:

$$hf = W + \frac{1}{2}mv^2$$

The zinc plate is attached to the positive side of a battery and the plate 'P' to the negative side. As the battery voltage is increased, a voltage is reached (called the stopping potential '$V_{st}$') where the potential difference across the two plates is sufficient to stop the electrons reaching the plate 'P'. The ammeter will then read zero. Work is done by the battery on the electrons to bring them to a stop:

$$eV_{st} = \frac{1}{2}mv^2$$

$$hf = W + \frac{1}{2}mv^2 = hf = W + eV_{st} \quad \Rightarrow \quad V_{st} = \frac{h}{e}f - \frac{W}{e}$$

According to Einstein, a plot of stopping potential '$V_{st}$' against the frequency '$f$' of the ultraviolet radiation will give a straight line of slope '$h/e$'. According to classical theory, the energy of a wave depends on the amplitude squared, not the frequency, so the way to increase the current of electrons is to increase the intensity of the light. But, the frequency-dependent prediction of Einstein was confirmed by

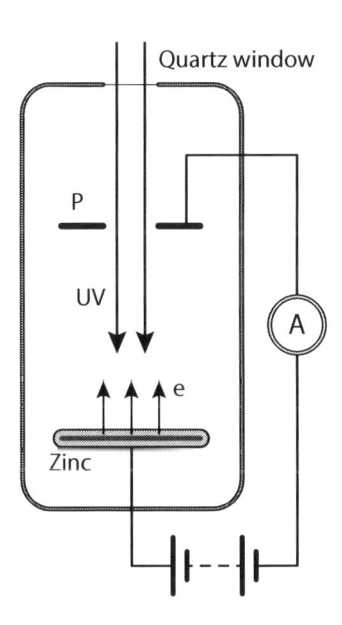

Millikan in 1916. Increasing the intensity does not alter the number of electrons liberated from the zinc plate. This was a heavy blow against the sceptics and supported Einstein's idea of radiation as quanta. It also allowed a measurement of the ratio 'h/e' from the slope, for electrons, and hence Planck's constant itself since the charge on the electron had already been measured. This is Millikan's original graph. The

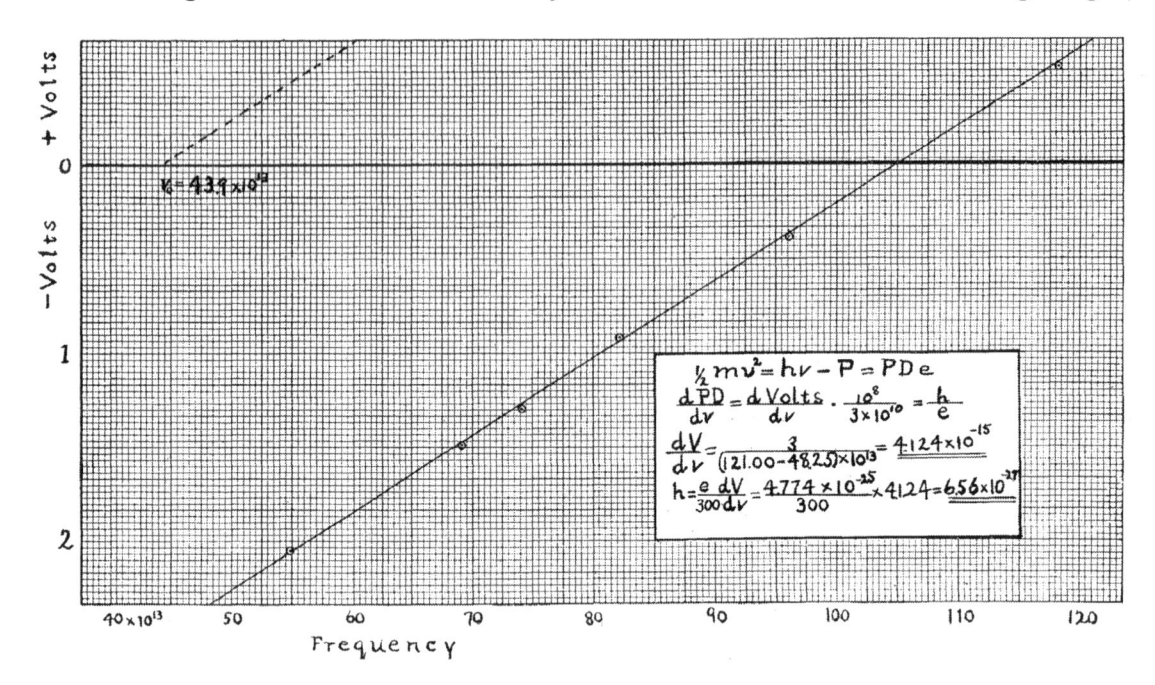

points are his data values and the straight line is his best fit. His value for Planck's constant compares favourably with the modern accepted value ($6.63 \times 10^{-34}$, he used cgs units).

## The Böhr Atom

The holy grail of physics today is a theory of quantum gravity. The holy grail a century ago was the structure of the atom, and the clue to its discovery came from spectroscopy. JJ Balmer had arrived at a formula through trial and error in the 1880's for the visible wavelengths of the emission lines in the hydrogen spectrum:

$$\lambda = k \left( \frac{n^2}{n^2 - 2^2} \right)$$

The 'n' is an integer which can take any positive value greater than 2. It gives a series of wavelengths which were an excellent match to the experimental values. The constant 'k' was his 'fundamental number for hydrogen'. The spectrum is shown below. The 3 → 2 line at 656nm is important in astrophysics

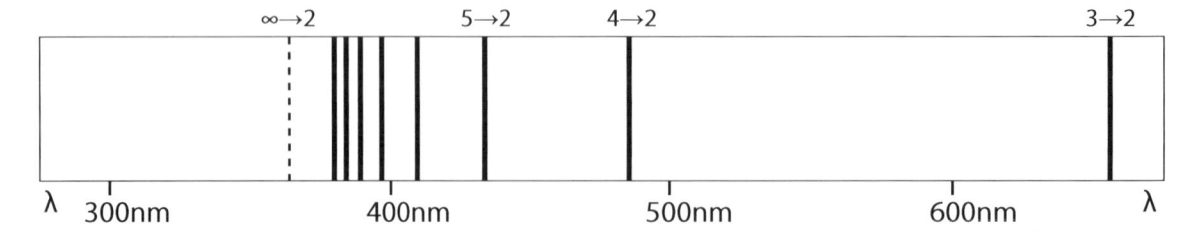

since hydrogen is common throughout the universe. Astronomers use filters which block out wavelengths from other elements to obtain images of hydrogen distribution in the nebulae of our galaxy.

It was known that the recently discovered 'electron' must have something to do with atoms, and that it must be much lighter than a single hydrogen atom (roughly 1/2000th of its mass). Did this mean there might be as many as 2000 electrons in a hydrogen atom? The answer came from JJ Thomson's scattering experiments where X-rays were scattered off thin films of material. There weren't thousands of them, but the number was roughly half of the atomic weight. Combined with the low mass of the electron, it means that most of the mass of an atom resides within the positive charges (atoms must

## Quanta & Waves

normally be neutral, if they weren't, the universe would be a lot different). The question then becomes; how is the mass and electric charge distributed in an atom? Thomson himself came forward with his 'Plum Pudding model', unfairly thought of as a randomly arranged splodge of material, but in actual fact, a cleverly ordered system calculated to cancel unwanted classical crashes. Ernest Rutherford had established a laboratory with two capable assistants in Geiger and Marsden at the University of Manchester. Between 1909 and 1911, they bombarded thin metal films with alpha particles and reached the conclusion that an atom was mostly empty space. Most of the alpha particles went through the thin metals with only a few being scattered, and even fewer coming backwards. He formed the idea of a very small central core containing the positive charges, but neglected to mention this to his fellow professors at the first Solvay conference he attended in Brussels during 1911. It wasn't picked up by the majority, but it did get the attention of Niels Böhr.

Böhr worked with JJ Thomson at the Cavendish laboratory at Cambridge for over 6 months and for 4 months with Rutherford at Manchester. He was clearly impressed by Rutherford's model of the atom and understood that the chemical properties of the atom were determined by the electrons while the nucleus was the source of radioactivity. He also suspected that classical physics was inadequate for its description, so turned to the ideas of Planck and Einstein.

Model building was a tricky business in those days. Earnshaw's Theorem on the instability of a static distribution of charges, meant that the electrons had to be moving. Böhr tried a central positive nucleus with a single orbiting electron. The problem was how to incorporate quantum ideas into the atom. He made an early attempt trying to establish a connection between the kinetic energy and Planck's constant, but it wasn't until he came across the phenomenology of Balmer's spectroscopy formula that '*the whole thing was clear to me*'. A colleague of his at Cambridge, John Nicholson, had come up with the idea that the angular momentum should be quantised. Böhr combined this with Balmer's empirical formula for the wavelengths of the hydrogen

*Bohr and Einstein 1925*

emission lines to derive what is now called the Böhr Model of the Atom. He starts with classical expressions for the forces and the total energy (sum of kinetic and potential energies):

$$\frac{mv^2}{r} = \frac{1}{4\pi\varepsilon_o}\frac{Qq}{r^2} \qquad E_{Tot} = \frac{1}{2}mv^2 - \frac{1}{4\pi\varepsilon_o}\frac{Qq}{r}$$

Capital 'Q' is the charge of the nucleus and small 'q' is the charge of the electron. He then takes a quantum mechanical expression for the angular momentum:

$$mvr = \frac{nh}{2\pi}$$

The undesirable quantity in these three equations is the speed 'v' of the electron in its orbit, so eliminate it using the forces equation and the angular momentum equation:

$$mvr = \frac{nh}{2\pi} \Rightarrow v = \frac{nh}{2\pi mr} \qquad \frac{mv^2}{r} = \frac{1}{4\pi\varepsilon_o}\frac{Qq}{r^2} \Rightarrow \frac{m\left(\frac{nh}{2\pi mr}\right)^2}{r} = \frac{1}{4\pi\varepsilon_o}\frac{Qq}{r^2}$$

$$r = \frac{\varepsilon_o n^2 h^2}{\pi m Q q} = \frac{8.854\times 10^{-12} \times n^2 \times (6.626\times 10^{-34})^2}{3.142 \times 9.109\times 10^{-31} \times (1.602\times 10^{-19})^2} = 5.29\times 10^{-11}\, n^2 \text{ metres}$$

The numbers are for a hydrogen atom (Q = 1e) and for the lowest orbit n = 1, giving a diameter of just over 0.1 nanometer. Knowing the radius, Böhr proceeded to calculate the total energy of an electron in an orbit of number 'n':

$$\frac{mv^2}{r} = \frac{1}{4\pi\varepsilon_o}\frac{Qq}{r^2} \Rightarrow \frac{1}{2}mv^2 = \frac{1}{2}\times\frac{1}{4\pi\varepsilon_o}\frac{Qq}{r}$$

$$E_{Tot} = \frac{1}{2}mv^2 - \frac{1}{4\pi\varepsilon_o}\frac{Qq}{r} = \frac{1}{2}\times\frac{1}{4\pi\varepsilon_o}\frac{Qq}{r} - \frac{1}{4\pi\varepsilon_o}\frac{Qq}{r} = -\frac{1}{2}\times\frac{1}{4\pi\varepsilon_o}\frac{Qq}{r}$$

$$E_{Tot} = -\frac{1}{2}\times\frac{1}{4\pi\varepsilon_o}\frac{\pi m Q^2 q^2}{\varepsilon_o n^2 h^2} = -\frac{m Q^2 q^2}{8\varepsilon_o^2 n^2 h^2}$$

He used Planck's expression for the energy of a photon to match this with Balmers expression for the hydrogen atom spectrum (rearranged by Rydberg, $R_H$ is the Rydberg constant):

$$\frac{1}{\lambda} = R_H\left(\frac{1}{2^2} - \frac{1}{n^2}\right)$$

The photon energy is the difference in energy between an electron in orbit 'n' jumping to orbit n = 2.

$$\Delta E = (E_n - E_2) = \left(-\frac{mQ^2 q^2}{8\varepsilon_o^2 n^2 h^2}\right) - \left(-\frac{mQ^2 q^2}{8\varepsilon_o^2 2^2 h^2}\right) = \frac{mQ^2 q^2}{8\varepsilon_o^2 h^2}\left[\frac{1}{2^2} - \frac{1}{n^2}\right]$$

$$(E_n - E_2) = hf = \frac{hc}{\lambda} = \frac{mQ^2 q^2}{8\varepsilon_o^2 h^2}\left[\frac{1}{2^2} - \frac{1}{n^2}\right] \Rightarrow \frac{1}{\lambda} = \frac{mQ^2 q^2}{8\varepsilon_o^2 c h^3}\left[\frac{1}{2^2} - \frac{1}{n^2}\right]$$

Rydberg's constant '$R_H$' from experiment agreed with Böhr's theoretical value. This was a great triumph for him, but some of the sceptics would only be shifted by dynamite, and the 'explosion' came with the prediction for a singly ionised helium atom. Being a single electron orbiting the nucleus, this should be similar to a hydrogen atom. With double the charge 'Q' in the helium nucleus and 'Q²' in the expression, the Rydberg constant for helium should be four times bigger than the Rydberg constant for hydrogen. It wasn't quite right at first until Böhr remembered to take the radius about the centre of mass instead of the centre of the nucleus. The experimental value was $R_{He} = 4.00163 R_H$, the theoretical value was $R_{He} = 4.00160 R_H$. Checkmate by Böhr.

Böhr had used a combination of classical and quantum expressions, so the Böhr Atom isn't a fully quantum mechanical system, but the door was now open and other players entered the scene to add their contributions..........de Broglie, Schrödinger, Heisenberg, Dirac, Pauli. They were in for an intellectually uncomfortable experience, and even today we still haven't emerged into the light.

# Quanta & Waves

**Example** Calculate the speed, the kinetic energy and the total energy of an electron in the lowest orbital of a hydrogen atom of radius $5.29 \times 10^{-11}$ m.

$$mvr = \frac{nh}{2\pi} \implies v = \frac{nh}{2\pi mr} = \frac{1 \times 6.626 \times 10^{-34}}{2 \times 3.142 \times 9.109 \times 10^{-31} \times 5.29 \times 10^{-11}} = 2.19 \times 10^6 \text{ m s}^{-1}$$

$$E_K = \frac{1}{2}mv^2 = \frac{1}{2} \times 9.109 \times 10^{-31} \times (2.19 \times 10^6)^2 = 2.18 \times 10^{-18} \text{ J} = \frac{2.18 \times 10^{-18}}{1.602 \times 10^{-19}} = 13.6 \text{ eV}$$

The total energy is equal in magnitude but opposite in sign to the kinetic energy (see previous page, and it's also the case with satellite motion in a gravity field, see page 71), so the total energy will be -13.6eV. The negative sign means the electron is trapped (it's in a potential well) and you have to supply 13.6eV of energy to free it from the electrostatic field of the nucleus ( a friendly passing photon of wavelength 91nm will do the trick).

## de Broglie Matter Waves

Einstein's bold proposal in 1905 of radiation as discrete objects (what we now call photons), split the physics community into two camps; him and the rest. His ideas were eventually given solid experimental backing by Millikan's photoelectric experiments in 1916 and by Compton's scattering experiment. By 1923, many of the 'eminents' had been thoroughly hosed, crowbarred out of the solid ground of common sense set in concrete during the Victorian era, and strapped onto a conveyer belt heading for the unknown. Experiment is always the final judge. No matter how eminent the physicist or how distinguished the record or how many of them there are (science isn't a democracy), if experiment proves you to be wrong, you eat humble pie, take a shower and move on. The discussion over what we have stumbled across, and what Quantum Theory reveals about our world, continues to this day.

Louis de Broglie's Doctoral Thesis of 1924 introduced the concept of wave/particle duality. An equation like $v = f\lambda$ contains only wave quantities and an equation like $F = ma$ is applied to particles. The de Broglie equation is very simple and contains a particle quantity on the left side and a wave quantity on the right side:

$$p = \frac{h}{\lambda}$$

You can derive it from Special Relativity (with massless photons), and Planck's energy equation:

$$E^2 = p^2c^2 + m_o^2c^4 \implies E^2 = p^2c^2 \implies E = pc = hf \implies p = \frac{hf}{c} = \frac{h}{\lambda}$$

It contains the only constant in Quantum Theory, Planck's constant 'h'. This constant happens to be extremely small, $6.626 \times 10^{-34}$ Js, and it means that we aren't directly aware of the quantum nature of the world. The de Broglie equation says that a particle with a given momentum will have a wavelength. By 'particle having a de Broglie wavelength', I don't want you to think of a particle jiggling up and down. It means that some experiments with these particles require wave equations to describe their behaviour.

**Example 1** Calculate the wavelength of an electron which has a speed of $5 \times 10^6$ m s$^{-1}$.

$$p = mv = 9.109 \times 10^{-31} \times 5 \times 10^6 = 4.55 \times 10^{-24} \text{ kgms}^{-1} \implies \lambda = \frac{h}{p} = \frac{6.626 \times 10^{-34}}{4.55 \times 10^{-24}} = 1.46 \times 10^{-10} \text{ m}$$

This wavelength is very short (about the size of an atom), and to reveal the wave aspect of electrons of this speed would require comparably small interference gaps. You can't manufacture 'gaps' of this size so have to look for alternatives.

This cuts both ways. The de Broglie equation also says that a wave with a given wavelength will have particle properties with a momentum.

**Example 2**   Calculate the momentum of a gamma-ray photon of frequency 7 x 10²⁰ Hz.

$$\lambda = \frac{v}{f} = \frac{3\times10^8}{7\times10^{20}} = 4.29\times10^{-13}\,\text{m} \quad\Rightarrow\quad p = \frac{h}{\lambda} = \frac{6.626\times10^{-34}}{4.29\times10^{-13}} = 1.54\times10^{-21}\,\text{kg m s}^{-1}$$

Compton in 1923 used this 'bullet like' property of gamma rays to knock electrons from atoms. The 'reflected' gamma ray had a lower frequency than the incident gamma ray, something which is impossible for a classical wave (where reflection can reduce the amplitude, but not the frequency).

Usually, you apply the de Broglie equation to quantum objects like electrons, photons or atoms. This next bit is disputed, but many physicists believe you can apply it to any object.

**Example 3**   Walking down the corridor with a speed of 2m s⁻¹, you would have a de Broglie wavelength of:

$$p = mv = 60\times 2 = 120\,\text{kgms}^{-1} \quad\Rightarrow\quad \lambda = \frac{h}{p} = \frac{6.626\times10^{-34}}{120} = 5.5\times10^{-36}\,\text{m}$$

With a wavelength so short, you are safe from diffraction effects. But suppose you entered a mysterious school corridor where $h = 100\,\text{Js}$? Would it help if you started running?

## The Davisson / Germer Experiment (1927)

This is the first of two famous experiments showing that electrons have wave properties. Three years after de Broglie proposed his equation, Davisson and Germer sent a beam of electrons towards a Nickel crystal. The electrons had been 'boiled off' a hot filament and accelerated towards an anode through a potential difference '$V$'.

The Work Done by the electric field on the electrons gives them kinetic energy:

$$qV = \frac{1}{2}mv^2$$

Rearranging the de Broglie relation for the speed gives:

$$\lambda = \frac{h}{p} = \frac{h}{mv} \quad\Rightarrow\quad v = \frac{h}{\lambda m}$$

Substitute for the speed into the kinetic energy:

$$qV = \frac{1}{2}mv^2 \quad\Rightarrow\quad qV = \frac{1}{2}m\left(\frac{h}{\lambda m}\right)^2 \quad\Rightarrow\quad \lambda = \frac{h}{\sqrt{2mqV}}$$

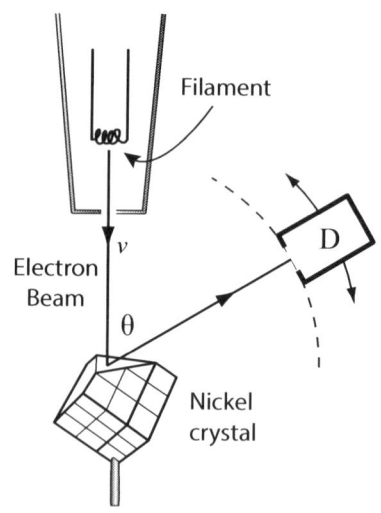

**Example**   Calculate the wavelength of the electrons if they are accelerated through a potential difference of 100 volts.

$$\lambda = \frac{h}{\sqrt{2mqV}} = \frac{6.626\times10^{-34}}{\sqrt{2\times9.109\times10^{-31}\times1.602\times10^{-19}\times100}} = 1.23\times10^{-10}\,\text{m}$$

This wavelength is comparable to the spacing of the atoms (9.1 x 10⁻¹¹ m) in a crystal of Nickel. It turns this into a diffraction grating experiment (reflection type, rather than a 'passing through' type). This is just like a standard X-ray diffraction experiment, but instead of X-rays, it's a beam of electrons whose wavelength is controlled by adjusting the voltage. For a fixed electron wavelength, the detector 'D' picked up stronger signals at certain angles which obeyed the standard relationship for a diffraction grating $n\lambda = 2d\sin\theta$. This is good evidence for electrons showing wave properties. After some head-scratching, Davisson concluded his report with these words:

*I believe, however, that for the present and for a long time to come we shall, in describing experiments, worry but little about ultimate realities and logical consistency. We will describe each phenomenon in whatever terms we find most convenient.*

## The G.P.Thomson Experiment (1928)

There were quite a few Thomsons' around at that time. There was William Thomson, better known as Lord Kelvin, who was Professor of Natural Philosophy at Glasgow University and who died at Largs in 1907. He spent his summer holidays at Lamlash on the Isle of Arran, but is more famous for the Kelvin temperature scale and proclaiming that 'heavier-than-air flying machines are impossible'. There was J.J.Thomson, who discovered the electron and worked at the famous Cavendish Laboratory at Cambridge University. He married another physicist, herself the daughter of a Professor of Physics at Cambridge, so it's little surprise that their son went on to do physics.
Father and son both won the Nobel Prize for Physics. It is the son, G.P.Thomson, who is our subject.

Thomson and his research student Andrew Reid initially fired electron beams at celluloid but with only partial success. After Reid died in a motorcycle accident, Thomson continued on alone and directed a beam of electrons towards very thin metal films of gold and aluminium. The beam passed through the metal and was detected by use of a photographic plate on the other side. This diagram illustrates the results of one such experiment. The circles are caused by a wave effect, diffraction, and once again demonstrate the wave properties of electrons. As before, the diffraction equation $n\lambda = 2d\sin\theta$, called Bragg's Law, was used to relate the wavelength to the geometry of the experiment.

George Paget Thomson was Professor of Natural Philosophy at Aberdeen University at the time and shared the Nobel Prize for Physics with Clinton Davisson in 1937. George's father doggedly refused to renounce classical physics right up to his death in 1940.

## Quantum Interference........The Double-Slit Experiment

The classic experiment of Thomas Young in 1810 (see later, page 146), demonstrated wave interference by passing light through a double slit. A century and a half later, Richard Feynman gave a series of lectures to undergraduates at CalTech in 1962. With his usual flamboyant style, he described how Young's experimental setup provided the ideal setting to illustrate the basic difference between classical and quantum physics. Imagine firing bullets at a steel plate with two holes in it (left diagram). The gun is very inaccurate and sprays bullets at random all over the plate. Some bullets go straight through and some glance off the side and get through. With both holes open, the distribution of bullets arriving at a screen behind the holes is a large central hump. If hole $S_1$ is closed, the distribution has a lower hump offset to the right. And if $S_2$ is closed, the distribution has a lower hump offset to the left. It's all pretty obvious, and its obvious because the bullets behave according to classical physics.

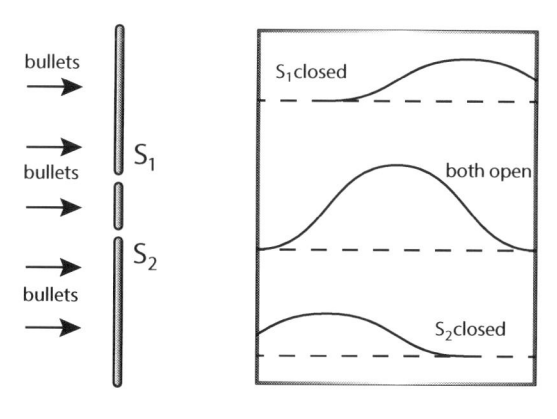

Mathematically, the probability of hitting a particular spot on the screen with both holes open is the sum of the individual probabilities with first one hole open, then the other. Adding individual probabilities to get the total probability is the trademark of classical physics. And there's no interference since bullets aren't waves! Using waves instead of bullets and parallel slits instead of holes (as Young did), gives the standard classical interference pattern for the intensity, shown below.

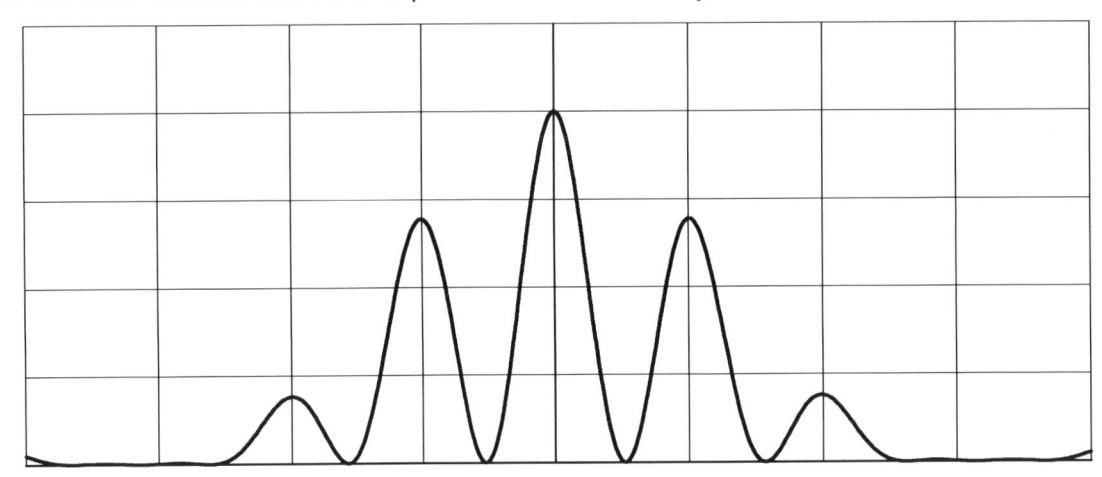

Feynman then imagines repeating the experiment using quantum objects in place of classical bullets or classical waves. His quantum 'bullets' were electrons. The experiment was being performed at the University of Tübingen by Claus Jonsson about the same time Feynman was delivering his lectures. Jonsson used electrons of energy 50keV which have a de Broglie wavelength of less than $10^{-11}$m. This required an unusually narrow 'slit'. In fact, it wasn't a 'slit'; it was a charged wire which the electron beam bent around either side of, to meet and interfere on the other side. Jonsson and his boss made the 'wire' from a spider's thread coated with gold.

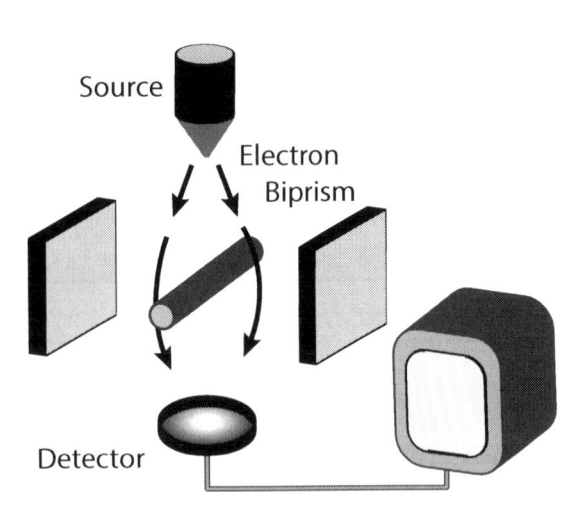

The experiment was repeated and improved by Tonomura in 1989 where the electron flux was reduced to less than 10 electrons per second. The top-to-bottom sequence of images on the right was built-up over a period of 20 minutes. Beside each image is the number of electrons detected. There's a clear interference pattern on the bottom image. Since then, single particle interference has been demonstrated using neutrons, atoms and buckyballs (C-70).

What the quantum world has presented us with is interference even when particles go through the apparatus **one at a time**. This is one of the weirder aspects of quantum theory.

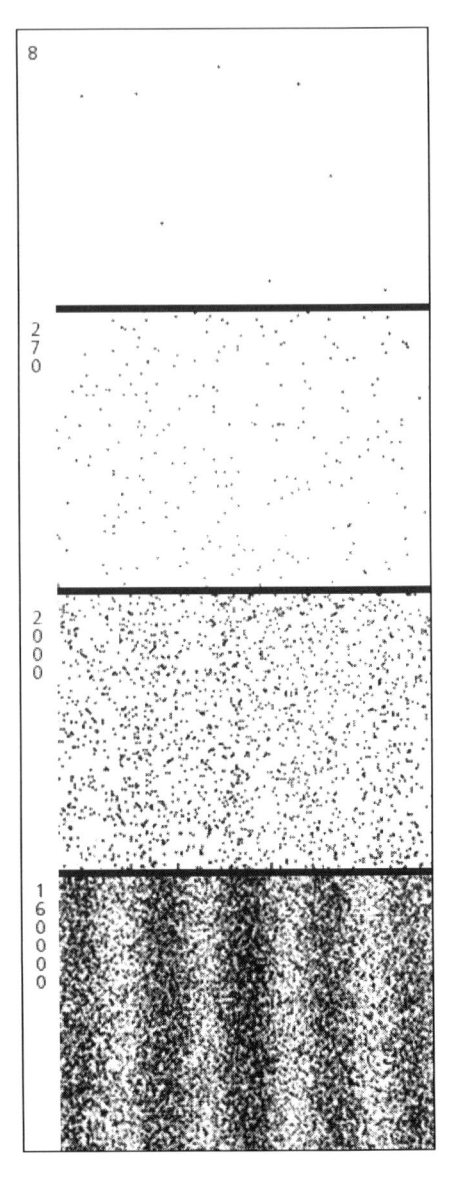

**Quanta & Waves**

Surely an interference pattern requires two things to be 'interfering'? Classically, yes; quantum mechanically, no! How do we explain this? The favoured view at present is Feynman's idea of paths. We know where the electron started from (the source) and where it ended (the detector), but we don't know what happened in between. Call these points 'A' and 'B'.

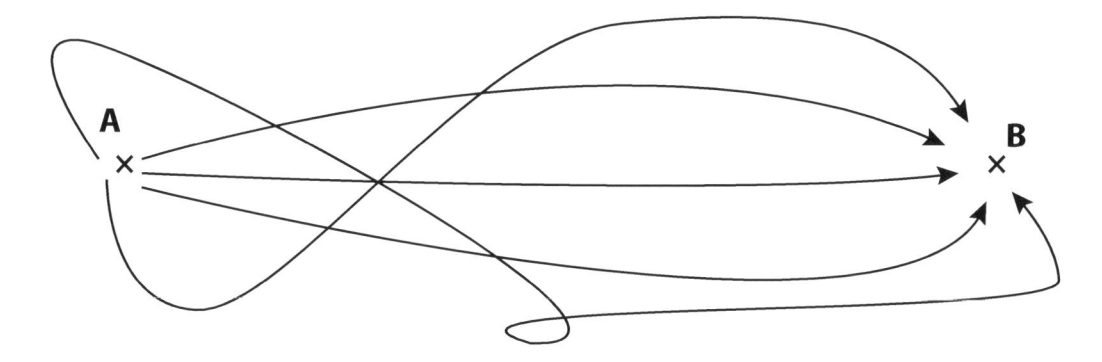

All paths between 'A' and 'B' are possible. Every path (billions of them) has a mathematical expression which quantifies how many lots of Planck's constant it takes to get there (it's called the 'action'). In addition each path has a different phase (so neighbouring paths could add-up or cancel). This gives what's called the 'amplitude' for a path. You then add up the amplitudes for the billions of paths, and in the process almost all of them cancel (due to the phases), except along the actual path taken. The probability is calculated by squaring the resultant amplitude (bit like the intensity in optics is the square of the amplitude of the wave). So it's not the electrons which are interfering with each other, it's the possible paths between the start and finish which interfere!!! That's an 11 on the weirdness scale.

Classical physics calculates the amplitude of each individual contribution, squares each one to get the individual probabilities, then adds them to get the overall probability. With quantum mechanics, you calculate the amplitude for each contribution, add the amplitudes, then square the result to get the overall probability. It's the order you do it in that counts.

**Example**   Three amplitudes: 4,7 and 5.

Classical:  square first then add: $4^2 + 7^2 + 5^2 = 90$

Quantum:  add first then square: $(4 + 5 + 7)^2 = 256$

## The Uncertainty Principle

Part of your Advanced Higher Physics course is a project. In it you will have to consider the uncertainties of your measurements. It might be hand timing an event between the start and the finish, or measuring the distance between two points (like the distance between the goalposts in a football pitch?). What you'll do is repeat the measurement many times and express the answer as result ± uncertainty. The uncertainty comes from human error, reading error, cheap instruments etc. It might also be because the repeat experiment didn't start off exactly the same as the previous one ('different initial conditions'). When you released that ball, you might have given it a little nudge? A bit of geology going on under the ground between measuring the goalposts?

Quantum uncertainty isn't like that. Make ten measurements of the energy of an electron under identical initial conditions and you will get ten definite results. By a 'definite result', I mean an exact answer, not a fuzzy one. There is no uncertainty with an individual result; it's 3.2 ± 0. But the ten results won't all be the same, *even under identical initial conditions*. The 'spread' in results will have what the mathematicians call a standard deviation, and what phyicists call the uncertainty.

In classical physics, identical initial conditions give identical outcomes. The French physicist Laplace said (roughly translated) that if he knew the initial positions and momenta of all the particles in the universe, he could predict their locations and momenta at any time in the future. In quantum processes, we can only predict probable outcomes. But Planck's constant is very small and quantum processes don't impinge upon our perception of the world. We only 'see' the result of an enormous number of quantum processes; what we call 'classical' physics.

Imagine holding one end of a long rope and making a wave by shaking it up and down continuously. If I ask you 'where is the wave?', you can't answer precisely; it's just all along the rope. But if I ask 'what is the wavelength?', you can give a good answer.

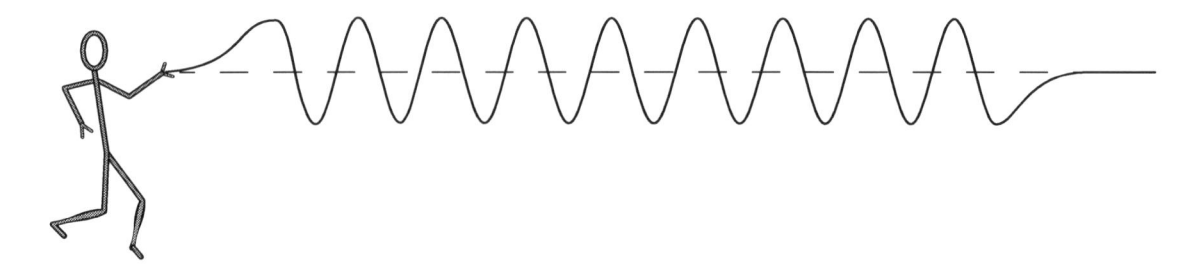

Instead of waggling the rope up and down continuously, suppose we give it a jerk. The first question 'where is the wave?' makes more sense this time. The second question 'what is the wavelength?' becomes a bit woolly.

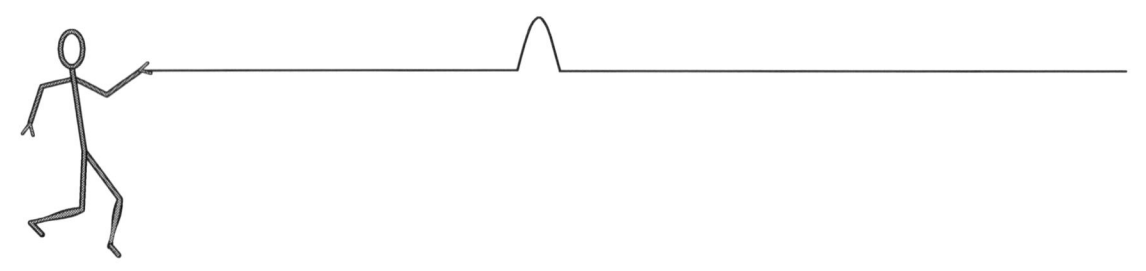

The more precise the wave's position, the less precise its wavelength (bottom illustration), and the more precise its wavelength, the less precise its position (top illustration). This works for any wave, classical or quantum mechanical.

The wavelength is related to the momentum through the de Broglie relation:

$$p = \frac{h}{\lambda}$$

A spread in wavelength corresponds to a spread in momentum, so we can also say that the more precise its momentum, the less precise its position. This is embodied in Heisenberg's Uncertainty Relation:

$$\Delta x \, \Delta p \geq \frac{1}{2} \hbar$$

The product of the two numbers must be greater than a certain minimum size. It means that you can't make both of them as small as you like. The $\Delta x$ is the standard deviation of many experiments of the position of an object, and the $\Delta p$ is the standard deviation of many experiments of its momentum. The constant $\hbar$ (pronounced 'h bar') is Planck's constant divided by $2\pi$.

You can devise and repeat (with identical initial conditions) an experiment to locate the position of a particle such that the spread in values of its position will be very small. But you will pay a price by having the momentum values widely scattered.

This isn't the case with all pairs (A,B) of measurable variables in quantum mechanics. It's only the ones whose product AB has the same units as Planck's constant (Js), and whose product does not commute AB ≠ BA (yes, that's another bit of weirdness).

**Example** Calculate the minimum uncertainty in the position of an electron if the experiments to measure its momentum produced an uncertainty (standard deviation) in speed of ±0.05c.

$$\Delta p = \Delta(mv) = m\Delta v = 9.109 \times 10^{-31} \times 0.05 \times 3 \times 10^8 = 1.37 \times 10^{-23} \text{ kg ms}^{-1}$$

$$\Delta x \Delta p \geq \frac{1}{2}\hbar$$

$$\Delta x \times 1.37 \times 10^{-23} \geq \frac{1}{2} \times \frac{6.626 \times 10^{-34}}{2\pi} = 5.27 \times 10^{-35} \text{ Js}$$

$$\Delta x \geq \frac{5.27 \times 10^{-35}}{1.37 \times 10^{-23}} = 3.8 \times 10^{-12} \text{ m}$$

That's the standard deviation in the spread of many measurements of the position. It's an example of a large uncertainty in momentum giving a small uncertainty in position.

Another pair of quantities which have an uncertainty relation is energy and time.

$$\Delta E \, \Delta t \geq \frac{1}{2}\hbar$$

Textbooks often write this relation down, add a few sentences, then move quickly on as if it was like the Δx, Δp relationship. It's not. Time plays a role in quantum theory which is different from things like energy, momentum, position, angular momentum. In this inequation, the Δt is the time taken for the energy value to change by one standard deviation. Take the n = 3 to n = 2 transition in the hydrogen atom. When the transition begins, the energy will change and the atom will start to emit a photon. The time Δt is the time it takes the energy of the atom to drop by one standard deviation of the spread of energy measurements. So in this relationship, Δt is a *duration* rather than an uncertainty. Another misuse of the relationship you often encounter is the assertion that energy conservation can be violated for a short time Δt. The word 'borrowed' is common to describe it. This is nonsense; nowhere in quantum mechanics is the Law of Conservation of Energy broken.

A valid use is in particle physics with the lifetimes of exotic short-lived particles. The Delta particle is a baryon composed of three quarks. One such combination is the Δ⁺ which is the combination 'uud'. Repeat measurements of its mass give the distribution shown on the diagram. It's centred on a mass of 1232 MeV/c² with a standard deviation of Δm = 60 MeV/c². For comparison, the proton has a mass of 931 MeV/c². The uncertainty relation can be used to calculate its lifetime:

$$\Delta E = 60 \text{MeV} = 60 \times 1 \times 10^6 \times 1.6 \times 10^{-19} = 9.6 \times 10^{-12} \text{ J}$$

$$\Delta E \, \Delta t \geq \frac{1}{2}\hbar \quad \Rightarrow \quad \Delta t \geq \frac{1}{2} \times \frac{6.626 \times 10^{-34}}{2 \times 3.14 \times 9.6 \times 10^{-12}}$$

$$\Delta t \geq 5.5 \times 10^{-24} \text{ s}$$

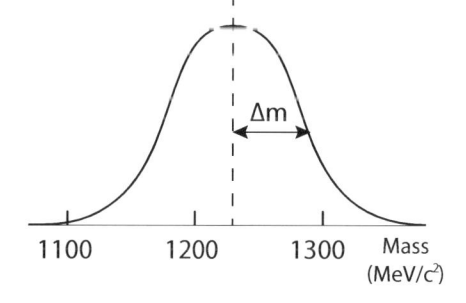

Its mean lifetime is close to this value, so it only exists for the minimum time available. During this time, it can hardly cover the width of an atomic nucleus before decaying into a neutron and a pion:

$$\Delta^+ \rightarrow {}^1_0 n + \pi^+$$

# Quantum Tunnelling

An essential feature of quantum mechanics is the use of complex numbers in the mathematics. This allows it to go places that real numbers can't reach. An example is quantum tunnelling.

If you're 1.80m tall and confronted by a 4m high smooth, vertical brick wall, you won't get to the other side. It's because you are a classical object. There's a zero probability of you being inside the wall or getting to the other side. However, if Planck's constant was a lot bigger, you'd be a quantum object and there's a chance you'd get through to the other side. The behaviour of quantum objects is dictated by complex numbers and they give you a finite probability of being found on the other side of the wall.

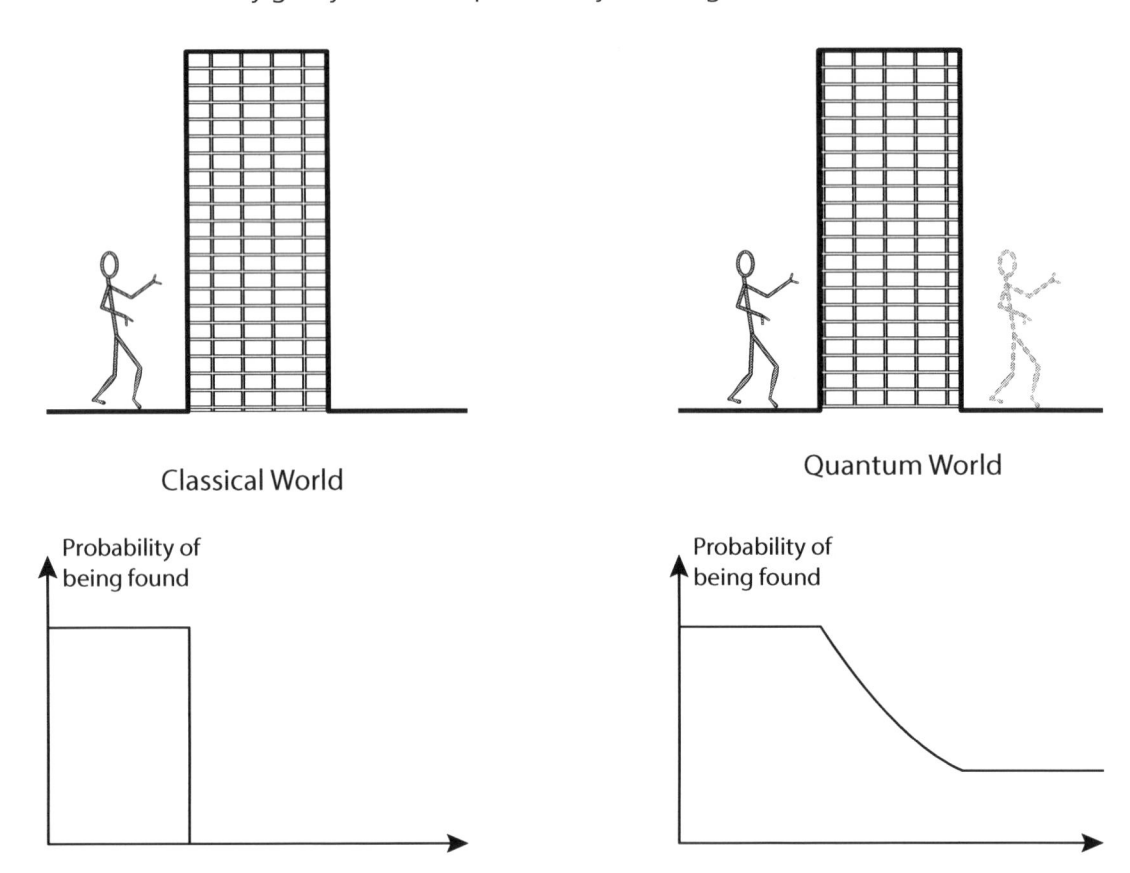

Classical World

Quantum World

Atomic nuclei are quantum objects and radioactive decay (like the emission of an alpha particle) takes place due to quantum tunnelling.

In 1928, George Gamow applied quantum mechanics to the atomic nucleus for the first time. An alpha particle within the nucleus isn't a free particle, it moves within a force field derived from two sources. There's a strong, attractive, short range nuclear force (modelled by a deep potential well), and a repulsive long range electrostatic force (modelled by a $1/r$ potential). The bottom drawing shows the amplitude for finding the particle as a function of the distance from the centre of the nucleus. Remember that you square the amplitude to get the probability of locating the alpha particle, so there is a finite chance of the particle finding itself outside the nucleus. It's like a throw of the dice; when the number comes up, the alpha particle is off like a shot (with energy 'E').

This short introduction to Quantum Theory shows you how weird it all is. But there's more. If you want the full weird, Google 'quantum entanglement'. It'll dynamite your socks!

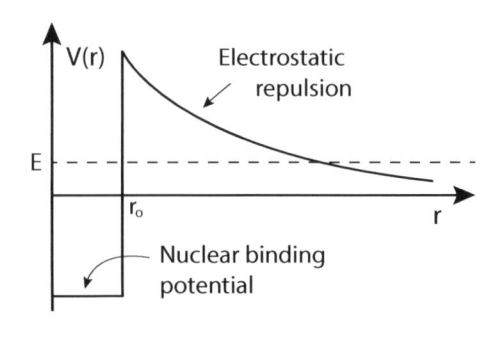

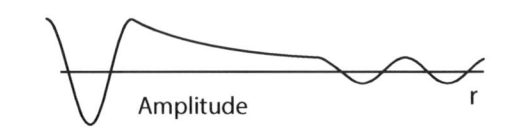

# Quanta & Waves

## Section 2.2 Particles from Space

It's problem solving time. Cosmic rays are particles (like protons and alpha particles) that come from space and hit the top of the atmosphere. They have a range of energies, with the highest energy particles being very rare. So rare that on average, the highest energy ones only strike above the Isle of Arran once every three months. How would you detect them? You could hardly use ordinary detectors since they'd be too small. Even the biggest ones at Cern are no more than 10m in size (so you'd have a long wait). Ideas? (Spoiler alert: they have been detected, read on).

### Cosmic Rays

Particles and radiation hitting the top of the atmosphere come from a variety of sources, and with a range of energies. The task of the experimental physicist is to detect them, and for the theoretical physicist to disentangle them and work out the different processes that produced them.

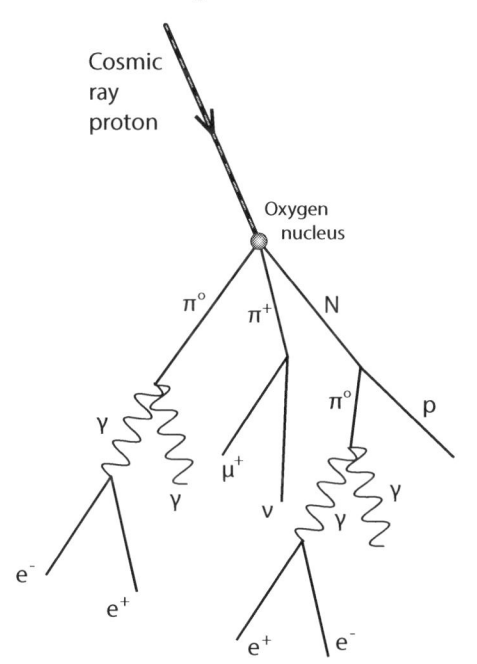

One source of radiation and particles is the Sun. This is mainly low energy, keV to MeV, though with a few up to 1 GeV. Most physicists see this as a separate area of study. The true 'cosmic rays' originate from outside the solar system, with some of them travelling a very long distance over a very long time.

The diagram on the left shows a typical scenario. The cosmic ray is a highly relativistic proton (that means its kinetic energy is much greater than its rest mass-energy of 931MeV) and it slams into an oxygen nucleus about 100km above ground level. There's plenty of spare energy to create a large number of particles in the collision. Common processes are:

- large number of pions produced in the initial blast
- neutral pion decays to two gamma rays
- gamma ray passes close to the nucleus of an atom of air and creates an electron-positron pair.
- charged pion decays to a muon and neutrino

The particles which hit the top of the atmosphere are called primary cosmic rays. Due to the collision with an air molecule, hundreds or even millions of particles can be produced in a shower spread over several square kilometres. These are called secondary cosmic rays and spread out in a cone only a few degrees wide (the diagram has exagerrated the angle). Being highly relativistic, many of the muons produced will reach the ground even though they have a mean lifetime (in their rest frame) of 2.2μs. Without time dilation, they'd only travel a distance of 2.2μs × 3×10$^8$ = 660m. On average about 100 muons hit every square metre of ground every second.

Primary cosmic rays are 90% protons, 9% helium nuclei, 1% electrons and tiny amounts of heavier nuclei. The number of protons within a certain energy range drops off steeply as the energy increases (graph on right). It's wiggly due to cosmic rays having a variety of origins. The 'knee' is the transition between particles which originated within our own galaxy, and those of extragalactic origin. A proton at the extreme energy end of the scale has the same energy as a soccer ball with a speed of 20mph. What's known as the 'Oh-my-God' particle was detected in Oct. 1991 over Utah in the US with an energy of 50J.

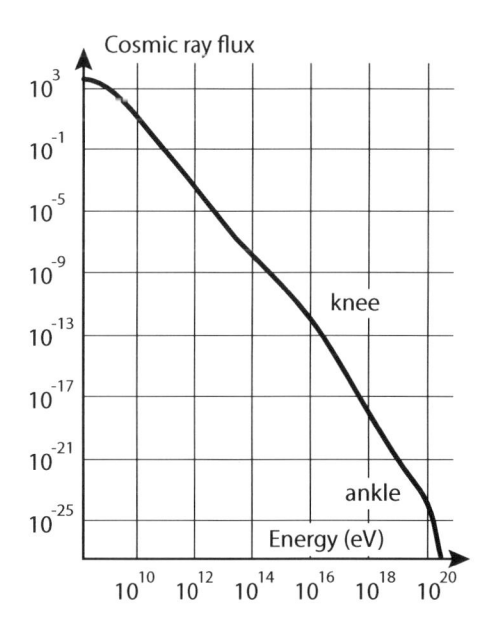

The primary cosmic rays have travelled long distances through space, but that space isn't empty. It contains low density gas (on average, about $1.1 \times 10^{-5}$ nucleons per cm³), neutrinos (about 340 per cm³) and the cosmic microwave background radiation (about 410 photons per cm³). These numbers are all averages over the whole universe. What would happen if a cosmic ray hit one of these things? If it hits the nuclei of a gas atom, it's the same as hitting one in the atmosphere, but without the gamma ray creating an electron positron pair (since there won't be a nearby handy electric field to act as a catalyst). Neutrinos just don't want to interact, so that leaves the CMB radiation.

Remember the atomic process that produced an absorption spectrum? A photon of just the right wavelength collides with an atom, and the atom takes the energy of the photon and goes into an excited state. You may have seen it demonstrated using sodium. This collision is between a cosmic ray proton and a microwave photon from the CMB, and the thing that goes into its excited state is the proton. The quark content of the proton is two 'u' quarks and one 'd' quark. When you have structure, you get excited states, and we've already met the first excited state of the proton. It's the Delta particle described on page 109. Its mean rest mass is 1232 MeV/c². The collision between the relativistic proton and the microwave photon has got to transfer enough energy to the three quarks to flip them into this excited state. The calculation predicts that the proton needs a minimum energy of about $10^{20}$ eV. The Delta resonance is briefly formed then decays by two possible routes:

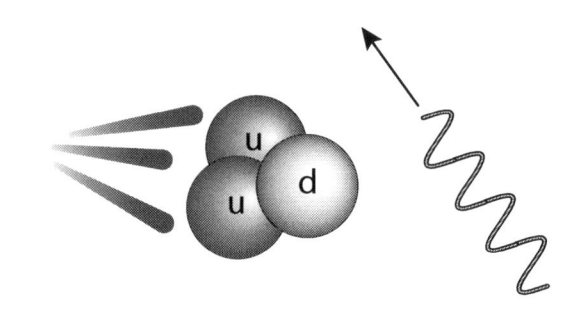

$$\gamma + p \rightarrow (\Delta^+) \rightarrow p + \pi^o$$

$$\gamma + p \rightarrow (\Delta^+) \rightarrow n + \pi^+$$

If the reaction does occur, there will be a shortage of cosmic ray protons above this cutoff energy. It's called the GZK cutoff after a 1966 prediction by Greisen, Zatsepin and Kuzmin.

## Detection of Cosmic Rays

You can use a charged electroscope. Victor Hess did this in a hot-air balloon in 1912 and noticed that it discharged twice as fast at 5km altitude as at sea level. What was responsible must be coming from above. Modern methods scatter detectors over large areas of deserted bits of the planet. There's one in Argentina called the Pierre Auger Observatory consisting of 1600 (yes, 1600) tanks of water each of volume 3000 gallons. Each tank is 1.5km from its neighbour; so that's a lot of area. The idea is that a secondary cosmic ray enters the water faster than a ray of light could travel through the water (that's $3 \times 10^8/1.33 = 2.25 \times 10^8$ m/s). When this happens, the cosmic ray crashes through the surrounding water molecules which then emit a characteristic light known as Cherenkov radiation (it makes the water in nuclear reactors look blue and creepy). Photomultiplier tubes inside the dark tank detect the light emitted. The secondary cosmic ray shower is scattered over many square kilometres, as are the water tanks. Simultaneous detection of an event in many tanks is a signal for a cosmic ray shower. A slight time delay in detection can give directional information.

There is another method based on 'fluorescence' and used by the Auger Observatory. Secondary cosmic rays crash into and excite the air molecules on their way through the atmosphere. The molecules then emit a bluish light which can be detected on the ground. But it's so faint, you need moonless and cloudless nights.

## The Origin of Cosmic Rays

# Quanta & Waves

Cosmic rays have a variety of origins. Those with medium to high energies (up to ≈ $10^{18}$ eV) probably have their origin within our own galaxy. Higher energy cosmic rays are probably extra-galactic and the mechanism by which they gain such enormous energies is unknown at present. The problem isn't so much where they come from (stars spew them out all the time), but how they get their energy.

Only charged particles can be accelerated to higher energies after they have been produced. Only stable particles (like the proton, electron or helium nucleus) will live long enough for the acceleration to build up sufficient energy. The obvious way to accelerate a charged particle is through an electric field. The problem is that although there are plenty of charged particles about in the universe (it's called a plasma), the universe is neutral on a large scale and a small scale. You don't come across large scale electric fields out in the cosmos. But you do encounter large scale magnetic fields. The problem is that magnetic fields don't change the speed of a charged particle, only its direction. So how do you increase the speed of a charged particle out in the cold darkness of space?

Enrico Fermi had the idea of a 'magnetic mirror'. You start with a plasma of equal numbers of positive and negative charges spread throughout a large region of space. A nearby supernova sends a magnetic shockwave through the plasma. A cosmic ray proton which has an energy (a fair bit) bigger than the particles of the plasma, just happens to be heading towards the shockwave and gets reflected backwards (hence 'magnetic mirror'). The proton 'interprets' the changing magnetic field as an electric field (think of waggling a magnet to induce a current). It's like the gravitational slingshot effect of a flyby past Jupiter (see page 70). The satellite picks up some momentum from the moving planet, and the cosmic ray picks up momentum from the advancing shockwave of the supernova. On average, supernovae occur every 50 years in our galaxy and some protons will receive multiple 'Fermi accelerations'.

Light travels in straight lines (unless passing through a strong gravitational field), so it's easy to spot where the light came from. Cosmic rays are electrically charged and their paths get deflected (remember, speed stays the same but direction changes), so its difficult to locate their origin in the sky.

## The Solar Wind

On the grand scale of things, gravity is in charge of the Sun. But it isn't obvious. Changes due to the battle between gravity and nuclear energy take place over very long periods of time. We humans live much shorter lives and only notice changes over periods of days to years. The key to understanding these changes is the interplay between convection and magnetism.

The earliest change recorded was the frequency of dark blotches moving across the face of the Sun as it rotated on its axis about once a month. These are 'sunspots' and are slightly 'cooler' regions of the Sun's surface (about 4500K compared to 5800K for the normal areas). The frequency of the number of sunspots varies over a regular period of 11 years (there was a maximum in the year 2000, so count from there).

The surface of the Sun isn't like the surface of the Earth, where you meet a sudden boundary between gas and solid or liquid. The Sun's 'surface' is called the photosphere and it's the surface where the material of the Sun becomes opaque to visible light. The actual material of the Sun is a hot mixture of electrically charged ions; things like protons, electrons, helium. It's called a plasma, sometimes described as a fourth state of matter (to go along with solid, liquid and gas). And it's hot; hot enough to strip eleven electrons from an atom of iron.

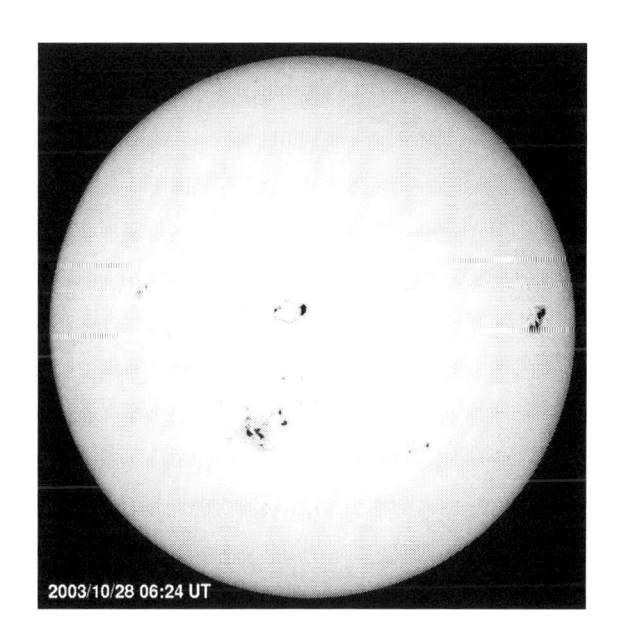

The physics of the Sun is full of mysteries, so it's a good area for research. It's also got important practical applications due to our reliance on satellite communication (see later for more on this). One of these mysteries is the mechanism for sunspot cooling, and this is one area where magnetism comes into things. A sunspot is like the end of a bar magnet, either a north end (where magnetic field lines come out), or a south end (where magnetic field lines go in). Somehow, the presence of the magnetic field under the sunspot makes the plasma cooler and hence darker relative to the surroundings. It must impede the flow of heat to the 'surface'.

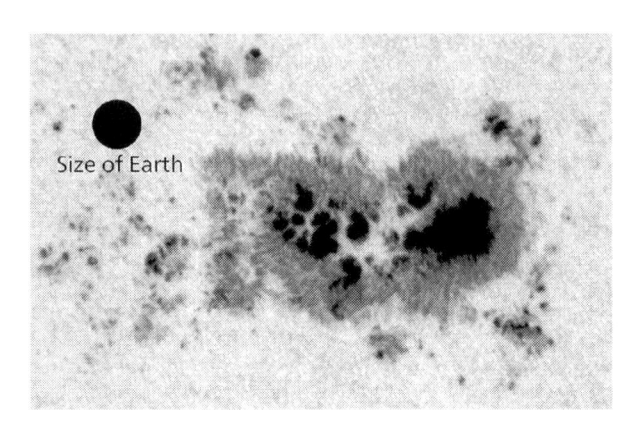

There's more to solve! The leading sunspots in a group **above** the equator all have the magnetic field lines coming out of them, and the ones **below** the equator have the magnetic field lines going in. The next sunspot cycle reverses the directions, so the sunspot cycle isn't 11 yrs, it's 22 yrs!

The magnetic field of the Earth has a simple overall pattern. The field lines come out of the top, swing around in big arcs, and go in at the bottom. The electrical currents deep inside the Earth support this magnetic field and must follow a simple pattern. The Sun is a plasma and that allows complicated convection currents to move the ions around in complicated ways. Magnetic field lines can appear locally on the photosphere, then disappear, over a period of days or weeks. Sunspots are a visible indicator of the Sun's magnetism with a 22 yr magnetic cycle.

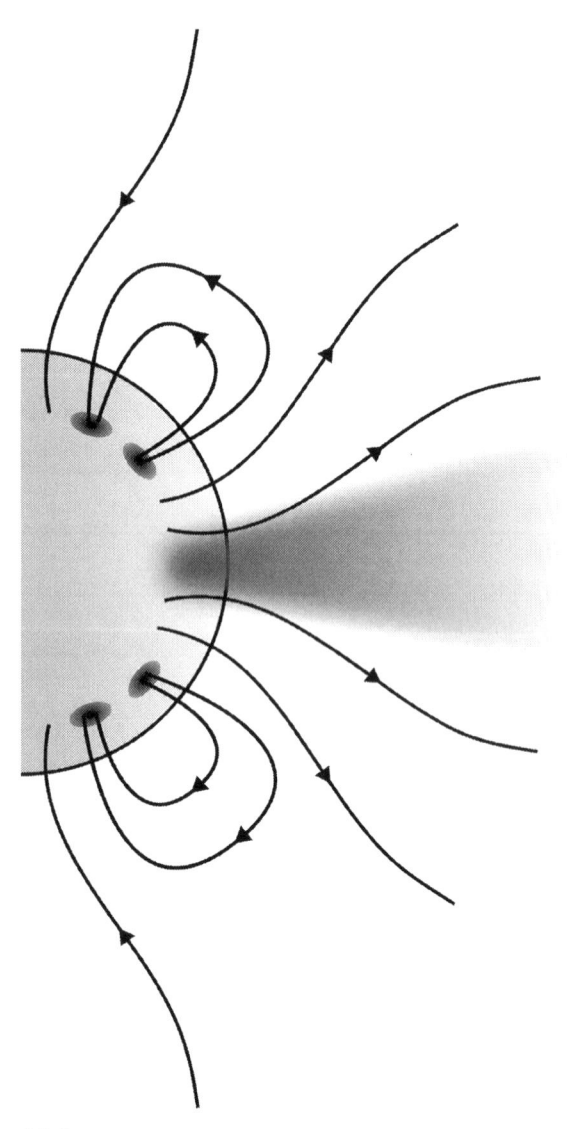

The image above left shows two distinct sunspots, roughly circular, and next to each other. When they occur in pairs like this, the magnetic field lines come out of one sunspot and go into the other. Imagine horseshoe-shaped field lines in the space above them (diagram on left). Any charged particles of the plasma travelling outwards from a sunspot, tend to move in spirals along these field lines (see later on page 120 for the mathematics).

The field lines go out through the Sun's outer atmosphere (called the Corona) carrying charged particles with them. These charged particles move around the closed loops above the sunspots and accelerate giving off electromagnetic radiation. We see these radiating loops as 'solar prominences', though they can emit a range of wavelength down to x-rays. The field lines can get very complicated. On page 182, you will learn that field lines don't have to come out of north poles and go into south poles. The Sun forms field lines as closed loops, figures of eight and closed coil shapes. These shapes are called 'flux rope', become detached from the Sun, and move off into space taking billions of tons of plasma with them (a process known as a 'coronal mass ejection'). The particles going out through the coronal holes can be at temperatures up to 10million Kelvin and add to the general Solar Wind. It's this which can cause havoc to satellites and send astronauts scurrying to shielded areas of their spacecraft. On Earth, we would witness this as an aurora. In

# Quanta & Waves

the upper atmosphere the nitrogen atoms (glowing bluish) and the oxygen atoms (giving greens and reds) get hammered by the protons and electrons of the Solar Wind.

The Solar Wind contains roughly equal numbers of protons and electrons (if it didn't the Sun would become charged and self-correct the imbalance). They have speeds of between 300km/s and 800km/s, thus taking about 3 to 4 days to reach us. Adding it all up, it's a mass loss from the Sun of about 1 million tons each second. Most of it escapes through the coronal holes, and most of the time these holes are located at the poles of the Sun. During active times, coronal holes can erupt anywhere and persist through 5 or 6 solar rotations.

Which takes us to the next mystery. Every point on Earth takes 23hrs 56mins to make one full rotation relative to the distant stars. The Sun isn't solid like the Earth, and its rotation period is 25days at the equator, increasing with latitude to 36days near the poles. The coronal holes have a period of 27½days not matter what the latitude. Solve that one!

The most spectacular solar event for at least the last 500 years (called the 'Carrington Event') occurred on Sept.1 1859. Communications were less electronic in those days, but it still managed to give telegraph operators electric shocks and produce fantastic displays of the aurora as far south as Cuba. A memorable recent solar storm was seen by millions of people at the end of October 2003. Scotland witnessed bright green auroral colours across wide areas of the country, even under a cloudy sky!. Solar physicists named it the 'Halloween event'.

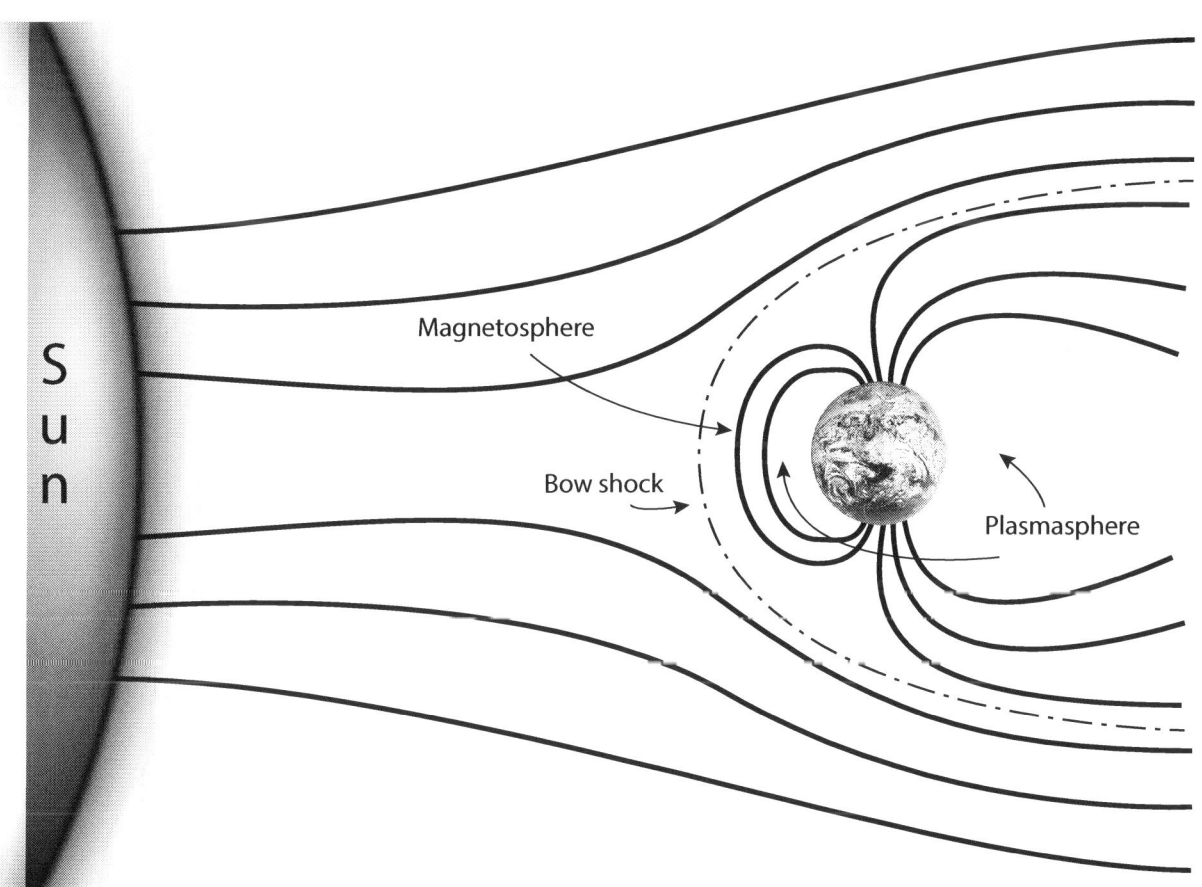

The magnetic field lines of the Sun and Earth combine to give the pattern above. Charged particles can change direction in a magnetic field and tend to follow the lines in spirals. This directs most of them to the polar regions, where aurora are common. Electronics and humans are sensitive to radiation. The magnetic field of the Earth provides some shielding for these, but the big problem is extended tours in deep space. Nasa has set a dose limit of 1Sievert over the lifetime of an astronaut (this gives a 3% chance of developing cancer). The Mars Curiosity mission measured the dose enroute to Mars, and an astronaut would receive about 0.66Sv on a 360 day return mission. Shielding is the key, but it's heavy!

## Moving Electric Charges in a Magnetic Field

Later in the course (page 177) we'll learn that a current carrying wire in a magnetic field 'B' experiences a force. Current is simply the movement of electric charge, so a moving electric charge in a magnetic field should also experience a force. We expressed our equation for the force $F = BIL\sin\theta$ in terms of currents and lengths of wire. With moving electric charges (like the particles of the solar wind), we require a companion equation for the force in terms of electric charge and speed. It's one of the easiest derivations you'll come across (but see the note after it). Take a length of copper wire with current 'I'.

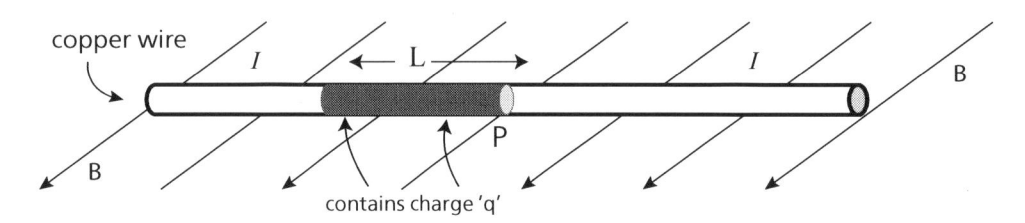

Consider a short section of length 'L' containing moving electric charge 'q' (the dark shaded bit). That dark shaded section with charge 'q' will take a time 't' for all of it to pass point 'P'. This gives a current of $I = \frac{q}{t}$. The charges have moved distance 'L' in that time, so the speed of the charges is $v = \frac{L}{t}$. That's all we need! Now just substitute:

$$F = BIL\sin\theta = B\left(\frac{q}{t}\right)(vt)\sin\theta \quad \Rightarrow \quad F = qvB\sin\theta$$

*Nerdy Note:* The equation we derived (with the charges and speed) is actually the fundamental equation. It should be used to derive the equation with the current and length. The second point is more serious. In the above derivation, I took the charge to be smeared uniformly throughout the section of length 'L'. In reality, it's made of many discrete charges (the electrons). When an electron passes point 'P', how do you define the current? How much time does it take a point particle to pass a point? In a typical wire with billions of electrons you have a quantity of charge passing in a finite time, so defining a current makes sense. Relating the movement of a single point charge to a current doesn't make sense. This is why the equation with the electric charge and velocity is the fundamental equation.

### Direction of the Force

Take the three fingers of your right-hand. Hold them as in the diagram below (the one on the right). The first finger points along the direction of the magnetic field lines (from north to south). The second finger shows the direction that a negative charge is moving. Your thumb will now be pointing in the

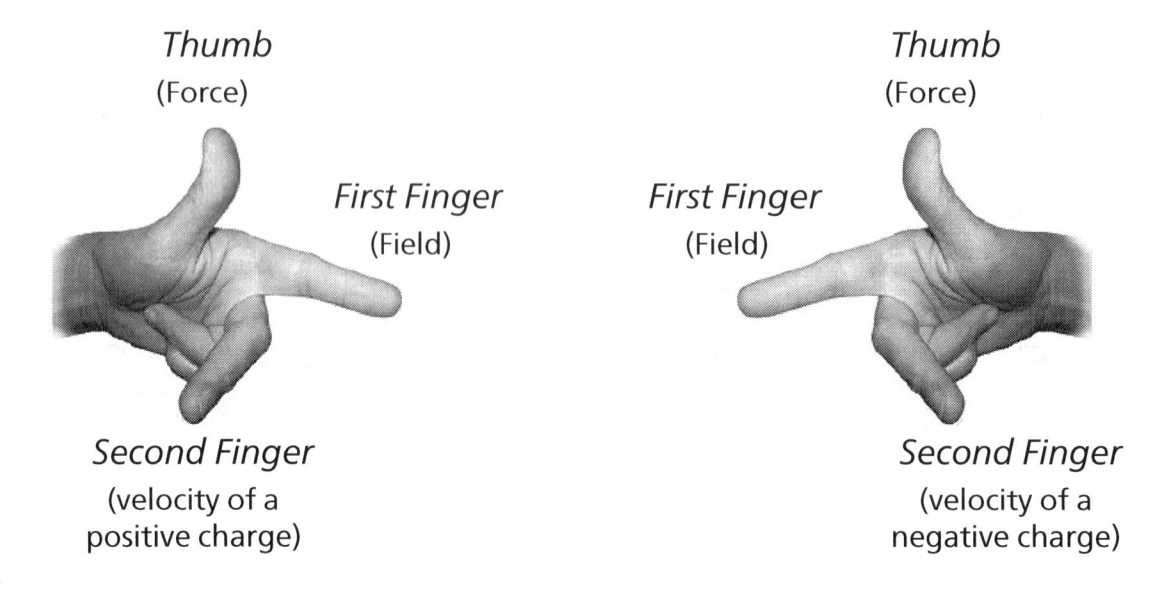

*Thumb* (Force) — *First Finger* (Field) — *Second Finger* (velocity of a positive charge)

*Thumb* (Force) — *First Finger* (Field) — *Second Finger* (velocity of a negative charge)

**Quanta & Waves**

direction of the force on the electric charge. The right hand is for negative charges. For the diagram at the top of page 116, your first finger goes along the direction of the 'B' arrows, your second finger goes left to right along the current arrow. The thumb of your right hand should be pointing upwards (just like the lower right drawing on the bottom of the page).

You might also get questions using positive charges like protons and alpha particles. If it's a positively charged particle, you have a choice. Use your right-hand and take the opposite direction for the thumb, or just use the left-hand (as shown in the diagram, page 116 bottom left).

The angle 'θ' is the angle between the velocity 'v' and the magnetic induction 'B'. The force on the charge depends upon the sine of the angle so it's at its maximum at θ = 90° and is zero when the velocity is aligned with the magnetic field θ = 0° or 180°. Notice that the force is at right-angles to the velocity; this should remind you of centripetal force, a fact we shall use shortly.

**Example 1**  This is an example with a negative charge. An electron travels at a velocity of 4 x 10⁵m s⁻¹ in a uniform magnetic field B = 0.18Tesla as shown. Calculate the force on the electron.

The angle given in the diagram is 20°. This means the angle between the velocity and the magnetic field is 70°.

$F = qvB\sin\theta = 1.6\times 10^{-19}\times 4\times 10^5 \times 0.18\times \sin 70°$

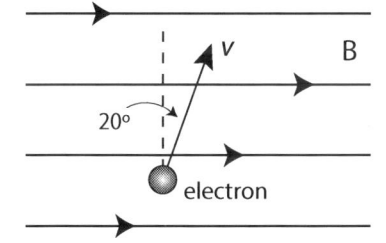

$F = 1.08\times 10^{-14}\,\text{N}$

Use the right-hand rule for the direction; first finger 'field' to the right, second finger 'velocity' to top of page, and your thumb should be pointing out of the page.

**Example 2**  This is an example with a positive charge. An alpha particle enters a uniform magnetic field at right-angles to the magnetic field lines as shown. It has a speed of 3.75 x 10⁶m s⁻¹ and the magnetic induction is 2.5Tesla. Calculate the force on the alpha particle.

The circles with crosses inside them signify something going away from you (like the tail feathers of an arrow), in this case the direction of the magnetic field lines.

$F = qvB\sin\theta = 2\times 1.6\times 10^{-19}\times 3.75\times 10^6 \times 2.5\times \sin 90°$

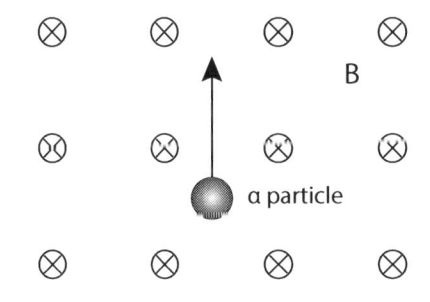

$F = 3\times 10^{-12}\,\text{N}$

For direction, either use the right-hand (first finger 'field' into the page, second finger 'velocity' to top of page, thumb points to the right so the alpha particle goes to the left), or use the left-hand (first finger 'field' into the page, second finger 'velocity' to top of page, thumb points to the left). Same answer, either way.

**Example 3**  Describe how a charged particle can move through a magnetic field without being deflected.

The sine of the angle between the velocity and magnetic field should be zero. So the charged particle should travel parallel to the magnetic field lines (θ = 0° or 180°).

117

## Components of a Vector

There's no new physics here. This is just an alternative notation. Take the case of an electron travelling at a slanty angle to the magnetic field. The diagram shows an angle 'θ' between the velocity vector 'v' and the magnetic induction vector 'B'. The velocity vector can be split into two components just like in maths. To keep things simple, the components are chosen to point along the direction of the magnetic field, and at right angles to the magnetic field. The component of the velocity parallel to the field lines is 'vcosθ' and the component of the velocity at right angles to the field lines is 'vsinθ'. That last combination appears in our expression for the force on a charged particle. It's often written using the shorthand notation $v_\perp$ (called 'vee perpendicular'). The formula for the force can then be written as:

$$F = qvB\sin\theta = q(v\sin\theta)B = qv_\perp B$$

If you had plenty of time on your hands, you could've split the magnetic induction vector 'B' into two components, one parallel to and one at right angles to, the velocity of the electron. This pairs-up the angle with the magnetic field instead of the velocity to get an alternative arrangement:

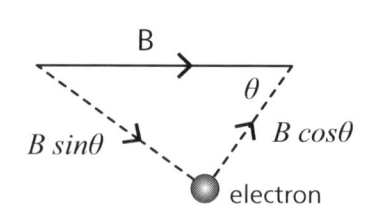

$$F = qvB\sin\theta = qv(B\sin\theta) = qvB_\perp$$

You'll come across these every so often, but it hardly seems worth the effort. Bit like rearranging chairs.

## Circular Motion in a Magnetic Field

A magnetic field produces a force on a moving charged particle which is at right-angles to its velocity (test out your right-hand rule on this diagram). This is what a centripetal force does; it always forces you sideways. If the force is constant, it makes the charged particle move in a circle. A constant sideways force will be produced by a constant magnetic field. We can calculate the frequency of the orbit and the time taken to go once around the circle. Keep life simple by using a non-relativistic analysis and taking the velocity at right-angles to the magnetic field (on the diagram, the velocity vector is on the plane of the page, sin θ = 1).

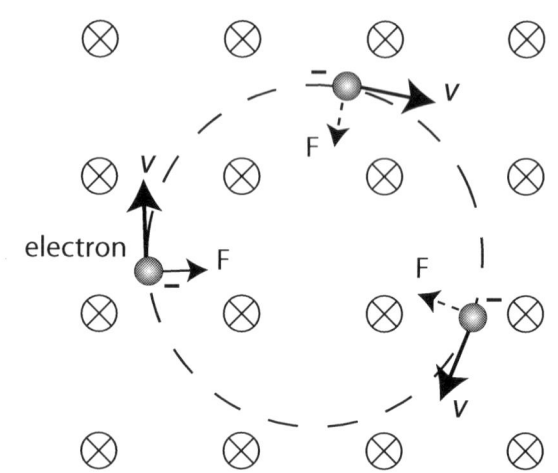

Equate the magnetic force on the charged particle with the expression for the centripetal force:

$$\frac{mv^2}{r} = qvB\sin\theta \quad \Rightarrow \quad \frac{mv^2}{r} = qvB$$

Cancel a 'v', then use $\omega = \frac{v}{r}$, to obtain:

$$\frac{mv^2}{r} = qvB \quad \Rightarrow \quad \frac{mv}{r} = qB \quad \Rightarrow \quad m\omega = qB \quad \Rightarrow \quad \omega = \frac{qB}{m}$$

This is the angular velocity (in radians per second) of the charged particle moving in a circle. We can use the expression $\omega = 2\pi f$ to get the frequency (in hertz):

$$\omega = 2\pi f = \frac{qB}{m} \quad \Rightarrow \quad f = \frac{qB}{2\pi m}$$

Then the period (in seconds):

$$T = \frac{1}{f} \quad \Rightarrow \quad T = \frac{2\pi m}{qB}$$

Let's pause for a moment and see what we've got. The period (T) doesn't depend upon the radius of the orbit, or the speed of the charged particle. It does depend upon the magnetic induction 'B', with a stronger field giving a briefer period. It also depends upon the charge to mass ratio of the particle. We will see the implications of this shortly. Compare this magnetic force with the force of gravity. Kepler's 3rd Law (page 68) expresses the period of a planetary orbit due to gravity $T^2 \propto r^3$. The force of gravity is a radial force and the period depends on the radius of the orbit. Okay, let's get a feel for the numbers.

**Example 1** An electron moving at right angles to a moderately strong magnetic field of 0.25T.

$$\omega = \frac{qB}{m} = \frac{1.6 \times 10^{-19} \times 0.25}{9.1 \times 10^{-31}} = 4.4 \times 10^{10} \,\text{rad s}^{-1}$$

$$f = \frac{\omega}{2\pi} = \frac{4.4 \times 10^{10}}{2\pi} = 7.0 \times 10^{9} \,\text{Hz} = 7.0 \,\text{GHz}$$

$$T = \frac{1}{f} = \frac{1}{7.0 \times 10^{9}} = 1.4 \times 10^{-10} \,\text{seconds}$$

As always, when we calculate numbers for fundamental particles, the answers are huge or tiny. The sizes we are familiar with (millimetres up to kilometres, seconds to days) are very different from the world of the fundamental particles.

## Radius of the Orbit

To calculate the radius of the circular orbit, start from the equation relating the forces:

$$\frac{mv^2}{r} = qvB \quad \Rightarrow \quad \frac{mv}{r} = qB \quad \Rightarrow \quad r = \frac{mv}{qB}$$

We've seen that the period is independent of the speed of the particle, but from the above equation we see that the radius does depend on the speed. The charged particle is usually produced outside the magnetic field by accelerating it in an electric field and then sending it into the magnetic field. This makes it easy to calculate its speed, using $\frac{1}{2}mv^2 = qV$.

**Example 2** An alpha particle is accelerated through a potential difference of 500 volts then sent into a magnetic field of 1.45T at right angles to the field lines. Calculate the radius of its orbit and the frequency and the period of its motion in the magnetic field.

In the electric field:

$$\frac{1}{2}mv^2 = qV \quad \Rightarrow \quad v = \sqrt{\frac{2qV}{m}} = \sqrt{\frac{2 \times 2 \times 1.6 \times 10^{-19} \times 500}{6.64 \times 10^{-27}}} = 2.2 \times 10^5 \,\text{m s}^{-1}$$

In the magnetic field:

$$r = \frac{mv}{qB} = \frac{6.64 \times 10^{-27} \times 2.2 \times 10^5}{2 \times 1.6 \times 10^{-19} \times 1.45} = 0.0031 \,\text{m} \;(= 3.1 \,\text{mm})$$

Frequency:
$$f = \frac{qB}{2\pi m} = \frac{2 \times 1.6 \times 10^{-19} \times 1.45}{2 \times 3.14 \times 6.64 \times 10^{-27}} = 1.1 \times 10^7 \, \text{Hz}$$

Period:
$$T = \frac{1}{f} = \frac{1}{1.1 \times 10^7} = 9.0 \times 10^{-8} \, \text{seconds}$$

In a magnetic field, a moving charged particle doesn't speed up or slow down. It can change direction, and therefore its velocity, but not its speed. In the example above, changing the speed requires an electric field. There is also a more subtle point. Electric fields do Work (as in *Work Done*) on charged particles, but magnetic forces don't. The magnetic field does no Work because the Work Done is the scalar product of force and displacement, and the magnetic field produces a force at right-angles to the displacement. This gives zero for the scalar product. If no Work is done on the particle it can't change its kinetic energy. An unusual 'exception' to this is the Fermi Acceleration of cosmic rays to ultra-high energy. In the rest frame of the approaching supernova shockwave, the cosmic protons 'rebound' elastically (initial speed equals final speed). They take their increase in momentum from the shockwave.

## Circles to Spirals

The diagram on page 118 illustrated how we can make charged particles move in a circle. The particle moved around the flat plane of the page. What if the particle also had a small component of its velocity going into the page? You'd still expect it to go around in a circle, but in addition it would drift downwards. It moves like the particle in the diagram below. It's called a helix ('spirals' have a changing radius). The side view shows it was angled into the page at an angle of 5°.

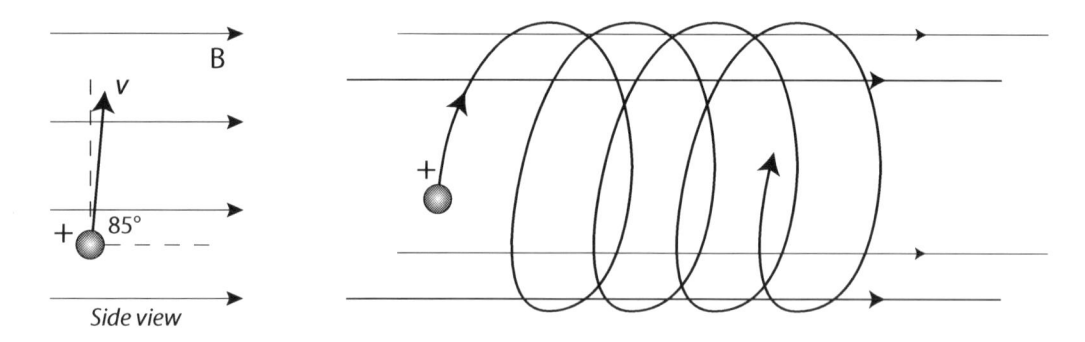

Given the initial velocity of the charged particle, we have to separate it out into components parallel to the magnetic field lines (for calculating the sideways drift), and at right angles to the field lines (for calculating the radius of the circle).

**Example**   The magnetic induction of the uniform field in the diagram above is 0.38T and the speed of the proton is 6 x 10⁴ m s⁻¹ at an angle of 85° to the field as shown.

Calculate the components of the velocity:

$$v_\perp = 6 \times 10^4 \sin 85 = 5.98 \times 10^4 \, \text{m s}^{-1} \qquad \text{(used to calculate radius)}$$

$$v_\parallel = 6 \times 10^4 \cos 85 = 5.23 \times 10^3 \, \text{m s}^{-1} \qquad \text{(used to calculate drift sideways)}$$

The radius of the spiral is:

$$r = \frac{mv_\perp}{qB} = \frac{1.67 \times 10^{-27} \times 5.98 \times 10^4}{1.6 \times 10^{-19} \times 0.38} = 0.0016 \, \text{m} \; (=1.6 \text{mm})$$

The period of the orbit is:

$$T = \frac{2\pi m}{qB} = \frac{2 \times 3.14 \times 1.67 \times 10^{-27}}{1.6 \times 10^{-19} \times 0.38} = 1.73 \times 10^{-7} \text{ seconds}$$

During one orbit, it has a sideways displacement of:

$$x = v_{\parallel} T = 5.23 \times 10^3 \times 1.73 \times 10^{-7} = 0.0009 \text{m } (= 0.9 \text{mm})$$

The helix corkscrews like a left-handed screw ie. the opposite of a normal screw thread. If it had been an electron instead of a proton, the helix would be like a right-handed corkscrew. Notice that the drift of the helix is along the magnetic field lines. This is important for life on Earth.

## Planetary Magnetism

Planetary magnetic fields provide a perfect example of charged particles travelling in spirals (not helixes, since the magnetic fields aren't uniform). Together with its atmosphere, Earth's magnetic field protects us from solar particles. These charged particles from the Sun consist mainly of protons and electrons travelling at speeds below about 800km s$^{-1}$. Whenever they meet a magnetic field, they travel in spirals along the field lines. Most planets have magnetic fields like a bar magnet. This deflects the solar wind towards the magnetic poles and causes spectacular aurora ('borealis' in the north and 'australis' in the south). The picture on the right was taken through the window of a NASA spacecraft and shows a spectacular 3-dimensional view of an aurora above Antarctica.

Venus has a very weak magnetic field and is thus unable to repel the solar wind (in the process generating spectacular lightning discharges in the atmosphere). Mars has a weak magnetic field though it was stronger in the past (being smaller than Earth, its core cooled quicker and shut down its internal current dynamo). The gas giants have strong magnetic fields, partly due to their rapid rotation. Jupiter's magnetic field is about twice as strong as Earth's field at the surface. The photo of Saturn on the left was taken by the Hubble Space Telescope. It records the ultraviolet emissions from Saturn and clearly shows aurora at both poles.

Whereas on Earth the charged particles collide with nitrogen and oxygen atoms, on Saturn the collisions are with hydrogen atoms. The appearance of the aurora at the poles shows that the north-south magnetic axis is aligned with the rotation axis. Unlike Uranus, which is a very strange place. It's magnetic poles are aligned at 60° to the rotation axis, and they don't even pass through the centre of the planet. The magnetic field on one half of the planet is ten times stronger than the other half. Our own Moon has a weak field globally, but strong over some small areas. There is at least one area on the surface about 100km in diameter (probably the result of an iron rich meteoritic impact) which could stand-off the solar wind and provide some protection for astronauts!

# Section 2.3 Simple Harmonic Motion

Many younger pupils enjoy banging tuning forks off benches and holding them against the end of their friend's nose. The barely visible vibration of the prongs of the tuning fork produces a memorable tickly feeling. Usually this is followed by experiments on the earlobes (still tickly) and the teeth (bit different but definitely not tickly). After castigating pupils for using the bench rather than the cork they were provided with, the teacher will demonstrate the vibration of the prongs by holding the tip of the tuning fork on the surface of a beaker of water or against a table tennis ball suspended on a thread.

The vibration of the prongs represents a new type of motion for us. It includes many types of regular to and fro motion about an equilibrium point: loudspeaker cone, molecule in a solid, piston in an engine, oscillating column of liquid in a 'U' tube, a point on a cello string etc. A pendulum swings along a curved path (as do points on the prongs of the tuning fork). If you take only small swings, the motion of a particle of the fork approximates a straight line. The name for all of this is 'oscillation' or 'harmonic motion'. In this course, we only study the simplest type of harmonic motion; hence the title.

## Analysing the Forces

When a mass 'm' oscillates to and fro, it won't have a constant velocity. Its greatest speed is when it passes the midpoint (usually taken as the origin), and it's momentarily at rest at the furthest points left and right (the maximum displacement of the mass). Constant velocity implies balanced forces (or no force) so there must be an unbalanced force acting on the mass. When the mass is on one side of the midpoint, the force must be directed back towards the midpoint. This will ensure the mass remains trapped. The force is called a restoring force.

Take $\underline{x}$ as the displacement vector of the mass 'm' which oscillates between x = +A and x = -A. For example $\underline{x} = 3\underline{i}$ places the mass at 3 metres on the positive side of the x-axis and $\underline{x} = -2\underline{i}$ places the mass 2 metres on the other side of the origin. We can trap the mass by applying a force which points to the left in the first case (when $\underline{x} = 3\underline{i}$) and to the right in the second case (when $\underline{x} = -2\underline{i}$). The force vector must have the opposite sign from the displacement vector.

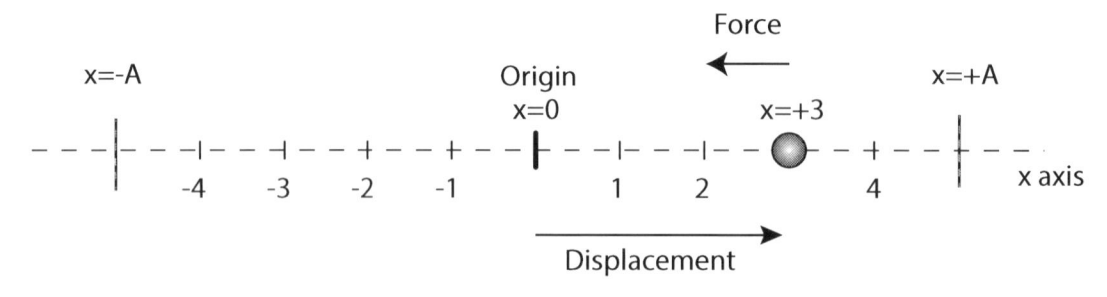

How the force depends upon the displacement is the next choice. The simplest choice is to make them proportional to each other. The way to express this mathematically is:

$$\underline{F} \propto -\underline{x} \quad \Rightarrow \quad \underline{F} = -k\underline{x} \quad \left( |F|\underline{i} = -k|x|\underline{i} \right)$$

Being one dimensional, the sign will reveal the vector nature of the quantities and we can use the scalar version: $F = -kx$ without losing any information. So taking 'x' positive makes the force negative and taking 'x' negative makes the force positive.

Directly proportional is the simplest relationship, so it's called Simple Harmonic Motion (SHM), and it's the only one we consider in this course. The force responsible for keeping the object trapped might be

# Quanta & Waves

due to only one thing, like tension in a spring. In some problems, the restoring force will come from a combination of two forces, like gravity and tension in a pendulum. An atom in a solid is trapped by electromagnetic forces as it vibrates between its neighbours. No matter how many forces are responsible, you can add them up to get a resultant. This is the 'F' in $F = -kx$ and we can now use it with Newton's 2ND Law to calculate the motion of the vibrating mass.

$$F = ma = -kx$$

This is so simple that it's easy to miss a useful conclusion; the acceleration is of the opposite sign to the displacement and proportional to it. So if you have an expression for the displacement 'x', multiply it by the factor k/m, change the sign, and you've got the acceleration. Forget this at your peril!

We now have to solve the equation. This means locating its position and velocity as a function of time. The motion keeps on repeating itself in time, so the solution must be a function which repeats itself. You can't use our old friend $x = ut + \frac{1}{2}at^2$ since this only works for constant acceleration. For SHM the acceleration is related to the displacement. Try expressing the acceleration in its differential form:

$$ma = m\frac{d^2x}{dt^2} = -kx$$

In words, we see the problem is to differentiate the solution x = f(t), twice, and get back to minus what we started with (give or take, a constant). Functions which do that are the sine and cosine functions. We usually associate them with angles, as in $\sin\theta$, but we want it as a function of time, so we try the solution: $x = \sin t$. There are two difficulties with this form. Firstly, the bit inside the sine must have no dimensions. Time has dimensions of time (doh!), so write the solution as $x = \sin bt$ where the constant 'b' has units of s⁻¹. Secondly, the dimensions on the left are 'metres', and on the right, 'no dimensions'. So we have to insert a 'metres thing' on the right. Using a sine function limits the 'x' value to between -1 and +1, so we multiply it by a constant 'A' to obtain the form $x = A\sin bt$. It now limits the 'x' values to between '-A' and '+A'. This is the 'metres thing' and 'A' is called the amplitude of the motion.

Ok, here goes. Differentiate the displacement to get the velocity:

$$x = A\sin bt \qquad v = \frac{dx}{dt} = \frac{d}{dt}(A\sin bt) = Ab\cos bt$$

Differentiate again to get the acceleration:

$$a = \frac{d^2x}{dt^2} = \frac{dv}{dt} = \frac{d}{dt}(Ab\cos bt) = -Ab^2\sin bt$$

Substitute the acceleration and displacement into our equation of motion:

$$m\frac{d^2x}{dt^2} = -kx \quad \Rightarrow \quad m(-Ab^2\sin bt) = -kA\sin bt \quad \Rightarrow \quad b^2 = \frac{k}{m} \quad \Rightarrow \quad b = \sqrt{\frac{k}{m}}$$

We now have the solution: $x = A\sin bt$ where $b = \sqrt{\frac{k}{m}}$ and 'A' is the amplitude.

**Example**   A 250g mass oscillates with Simple Harmonic Motion under the action of a force with a force constant k = 9N m⁻¹. (That's what it's called and that's its unit). The maximum displacement is 0.5m. Calculate the frequency of the motion.

$$b = \sqrt{\frac{k}{m}} = \sqrt{\frac{9}{0.25}} = 6s^{-1} \quad \Rightarrow \quad x = 0.5\sin 6t$$

Now sketch this sine graph of displacement (vertical axis) as a function of time (horizontal axis):

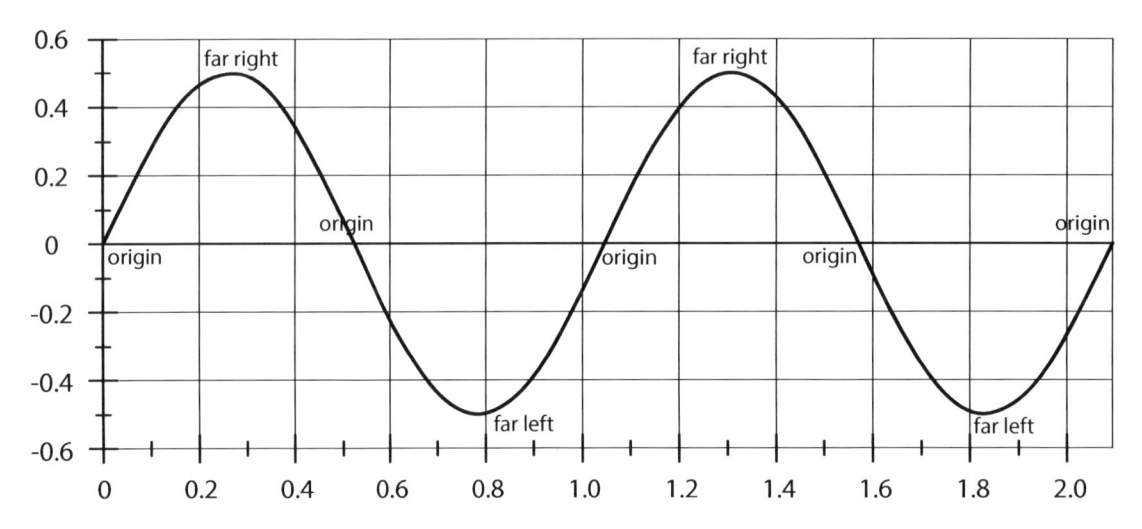

The displacement varies between +0.5m and -0.5m. A sine function sin θ will repeat itself every 2π, so sin 6θ will repeat itself every 2π/6. This is confirmed on the horizontal scale with a value just over 1. Choosing the sine function as a solution means that the clock started when the mass passed the origin and was moving to the right. The alternative solution was a cosine function. This works just as well, but the clock starts when the mass is at the far right x = +A. From the graph, we can read off the period (T), the time taken for one complete cycle. It's about 1.05s. This gives a frequency of $f = 1/T = 1/1.05 = 0.95 \text{Hz}$.

## Frequency of the Motion

The solution $x = A \sin bt$ can be written in a way which shows the frequency. It's hidden in the constant 'b'. When the time is at one quarter period t = T/4, the particle is at the far right x = +A. To get this you must have $x = A \sin\left(\frac{\pi}{2}\right)$. Matching up what goes in the brackets: $\frac{\pi}{2} = bt = b \times \frac{1}{4}T \Rightarrow b = \frac{2\pi}{T}$

This is just our old friend the angular velocity 'ω'. So we can write the solution in three ways:

$$x = A \sin \omega t \qquad x = A \sin 2\pi f t \qquad x = A \sin\left(2\pi \frac{t}{T}\right)$$

In the example above, the period of 1.05s was estimated from the graph. We can calculate it more accurately from the values for k and m:

$$b = \omega = \frac{2\pi}{T} = \sqrt{\frac{k}{m}} \Rightarrow T = 2\pi\sqrt{\frac{m}{k}} = 2\pi\sqrt{\frac{0.25}{9}} = 1.0472\text{s}$$

In SHM, don't call 'ω' the angular velocity. We've got a scalar quantity here and angular velocity is a vector. In this context we call it the angular frequency. It still has the same symbol 'ω'. Don't confuse it with frequency 'f'. The frequency is the number of turns gone through per second, the angular frequency is the number of radians gone through per second.

## Graphs of Displacement, Velocity and Acceleration

Starting from the sine solution to the equation of Simple Harmonic Motion, we can plot graphs of displacement against time, velocity ($v = \frac{dx}{dt}$) against time and acceleration ($a = \frac{dv}{dt} = \frac{d^2x}{dt^2}$) against time.

Plotting acceleration against **displacement** is also common. On page 123, we noted that the relationship was one of proportionality $ma = -kx$. This gives a straight line with a negative gradient. The graphs are shown on the next page and have an amplitude of 5cm and a period of 0.25s.

**Quanta & Waves**

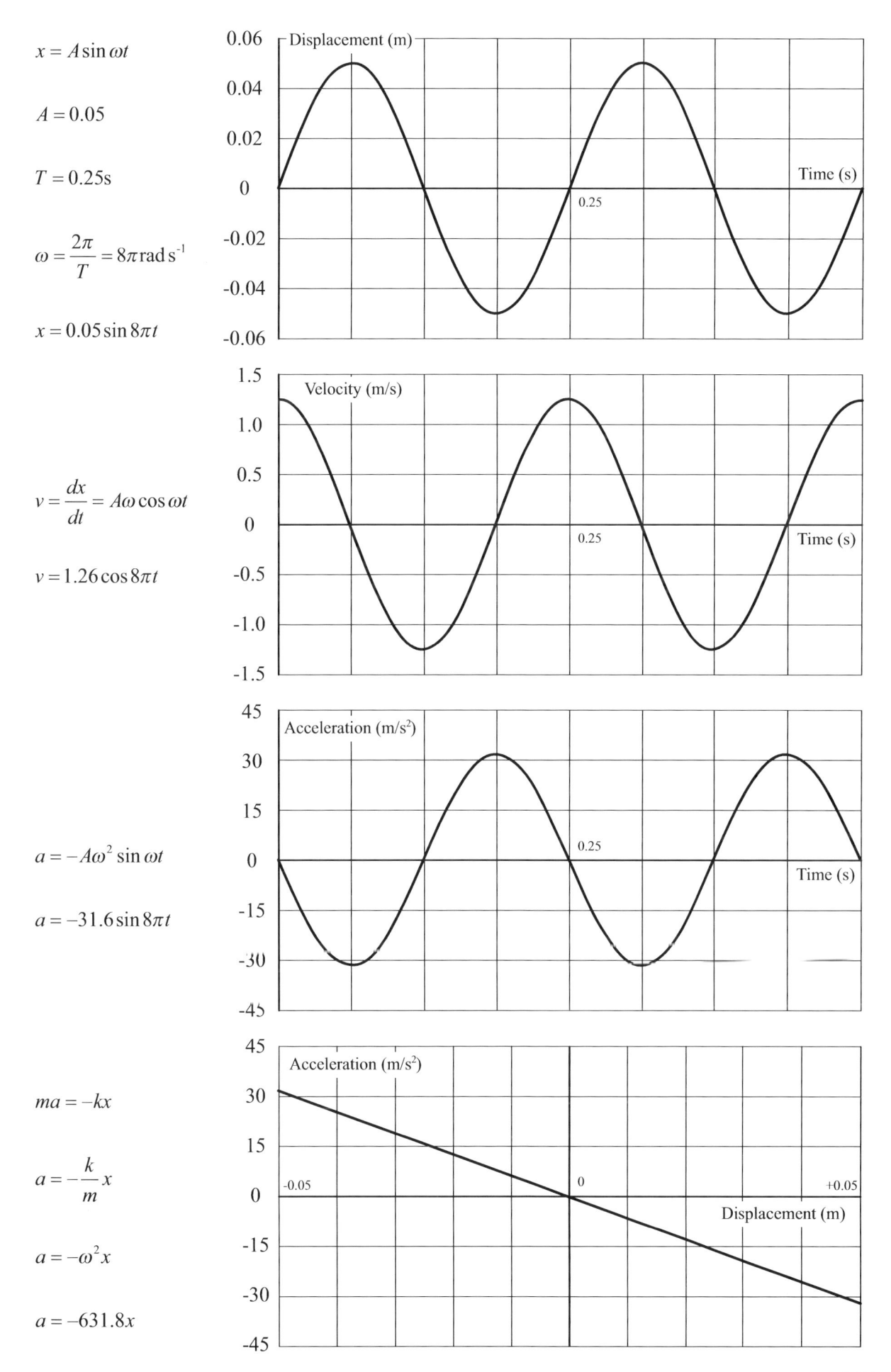

$x = A \sin \omega t$

$A = 0.05$

$T = 0.25\,\text{s}$

$\omega = \dfrac{2\pi}{T} = 8\pi\,\text{rad s}^{-1}$

$x = 0.05 \sin 8\pi t$

$v = \dfrac{dx}{dt} = A\omega \cos \omega t$

$v = 1.26 \cos 8\pi t$

$a = -A\omega^2 \sin \omega t$

$a = -31.6 \sin 8\pi t$

$ma = -kx$

$a = -\dfrac{k}{m} x$

$a = -\omega^2 x$

$a = -631.8 x$

125

## Functions of Position and Functions of Time

The solution $x = A\sin\omega t$ gives a velocity of $v = A\omega\cos\omega t$ and an acceleration of $a = -A\omega^2\sin\omega t$. These are all functions of time. Sometimes, it's useful to describe the velocity and acceleration in terms of the position 'x' rather than the time 't'. When you meet this for the first time, you might wonder how to proceed. With experience, you will build up a repertoire of techniques; and when a physicist sees a cosine and a sine together, the trigonometric relation $\sin^2\theta + \cos^2\theta = 1$ comes to mind. The velocity is a cosine function, so square it and then use the trig identity:

$$v = A\omega\cos\omega t \Rightarrow v^2 = A^2\omega^2\cos^2\omega t = A^2\omega^2\left(1 - \sin^2\omega t\right)$$

Multiply out the bracket and recognise the displacement function:

$$v^2 = A^2\omega^2 - A^2\omega^2\sin^2\omega t = A^2\omega^2 - \omega^2\left(A^2\sin^2\omega t\right) = A^2\omega^2 - \omega^2 x^2 = \omega^2\left(A^2 - x^2\right)$$

Remember that this is the velocity squared, so square root it:

$$v = \pm\omega\sqrt{A^2 - x^2}$$

The ± describes the motion for both directions, and you should be able to spot the thinly disguised formula $v = \omega r$, with 'r' dressed in a Pythagoras-like cloak. We already have the result for the acceleration. It's in the initial line, where $ma = -kx$. This gives:

$$a = -\frac{k}{m}x = -\omega^2 x$$

This table summarises the functions of position and time for Simple Harmonic Motion:

| Quantity | as Function of Position | as Function of Time |
| --- | --- | --- |
| Displacement | $x = x$ | $x = A\sin\omega t$ |
| Velocity | $v = \pm\omega\sqrt{A^2 - x^2}$ | $v = A\omega\cos\omega t$ |
| Acceleration | $a = -\omega^2 x$ | $a = -A\omega^2\sin\omega t$ |

## Simple Harmonic Motion using Phasors

The name is famous from Star Trek but they pinched it from mathematical physics. Simple Harmonic Motion along a straight line is a pattern of speeding-up and slowing-down. The phasor diagram is a way of mapping it to constant motion around a circle. It starts with a circle of radius 'A' (the amplitude). The line representing the radius (called a phasor) starts off pointing to the right (3 o'clock position) and rotates in an anticlockwise direction at a constant angular rate '$\omega$'. The displacement (symbol 'y') is given by the length of the side as shown in the diagram.

As the phasor rotates around the circle, its end point 'P' is mapped horizontally across onto a straight line as a dot 'Q'. The dot 'Q' describes simple harmonic motion between '+A' and '-A' (speeding-up and slowing-down).

Big deal you're thinking, but it's very useful if you have two objects undergoing SHM. They could be out of phase. Calculating the phase difference is easy on the circle but difficult on the line.

It's commonly used in AC circuit theory showing currents and voltages (see page 192).

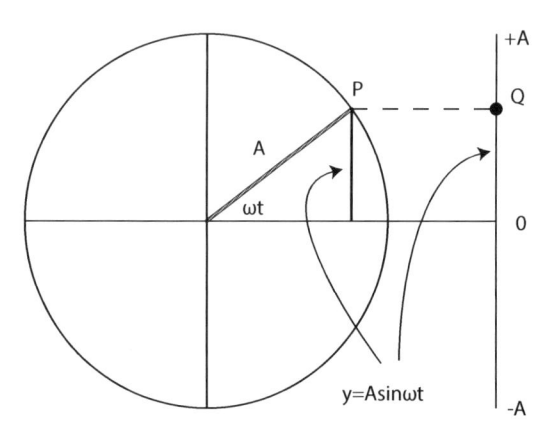

# Quanta & Waves

## Examples of Simple Harmonic Motion

**1. Pendulums** The common pendulum swings along an arc in a vertical plane. Arcs are curved, and the restoring force (due to gravity and the tension of the string) isn't exactly correct for Simple Harmonic Motion. It's close, but not exact. The longer the string, or shorter the arc, the better it approximates our ideal motion. For small oscillations, the path of the arc is nearly a straight line and the equation of motion approaches that of Simple Harmonic Motion.

What's usually taken as a pendulum is called the **Simple Pendulum**. And what most students remember about it is that the period of the oscillation doesn't depend upon the mass of the bob; it's just the length of the cord and the planet under it.

Refer to the force diagram on the right. The mass swings along part of an arc of a circle and at any instant, it moves in the direction of the tangent. We want the component of the force acting in that direction. From triangle PQR and the definition of the sine function, the component is: $mg \sin \theta$

The string tension is at right angles to the tangent so doesn't contribute directly to the (tangential) acceleration of the bob. Use Newton's 2ND Law:

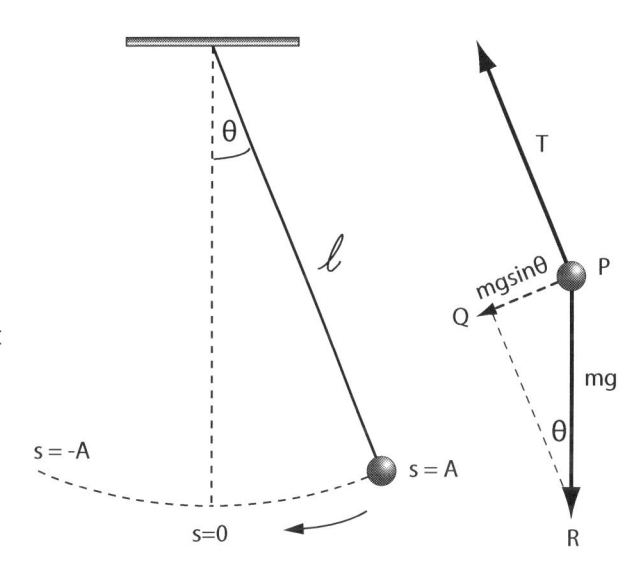

$$ma = mg \sin \theta$$

We want to form an equation in one variable, so express the tangential acceleration (the change in motion of the position along the arc) in terms of the changing angle. The above equation tells us that the acceleration depends upon the angle, so we use the differential form: $a = -\dfrac{d^2 s}{dt^2}$ with 's' the distance along the arc. Why the minus sign? The direction of increasing displacement (and angle) is opposite to the direction of the force (and hence acceleration), so we insert a minus sign on going from 'a' to 's'. Finally express the arc length in terms of the angle 'θ' in radians, $s = l\theta$. Putting it all together gives:

$$ma = -m\frac{d^2 s}{dt^2} = -m\frac{d^2(l\theta)}{dt^2} = -ml\frac{d^2\theta}{dt^2} = mg \sin \theta \quad \Rightarrow \quad \frac{d^2\theta}{dt^2} = -\frac{g}{l}\sin \theta$$

This equation has no analytic solution until we make the small angle approximation sinθ ≈ θ :

$$\frac{d^2\theta}{dt^2} = -\frac{g}{l}\sin \theta \quad \rightarrow \quad \frac{d^2\theta}{dt^2} = -\frac{g}{l}\theta$$

This may not look like it at first glance, but it's the equation of motion for SHM (in 'θ' rather than 'x'). Differentiating something twice with respect to time is proportional to the something you started with, and of opposite sign.

The solution for the angle can be expressed as a sine (starting the clock at s = 0) or as a cosine (starting the clock at s = +A). Last time we did a sine solution, so this time I'll make it the cosine.

$$\theta = A\cos \omega t \quad \Rightarrow \quad \frac{d\theta}{dt} = -A\omega \sin \omega t \quad \Rightarrow \quad \frac{d^2\theta}{dt^2} = -A\omega^2 \cos \omega t$$

Substitute in the equation of motion:

$$\frac{d^2\theta}{dt^2} = -\frac{g}{l}\theta \quad \Rightarrow \quad -A\omega^2 \cos \omega t = -\frac{g}{l} A\cos \omega t \quad \Rightarrow \quad \omega^2 = \frac{g}{l}$$

Finally, in terms of the period:

$$\omega^2 = \left(\frac{2\pi}{T}\right)^2 = \frac{g}{l} \quad \Rightarrow \quad T = 2\pi\sqrt{\frac{l}{g}}$$

This is for small angles. Putting in a length of 24.8cm gives a period of 1 second, so would act as a (short term) clock. Testing the formula with very long pendulums is instructive.

**The Foucault Pendulum** is one of these long pendulums. Pendulum experiments at school are usually timed over 10 or 20 swings, possibly about 50cm long, with a period of a second or two. A Foucault pendulum could have a 20kg metal sphere on the end of a 60m long wire with a period of 15 seconds. You often find them in tall museums in big cities, where they arrange it so that the metal sphere knocks over dominoes or bits of card on a marbled floor. But it's not just that they're big. The dominoes are arranged in a circle and over a day and a bit (it's just under 29 hours at Glasgow) the sphere gets around the whole circle and knocks them all down. The plane of oscillation of the sphere isn't fixed.

It's due to the rotation of the Earth. The plane of oscillation of the pendulum is fixed with respect to the starry sky. You might think the time to knock down the whole circle of dominoes would be one day, but it can't be. If the pendulum was on the north pole, the distant star you stay aligned with will go horizontally around the horizon once in 24 hours (the pole star is directly overhead). If you are on the equator, a star on the celestial equator would rise due east, go straight overhead and set due west. Set the plane of oscillation towards that star and the pendulum will just keep passing the same domino over and over. What took 24 hours at the north pole takes an infinite time at the equator. The time to knock down all the dominoes depends on your latitude and is given in hours by 24/sin θ where 'θ' is the latitude.

2. **Weight and Spring**   This is a standard example in Simple Harmonic Motion. A weight suspended on a spring extends by a distance 'd' (middle diagram below). When it's at rest, the weight *'mg'*

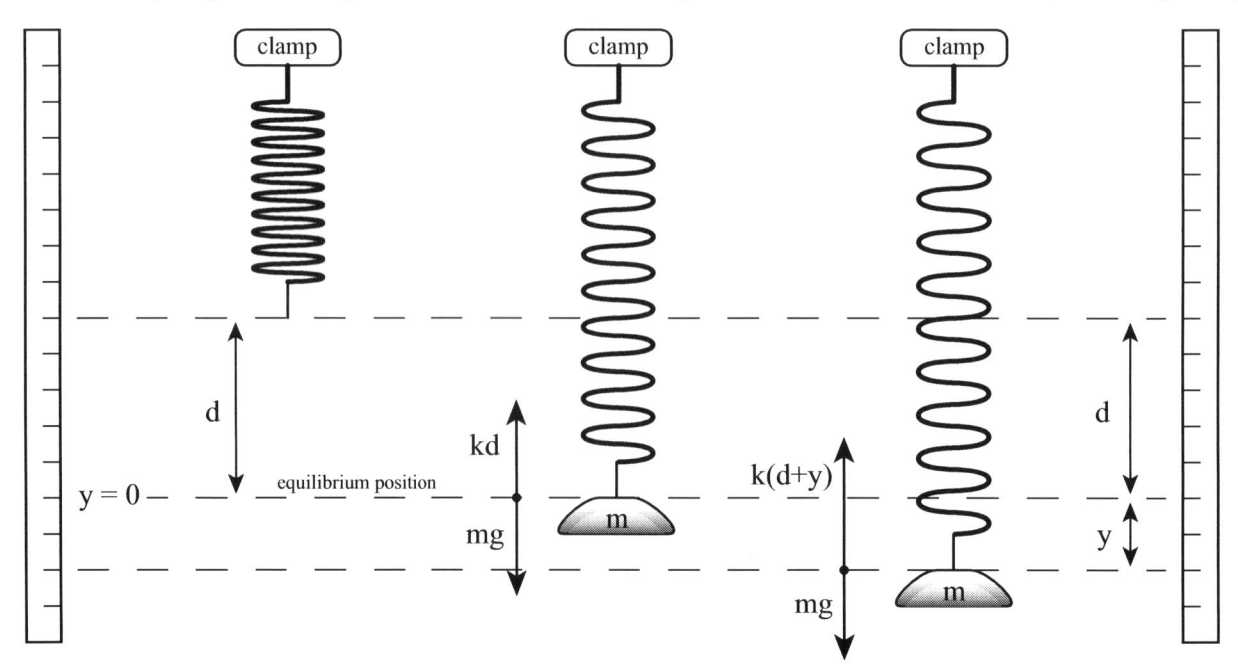

# Quanta & Waves

is balanced by the restoring force 'kd' due to the spring, mg = kd. This is the equilibrium position with the weight on the spring. Now pull it down, let it go, and it oscillates about this point. The right-hand diagram analyses the forces at a lower position. The spring is extended by $(d+y)$ and gives a restoring force due to the spring $k(d+y)$, which is greater than the weight. Taking the downwards direction as positive, the unbalanced force is $mg - k(d+y)$. Using Newton's 2nd Law:

$$ma = mg - k(d+y) = mg - kd - ky$$

With the differential form for the acceleration and remembering: $mg = kd$

$$m\frac{d^2y}{dt^2} = -ky$$

This is Simple Harmonic Motion about the point $y = 0$ with period $T = 2\pi\sqrt{\frac{m}{k}}$. A plot of $T^2$ against mass gives a straight line of slope $4\pi^2/k$.

## Kinetic and Potential Energy in SHM

Whether its a spring, a pendulum or an oscillating column of liquid, there is always an interchange between kinetic energy and potential energy. The sum of them gives the total energy. If no energy is lost to the surroundings, like heat energy and sound energy, the total energy will be constant at all times, and at all positions, of the oscillating mass. Special positions are at the centre, where it's all kinetic energy, and the end points, where it's all potential energy.

$E_p$ = max        $E_p$ = 0         $E_p$ = max
$E_k$ = 0          $E_k$ = max       $E_k$ = 0

x = -A             x = 0             x = +A
                   Equilibrium position

In the real world, oscillating systems gradually slow down and come to a stop. Like the ultimate fate of the universe, they eventually transfer all of their energy to the surroundings as heat. We start with a system where no energy is transferred to the surroundings (the system conserves energy).

The kinetic energy is $\frac{1}{2}mv^2$. On page 126, we derived an expression for the velocity in terms of the position. Multiply both sides of this by ½m:

$$v^2 = \omega^2(A^2 - x^2) \quad \rightarrow \quad E_k = \frac{1}{2}mv^2 = \frac{1}{2}m\omega^2(A^2 - x^2)$$

At x = 0, the kinetic energy is at its maximum:

$$E_k = \frac{1}{2}m\omega^2(A^2 - x^2) = \frac{1}{2}m\omega^2(A^2 - 0) = \frac{1}{2}m\omega^2 A^2$$

At x = 0, there is no potential energy, so this expression is also the total energy. Now use conservation of energy for any position 'x':

$$E_{total} = E_k + E_p \quad \Rightarrow \quad \frac{1}{2}m\omega^2 A^2 = \frac{1}{2}m\omega^2(A^2 - x^2) + E_p \quad \Rightarrow \quad E_p = \frac{1}{2}m\omega^2 x^2$$

A plot of the kinetic energy and potential energy as a function of position (x) on the same axes gives this graph.

Given an amplitude of 4m and a spring constant $k = m\omega^2 = 6\,\text{N m}^{-1}$, gives a total energy of 48 Joules. The two curves cross where the energies are both 24 Joules. Can you show that this occurs at $x = \pm \dfrac{1}{\sqrt{2}} A$ ?

Note that this is as a function of position. Plotting them as functions of time gives cosine squared and sine squared shapes.

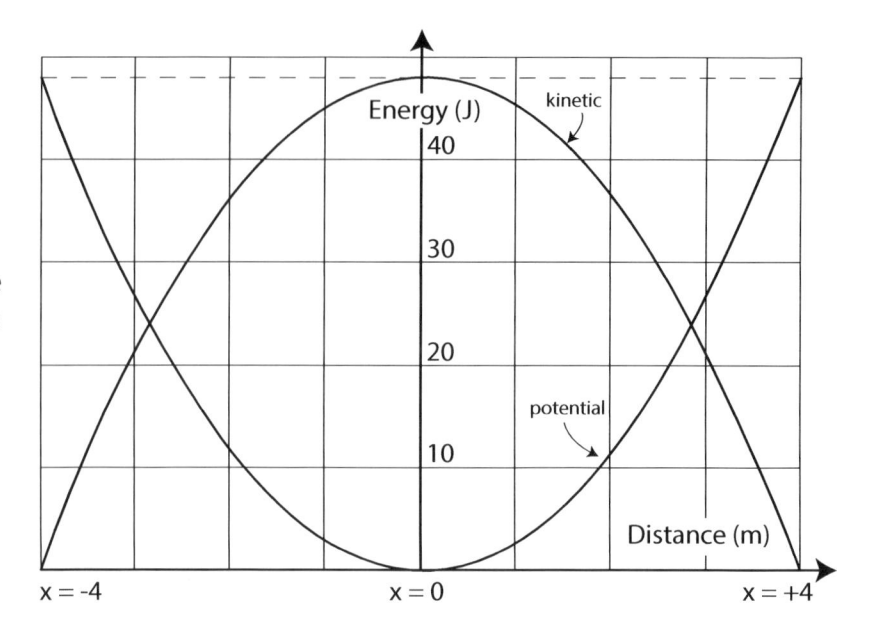

## Damped Simple Harmonic Motion

In the real world, systems lose energy to their surroundings and the oscillations decrease over time. Our simple harmonic motion so far has a restoring force related only to the displacement. Add in another force related to the velocity, and you have damped motion.

$$m\frac{d^2x}{dt^2} + b\frac{dx}{dt} = -kx \quad \Rightarrow \quad x = Ae^{-bt/2m} \cos \omega t \quad \text{where } \omega^2 = \frac{k}{m} - \left(\frac{b}{2m}\right)^2$$

The new term in the middle of the equation of motion introduces the velocity. The constant, 'b', controls how much of an effect it has; taking b = 0 means no effect due to the velocity and the equation of motion reduces to undamped SHM. The example of the spring on page 128 has a mass oscillating in air (this is b = 0). Put the mass in some liquid and you get a non-zero value for 'b'. Note that the solution (x), contains an angular frequency (ω) modified from the undamped value $\omega^2 = \dfrac{k}{m}$. The graph below shows three different 'b' values. In each case A = 1 metre, m = 0.5kg and k = 4N m⁻¹. If you were in a car going over a bump in the road, which graph would you prefer the suspension system to follow?

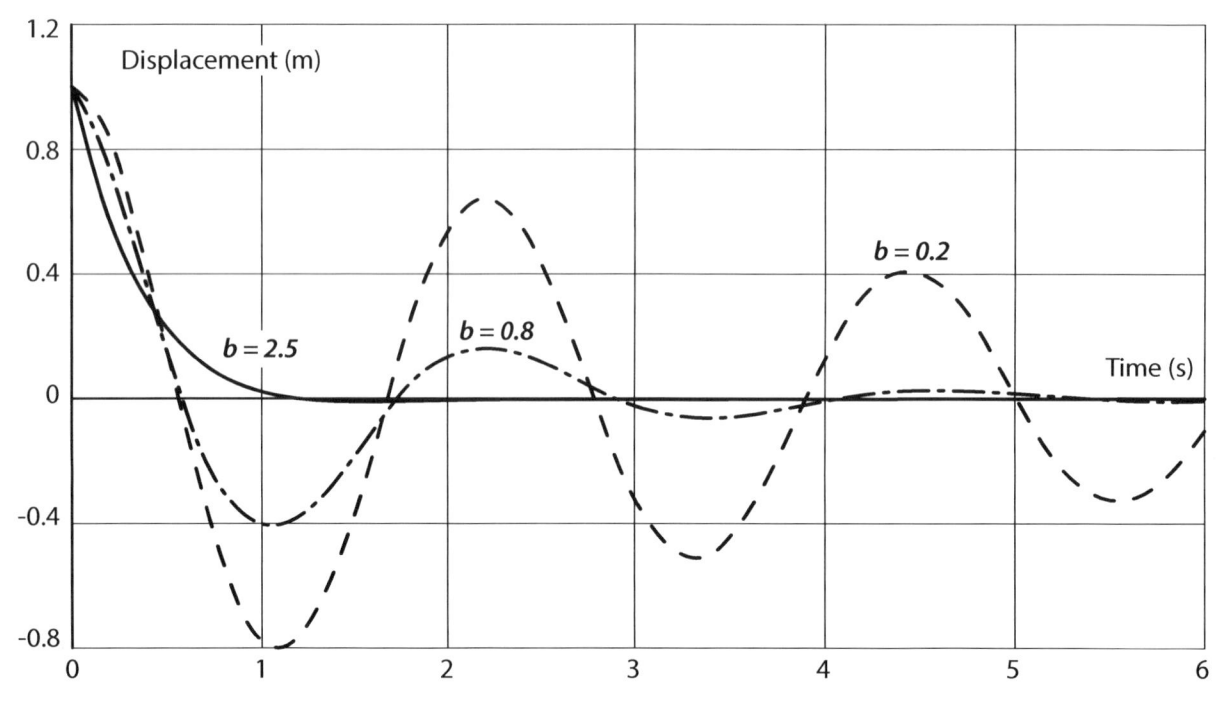

# Quanta & Waves

## Section 2.4 Travelling Waves

Think of a bright spot on an oscilloscope screen. It's at the centre of the screen and the timebase has been switched off (so the spot doesn't move across the way). Apply a sinewave a.c. signal with a frequency of 1Hz to the y-input. The spot bobs up and down (the top diagram). What you are observing is an example of Simple Harmonic Motion. Now bring out your *special* oscilloscope. This is one which shows two spots side-by-side. Apply the same a.c. signal to both and they bob up and down together as a pair. Now reach for your *very special* oscilloscope. This is one with 17 spots all side-by-side lined up along the x-axis. Apply the same a.c. signal to all of them and all the spots bob up and down together, like a horizontal line being lifted up and down.

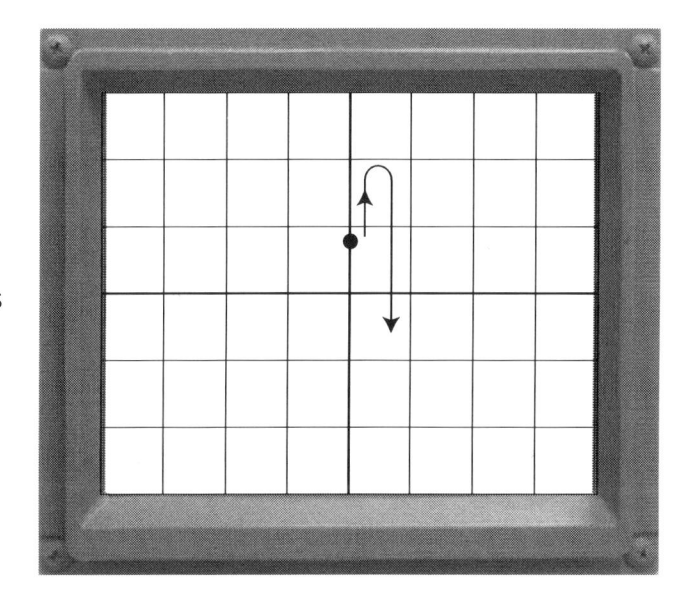

Now for the clever bit. With a frequency of 1Hz, it takes 1s to complete a full bob up and down. Take any spot and impose the condition that the spot on its immediate right is out of step by 0.125s. The spot on your right would reach the top 0.125s later than your spot, and the spot on your left would reach the top 0.125s earlier than your spot. Remember that this rule applies to every spot. If you could watch all 17 spots, what would you observe? The answer is that it would look like the diagram on the right, a sinewave. Two of the spots are arrowed to show where they are going, so the wave crests move rightwards. It's called a **Travelling Wave**. Think of it as a whole series of points following Simple Harmonic Motion with each point being slightly out of step with its neighbour.

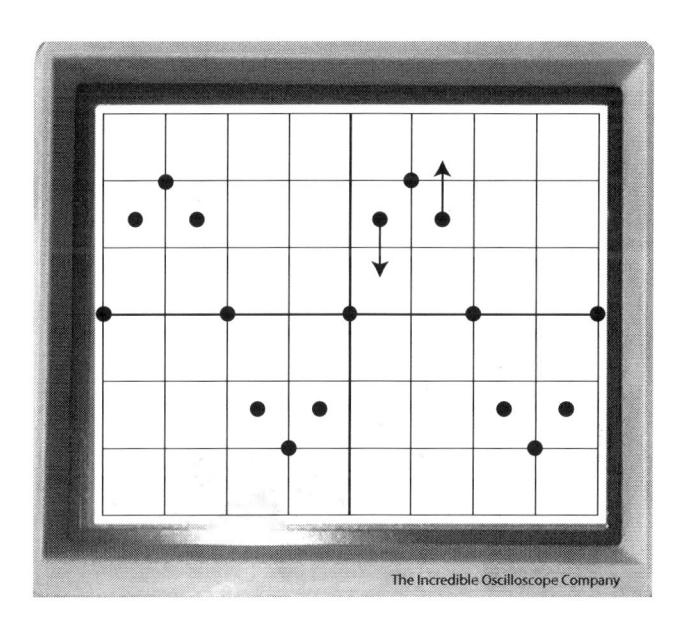

Take the spot in the centre of the screen. It bobs up and down with y-displacement $y = A\sin 2\pi ft$. At time = 0, the spot has a displacement of $y = A\sin 2\pi f \times 0 = 0$ (as in the diagram). How could you work out the y-displacement of the next spot along to the right? It's coming down towards the middle and will reach it at time t = 0.125s. The answer is $y = A\sin 2\pi f(0.125 - t)$. Let's check it. With an amplitude of 2 squares and a frequency of 1Hz, at t = 0 you get:

$$y = A\sin 2\pi f(0.125 - 0) = 2 \times \sin 2\pi \times 1 \times 0.125 = +1.41$$

This looks correct; the y-value is positive and the spot is above the middle line. For the next spot along:

$$y = A\sin 2\pi f(0.25 - 0) = 2 \times \sin 2\pi \times 1 \times 0.25 = +2$$

This is also correct; that spot is at its maximum displacement (above the middle line).

Now imagine not just 17 spots but an infinite number, all tight against each other. This could now be a continuous piece of string vibrating under the action of a sinewave.

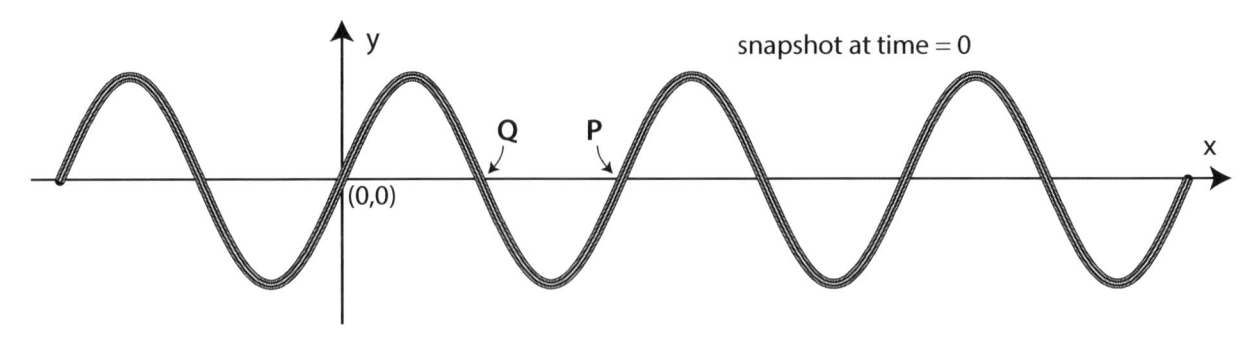

The above diagram shows a snapshot when the clock was started at t = 0. Remember that it's a moving wave; the crests and troughs are 'moving' to the right. The particles of the wave move up and down, but the crest (which is a mathematical point) moves to the right. We want an equation for the y-displacement of a molecule of rope for any 'x' position at any time, that is y = f(x,t). There are a few special 'x' positions and 't' times where we don't need an equation to work out the answer. How about x = λ at time t = T? Starting from the snapshot above, x = λ takes us exactly one wavelength along to the right of the origin, to point 'P'. So the question is, what is the y-displacement of that molecule of string exactly one period later? The answer is y = 0 since we started with y = 0 and went through one complete cycle. Here's another example. What is the y-displacement at x = ½λ at time t = ¼T? Point 'Q' on the diagram is the correct 'x' value, but we need the snapshot at time t = ¼T. If the crest moves to the right, this molecule gets lifted up. One quarter of a period later it will be at the top, so the answer is y = +A , where 'A' is the amplitude.

These were special places and times. To calculate the y-displacement for any 'x' and any 't' requires an equation. Here's a neat way to obtain it. Imagine two observers, OH and OH-Prime. They set up their own co-ordinate systems. OH uses the symbols x and y for his measurements, and stands beside his origin, legs apart. He will see the wave go past him. OH-Prime is energetic and decides to run along at the same speed 'v' as the wave. He has his own co-ordinate system and uses the symbols x' and y' to measure the wave points on the wave. To OH-Prime, it will look as if the wave isn't moving. He won't even need time 't' to describe it, (see the sequence of three diagrams top to bottom). OH-Prime sees a static sine shape with displacement:

$$y' = A\sin\frac{2\pi}{\lambda}x'$$

Now relate x' to x and y' to y using:

$$x' = x - vt \qquad y' = y$$

To give the answer:

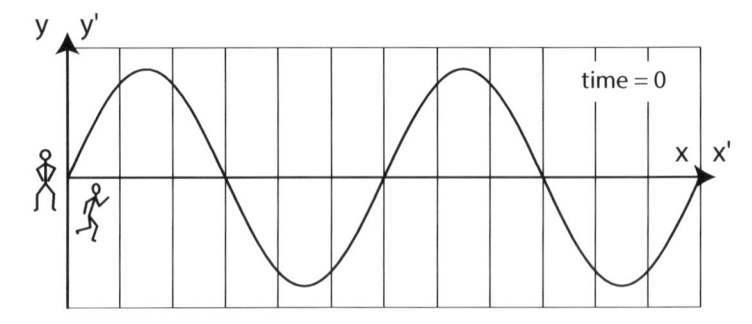

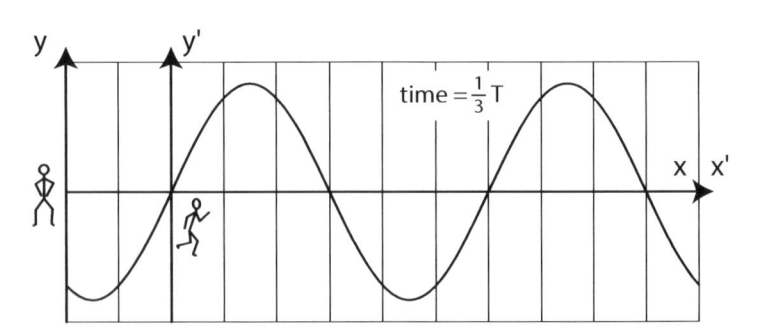

$$y = A\sin\frac{2\pi}{\lambda}(x - vt)$$

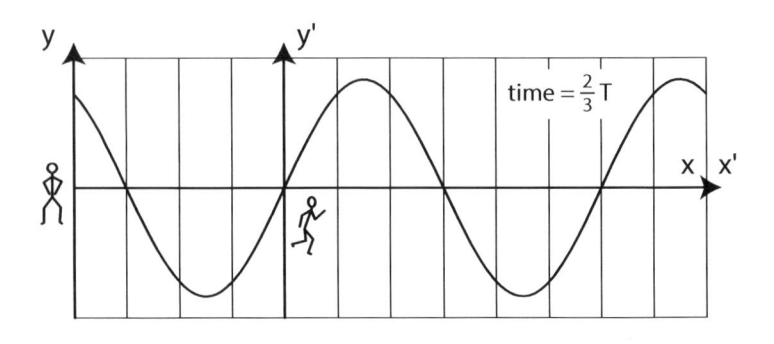

132

# Quanta & Waves

## Example of a Travelling Wave

This is our expression for the displacement: $y = A\sin\frac{2\pi}{\lambda}(x-vt)$. Suppose we have a travelling wave with a wavelength of 4m, an amplitude of 50cm and a wavespeed of 12m s$^{-1}$. Substitute to get:

$$y = A\sin\frac{2\pi}{\lambda}(x-vt) = 0.5\sin\frac{2\pi}{4}(x-12t) = 0.5\sin 2\pi\left(\frac{1}{4}x - 3t\right) = 0.5\sin(1.57x - 18.8t)$$

Notice how the result gets messy when you multiply out the π. It's a good tactic to leave the π in place (or better still, leave in the 2π). It makes it easier to read off the wavelength etc by inspection. You should be able to work both ways; start off with an equation and deduce the wavelength, frequency etc. Before we do that, here are a few alternative ways of expressing the 'y' displacement.

## Alternative Expressions for the Displacement

We can use $v = f\lambda$ and $f = \frac{1}{T}$ to obtain:

$$y = A\sin\frac{2\pi}{\lambda}(x-vt) \Rightarrow y = A\sin\frac{2\pi}{\lambda}(x - f\lambda t) \Rightarrow y = A\sin 2\pi\left(\frac{x}{\lambda} - ft\right) \Rightarrow y = A\sin 2\pi\left(\frac{x}{\lambda} - \frac{t}{T}\right)$$

All of the above describe a sinewave travelling to the **right**. If you imagine running time backwards, the crests would go to the left. This is like changing t → -t, to give the equations:

$$y = A\sin\frac{2\pi}{\lambda}(x+vt) \quad y = A\sin 2\pi\left(\frac{x}{\lambda} + ft\right) \quad y = A\sin 2\pi\left(\frac{x}{\lambda} + \frac{t}{T}\right)$$

These describe waves travelling to the **left** (the negative x-direction). For waves travelling to the right or left, we always have the 'x' part before the 't' part in the expression for the displacement. If you put t = 0 in these expressions, you get $y = A\sin\frac{2\pi}{\lambda}x$. This gives the standard looking sine wave graph. Some authors put the 't' first followed by the x; like this: $y = A\sin\frac{2\pi}{\lambda}(vt-x)$. These are perfectly acceptable, with the minus sign for waves travelling in the positive x-direction and the plus sign for waves travelling in the negative x-direction (as we have). However, there is a catch. At the start time t = 0, you get:

$y = A\sin\frac{2\pi}{\lambda}(0-x) = -A\sin\frac{2\pi}{\lambda}x$, which is an upside-down sinewave for waves travelling to the right. For sinewaves travelling to the left it gives $y = A\sin\frac{2\pi}{\lambda}(0+x) = A\sin\frac{2\pi}{\lambda}x$, which is a proper way-up sinewave. If you choose this system, make sure and draw the correct sinewave at the start time.

## Examples

Check through the three examples below and understand them. The technique is to take out a 2π and read off what's inside the bracket:

$$y = 6\sin 2\pi(0.1x - 25t) \leftrightarrow y = A\sin 2\pi\left(\frac{x}{\lambda} - ft\right) \Rightarrow A = 6\text{m} \quad \lambda = 10\text{m} \quad f = 25\text{Hz} \quad (v = f\lambda = 250\text{ms}^{-1})$$

$$y = 0.4\sin(3x - 7t) = 0.4\sin 2\pi\left(\frac{3}{2\pi}x - \frac{7}{2\pi}t\right) \Rightarrow A = 0.4\text{m} \quad \lambda = \frac{2\pi}{3}\text{m} \quad f = \frac{7}{2\pi}\text{Hz} \quad \left(v = f\lambda = \frac{7}{3}\text{ms}^{-1}\right)$$

$$y = 1.5\cos(0.2x + 15t) = 1.5\cos 2\pi\left(\frac{0.2}{2\pi}x + \frac{15}{2\pi}t\right) \Rightarrow A = 1.5\text{m} \quad \lambda = \frac{2\pi}{0.2}\text{m} \quad f = \frac{15}{2\pi}\text{Hz} \quad (v = f\lambda = 75\text{ms}^{-1})$$

In which directions are the crests moving? (answers: right, right, left).

*Nerdy Note:* Any self-respecting nerd will want to know that the displacement expression:

- Is a function of two variables f(x,t), so you must input two things.
- We've used a sine function, so y = 0 at x = t = 0.
- A cosine expression is just as good as a sine function, but y = A at x = t = 0.
- The formula isn't 'a wave equation'. The formula is the *solution* to a wave equation. The wave equation is: $\frac{\partial^2 y}{\partial x^2} = \frac{1}{v^2}\frac{\partial^2 y}{\partial t^2}$. The funny symbols are like 'differentiation', $\frac{d^2 y}{dx^2}$ etc. The constant '$v$' is the speed of the wave.
- The discussion so far has been about transverse waves. The same equation describes longitudinal waves (like sound waves). The solution is the same, but the displacement is along the x-direction (possible confusion with symbols).
- At university, they introduce the quantity $k = \frac{2\pi}{\lambda}$. Combined with $\omega = \frac{2\pi}{T}$ the displacement is then written as: $y = A\sin(kx - \omega t)$ or $y = A\sin(\omega t - kx)$.
- You already know that the angular frequency is the number of radians produced in unit time (the second). So ω = 4π rad s⁻¹ is two complete waves in one second. The '$k$' number is the number of radians produced in unit length (the metre). So $k$ = 8π rads m⁻¹ is four complete waves in one metre; a wavelength of 0.25m. Expressing it this way makes the distance and time parts look more symmetrical.

## Stationary Waves

Where two waves meet, interference takes place. When a crest from one wave momentarily lines up with a crest from another wave, we get constructive interference. When a crest from one wave meets a trough from another wave, we get destructive interference. If the waves are of equal amplitude, two crests will make a crest of twice the amplitude, and a crest and trough will cancel out.

Some waves need a medium ('stuff') to travel through, like sound waves or waves on a string. Other waves don't need a medium, like light waves. Consider a wave on a string. Suppose you attached a vibration generator to one end of the string and another identical vibration generator to the other end of the string. If money was tight, you could make-do with the apparatus shown below:

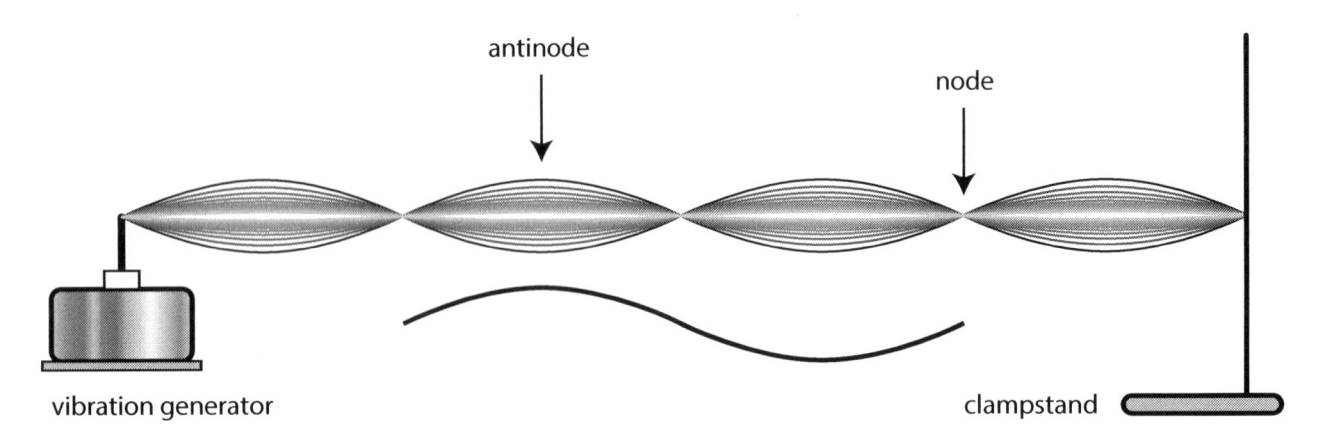

The wave sent out by the generator travels from left to right. We could model it mathematically with our travelling wave containing a minus sign in the bracket. The wave reflects off the clampstand and travels from right to left, so gets modelled by a travelling wave with a plus sign inside the bracket. What is the string to make of all this? What does it do? Does it get confused?

No, it's a simple physical object so obeys the laws of physics. This is the Principle of Superposition, which states: the resultant displacement at a point is the sum of the individual displacements from each wave.

# Quanta & Waves

What the result looks like on the string is shown on the diagram. It looks blurry because it's moving quickly and your eyes/brain can't keep up. The unexpected thing is that some points on the string don't move! They're called 'nodes' and are spaced half a wavelength apart. The in-between points are called 'antinodes' and locate the positions of maximum amplitude.

Here's the maths. Like good physicists, we keep things simple. Assume the waves are of equal amplitude (of magnitude 1 unit), which means no energy loss on reflection at the clampstand. You should keep the clampstand rigid, otherwise it will vibrate and remove energy from the wave. Okay, apply the Principle of Superposition (just add the amplitudes):

$$y_{result} = y_\rightarrow + y_\leftarrow = 1 \times \sin 2\pi \left( \frac{x}{\lambda} - ft \right) + 1 \times \sin 2\pi \left( \frac{x}{\lambda} + ft \right)$$

This is the answer. The problem is that humans aren't clever enough to be able to picture it as a shifting pattern on a string. A few lines of mathematics will change it to a form where we can picture the string. The difficulty comes from having distance and time variables in two separate places (one pair in each sine function). What we will do, is change it so that it is a product of two functions, one a function of time, and the other a function of distance. Once we've finished, you'll see how this is easy to visualise. You may remember these trigonometric identities:

$$\sin(P+Q) = \sin P \cos Q + \cos P \sin Q \qquad \sin(P-Q) = \sin P \cos Q - \cos P \sin Q$$

This is like our travelling waves; two sine functions, one with a plus sign, one with a minus. Add them:

$$\sin(P-Q) + \sin(P+Q) = \sin P \cos Q - \cos P \sin Q + \sin P \cos Q + \cos P \sin Q = 2 \sin P \cos Q$$

Now apply it to our waves with $P \equiv \frac{2\pi x}{\lambda}$ and $Q \equiv 2\pi ft$. This gives:

$$y_{result} = \sin 2\pi \left( \frac{x}{\lambda} - ft \right) + \sin 2\pi \left( \frac{x}{\lambda} + ft \right) = 2 \sin \frac{2\pi x}{\lambda} \cos 2\pi ft$$

- the '2' outside means the amplitude is double the individual waves
- the basic shape in space is a sinewave, $\sin \frac{2\pi x}{\lambda}$
- that basic shape is multiplied by a number (cos2πft) which varies between +1 and -1

| Time 't' | Basic sinewave shape | Multiplied by | Result on string |
|---|---|---|---|
| 0 | ∿ | cos 0 – 1 | ∿ |
| ¼T | ∿ | cos 2π¼ = 0 | — |
| ½T | ∿ | cos 2π½ = -1 | ∿ |
| ¾T | ∿ | cos 2π¾ = 0 | — |
| T | ∿ | cos 2π = 1 | ∿ |

The first column shows the times at simple fractions of a period 'T'. The second column is the basic sinewave shape. The third column works out the time dependent number, the number by which we multiply the basic sinewave shape. The last column is the result on the string. Imagine running it as a time sequence from top to bottom. In an experiment, the frequency is usually too high to see the motion of the string; it looks blurred. But what you don't see are crests travelling to the right or left. The antinodal points oscillate up and down between crest and trough. The diagram on page 134 also shows a snapshot of the middle part of the wave; it's exactly one wavelength long and goes from one nodal point through to the second node along (not just node to neighbouring node). If you measure this wavelength with a metrestick and read off the frequency from the signal generator, you can calculate the wavespeed of the interfering waves using: $v = f\lambda$. If you use white string, turn down the lights in the lab, and turn on a stroboscope with the same frequency as the generator, the string looks as if it has stopped moving. Can you explain why?

## Beat Frequency

The stationary waves were produced from two signals of the same frequency. You can use two signals with different frequencies but you usually get a complicated changing pattern along the string. This next section is an example of two waves of different frequency interfering at **one point** in space. We use the same travelling wave equations as before, and to make life easy, take the single point in space at $x = 0$. This gives:

$$y_1 = A \sin 2\pi f_1 t \quad y_2 = A \sin 2\pi f_2 t$$

Two signal generators provide the two different frequencies. They are attached to a loudspeaker, with the cone effectively the 'one point in space'. Take both amplitudes as $A = 1$ and apply the principle of superposition:

$$y_{result} = y_1 + y_2 = \sin 2\pi f_1 t + \sin 2\pi f_2 t$$

As before, we need a bit of trigonometry to get it in a form where we can 'picture' it. Use the identity:

$$\sin C + \sin D = 2\sin\frac{1}{2}(C+D)\cos\frac{1}{2}(C-D)$$

With our symbols:

$$y_{result} = 2\sin 2\pi\left(\frac{f_1+f_2}{2}\right)t \, \cos 2\pi\left(\frac{f_1-f_2}{2}\right)t$$

There are three parts to the answer.

- The '2' for the amplitude means the maximum displacement of the loudspeaker cone is twice that of any individual signal.
- The sine function contains half the sum of the two frequencies, that is, the average frequency.
- The cosine function contains half the difference of the two frequencies.

**Example** Frequencies of 20Hz and 21Hz would give the resultant displacement:

$$y_{result} = 2\sin 2\pi\left(\frac{21+20}{2}\right)t \, \cos 2\pi\left(\frac{21-20}{2}\right)t = 2\sin 2\pi 20.5t \, \cos 2\pi 0.5t$$

This is a high frequency sinewave (20.5Hz) modulated by a low frequency cosine (0.5Hz). Played through a loudspeaker, you hear a 'wow wow wow' sound, the noise of the beats. A loud 'wow' is heard when the crests of the two waves (21Hz and 20Hz) roughly coincide in time. Although the low freq-

# Quanta & Waves

uency cosine modulation has a frequency of 0.5Hz, the beats have a frequency of twice this, since a 'wow' also occurs when the two troughs line up. The two waves go through a cycle of: two crests line up, crest cancels trough, two troughs line up, trough cancels crest, etc. The beat frequency is ($f_1 - f_2$).

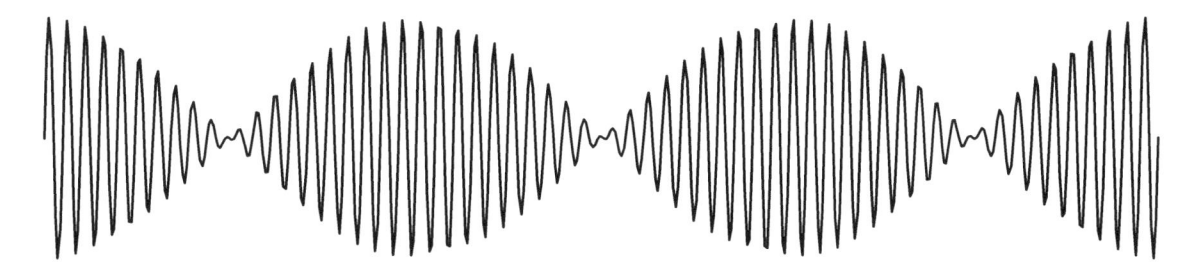

The diagram above is for equal amplitudes. If the 20Hz signal is halved in amplitude, you get this:

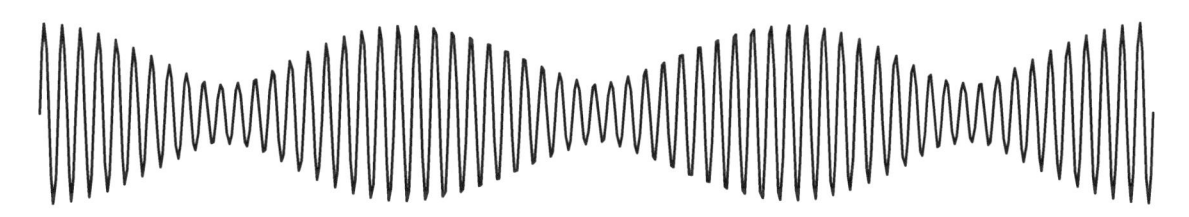

In both cases, the 'wow-wow-wow' sound of the beat frequency stays the same. With unequal amplitudes, the 'wow-wow-wow' is less distinct.

## Harmonics and Music

Whole number multiples of a pure note are called harmonics. A first harmonic of $f_1$ = 300Hz has a second harmonic of $f_2$ = 600Hz, a third harmonic of $f_3$ = 900Hz and so on. Musical instruments produce a first harmonic (also called the 'fundamental') with higher harmonics of reduced amplitude. Here is the result of starting from a fundamental frequency $f_1$ and adding harmonics:

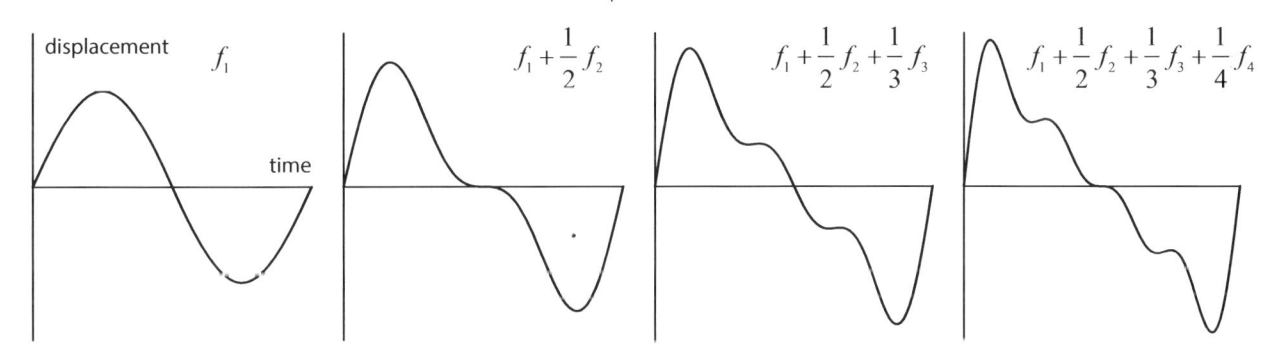

## Fourier Analysis

Any repeating waveform can be decomposed into a series of sine and cosine waves. The graph below is roughly a squarewave in shape and is the result of a sum of (odd numbered) sine functions:

$$y = \sin \omega t + \frac{1}{3}\sin 3\omega t + \frac{1}{5}\sin 5\omega t + \frac{1}{7}\sin 7\omega t + \frac{1}{9}\sin 9\omega t + \frac{1}{11}\sin 11\omega t \qquad \omega = 2\pi f$$

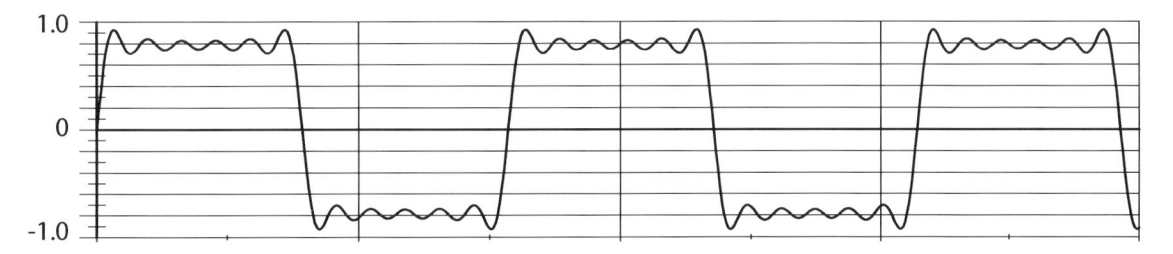

137

# Section 2.5 Interference

The study of optics is divided into geometrical optics (treating light as rays), physical optics (treating light as a wave) and quantum optics (the interaction of light with atoms). This chapter looks at the most important part of physical optics, the interference of light, and then concludes with an introduction to polarisation. Before launching into it, we must prepare the ground by learning about coherence, and understanding the importance of the different types and shapes of light source.

Interference is what you get when two waves meet at the same place at the same time. The wavelength of light is short (400nm – 700nm), and combined with its high speed ($3 \times 10^8$m s$^{-1}$), you get an extremely high frequency (about 600THz). This means that if two crests overlapped for one instant in time, then they won't stay like that for long, certainly not long enough for us to observe, before they get quickly out of step. Interference of waves takes place all the time, no matter what the waves are like. Our problem is to keep it constant for long enough so that we can make measurements. The short wavelength isn't just a problem, it's a gift. If the two waves move apart by only half a wavelength, you go from constructive to destructive interference, something which is easy to observe and measure. For red light, that's a distance of only 0.3μm, so interference is a very precise method for measuring changes in distance.

So how do you keep an interference pattern constant? For a start, interference patterns never stay frozen. Remember that these waves are moving in time; watching a region of constructive interference with two water waves doesn't produce a permanent big crest, it produces permanent rough water (cycling through big crests and deep troughs). The question becomes, how do you maintain this pattern? Keeping the frequency of the two waves the same is sensible. If the two crests coincide at one time, they will always stay in step. These waves are described as **coherent**; the phase relation of one wave to the other stays constant. An alternative definition of coherence comes from the way we calculate the intensity. You may recall that for a single wave, the intensity is proportional to the square of the amplitude. For two coherent waves, you add the amplitudes first, then square to get the total intensity. For two incoherent waves, you square the amplitudes first, then add to get the total intensity. How about the height of the wave? Two waves of different amplitude will never give complete cancellation even if 180° out of step; you need waves of equal amplitude.

This isn't the whole story. A filament lightbulb produces waves about 2 metres long (that's the length of the 'ray' from end to end, not the wavelength) and all these 'wavetrains', as they are called, are out of step with each other. So even if one pair of wavetrains produced constructive interference, the next ones along probably won't. This means that we have to consider the source and its characteristics.

A Laser is an ideal source. It produces (coherent) light of a single wavelength with every wavetrain in step. As a source, it is the first choice in laboratory experiments, but if it was the only possibility, there wouldn't be any interferometers used in Astronomy (which there are; see later on measuring the diameters of stars pages 148/149). Non-Laser sources, like filament lightbulbs or fluorescent tubes, consist of zillions of little atomic radiators (remember an electron jumping down to a lower orbital?) The atoms are completely unco-ordinated and emit a range of different wavelengths. An improvement would be a monochromatic incoherent source like a sodium lamp. This could be used if the interfering wavetrains can be made coherent. The solution is to do one of two things. These go under the heading of 'interference by division of amplitude' and 'interference by division of the wavefront'.

# Quanta & Waves

**Interference by Division of the Wavefront:** If you drop a stone into a pond of calm water, circular wave crests radiate outwards. Each point on a continuous crest is in step ('in phase'). This crest is an example of a 'wavefront'. A wavefront doesn't have to be a crest, but every point along the line should be in step. If you direct a wavefront towards two narrow gaps (in the simplest case, the wavefront would reach the two gaps at the same time, as in the diagram below), the two circular waves emerging on the other side would have a constant phase difference (and in the simplest case, be in phase). When the two parts of the wavefront go through the gaps, the wavefront gets 'divided up'; hence the name. Dropping the stone in the pond to produce circular wavefronts is like having a point source, and this would be the appropriate type of light source to use. The point source could be either a very small filament or it could be an extended source with a pinhole in front of it. The pinhole effectively becomes the source even though it doesn't produce the light energy. In addition, the wavefronts reaching the two gaps don't have to be circular; straight wavefronts would also work (in water, you could easily produce them using a ruler; with light you would use a convex lens). Our example of interference by division of the wavefront is the Young's Slits experiment (see later, page 146). One last point to consider. Would a star make a good point source? They look very point-like in the sky, but most of them are over one million miles in diameter. Point source?

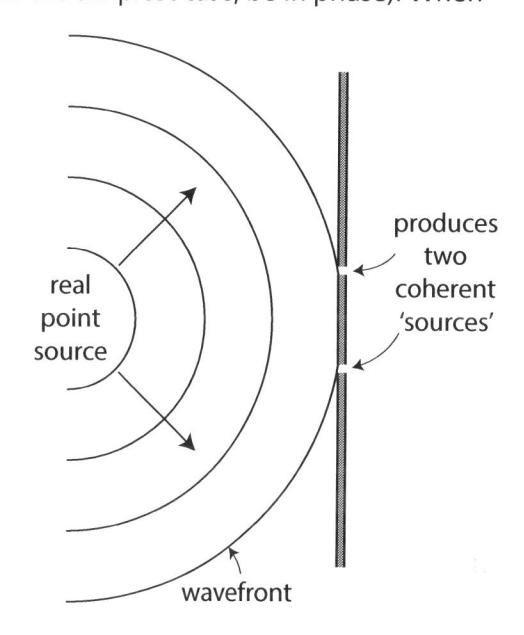

**Interference by Division of Amplitude:** This is where we take a ray of light from a source and split it into two by partial reflection/partial refraction at the surface of a block of glass (diagram below). The two split rays will be coherent since they started from the same initial ray. The source doesn't even have to be a point. Rays emitted from different positions on an extended source (like a discharge lamp) will all be split in two and thus always produce coherent pairs. Once split, the two coherent rays are made to traverse different paths. They are then recombined, where interference takes place. The type of interference produced, constructive or destructive, gives us information about the difference in path traversed by the two rays. The path difference between the two routes shouldn't be longer than the length of a wavetrain (about 2m). If it is too long, the wavetrain taking the shorter route will have passed through the interference area before its split partner reaches it. The ray taking the longer route will be incoherent with the next wavetrain. Most of this chapter is based on examples of interference by division of amplitude, but before we launch into it, we take a short diversion into 'path difference', and an unexpected complication with reflection.

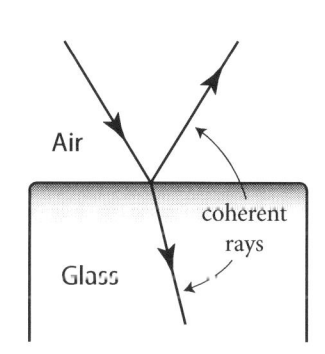

## The Path of a Ray

The wavelength of the wave below is 3cm in air, and the straight distance from point 'A' to point 'B' is 24cm. How many waves will fit between 'A' and 'B'? It's not a trick question; the answer is 8 waves.

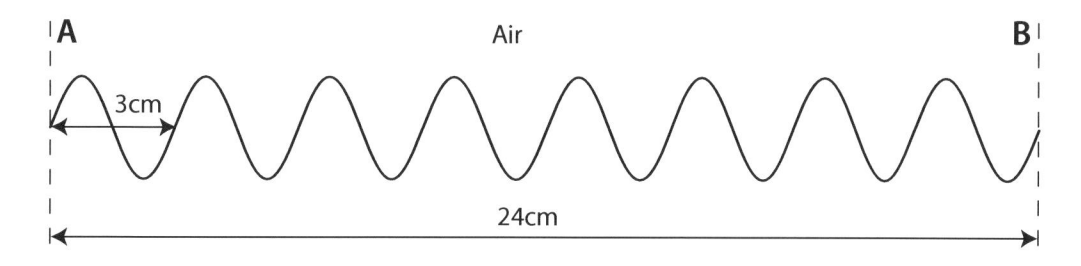

Suppose we now place a 12cm long block of glass in the middle. Does it still take eight complete waves to fit between 'A' and 'B'? You know that the wavelength is shortened in glass so the answer is no. The refractive index 'n' of the material gives us the relation between the wavelengths in air and glass:

$$n = \frac{\lambda_{air}}{\lambda_{glass}}$$

For glass of refractive index 1.5, a wavelength in air of 3cm will give:

$$n = \frac{\lambda_{air}}{\lambda_{glass}} \quad \Rightarrow \quad 1.5 = \frac{3}{\lambda_{glass}} \quad \Rightarrow \quad \lambda_{glass} = 2\text{cm}$$

In a 12cm long block of glass, this will fit 6 waves. The remaining 12cm of air between 'A' and 'B' will fit 4 waves of 3cm each. The exact position of the block doesn't matter; placed centrally it looks like:

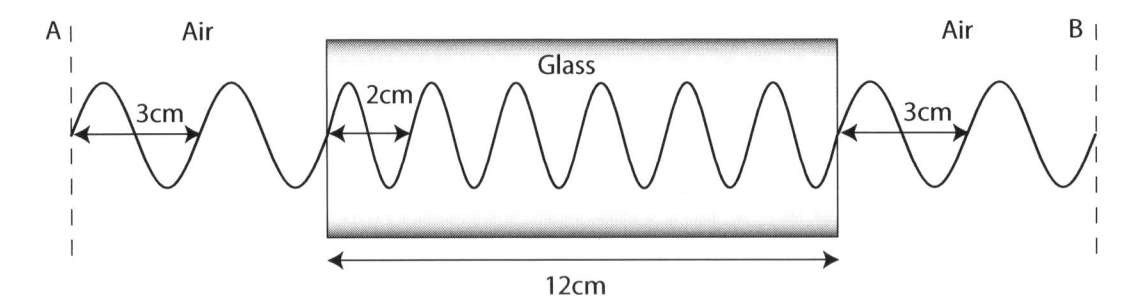

In air, it took eight waves to go from 'A' to 'B'. It takes 10 waves with the glass. Placing a ruler between 'A' and 'B' would give a reading of 24cm. This is called the **Geometric Path Length**. The wave has a wavelength of 3cm in air but requires 10 waves to reach point 'B'. Although it's 24cm from 'A' to 'B', it traverses the equivalent of 30cm of air to get from 'A' to 'B'. This is called the **Optical Path Length**.

Suppose we have two rays starting out in phase from A and A' (diagram below), with one going through a block of glass on the way, and the other going through air. On reaching the finish line, from B to B', they are brought to a focus at 'C' using a convex lens, where they interfere.

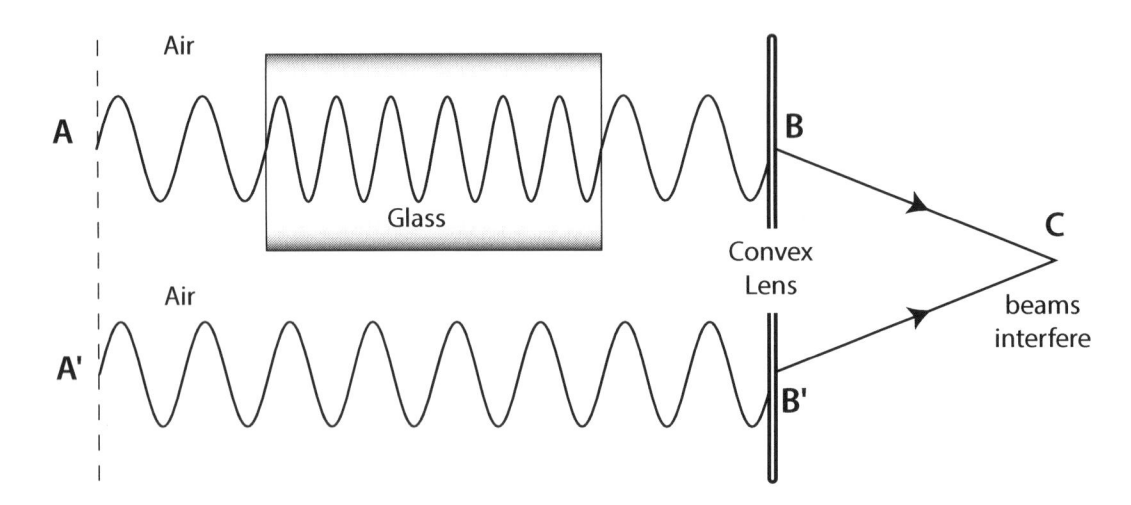

At 'C', is it constructive, destructive, or something in between, interference? What we need, is the difference between the two routes. From the diagram, we can see that the top route requires two more wavelengths than the bottom route (we can ignore B to C and B' to C since they are identical). The geometric path lengths are the same, but the optical path lengths are different (the top route is 'optically' longer by $2\lambda$). The **Optical Path Difference** equals $2\lambda$ and so produces constructive interference. Remember that the optical path is related to the geometric path through the refractive index '$n$'. (In the discussion, I've used air as the surrounding gas. Strictly speaking, it should be a vacuum.)

# Quanta & Waves

## Example 1

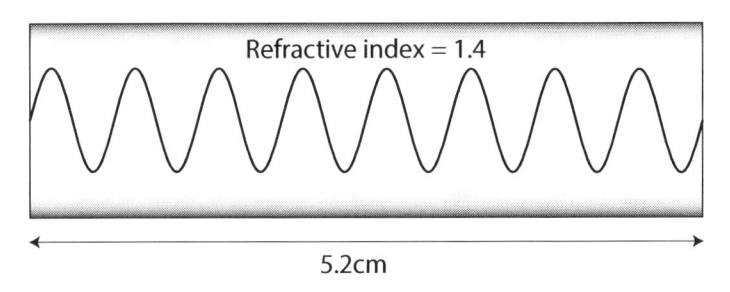

Geometric Path = 5.2cm

Optical Path = ☐× Geometric Path

$= 1.4 \times 5.2 = 7.28$cm

## Example 2

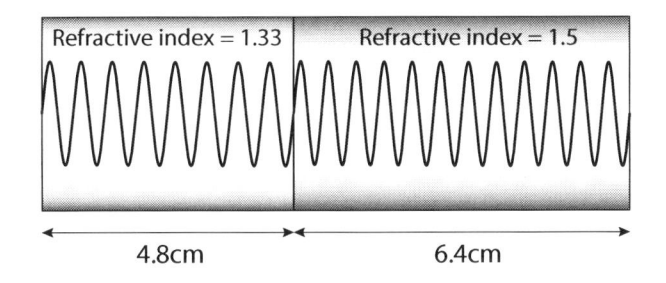

Geometric Path $= 4.8 + 6.4 = 11.2$cm

Optical Path $= 1.33 \times 4.8 + 1.5 \times 6.4$
$= 15.984$cm

## Complications on Reflection

I'll state the result first, then try to justify it. When a lightwave reflects off a surface of higher refractive index, it receives an additional phase shift of 180º (π radians). This doesn't happen if it reflects off a surface of lower refractive index (as in total internal reflection). This complication is important when calculating optical paths. What would have been constructive interference could become destructive interference (since the reflection corresponds to a phase shift of half a wavelength). Proving the statement requires Maxwell's Equations (about 3 years in advance of your present knowledge), so most authors resort to some dozy waffle about waves on a string reflecting off trees. But not us.

A better argument is due to Stokes, and relies upon the principle of the reversibility of light. Reflect a beam of light of amplitude 'a' off a surface of higher refractive index (left diagram). The symbols 'r' and 't' are fractions less than one, so the quantity 'ar' is the amplitude of the reflected wave and 'at' is the amplitude of the transmitted wave. The left diagram has two outgoing beams of light. The principle

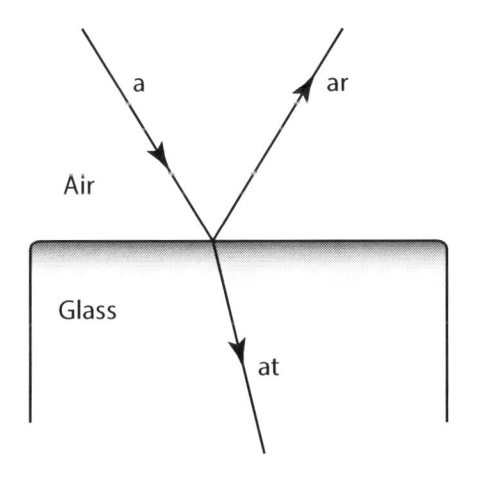

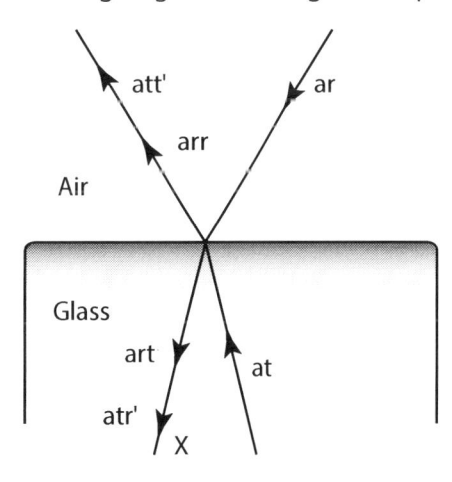

of the reversibility of light says that if we reverse these two beams, we should recover what we started with. This gives the right diagram. You'll notice an extra beam of light 'X'. It shouldn't be there, so the two amplitudes which generate it, must add up to zero:

$$art + atr' = 0 \quad \Rightarrow \quad at(r + r') = 0 \quad \Rightarrow \quad (r + r') = 0$$

141

Having two separate transmission fractions t and t', allows for the possibility that going from air to glass is different from going from glass to air. Similarly with r and r', where reflection on the air side may be different (which it is) from reflection on the glass side. Now recall that these beams represent wave motion. To prevent clutter on the diagram, I didn't write the incident beam as $a\sin\omega t$. I just wrote the amplitude 'a'. If you write the sine functions back in for all the beams, destructive interference for beam 'X' is achieved by adding a 180º phase shift to one of the beams:

$$r\sin(\omega t + \pi) + r'\sin\omega t = 0 \qquad |r| = |r'|$$

Adding in the π phase shift is the only way to get rid of beam 'X'. This shows that reflection from the top surface is 180º out of step with reflection from inside the glass. However, it doesn't reveal which reflection gets the shift; you have to supplement Stokes' analysis with experimental observation. Now reread the first three sentences of this section again.

## Interference by Division of the Amplitude

Here are three examples: the thin film, the air wedge and Newton's Rings. This is the basic diagram for the thin film:

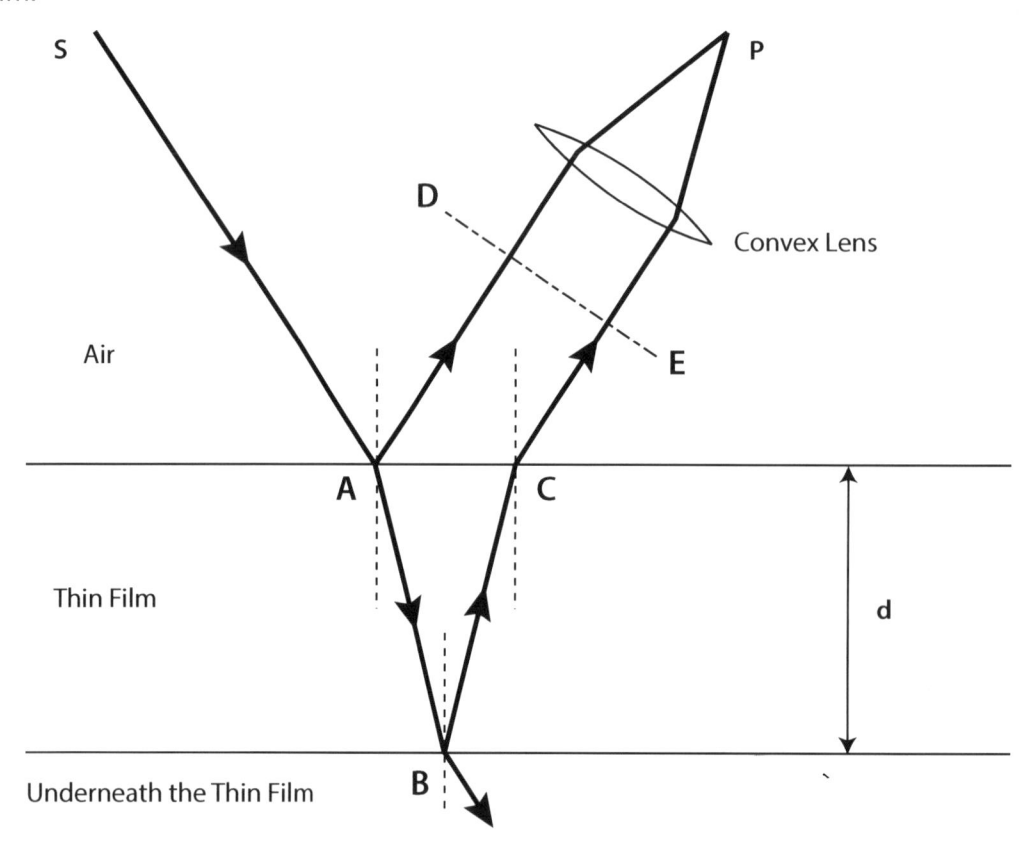

A monochromatic, moderately extended source is suitable. A beam (wavetrain) from 'S' strikes the top surface of a thin transparent layer (the 'thin film') at 'A'. The beam is partly reflected and partly transmitted (division of amplitude). The transmitted beam is then (partly) reflected from the bottom surface of the thin film back up to point 'C', where it is refracted into the air. The two emerging beams are parallel. What is the phase relation of the two beams where they cross the line DE? If they are in phase along this line, the line will be a wavefront, and the convex lens will produce constructive interference when the beams are focussed at 'P' (the convex lens could be your eye lens and point 'P' could be on your retina). We need to calculate the optical path difference between the two beams. We expect it to depend upon the thickness of the thin film, the refractive index of the thin film, the angle of the initial beam, and possibly the complication of the extra 180º phase shift on reflection. In this course, we make life easy and only consider an angle of incidence of zero degrees (point 'S' vertically above point 'A'). This is described as 'normally' incident light. Drawn this way, the diagram would have all the beams on top of each other and obscure the physics, so let's redraw the diagram with the beam slightly tilted.

# Quanta & Waves

The geometric path difference is due to the beam in the thin film having to go down and back up, a distance of 2d. The thin film has refractive index 'n ', so the geometric path difference of 2d becomes an optical path difference of 2nd. Lastly, there is the phase shift on reflection. Starting from air, there will always be a 180º shift to the reflected beam. The question is; what happens at the bottom surface 'B'? The answer is; it depends on the material underneath. If its refractive index is greater than the thin film, there will be a phase shift of 180º at 'B' (resulting in a phase shift at both reflections, so they cancel out and you can ignore it). If the refractive index of the material underneath is less than the thin film, there will not be a phase shift (so it only occurs at the top surface).

The most common case is where the refractive index of the material underneath is greater than that of the thin film. This is used in camera lens coatings where a thin film (usually of magnesium fluoride, refractive index n = 1.38) is deposited onto the glass lens (of n = 1.52). There is no 'π' phase shift to worry about. In lens coatings, the idea is to reduce reflections, thereby increasing transmission through the lens. This requires destructive interference of the reflected beams, so the optical path difference should be a half integer number of wavelengths:

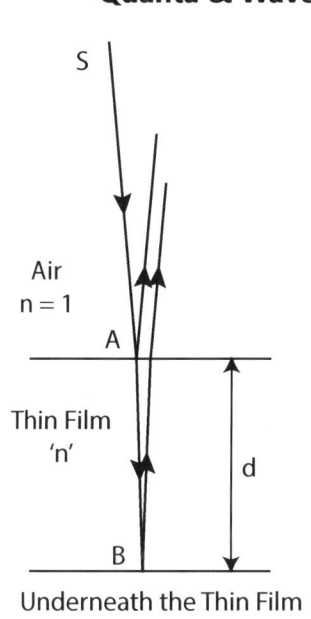

$$2n_{film}d = \frac{1}{2}\lambda \quad \Rightarrow \quad d = \frac{\lambda}{4n_{film}}$$

**Example** Calculate the thickness of the magnesium fluoride coating required to cause destructive interference of reflected light of wavelength 550nm.

$$d = \frac{\lambda}{4n_{film}} = \frac{550 \times 10^{-9}}{4 \times 1.38} = 1.0 \times 10^{-7} \text{m} \quad (= 0.1 \mu\text{m})$$

This thickness of coating will destructively interfere the reflected light of that specific wavelength. It will be less effective as you move to longer or shorter wavelengths. If white light is shone on the lens, the reflected light will have a purple cast to it ('purple' = an arty combination of blue and red), and the transmitted light will have a slight greeny-yellow cast. We also assumed normally incident light, so the coating is also less effective for light coming in at an angle. To give you an idea of the figures, an uncoated lens reflects about 4% of the light, a lens with a single layer coating reflects about 1% of the light, and a lens with an expensive multi layer coating (each one of different thickness) reflects only about 0.1% of the incident light.

*Nerdy Note* Nerds will be asking how it's possible for more light to be transmitted when the reflected beams cancel. The answer is 'wavetrains'. A 2m long wavetrain is composed of many sine and cosine waves. Part of a wavetrain is in the reflected beam and part of it is in the transmitted beam. When destructive interference occurs in the reflected part, the sine and cosine waves rearrange themselves along the length of the wavetrain, resulting in a greater amplitude in the transmitted part.

## Petrol Stains & Soap Bubbles

Both provide thin, parallel, reflecting interfaces for an interference effect. Road surfaces are rough. A shower of rain leaves a puddle of water and makes the surface smooth. A car leaving a petrol stain on top of the puddle provides the thin film. The sun shines white light on the thin film. With the refractive index dependent upon the wavelength of light, you get different optical path lengths, producing constructive interference at slightly different angles for each colour of light.

Soap films have air on each side of the film. If the bubble expands, it will change the thickness of the film and the angles at which the different colours constructively interfere.

## The Air Wedge

The thin films we've discussed were of uniform thickness. The next example is a 'thin film' of air wedged between two flat glass slides with the air gap getting progressively wider. The arrangement is shown below, with the glass slides touching at one end and held apart at the other end by something very small (tradition demands a human hair which varies from 20-50μm for fair hair, to 50-180μm for black hair). The angle 'θ' is greatly exaggerated in the diagram.

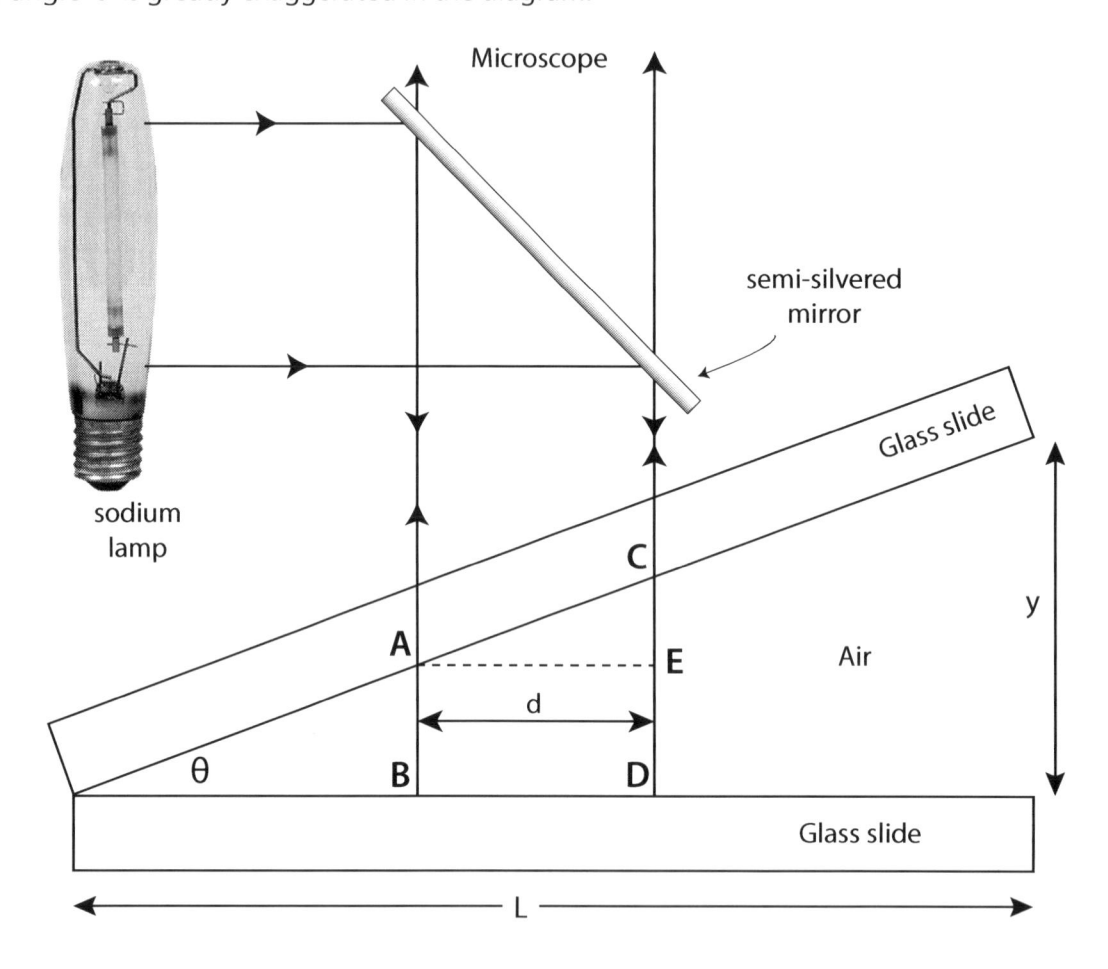

With four surfaces, there are several possibilities for interference. We consider the interference taking place between the beams reflected from the bottom surface of the top glass slide (like 'A' and 'C') and the top surface of the bottom glass slide (like 'B' and 'D'). The problem of having a source and an observer directly above (so we can have normal incidence) is solved by using a semi-silvered mirror. This lets half the light through (so you can see with the microscope) and reflects the other half (so the source can illuminate the air wedge). Two beams are shown. The left-hand beam conceals a beam reflected at 'A' plus the beam reflected from 'B', the latter having gone through a thickness of air from 'A' to 'B' and back up to 'A'. Assume the optical path difference produces constructive interference for this beam. If we move along to the right, the air wedge gets thicker and the optical path difference will increase. When we reach the right-hand beam (CD), we will have increased the optical path by a whole wavelength. Once again, we achieve constructive interference.

The question is, how far along do we have to move? In the diagram, this has the symbol 'd'. The additional path required is from point 'C' to point 'E' and back up to 'C'. By trigonometry:

$$\tan\theta = \frac{CE}{\Box} \quad \text{but,} \quad 2CE = \lambda \quad \Rightarrow \quad \Box = \frac{\lambda}{2\tan\theta}$$

If the length of the glass slide is 'L' and the human hair at the right hand end has thickness 'y', this gives:

$$\tan\theta = \frac{y}{L} \quad \Rightarrow \quad d = \frac{\lambda L}{2y}$$

# Quanta & Waves

Notice that we didn't have to bother about phase shifts at the reflections. Both left and right beams have to undergo the same process, so any differences cancel out. If you look down the microscope, what do you see? The glass slides are hinged at the left end. Constructive interference will occur where the path through the air has a constant thickness. This is parallel to the hinge, so you will see straight bright parallel lines (called 'fringes').

In practice, you have to keep the glass slides very clean, but with the wavelength of light being so small, the slightest blemish away from a mathematically perfect wedge usually produces clapped-out angled fringes. The photo opposite is fairly typical.

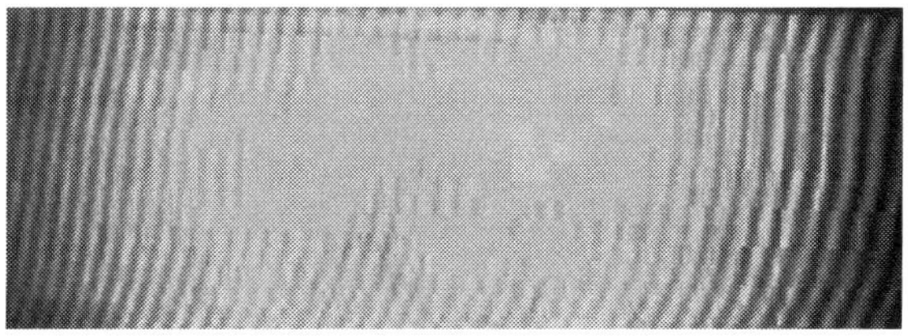

When observing through the low power microscope, focus on the air wedge. One final point. The dark and bright fringes are observed with the highest contrast, not only when the amplitudes of the interfering waves are equal, but also when other bright reflections don't flood the field of view.

## Newton's Rings

This is a variation on the air wedge. Instead of two flat glass slides, we have one flat surface and one curved. The flat surface is a plain piece of glass and the curved surface is usually a plano-convex lens sitting on top. They make a single point of contact. The fringes will be circular since this is the locus of points of constant air thickness (optical path difference).

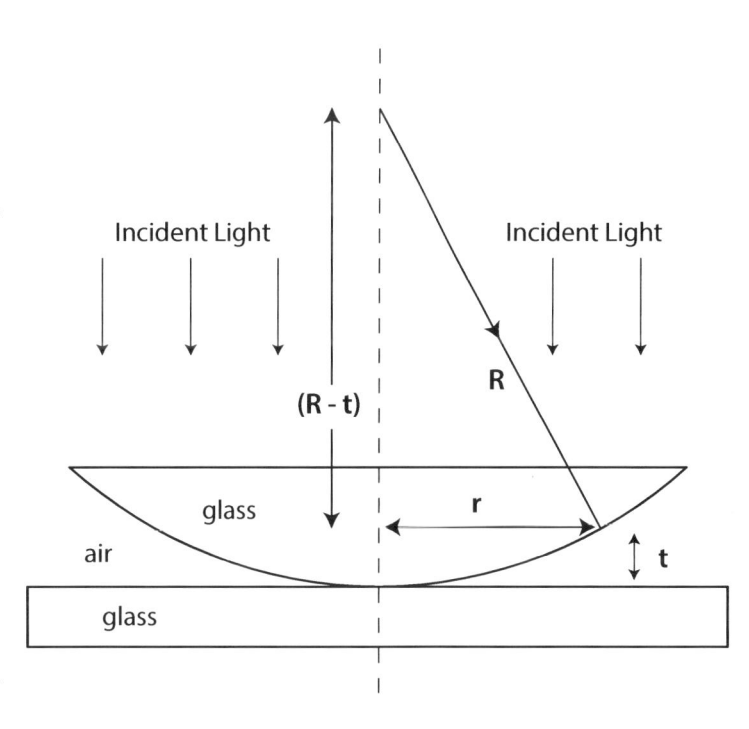

At the point of contact of the two glass surfaces, there is no geometric path difference so you would expect to see a bright spot. But a phase change of 180° is added to the beam reflected off the flat glass plate and this makes the central spot dark.

The radius of the curved glass surface is 'R' and a circular dark fringe of diameter d = 2r is observed (see diagram). For two neighbouring **dark** fringes (with subscripts 1 and 2) use Pythagoras Theorem on the triangles:

$$R^2 = (R-t_1)^2 + r_1^2 \qquad R^2 = (R-t_2)^2 + r_2^2$$

Subtract one equation from the other, expand out the brackets and ignore tiny terms like $t^2$ to give:

$$2Rt_2 - 2Rt_1 = r_2^2 - r_1^2 \qquad d_1 = 2r_1 \quad d_2 = 2r_2$$

$$2(t_2 - t_1) = \lambda \implies d_2^2 - d_1^2 = 4R\lambda \qquad d_n^2 = 4n\lambda R$$

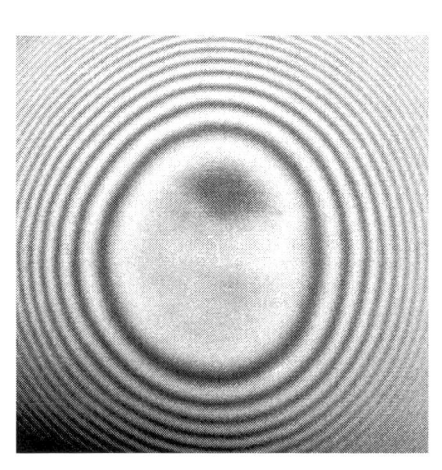

Measuring the diameter means you don't have to locate the centre. The picture shows some real Newton's Rings; they aren't quite circular and the dark spot isn't quite centred. The shape of the rings can be used to determine the optical accuracy of curved surfaces such as lenses and mirrors to within a small fraction of λ.

# Interference by Division of the Wavefront

This is the alternative method for producing interference. Two small slits in a barrier act as sources producing circular wavefronts which interfere with each other. The diagram below is a snapshot showing the wavefronts (take them as crests). It also shows how to ensure the slits produce circular waves which are coherent, in this case by directing plane waves onto them. (An alternative is an extended source behind a small circular aperture, a.k.a. a tiny hole).

Ideally, the width of each slit should be about the same size as the wavelength of the monochromatic source. In practice, you end up with a combination of interference from the two slits and diffraction effects due to the width of each slit. I'll consider the ideal case of tiny slits first, then show you what you get when you do a real experiment.

The diagram opposite has the two sources in phase, and if you go horizontally across from the midpoint of the slits, you get constructive interference (at the moment of the snapshot, the point on the screen at 'O' has the two crests adding up). Showing all the wavefronts like this clutters up the diagram, so usually we just draw lines like the two shown reaching point 'P'. These are the paths from the two sources to the point on the screen, and the type of interference will be determined by the path difference.

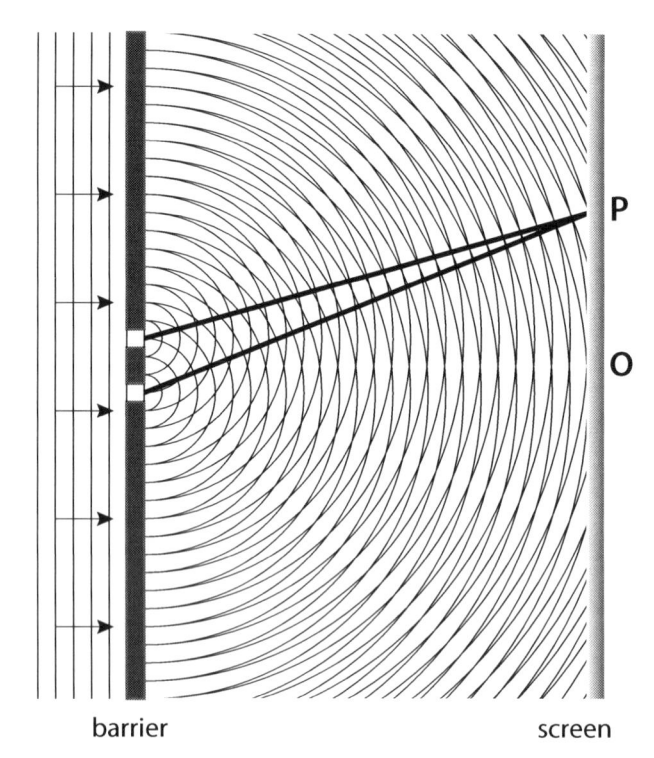

The diagram below shows the paths of the light rays for constructive interference at point 'P'. Thomas Young used this apparatus with sunlight on a pinhole as his source of coherent light. He wanted to show that light was a wave, thereby disproving the Newtonian view that light consisted of particles. The diagram is not drawn to scale; what you normally have with light is a screen distance 'D' of about one metre and a slit separation 'd' of less than one millimetre. This will allow us to make some useful approximations.

What we will derive is an expression for the distance 'x' to point 'P' on the screen. To produce constructive interference, path $S_2P$ must be one wavelength longer than path $S_1P$: $S_2P - S_1P = \lambda$

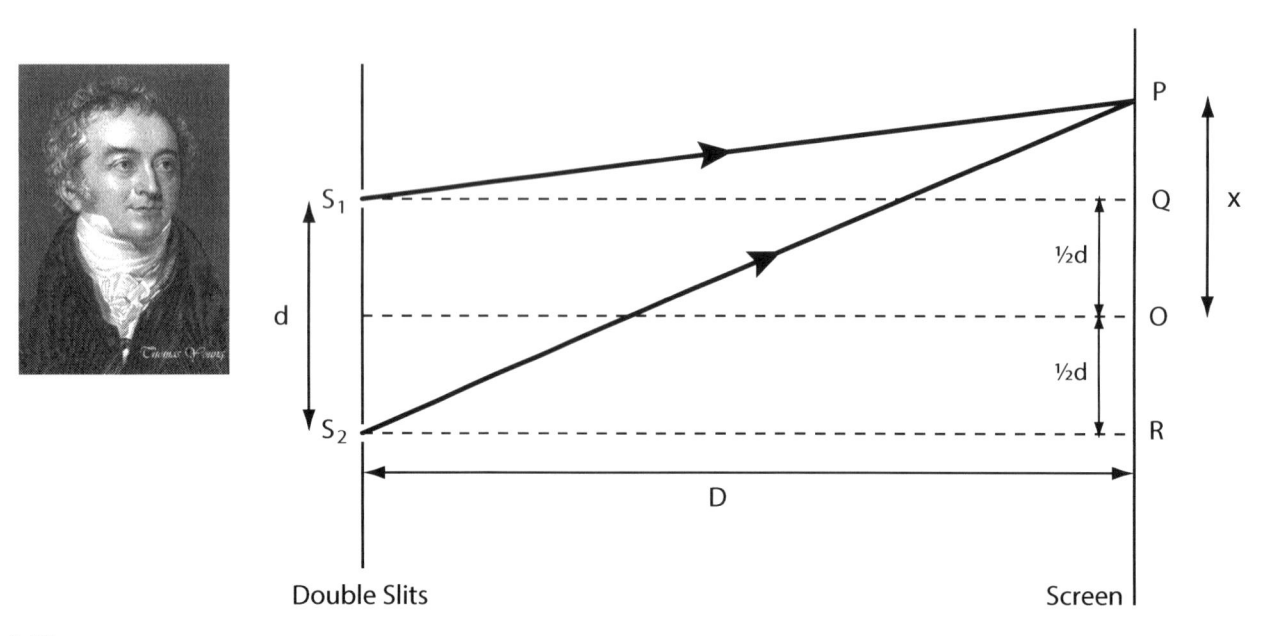

Consider triangles S$_1$PQ and S$_2$PR and apply Pythagoras Theorem:

$$(S_1P)^2 = (S_1Q)^2 + (PQ)^2 \quad \Rightarrow \quad (S_1P)^2 = (S_1Q)^2 + \left(x - \frac{d}{2}\right)^2 = D^2 + \left(x^2 - xd + \frac{d^2}{4}\right)$$

$$(S_2P)^2 = (S_2R)^2 + (PR)^2 \quad \Rightarrow \quad (S_2P)^2 = (S_2R)^2 + \left(x + \frac{d}{2}\right)^2 = D^2 + \left(x^2 + xd + \frac{d^2}{4}\right)$$

If we subtract one line from the other, we get the difference of squares: $(S_2P)^2 - (S_1P)^2$. If we then factorise this, we get the product of the sum and the difference:

$$(S_2P)^2 - (S_1P)^2 = (S_2P + S_1P)(S_2P - S_1P)$$

For point 'P', the difference $S_2P - S_1P$ is one wavelength, and if we remember the scale of the drawing, the sum $S_2P + S_1P$ is approximately twice the screen distance. Putting it all together gives:

$$(S_2P)^2 - (S_1P)^2 = D^2 + \left(x^2 + xd + \frac{d^2}{4}\right) - \left(D^2 + \left(x^2 - xd + \frac{d^2}{4}\right)\right) = 2xd$$

$$(S_2P)^2 - (S_1P)^2 = (S_2P - S_1P)(S_2P + S_1P) \approx 2D\lambda$$

Hence:

$$2xd = 2D\lambda \quad \Rightarrow \quad x = \frac{D\lambda}{d}$$

Point 'P' was the first area of constructive interference above the centre. The next one out will have a path difference of two wavelengths, and the one after that will have a path difference of three wavelengths, and so on. Using the letter 'n' for the numbers 1,2,3,4.... (not to be confused with the refractive index; we always take air between the slits and the screen), the wavelength in the formula is replaced by: $\lambda \Rightarrow n\lambda$. So the distance from the centre (n = 0) to the nth bright area is:

$$x = \frac{n\lambda D}{d}$$

The distance 'x' is proportional to 'n', so the bright areas (everyone calls them 'bright fringes') will be evenly spaced. (This is only true since we made an approximation in the derivation; in reality the separation will increase slightly). Identifying the centre bright fringe amongst many is difficult, and it won't even be central if the two coherent sources are out of phase, so it's much better measuring the fringe separation $\Delta x$. For example, for fringes 4 and 5:

$$\Delta x = \frac{5\lambda D}{d} - \frac{4\lambda D}{d} = \frac{\lambda D}{d}$$

Obviously, the formula works for any neighbouring pair of fringes. It's similar to the last formula, but without the 'n'. Here is what the bright fringes look like for the ideal case where the slit widths are tiny and the fringes are evenly spaced:

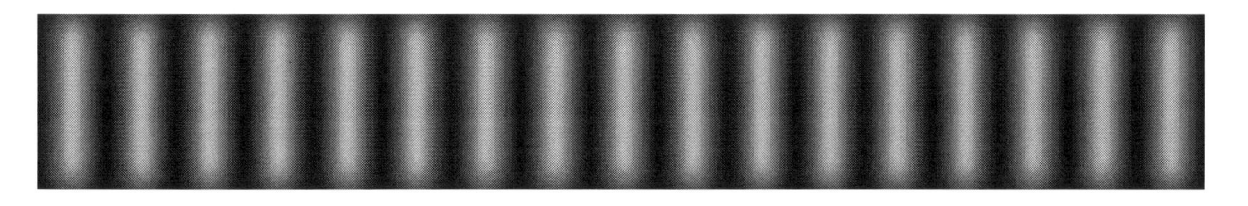

A plot of intensity against distance is a cosine squared function like this:

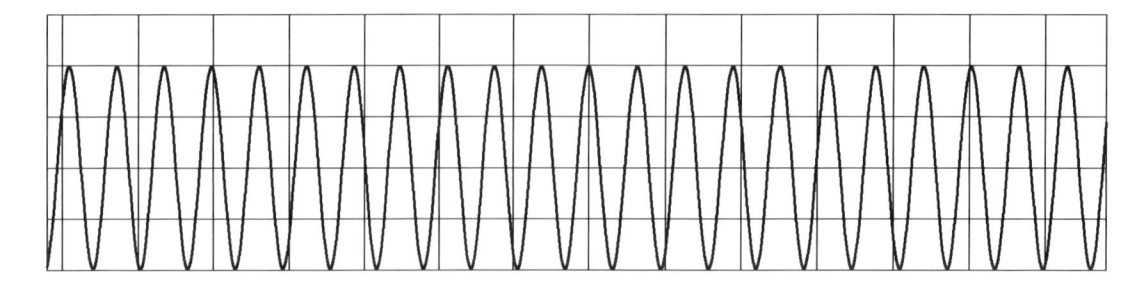

**Example** Calculate the spacing of the bright fringes where the slit separation is 0.25mm, the screen distance is 1.5m and a sodium source is used (λ = 589nm).

$$\Delta x = \frac{\lambda D}{d} = \frac{589 \times 10^{-9} \times 1.5}{0.25 \times 10^{-3}} = 0.0035\text{m} \quad (3.5\text{mm})$$

(Notice how small this is; you normally measure 10 spacings then divide by 10).

At the start, I mentioned that in practice, each slit will be wider than one wavelength. Having a wider slit opening brings in additional diffraction effects and modifies the interference pattern on the screen. Typically, the slit separation is about five to ten times the width of a single slit. This is what you see when the slit separation is six times the slit width:

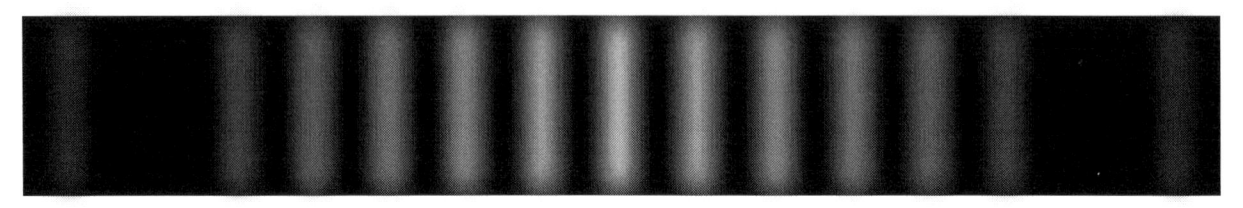

This is its intensity distribution:

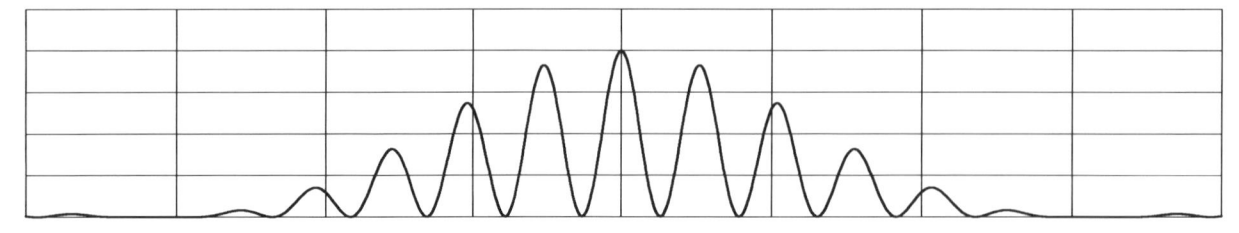

In school, you can make your own double slit using a glass slide which has been spray-painted black on one side. Use a straight edge and sharp craft knife to draw two parallel lines across the width of the glass slide as close as possible (if you do ten pairs, you might get a few decent examples). Place the double slit in front of a helium-neon laser and project onto a white screen about one metre away.

## Stellar Interferometry

Stars are so far away, that they are considered to be points of light. Not counting the Sun, the nearest is at a distance of $4 \times 10^{16}$m. The angle subtended by the diameter of the star is just too small. To get an idea of the scale, the moon subtends an angle of half a degree, and planet Jupiter subtends an angle of about 0.008 degrees (this is about half what the human eye can reveal, 0.016°). Astronomers don't use degrees for small angles. They divide one degree into 60 parts (called minutes of arc) then divide each minute into 60 parts (called seconds of arc). With this system, Jupiter makes an angle of 30 arc seconds at its closest approach, and the stars, as we will discover, are in the range of milli-arc seconds and below.

# Quanta & Waves

Being as small as they are, no-one has ever looked at a star through a telescope and seen a disc. A larger diameter telescope mirror is better than a small one, but the atmosphere makes the stars twinkle, and in any case it would need a mirror bigger than we could build. That should be the end of the story, but for that interesting wave effect called interference. Albert Michelson measured the diameter of a star using this effect in 1920. His target was the star on the top left of the constellation of Orion, called Betelgeuse. The famous astronomer Arthur Eddington had predicted its diameter from theoretical considerations, and was keen to be proven correct. Eddington was talented but vain. On being informed that only three people understood Einstein's General Theory of Relativity, Eddington replied "who's the other person?"

Michelson's design is shown below. The two mirrors M1 and M2 were mounted on a moveable track above the telescope. Imagine the star as a disk and ignore the fact that it doesn't emit monochromatic light and that the light is only partially coherent. Light from one side of the star follows the solid path (AA) and is focussed at the eyepiece. Being aligned as shown, there is no path difference at the double slit and we get constructive interference (and a cosine squared intensity distribution). Light from the other side of the star follows the dotted path (BB) and is focussed at a slightly different position at the eyepiece. Here's the clever bit. You move the mirrors M1 and M2 apart, until the top dotted beam has a path length from the star exactly one wavelength longer than the bottom dotted beam. This makes the fringes disappear at the eyepiece. At this point (some maths/physics needed), the angle subtended by the star's diameter is $\theta = 1.22\lambda/D$. For Betelgeuse, Michelson had to move the mirrors D = 307cm apart. This gave an angle of 47 milli-arc-seconds (mas); the same angle a £1 coin held up at Perth would subtend when viewed from Glasgow. Eddington had predicted 51 milli arc-seconds.

Since then, more accurate instruments have been built. The photo below left shows one telescope from an array of six, called the CHARA Array on Mt Wilson just north of Los Angeles. The tube coming out on the left is a vacuum light pipe carrying one of the beams to the interference point. The separation of the small telescopes (they are like the mirrors M1 and M2) can reach 330metres, allowing an angular resolution of 20 micro-arc-seconds). This has revealed that the star Vega (overhead on summer nights) at a distance of 25.3 lightyears, is 20% wider at its equator than the poles, with a diameter of 2.7 times that of the Sun.

The Very Large Telescope (VLT) on Cerro Paranal in the Atacama Desert in Chile consists of 4 mirrors each of 8.2m diameter. You may have seen one of the on-site facilities in the James Bond movie, Quantum of Solace. When not taking images of very distant galaxies, the four telescopes are combined into a sophisticated interferometer with a resolution of 1 mas.

# Laser Interferometry

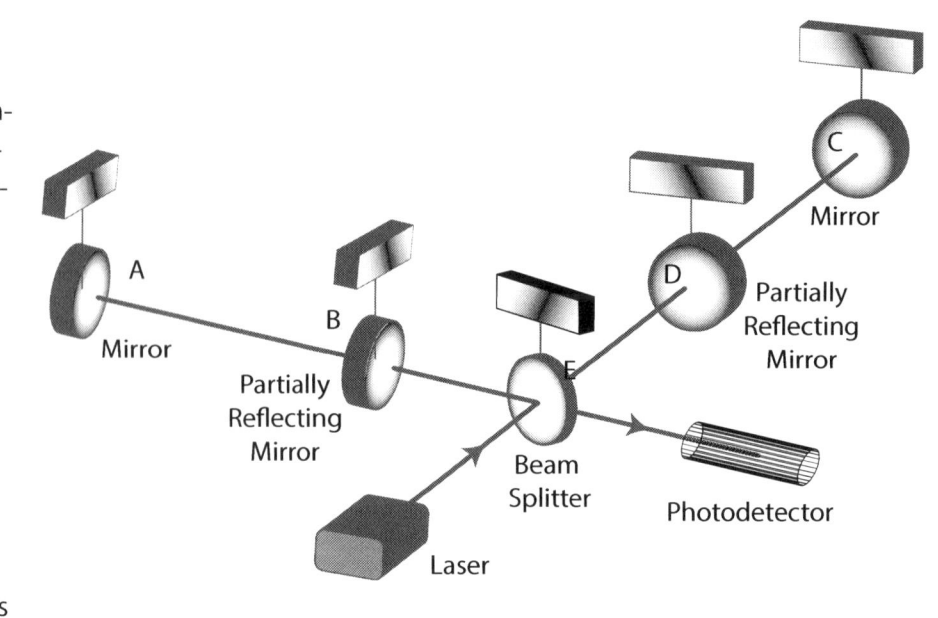

This is an interesting application of interferometry. It makes use of the extreme sensitivity of an interference pattern to changes in path difference; in this case, the change in the spacetime distance between two points when a gravitational wave passes by. The interferometer is laid out in a 90 degree 'L' shape as shown. An event like the merging of two black holes, will send out gravitational waves which ripple through spacetime. When these waves pass the interferometer, one arm will shorten then lengthen while the other arm lengthens then shortens. The laser sends out a coherent infrared beam of wavelength 1064nm. It is split by division of amplitude at the beam splitter 'E'. The two beams are sent to mirrors 'A' and 'C', 4km away at the end of each arm. The beam splitter and the two mirrors are the masses which the gravitational wave displaces as it passes. Each mirror, 10.7kg in mass and with a diameter of 25cm, is suspended like a pendulum (with a length equivalent to a period one second). The signals recombine at the photodetector where interference takes place. A change in the path difference as the wave passes, will alter the interference pattern.

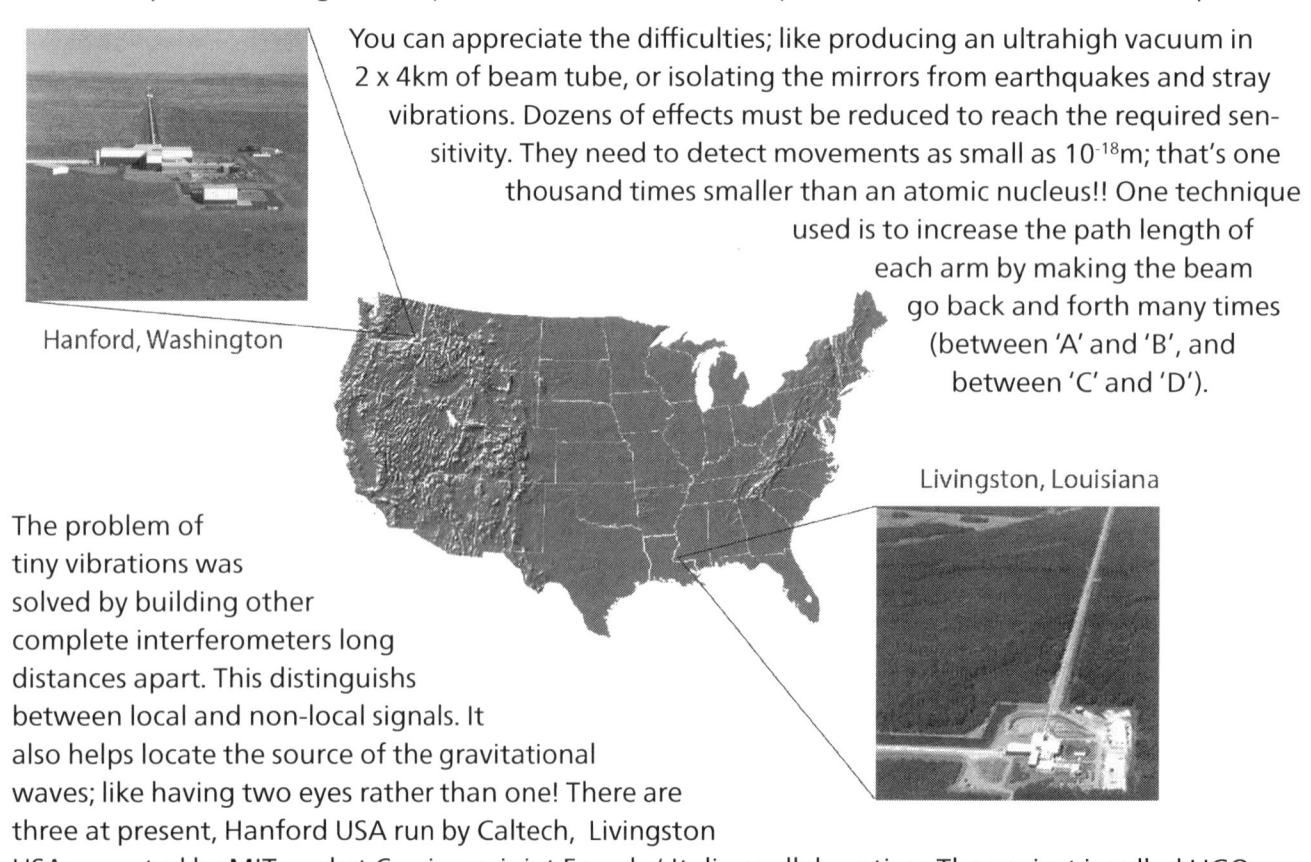

You can appreciate the difficulties; like producing an ultrahigh vacuum in 2 x 4km of beam tube, or isolating the mirrors from earthquakes and stray vibrations. Dozens of effects must be reduced to reach the required sensitivity. They need to detect movements as small as $10^{-18}$m; that's one thousand times smaller than an atomic nucleus!! One technique used is to increase the path length of each arm by making the beam go back and forth many times (between 'A' and 'B', and between 'C' and 'D').

Hanford, Washington

Livingston, Louisiana

The problem of tiny vibrations was solved by building other complete interferometers long distances apart. This distinguishs between local and non-local signals. It also helps locate the source of the gravitational waves; like having two eyes rather than one! There are three at present, Hanford USA run by Caltech, Livingston USA operated by MIT, and at Cascina, a joint French / Italian collaboration. The project is called LIGO, the Laser Interferometer Gravitational-Wave Observatory. The first signal (Livingston first, then Hanford 7ms later) was received on 14th Sept. 2015 and recorded the inspiral of two 30 solar mass black holes as they coalesced into one, taking 0.2 sec to rotate about each other from 35Hz, to 250Hz as they merged.

# Quanta & Waves

# Section 2.6 Polarisation

So, what is 'light'? We know it's produced by an electron dropping down from an outer shell to an inner shell in an atom. Each excited atom sends out its own little burst of light, called a 'wavetrain' (or a 'photon', using quantum language). In a filament lamp, like the one in a RayBox, zillions of atoms do this each second. The whole lot are completely unco-ordinated, each wavetrain about 2 metres long, producing a beam which is non-coherent. So, what is the nature of a wavetrain, this 2 metre long 'thing' emitted by a single atom? Here are some facts:

- it can produce interference, so its a wave rather than a particle (this is classical physics talk).

- it travels in straight lines (there is a of law in physics that says: the path of a beam of light is such that it always takes the shortest time to get from 'A' to 'B'; you can derive Snell's Law from it).

- it travels through a vacuum (unlike sound, which needs a material medium; this gave the Victorian physicists a very bad time).

- it requires vectors for its description (unlike sound waves, which only require scalars).

Étienne-Louis Malus (1775-1812) was an engineer, and amongst other distractions, like Napoleon's expedition to Egypt, found time to conduct 'optical researches'. One of these demonstrated the vector nature of light, the importance of which was was unrecognised until decades later.

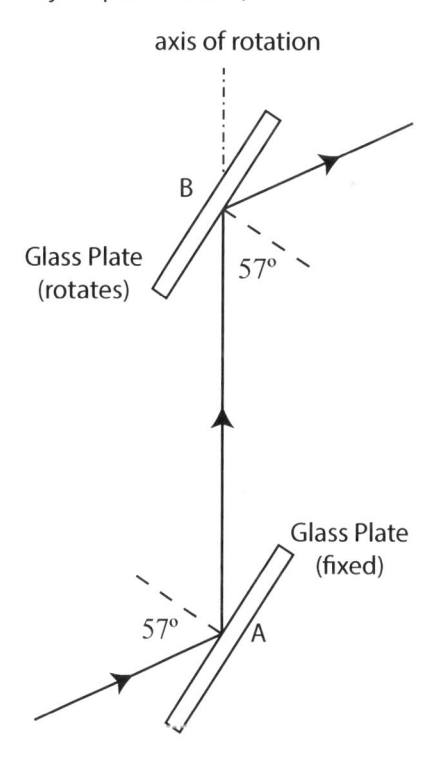

On the diagram, a beam of ordinary light enters along the bottom and strikes a fixed glass plate at an angle of 57°. It reflects upwards to another glass plate. This top glass plate can be rotated about a vertical axis (shown with a dot dash pattern). As drawn, the beam reflects off the top plate and emerges just as you'd expect. Malus then rotated the top glass plate (imagine it going anti-clockwise as you look down along the axis of rotation), and noticed that the reflected beam gradually reduced in brightness, until it vanished when the plate had been rotated through 90°! Continuing on around, the beam built-up to full brightness again at 180°, vanished again on reaching 270°, then back to full brightness at 360°. It seems that directions are important, thus requiring a vector description for light rays. A similar experiment using sound instead of light, would find no variation in the intensity of the reflected beam, and hence only require scalar quantities for its description. (We shall return later to the 57° on page 154).

**Transverse Waves & Longitudinal Waves**

Given that a soundwave requires scalars for its description, the only way to achieve this is by longitudinal motion of the wave; the vibrations go back and forth along the same direction as the direction of energy flow. All you need to do is put in the x co-ordinate of the particle of the medium into your (scalar) wave function and you get the x displacement of the particle.

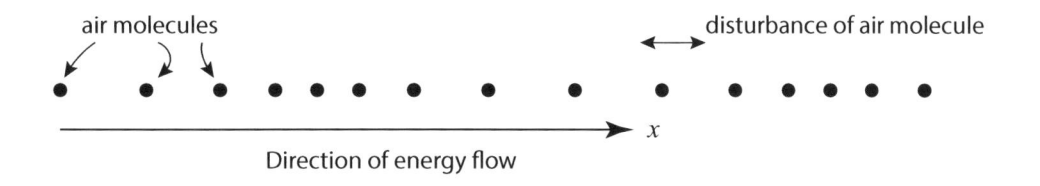

Given Malus' result, the only way to get a vector description of a wave is through transverse motion. When the vibration is at right angles to the direction of energy flow, you have the freedom to move on a two dimensional plane, rather than a one dimensional line as with longitudinal motion. Its transverse character is the origin of the vector nature of light.

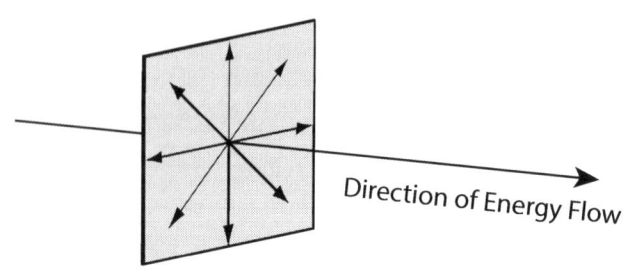

The 2D plane on the diagram shows four possible vibration directions. In practice, there are an infinite number, covering every possible angle in between. If zillions of wavetrains were emitted from a special source, all vibrating in the same direction, they would be described as plane polarised. The wavetrains emitted by a source like a filament bulb all vibrate in different directions on the 2D plane; the light is called unpolarised. It's also possible to get a beam of light which is partially polarised. This is where you still find all directions of vibration in the wavetrains, but they aren't distributed evenly across all the angles; one particular angle is favoured (the sunlight entering your eye is like this).

Here are a few diagrams comparing coherence and polarisation. The arrow shows the y-displacement for each wavetrain at one particular instant:

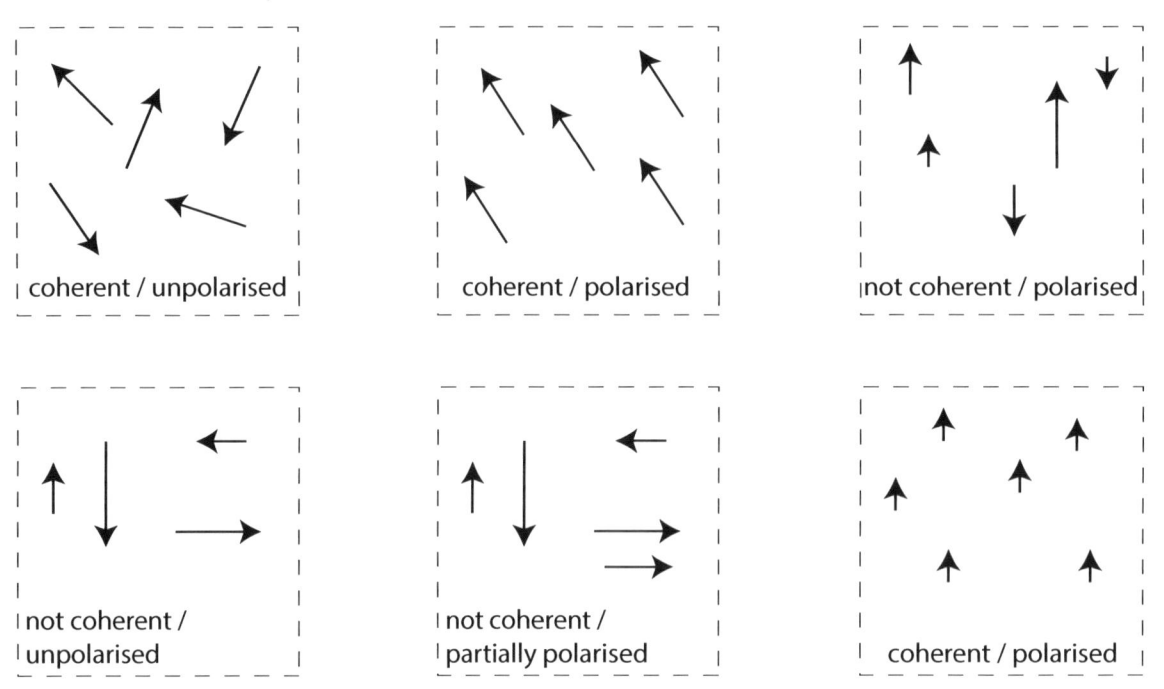

| coherent / unpolarised | coherent / polarised | not coherent / polarised |
| not coherent / unpolarised | not coherent / partially polarised | coherent / polarised |

### Light as an Electromagnetic Wave

James Clerk Maxwell, the dull, shy boy at school, first discovered what it was that was vibrating in a beam of light. It turned out to be electric **'E'** and magnetic **'B'** fields. From the diagram, you can see that these fields vibrate at 90° to each other. When passing through an insulator they are in step (like the diagram), but when passing through a conductor, the magnetic field lags behind the electric field. In general, it is the electric field which interacts with a material (like your retina), and defines the direction of polarisation. (If you're wondering how it travels through a vacuum, the answer is that a vacuum isn't 'nothing'; it's a stormy quantum ocean).

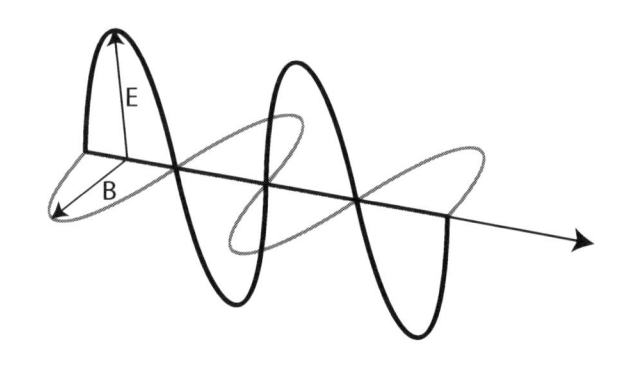

# Quanta & Waves

**Polaroid Sheets**

Polaroid sheet is a plastic material. It is transparent to light where the electric field vibration is in a certain direction, and blocks out other directions. On the diagrams below, this direction is shown by parallel lines on the sheet:

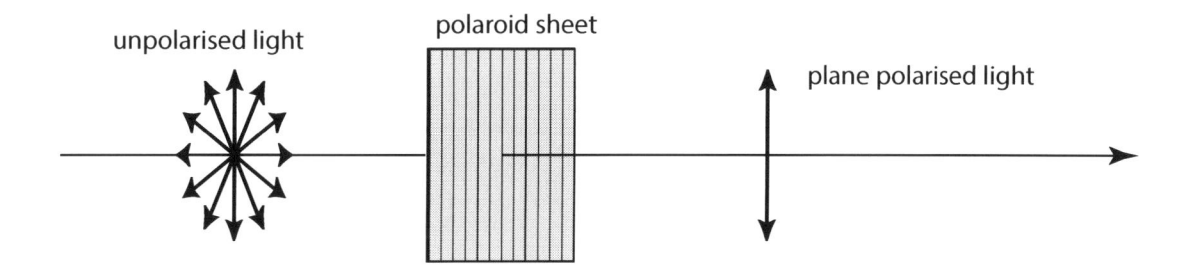

You can combine two Polaroid sheets, set at an angle to each other. Then look through the end.

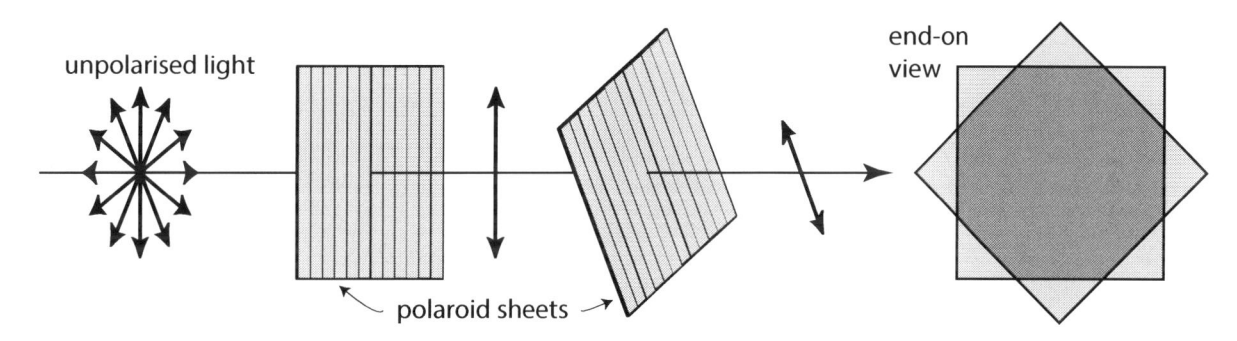

No light will pass through to the end if the sheets are set at 90° to each other. For angles in between, the intensity transmitted is proportional to the cosine squared. It is the component of the electric field vector parallel to the polarising direction of the sheet which is transmitted. On the diagram, AB is the incident electric field amplitude, and BC is the component along the polarising direction of the sheet, which gets transmitted:

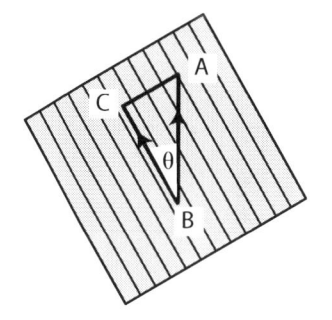

$$\cos\theta = \frac{BC}{AB} \qquad \text{intensity} \propto (BC)^2 = (AB)^2 \cos^2\theta$$

Here's a interesting effect using 3 Polaroid sheets. As before take two sheets and set them at 90° to each other so that no light passes through the last one. Now take a third Polaroid sheet and hold it in between the other two sheets. Some light will emerge from the last sheet!

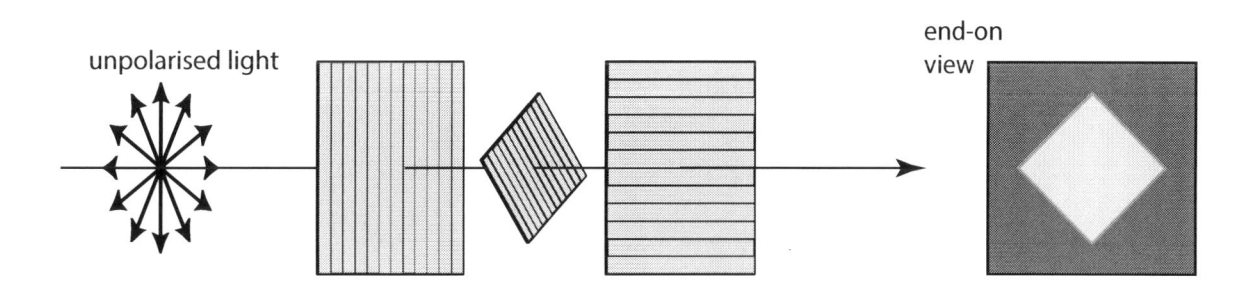

Can you explain it? Think of components passing through at each stage.

## Brewster's Angle

Sir David Brewster (1781-1868), man of Jedburgh, was part Church of Scotland Minister, part Principal of Edinburgh University, and was renowned for his temperament, (to such a degree that opponents would provoke him then stand back). He had an especial talent for inventing optical gadgets, and while doing so, stumbled upon polarisation. Brewster was also, for a time, a Professor of Physics at St. Andrews University. Yet, despite his great breadth of experience, he shared the 'poor' judgement of many other Victorian scientists over the thorny question of whether light is a particle or a wave. Regardless of the great advances in the wave theory of light, he was dead against it. Like Faraday, he collected many medals and awards, and also, like Faraday, wasn't at home with mathematics. Despite this, (or is it because of this?) he made important discoveries over a wide range of fields of study.

If you recall the experiment of Malus with the two glass plates, then you will remember the angle of 57° to the normal. That angle is known as Brewster's Angle for that particular type of glass. A ray of ordinary unpolarised light (sunlight or filament bulb), is directed onto a block of glass as shown below. The square dotted boxes show the polarisation of the beams (it's what you would 'see' if you looked along the beam). This is the direction of vibration of the electric field vector. The incoming beam 'A' is unpolarised. If the angle of incidence is 57°, the reflected beam is plane polarised, and the refracted beam is partially polarised. The reflected beam has no component along the plane of this page (called the plane of incidence). The arrowed direction in the dotted box (top right) comes out of the page. Brewster noticed that the reflected and refracted beams were at right-angles to each other. This allows us to relate Brewster's Angle (also called the polarising angle $i_p$) to the refractive index, as follows:

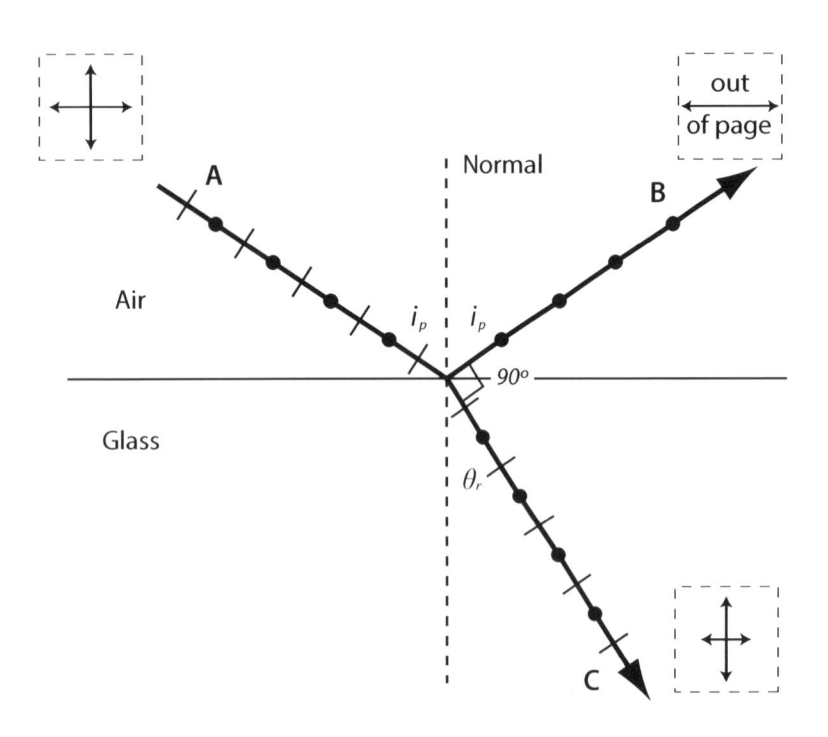

Start from Snell's Law:

$$n = \frac{\sin \theta_i}{\sin \theta_r}$$

Relate the angle of refraction to the angle of incidence:

$$\theta_r + 90° + i_p = 180°$$

$$\theta_r = 90° - i_p$$

Substitute in Snell's Law:

$$n = \frac{\sin \theta_i}{\sin \theta_r} = \frac{\sin i_p}{\sin(90 - i_p)}$$

$$= \frac{\sin i_p}{\cos i_p} = \tan i_p$$

**Example** Calculate the Brewster Angle for glass of refractive index 1.54.

$$n = \tan i_p \quad \Rightarrow \quad 1.54 = \tan i_p \quad \Rightarrow \quad i_p = \tan^{-1} 1.54 = 57°$$

and that's where the 57° came from!

# Quanta & Waves

## Examples of Polarisation

When a beam of plane polarised light goes through a transparent material, it usually keeps vibrating in the same direction. In a few materials, it doesn't do this, and rotates in the 2D plane. Quartz is like this; it rotates the plane of vibration by about 22° for every millimetre it goes through.

A Liquid Crystal Display uses this effect (it's called Optical Activity). The two photos on the right show an LCD screen with a circle of Polaroid sheet on top. The bottom sheet was rotated until the light from the display was absorbed. This shows that the light emitted by the LCD screen is polarised. The calculator requires to convert electrical signals into optical signals and achieves this by triggering an optically active liquid with an electric field. A plane polarised beam of light entering from behind has its plane of vibration rotated / not rotated as it passes through the liquid. This will either be blocked or transmitted by a Polaroid sheet on the top surface. If blocked, it produces a dark patch on the screen, one block of the seven segment display.

The day sky should look black, just like the night sky, except when you look straight at the Sun. The fact that it doesn't is due to sunlight scattering off the air molecules. The amount of scattering is strongly dependent upon the wavelength with blue light scattered about ten times more strongly than red light. That's why the sky is blue (and also why tobacco smoke has a blue tinge).

'Scattering' of a wavetrain of light by an air molecule isn't like 'bouncing off' it. The (photon of) light is absorbed by the air molecule which then re-radiates another photon of the same frequency. With many molecules, the light is emitted in all directions. The light emitted along the line from the Sun is unpolarised, but as you swing around until you are at right-angles (making a 2D plane facing the Sun), the scattered light becomes partially polarised. On a clear day, stand with the Sun to your left or right and hold up a Polaroid sheet to the blue sky in front of you. Rotate it and you'll see the sky darken. Photographers use this effect (compare the cloud photos above).

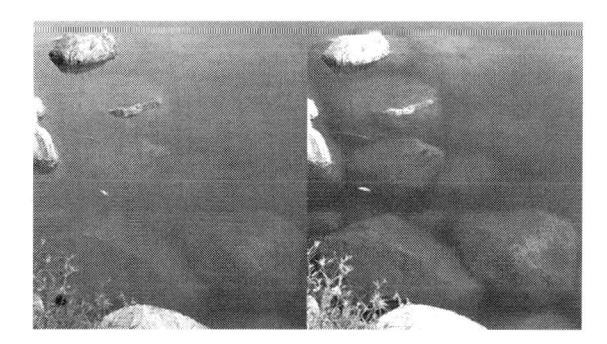

Brewster and Malus showed that unpolarised light reflected from an insulator is plane polarised if reflected at a special angle given by $n = \tan i_p$. Water has a refractive index of 1.33 and gives a Brewster Angle of 53°. Stand in front of a water surface facing towards the Sun. A Scottish loch on a calm day will do. Look onto the water surface and you will get lots of reflection. The light coming from the bottom of the loch is masked by the reflection from the surface. Now look at it through a Polaroid sheet and hold it so that its polarising direction is vertical. The surface reflection (plane polarised horizontally) is cut out, letting you see under the water to the rocks below.

The light from a rainbow is polarised along the tangent to the bow. Hence a single sheet of Polaroid cannot make the whole rainbow disappear.

# Section 3.1a Electric Fields

Atoms are made of particles which have mass and electrical charge. Mass comes in only one variety but electric charge comes in two varieties (labelled positive and negative). Both properties produce effects which act over long distances. The natural world of our everyday experience is dominated by these simple facts. As we will discover, the forces due to electrical charges are much greater than those due to masses. It is the result of electrical charges coming in two varieties, allowing for the possibility of cancellation of the enormous forces, which conceals their presence from us. While the effects of gravity are constantly and obviously with us, the effects due to the electrical charges show up in unexpected ways. The force of friction, the tension in a rope, the viscosity of a liquid, a chemical reaction, a ray of light, would all seem to be remote from an electrical explanation; and yet, it is their origin. The other fundamental forces (the strong and weak nuclear forces), whilst important at the birth of the universe, in keeping our planet warm and holding nuclei together, only act over very short distances and are of minor importance to most people in everyday life.

The good news is that the gravitational and electrostatic forces share many of the same concepts which we've already covered. Notice that I use the word 'electrostatic' rather than 'electromagnetic'. When electrical charges are moving, we observe an additional phenomenon, called magnetism. We begin with the study of stationary charges then consider the effects of moving charges (currents).

## The Force of one Charge on another Charge

Regardless of how long you spend studying electricity, it still seems weird. You can plug a kettle of water into a mains socket, watch it for a few minutes, then observe steam coming out of the spout. Everyone's done it, and they think nothing of it. There's a spectacular lack of action from the cable, there's nothing 'electrical' to observe. Unlike gravity, it all seems so secretive, and this is the main difficulty in learning about it; we deal in concepts, not concrete.

The place to start is with the forces of attraction and repulsion between electrical charges. Newton's Inverse Square Law of Gravitation had been discovered the best part of a century before all this stuff, when in 1767, Joseph Priestley applied the same thing to electrical charges. Before this time, the two types of charge were known as 'vitreous' and 'resinous'. It wasn't until Benjamin Franklin came on the scene that they were called 'positive' and 'negative', and planted ideas in Priestley's head. Inevitably, Cavendish was involved, but it was the Frenchman, Charles Coulomb who performed the crucial experiment in 1785. This led to Coulomb's Law of electrical charges:

$$F \propto \frac{q_1 q_2}{r^2}$$

The apparatus is shown on the right. It's the torsion balance, of which Coulomb was the inventor. We've met it before in gravitation on page 53 with the measurement of big 'G'. The two small charged spheres will repel each other and twist the fibre. The top of the fibre is attached to a pointer with a scale, and rotated to bring the spheres closer together. The separation of the spheres can be read-off from a scale around the circumference of the draught proof container. The relationship demonstrated is only one of proportionality so you don't need to calibrate the twist of the fibre, you just assume that twisting it through twice

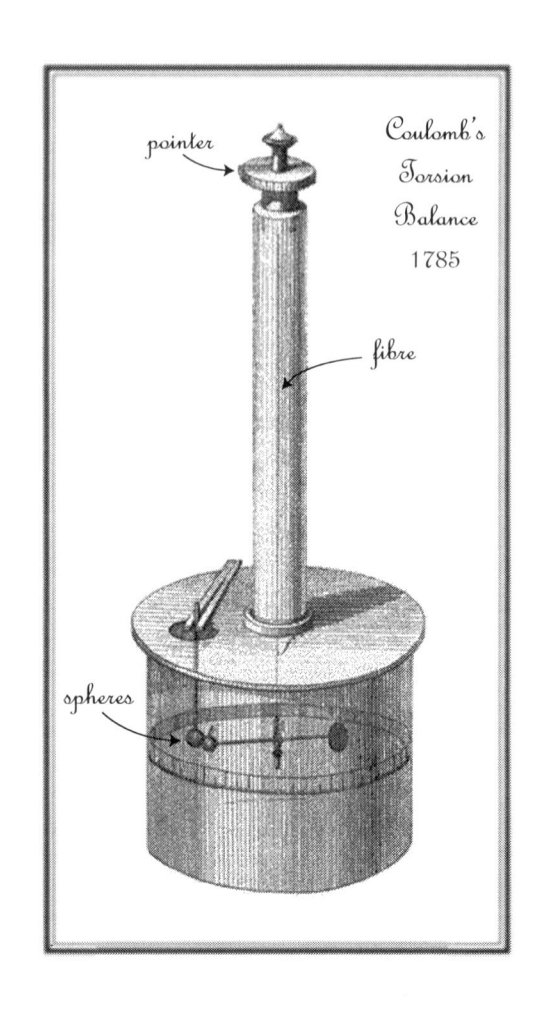

# Electromagnetism

the angle requires twice the torque. Similarly with the scale around the side of the container. The reading on the scale in centimetres will be proportional to the actual separation. Why bother calibrating it when it just introduces more errors? Apart from stray electric charges in the vicinity, the main problem is that the two small spheres don't act as points. Unlike gravity, where the masses stay in place, the electric charges repel each other to the opposite sides of the spheres. The force doesn't come from the centre of each sphere. Keeping the spheres small and not too close will reduce the error.

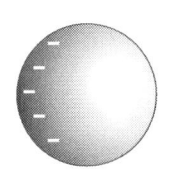

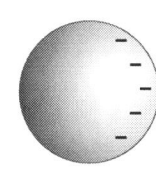

Coulomb's experiment tested both $F \propto q_1 q_2$ and $F \propto \dfrac{1}{r^2}$.

In the decade before this, Cavendish performed an experiment which tested only the inverse square law part of it. A charged inner sphere over 25cm in diameter was held in place by an insulating stand (diagram on right). Two uncharged pasteboard hemispheres of a slightly larger size than the inner sphere, were covered in tinfoil *'to make them the more perfect conductors of electricity'*. When the hemispheres were closed over the inner sphere, a small conducting wire transferred the charge onto the hemispheres. The hemispheres were then opened and the inner sphere tested for any residual charge. None was found.

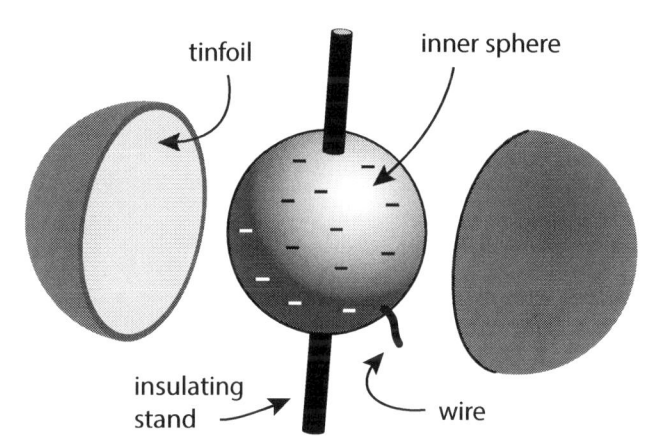

The reasoning is the same one Newton had used to show that there is no force on a small mass placed within a hollow sphere. The pull on the small mass from the left cancels the pull from the right, no matter where you are inside the sphere. But it only works if the force obeys an inverse square law (page 174). Cavendish applied it to electricity. If the power was greater than inverse square eg. inverse cube, the discharge would have stopped before completion. If the power was less than inverse square eg. inversely proportional, the transfer of charge would continue until the inner sphere had the opposite charge. Cavendish concluded that the inverse power was 2.000±0.017. The latest experiments indicate that the power is 2.0 accurate to at least sixteen decimal places. When Quantum Theory is introduced into electricity, an inverse square law of force implies a massless photon. The importance of Cavendish's method is that it is used to place an experimental upper limit on the mass of a single photon. The most recent (2003) experiment gave an upper limit of $10^{-54}$ kg. If the photon is really neutral has also been tested; the upper limit is $5 \times 10^{-52}$ Coulombs.

## The Constant of Proportionality

The force between two electric charges depends upon the magnitudes of the charges and the distance between their centres. We have units for all of these; newtons, coulombs and metres. But we can't hope that two charges of one coulomb each, placed one metre apart, would give a repulsion of one newton. After all, the newton was defined through a mechanical experiment $F = ma$, which has got nothing to do with electricity. Putting in a constant 'k' of the correct size lets you measure the force in newtons:

$$F \propto \frac{q_1 q_2}{r^2} \quad \Rightarrow \quad F = k \frac{q_1 q_2}{r^2} \quad \Rightarrow \quad F = \frac{1}{4\pi\varepsilon_0} \frac{q_1 q_2}{r^2}$$

The Greek-looking bit is called 'epsilon nought'. It's known as the *'permittivity of free space'* (and also, the electric constant). Writing it this way looks unnecessarily complicated but there is a reason for it (see page 183 where it cancels a $4\pi$ from the magnetic constant '$\mu_0$'). The size of the constant determines the strength of the force; and the force is big. If one coulomb of charge was superglued to each hand with your arms one metre apart, your arms would be wrenched out of their sockets.

$$\varepsilon_0 = 8.854 \times 10^{-12} \text{ Farads per metre} \quad \Rightarrow \quad \frac{1}{4\pi\varepsilon_0} = 8.988 \times 10^9 \quad \rightarrow \quad F = 8.988 \times 10^9 \times \frac{1 \times 1}{1^2}$$

That's a force of about nine billion newtons on each arm socket. The constant $\varepsilon_o$ hardly ever occurs on its own; it is frequently in the combination $\frac{1}{4\pi\varepsilon_o}$. This is $8.988 \times 10^9$, very close to $9 \times 10^9$ and it's sensible to use the rounded value in most calculations. In the 2011 final exam, the SQA explicitly accepted $9 \times 10^9$. They can be a bit fickle though, and whether this will continue is anyone's guess.

**Example 1** A coulomb of charge is a very large amount, so you often get electric charges given in millicoulombs (mC), microcoulombs (μC) and nanocoulombs (nC). Calculate the electrostatic force if a +5μC point charge is placed 45cm from a -8μC point charge.

$$F = \frac{1}{4\pi\varepsilon_o}\frac{q_1 q_2}{r^2} = 9\times 10^9 \times \frac{(+5\times 10^{-6})(-8\times 10^{-6})}{0.45^2} = -1.78\text{N}$$

The minus sign means that the force indicates 'attraction'.

**Example 2** Force is a vector; in this example you calculate both magnitude and direction. The three charges make an isosceles triangle as shown. Calculate the force on the -3μC charge.

There are two forces acting on the -3μC charge; one attractive ($F_1$) towards the +8μC charge, and one repulsive ($F_2$) away from the -6μC charge.

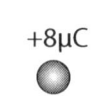

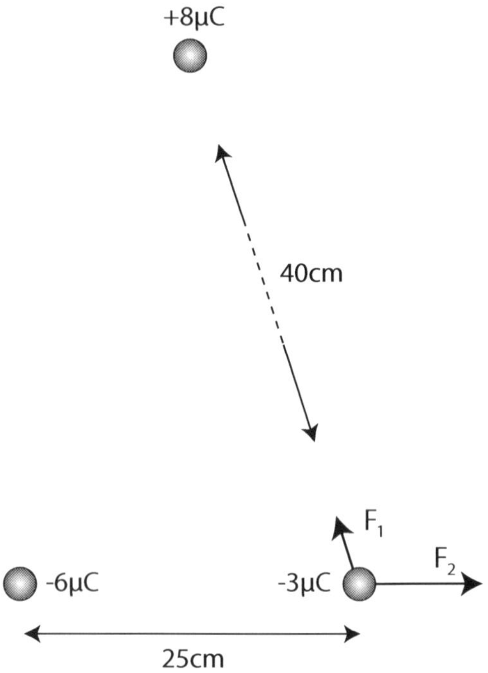

**Force ($F_1$):**

$$F = \frac{1}{4\pi\varepsilon_o}\frac{q_1 q_2}{r^2} = 9\times 10^9 \times \frac{(8\times 10^{-6})(-3\times 10^{-6})}{0.4^2} = -1.35\text{N}$$

The angle it makes with the vertical (bottom diagram) comes from the triangle:

$$\sin\theta = \frac{12.5}{40} \Rightarrow \theta = 18.2°$$

**Force ($F_2$):**

$$F = \frac{1}{4\pi\varepsilon_o}\frac{q_1 q_2}{r^2} = 9\times 10^9 \times \frac{(-6\times 10^{-6})(-3\times 10^{-6})}{0.25^2} = 2.59\text{N}$$

This points horizontally to the right.

Now add these two results as vectors. Use the cosine rule for the magnitude of the result:

$$F_{result}^2 = 1.35^2 + 2.59^2 - 2\times 1.35\times 2.59\times \cos 71.8$$

This gives 2.52N. Using the sine rule for the angle, the bearing is marked on the diagram (59.4°).

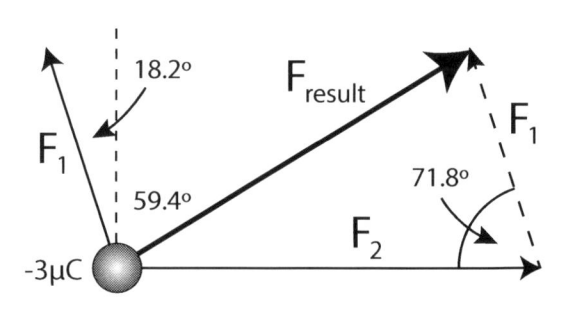

Work through all the details of the problem so that you understand it thoroughly. Using the sine and cosine rules is common in vector calculations; be comfortable with them!

# Electromagnetism

## The Electric Field

This is handled in a similar way to the gravitational field. The difference being that arrows on gravitational field lines only go **into** masses whereas arrows on electric field lines come **out of** positive charges and **into** negative charges. The definition of the field is similar:

$$g = \frac{F}{m} \quad \Rightarrow \quad E = \frac{F}{q}$$

In the diagram above right, the electric charge capital 'Q' produces the electric field and the test charge '+q' experiences a force 'F'. For example, if you place a test charge of q = +4coulombs in an electric field and it experiences a force of 20N, the electric field at that point is 5 Newtons per Coulomb (N C$^{-1}$). The force and the electric field are both vectors.

We have rules for drawing gravitational field lines (pages 53/54). Having two types of electric charge modifies these rules slightly for electric field lines. Electric field lines start on positive charges and end on negative charges. Page 54 shows a diagram of the gravitational field line pattern for two identical masses. It would be the same diagram for two identical negative charges, and if you changed the direction of the arrows, also give the pattern for two positive charges. The third combination of one positive and one negative charge, only possible in the electric case, gives the pattern on the right.

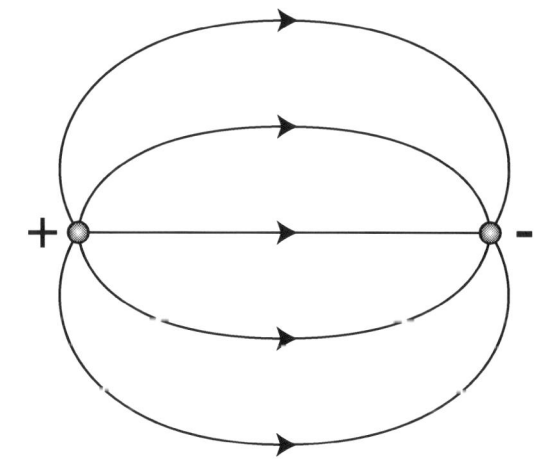

### The Electric Field due to a Point Charge

A point charge produces an electric field with a radial pattern. The expression for the electric field strength at a distance 'r' from the point charge is derived from Coulomb's Law:

$$F = \frac{1}{4\pi\varepsilon_o}\frac{Qq}{r^2} = \left(\frac{1}{4\pi\varepsilon_o}\frac{Q}{r^2}\right)q = Eq \quad \Rightarrow \quad E = \frac{1}{4\pi\varepsilon_o}\frac{Q}{r^2} \qquad \left[\mathbf{E} = \frac{1}{4\pi\varepsilon_o}\frac{Q}{r^2}\hat{\mathbf{r}}\right]$$

Charge 'Q' produces the electric field and the last expression is the vector form (like top of page 51).

This is like the expression for the force but without the little 'q'. Remember it only applies to point charges. It's a common mistake to apply the formula to charged parallel plates (where the field is constant between the plates). Notice that it's another example of the inverse square law; moving out to twice the distance produces one quarter of the effect.

159

Let's get a feel for the numbers and work through an example. The electric field strength at a distance of 1m from a +1µC charge is:

$$E = \frac{1}{4\pi\varepsilon_o}\frac{Q}{r^2} = 9\times10^9 \times \frac{(+1\times10^{-6})}{1^2} = +9000\,\text{NC}^{-1}$$

Notice the units, newtons per coulomb. An electric field strength of 9000 NC$^{-1}$ means that if you place a positive charge of one coulomb at that point, it experiences an initial force of 9000N in the direction of the field line. Two coulombs would be whacked with 18000N.

**Example**  A common question is to calculate the electric field strength at certain positions 'A' and 'B' due to four charges laid out in a square. Point 'A' is at the mid-point of a side and 'B' is in the middle of the square. Treat each charge as a point.

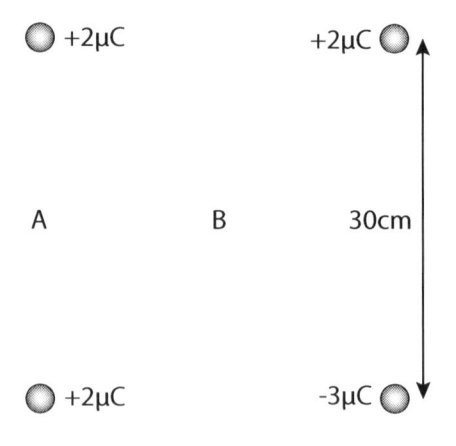

There's always a bit of geometry to get out of the way first. The distance from any charge to point 'B' using Pythagoras Theorem is 21.2cm. The distance from point 'A' to the nearest charges is 15cm and to the far away charges is 33.5cm. There will be angles to calculate (usual sin tan cos stuff). Now look for symmetry. If an exam setter had a twisted sense of humour, all four charges would be different. This example has three charges all the same (sign and size) and one of the opposite sign / different size. Electric field strength is a vector, so the signs are important. Symmetry reduces the number of calculations. The method assumes the principle of superposition. You calculate each contribution as if the other charges didn't exist, then add the results vectorially. Finally, remember there are no charges at points 'A' or 'B'; you're working out the electric field strength at these points due to the four charges.

**Point 'A'**  The magnitudes of each contribution from the four charges are:

top left/ bottom left
$$E = \frac{1}{4\pi\varepsilon_o}\frac{Q}{r^2} = 9\times10^9 \times \frac{(+2\times10^{-6})}{0.15^2} = +8\times10^5\,\text{NC}^{-1}$$

top right
$$E = \frac{1}{4\pi\varepsilon_o}\frac{Q}{r^2} = 9\times10^9 \times \frac{(+2\times10^{-6})}{0.335^2} = +1.6\times10^5\,\text{NC}^{-1}$$

bottom right
$$E = \frac{1}{4\pi\varepsilon_o}\frac{Q}{r^2} = 9\times10^9 \times \frac{(-3\times10^{-6})}{0.335^2} = -2.4\times10^5\,\text{NC}^{-1}$$

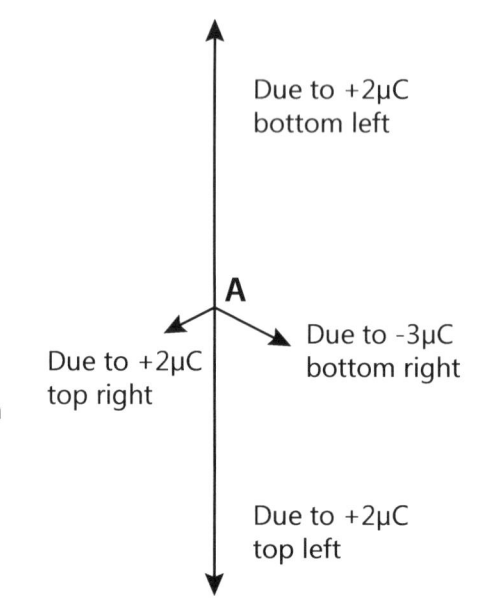

Now calculate the direction of each vector (diagram on right) then add them. Two of the contributions cancel (from top left / bottom left), leaving the resultant below:

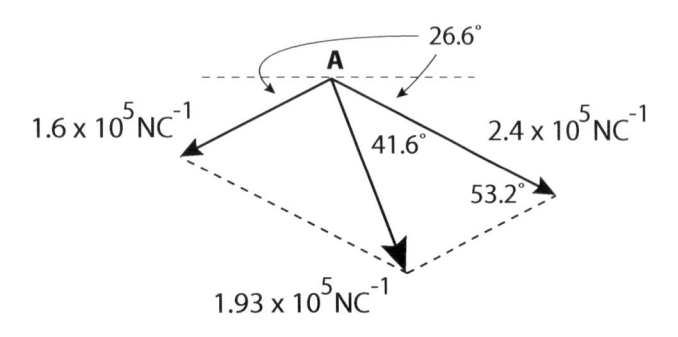

Use the cosine rule (with an angle of 53.2°) to calculate the magnitude, and the sine rule for the direction. Final result is 1.93 x 10$^5$ NC$^{-1}$ on a bearing of 158.2° from North.

Go through all the fiddly calculations yourself and make sure you understand it.

# Electromagnetism

**Point 'B'** This is the easy one. Two of the contributions cancel (from top right / bottom left). The other two point along the same line at 45°. The two contributions are:

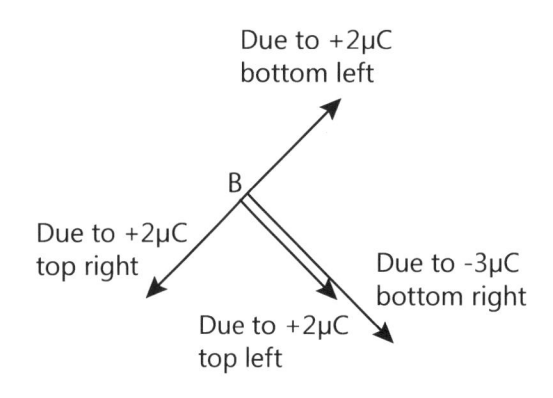

$$E = \frac{1}{4\pi\varepsilon_o}\frac{Q}{r^2} = 9\times10^9 \times \frac{(+2\times10^{-6})}{0.212^2} = +4.0\times10^5\,\text{N}\,\text{C}^{-1}$$

$$E = \frac{1}{4\pi\varepsilon_o}\frac{Q}{r^2} = 9\times10^9 \times \frac{(-3\times10^{-6})}{0.212^2} = -6.0\times10^5\,\text{N}\,\text{C}^{-1}$$

Note the signs. They are relative to the charge producing the field, out from the top left and in towards the bottom right. They point in the same direction. The result is 1.0 x 10⁶NC⁻¹ on a bearing of 135° from North.

## Conductors and Insulators

This is one of the main differences between gravity and electrostatics. The sources of the electric field (the charges), can redistribute themselves within some materials (called conductors), but not in others (insulators). Applying an external electric field to an insulator can distort the distribution of negative charge in the molecules of the material. If the centre of the positive charge of a molecule no longer co-incides with the centre of the negative charge, a dipole (opposite charges separated by a distance, like middle diagram on page 159) is formed. Molecules which are already dipolar in nature can be rotated by an external electric field and alter the total field. This leads on to the study of dielectrics. Remember putting an insulator between the plates of a capacitor, and how it affected the capacitance?

Fortunately for us, the world is electrically neutral. When charges do get separated, the results can be spectacular (as in thunder and lightning), or helpful (as in a laser printer). Charges can be separated by rubbing a material. Walking over a carpet is sufficient, and most people remember the shock received on sliding across a car seat and closing the door. Combing your hair? Removing your jumper over your head? I've never managed to get this to work, but some people see discharges when bringing their knees across the underside of the bed quilt (with the light out and your head also under the quilt).

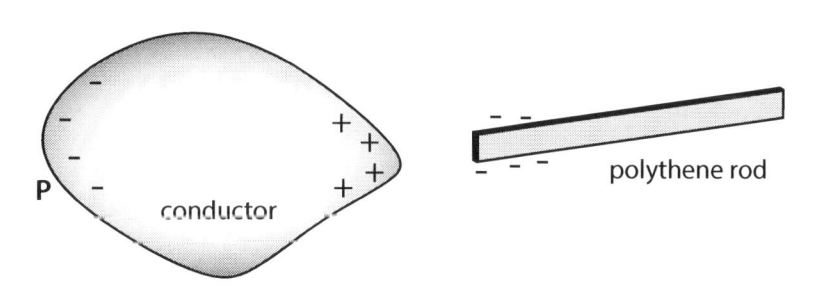

The time-honoured, school method of rubbing a polythene rod with a woollen cloth, leaves the rod negatively charged and ready for use. Brought close to (but not touching) a conductor, redistributes the charges in the conductor as in the diagram. The electrons are repelled to the far left leaving an excess of positive charge on the right side. If you remove the rod, the charges in the conductor return to their previous positions. But, if you leave the rod in place and touch point 'P' with your hand, the electrons can get further away from the rod and reach planet Earth through your body. If you now remove your hand from point 'P', the electrons can't get back to the conductor. This leaves the conductor with a net positive charge. Finally, remove the rod, and the remaining negative charges will be redistributed across the surface of the conductor, leaving it with an overall positive charge across the whole surface.

I've drawn the conductor with bumps. If it was a sphere, the positive charge would be uniformly distributed over its surface. With bumps on it, you get more charge at the pointy bumps and less charge on flatter parts. The electric field strength is higher near bumps (especially sharp bumps) and can cause discharges into the air. Roughly speaking, a bump is where charge can get further away from the other charges. The mutual repulsion of the charges, and the ability to move through a material, is what makes the charges end on the surface. Experiments show that the charge is within the top two atomic layers.

A similar effect happens to the charges in a conductor when it's placed in an **external** electric field (one which is a bit more extensive than the polythene rod). The external field is produced by a positive charge off to the left of the diagram. You can tell it's not a point charge since the field lines are parallel. It was produced by a flat conducting plate. The electrons within the conductor are attracted to the left, leaving the right side positive. These charges reside on the surface and produce a field which modifies the external electric field as shown. These field lines enter and leave the conductor's surface at an angle of 90°. If they weren't at 90°, the electric field lines would have a component parallel to the surface of the conductor. This would move the electric charges on the surface and redistribute them further. The fact that the charges are static, implies that the electric field is at 90° to the surface. In electrostatics, the actual surface of a conductor will always be an equipotential surface (touch any two places with the probes of a voltmeter and it will read zero volts). With gravity, the field lines will be at 90° to the equipotential surface (which may not correspond exactly with the actual surface you walk on!).

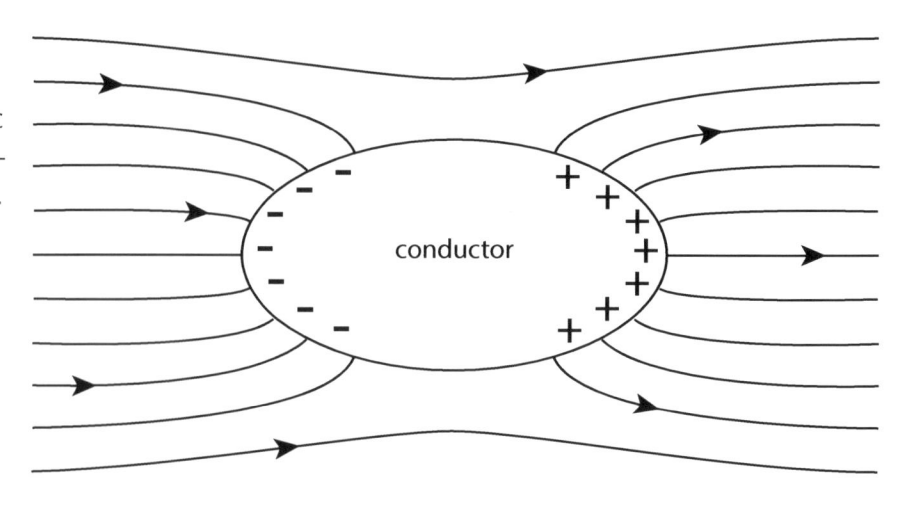

**Models and the Real World** Field lines are useful mathematical constructs, but don't exist in the real world. Pushing the model too far can lead to an apparent paradox until you remember that they aren't real. Take a point positive and point negative charge nearby. One of the rules says that lines leave the positive charge and **must** end on the negative charge. In the diagram, how does the line coming out of the left end up coming in on the right? (Assume no other charges in the universe, and that the universe isn't 'curved'). The answer is that it doesn't join up; the model has been pushed too far. The problem wouldn't arise if we used shading to illustrate the field strength.

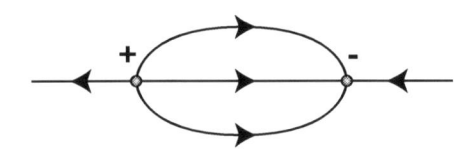

## The Electric Field between Parallel Plates

Lines getting further apart means a weaker electric field. Parallel lines imply a uniform (constant) electric field. The uniform field is very useful since it gives a constant force on any charged particle within it. It's also easy to produce. Use parallel conducting plates as in the diagram. The battery which supplies the energy to the electric field isn't shown, but the voltmeter which records the potential difference is connected across the plates. The electric field lines point from the positive to the negative plate. The small charged particle shown has a negative charge, so experiences a force in the opposite direction to the arrows. The electric field is constant so the force on the particle will be constant ($F = Eq$) and the acceleration will be constant ($F = ma$). You can use the equations of motion like $s = ut + \frac{1}{2}at^2$ to solve problems. Our definition of the electric field strength (page 159) comes from the force on a known charge ($F = Eq$). There is an alternative way to calculate it; one which involves voltage and distance. It's easy to derive for the special case of a uniform field and easy to write down for the general case of any shape of field.

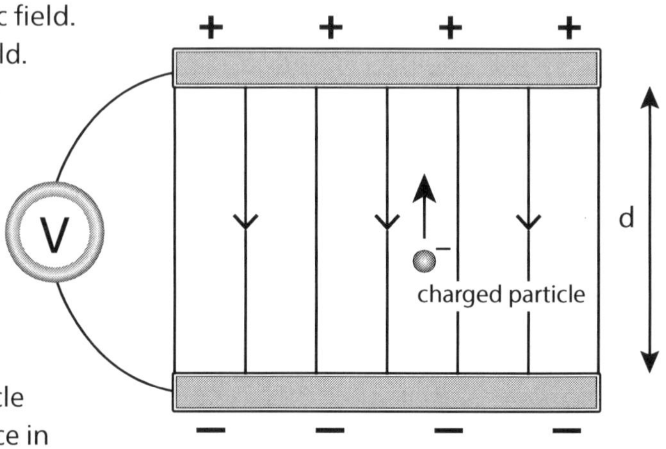

# Electromagnetism

Start off with the negatively charged particle at the negative plate and let it go (refer to previous diagram). The electric field is constant, so the force on the particle is constant, so the acceleration is constant, and so you could use your old favourite equations of motion. It then bashes into the positive plate. To form an equation, we say that the work done by the battery through the electric field is transferred into the kinetic energy of the charged particle. We have an expression for the work done (W.D. = Vq), and one for the kinetic energy ($E_k = \frac{1}{2}mv^2$), so equating them gives: $Vq = \frac{1}{2}mv^2$

We have uniform acceleration, so can use $v^2 = u^2 + 2as$ with $u = 0$, to give:

$$Vq = \frac{1}{2}mv^2 = \frac{1}{2}m(u^2 + 2as) = mas$$

Finally use Newton's 2nd Law (F = ma) and the definition of electric field strength (F = Eq):

$$Vq = mas = Fs = Eqs \qquad \Rightarrow E = \frac{V}{s}$$

We've used the symbol 's' for the distance moved. The usual symbol for the separation of the plates is 'd' and if the charged particle moves from one plate to another, the formula becomes:

$$E = \frac{V}{d}$$

Remember that it only works for **uniform fields**; don't apply it to a point charge. It also gives us an alternative unit for electric field strength. We're dividing a voltage (in volts) by a distance (in metres) so that unit is volts per metre (Vm⁻¹). Parallel plates with a voltage of 200volts across them and a separation of 5cm will have an electric field strength of 200÷0.05 = 4000Vm⁻¹ between the plates. You could also express it as 4000NC⁻¹.

Parallel plates are used in oscilloscopes and (were used) in old television tubes. This time, the electrons are fired in from the side (daigram below). As they pass through, they get deflected by the electric field and come out the other side where a fluorescent screen detects them as a spot of light. Waggle the

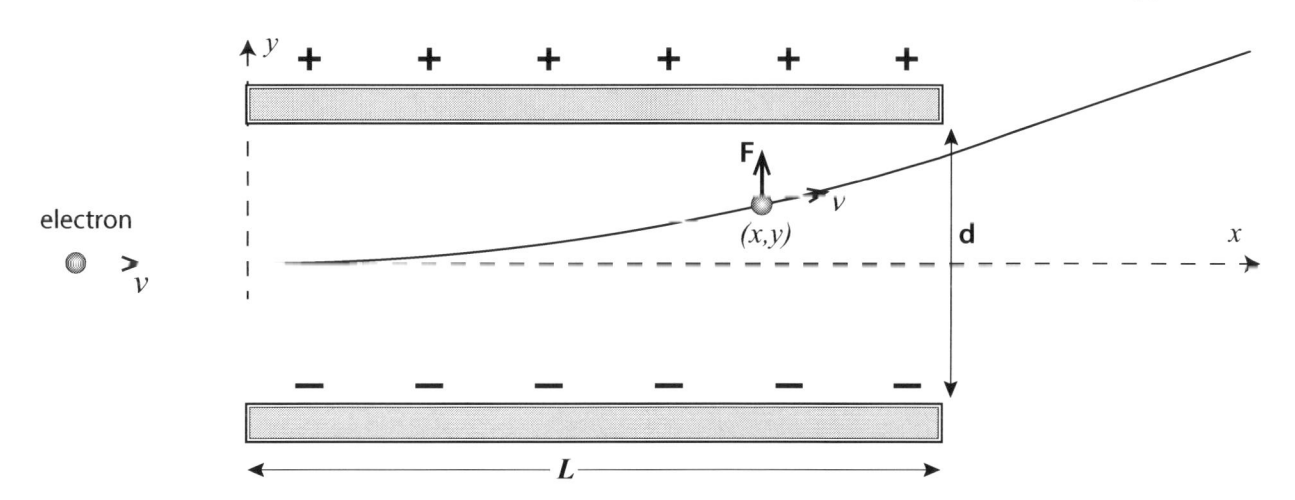

voltage dial and you could move the spot up and down within the top half of the screen. Reverse the connections and you could move it within the bottom half of the screen.

How much voltage would be needed to produce a given vertical deflection on the screen? Keep things simple and assume no electric field outside the plates and a perfectly uniform field between the plates. The plates are charged by voltage 'V', have length 'L' and separation 'd'. The electrons have speed 'v' and are aimed midway between the plates. A cartesian co-ordinate system is set-up as shown (origin begins at start of uniform field).

Here's the strategy. Determine the forces. Split the motion into horizontal and vertical components. Use the equations of motion to derive the horizontal and vertical displacements in terms of time. Eliminate the time to express the y-deflection in terms of the x-displacement.

The forces are due to a gravitational field (since the electron has mass) and an electric field (since the electron has charge). They both act vertically. Let's compare the sizes.

$$W = mg = 9.1 \times 10^{-31} \times 9.8 = 8.9 \times 10^{-30} \text{ N} \qquad F_{elec} = Eq = \frac{V}{d}q = \frac{V}{d} \times 1.6 \times 10^{-19}$$

With electrons as the charged particles, you can ignore gravity unless a stellar mass black hole is nearby. On Earth, V÷d would have to be very small to bring gravity into consideration. If the charged particle was on an oil drop as in the Millikan experiment (so it's not the mass of the electron, but the mass of the oil drop), gravity becomes important; always do a quick calculation. We ignore gravity and take the only force to be due to a uniform electric field. Use the equations of motion for constant acceleration:

Horizontal Motion: $v = \frac{x}{t}$ 	Vertical Motion: $s = ut + \frac{1}{2}at^2 \Rightarrow y = \frac{1}{2}at^2$

The t's are the same. Eliminate 't' by substitution:

$$v = \frac{x}{t} \Rightarrow t = \frac{x}{v} \qquad y = \frac{1}{2}at^2 = \frac{1}{2}a\left(\frac{x}{v}\right)^2 \Rightarrow y = \left(\frac{a}{2v^2}\right)x^2$$

This is the equation for the shape of the trajectory within the plates, a quadratic (parabola). We need an expression for the vertical acceleration 'a' in terms of things we can measure:

$$F_{elec} = Eq = \frac{V}{d}q = ma \Rightarrow a = \frac{Vq}{md}$$

We now substitute this acceleration into the quadratic. The electron leaves the plates when x = L, so the vertical displacement on leaving the plates is:

$$y = \left(\frac{Vq}{2mv^2 d}\right)x^2 \Rightarrow \left(\frac{Vq}{2mv^2 d}\right)L^2$$

Deriving this equation and understanding what you're doing is a good example of the academic standard you should be trying to achieve in this course.

**Example**  An electron enters the mid-point of parallel plates with a horizontal speed of 5 x 10⁶m s⁻¹. The potential difference across the plates is 40volts. They have a separation of 12cm and a length of 20cm. Calculate the vertical displacement and direction of travel on leaving the plates. State any assumptions you make.

Substitute the values into the quadratic equation:

$$y = \left(\frac{Vq}{2mv^2 d}\right)L^2 = \frac{40 \times 1.6 \times 10^{-19} \times (0.2)^2}{2 \times 9.1 \times 10^{-31} \times (5 \times 10^6)^2 \times 0.12} = 0.047 \text{m}$$

The angle on leaving the plates comes from the gradient $\frac{dy}{dx}$. So differentiate the quadratic! This gives:

$$\frac{dy}{dx} = \left(\frac{Vq}{2mv^2 d}\right) \times 2x$$

Evaluate at $x = L$ to obtain a gradient of tanθ = 0.47 which is an angle of 25°. An assumption is that the electron only experiences a force when it's between the plates.

# Electromagnetism

## Particle Accelerators

The acceleration of charged particles to high speeds has many applications; from the electron 'guns' in old fashioned television sets, to the destruction of cancerous cells in tissue, to the investigation of the structure of the atom. The machines used to achieve this provide a fascinating study in their own right. They range from simple parallel plate arrangements up to the most advanced technology on the planet, requiring thousands of highly trained scientists and engineers to design and operate. But before describing how they work, you must know about a new unit for energy.

## A New Unit for Energy

Particle Physicists don't use the joule as their unit of energy; it's too big and too inconvenient. They want something suitable for describing the energy of the particles they study, rather than something designed for use with electric kettles or tanks of petrol. To them, one unit of energy is what an electron gains when accelerated through a potential difference of one volt. It has a confusing name, the 'electron-volt' (eV), which leads some people to think that it's a voltage. But it's not a voltage; it's an energy. You can see why they called it the 'ee-vee', but they should have chosen another name. The energy gained by the electron (an energy of 1eV) in accelerating through a potential difference of one volt is:

$$\text{Work Done} = qV = 1.6 \times 10^{-19} \times 1 = 1.6 \times 10^{-19} \text{ Joules} \quad (\equiv 1\text{eV})$$

Multiples are commonly used:

$$1\text{keV} = 1,000\text{eV} = 1.602 \times 10^{-16} \text{ joules}$$
$$1\text{MeV} = 1,000,000\text{eV} = 1.602 \times 10^{-13} \text{ joules}$$
$$1\text{GeV} = 1,000,000,000\text{eV} = 1.602 \times 10^{-10} \text{ joules}$$
$$1\text{TeV} = 1,000,000,000,000\text{eV} = 1.602 \times 10^{-7} \text{ joules}$$

Through Einstein's equation $E = mc^2$ we can also use this energy unit to quantify the masses of the elementary particles.

**Example** The mass of a proton is $1.67 \times 10^{-27}$ kg. Multiply by the speed of light squared for the energy equivalent in joules:

$$E = mc^2 = 1.67 \times 10^{-27} \times (3 \times 10^8)^2 = 1.5 \times 10^{-10} \text{ Joules}$$

Then convert to our new unit:

$$1.5 \times 10^{-10} \text{ Joules} \quad \Rightarrow \quad \frac{1.5 \times 10^{-10}}{1.6 \times 10^{-19}} = 9.38 \times 10^8 \text{ eV} = 938 \text{ MeV}$$

This is the energy you would get if you converted the mass of a proton into energy. Its mass would be expressed as 938MeV/$c^2$. Other examples are the electron with a mass of 511keV/$c^2$ and the recently discovered Higgs Boson with a mass of 126GeV/$c^2$. In conversation, particle physicists don't even bother saying the $c^2$; it's just 'proton mass is 938MeV'.

The electron-volt is commonly used in chemistry where chemical reactions are of the order of eV. The ionisation energy for the lowest orbital of a hydrogen atom is 13.6eV, and visible light photons emitted from atoms are typically of a few eV energy. Anything to do with the nucleus has energies of the order of MeV (and hence nuclear explosions release about one million times more energy per atom than chemical explosions). The nuclear reactions in the Sun release particles with energies of a few MeV and a few days later, hit our atmosphere. The Large Hadron Collider at CERN collides 7TeV protons with 7TeV protons travelling in the opposite direction. Highest energy of all, are the cosmic 'rays' with energies up to $10^{20}$eV (the one place where the joule would be useful!)

# The Cyclotron

Accelerating an uncharged particle is difficult; that's why you don't find many high energy neutrons. They get their speed 'at birth' and that's pretty well that. Charged particles can be accelerated using electric and magnetic fields. The electric field changes their speed and the magnetic field changes their direction. The choice is to accelerate the particles in a single straight line or to go around in a circle many times. The longest straight-line accelerator is just south of San Francisco at Palo Alto and is 3km long. The largest circular accelerator is west of Geneva and has a diameter of 8.5km. In all cases, you have to accelerate the particles in a vacuum to prevent collisions with air molecules. With large machines, that's a lot of nothing!

The most basic type of circular design is the cyclotron. It started in the 1930's with a 20cm diameter (energy about 1MeV) and evolved up to 4.7m diameter (energy about 100MeV) by 1942. This diagram shows the basic design. It's in two halves, each called a 'dee' (shaded grey) with a small gap between them. If a proton is at position 'A', you make the top dee negative to accelerate it across the gap to position 'B'. A magnetic field makes it travel in a circular orbit to position 'C'. During this time you switch the polarity of the dees so that the top dee becomes positive and the bottom dee negative. Once again the proton gets accelerated across the gap to position 'D'. By the time it gets back to 'A', the polarity of the 'dees' has been reversed again. This is what the oscillator is for; it is an a.c. voltage supply which changes its polarity in step with the motion of the protons. Each time they cross the gap, the protons get faster, so you might think that the polarity of the oscillator would have to change at a complicated rate. It doesn't, and the reason is that the time for an orbit (or half orbit for each dee) is independent of the speed and radius (see page 119):

$$T = \frac{2\pi m}{qB} \quad \text{(full orbit)} \qquad t = \frac{\pi m}{qB} \quad \text{(time in each 'dee')}$$

As the proton gets faster, it moves outwards with a larger radius until eventually it can be deflected off to the side at a tangent towards an experiment. The above equations are non-relativistic. When the protons become relativistic, the time for an orbit depends upon the speed and the oscillator gets out of step with the protons. Another problem is being able to create a strong magnetic field over a large area; this limits the size, and led to the development of ring shaped accelerators.

The Large Hadron Collider is the latest in a series of ring-shaped accelerators called synchrotrons. The charged particles are accelerated along the circumference of a circle of fixed radius. This is different from the cyclotron where the radius increases with the speed, and a magnetic field is required across the entire area. In the synchrotron, the magnetic field need only be applied along the circumference of the ring, but it has to change as the particles speed-up. As before, an electric field is used to increase the energy of the particles. This is applied at one position on the ring (the north-west side) using a voltage of 16MV at a frequency of 400MHz. The magnets are of two main types: dipoles for bending the beam and quadrupoles for focussing the beam. If you're getting the impression that things are very complicated, you're correct! In fact, everything about this project invites superlatives. Go see it for yourself!

# Electromagnetism

## Millikan's Oil Drop Experiment

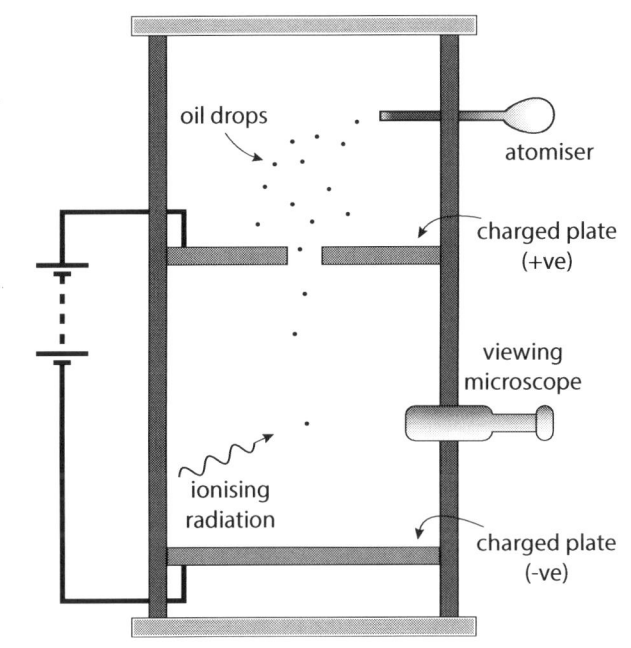

His most important contribution to science was on the photoelectric effect, but Millikan's most famous work is his oil drop experiment to determine the charge on the electron. In fact, he wasn't the first person to measure it. John Townsend (1897) had come up with a method involving passing an electrified gas into a damp atmosphere. Small water droplets formed around each elementary charge (like the idea behind the cloud chamber which was in the process of being developed by CTR Wilson). By measuring the mass of each drop, the total mass of water collected and the total charge on the gas, he estimated the charge on each drop. His answer was surprisingly accurate, $1.7 \times 10^{-19}$ Coulombs!!

Millikan started his investigations in 1908. He pumped a fine spray of oil drops through an aperture into a chamber (diagram above right). The pump charges-up many of the drops by friction. They then entered the chamber where they were exposed to ionising radiation. The ionising radiation changed the charge on the drop and it was this *difference* to the charge which Millikan measured.

The chamber is basically the space between parallel charged plates maintained at a potential difference of 'V'. A single drop is viewed using a microscope and the voltage increased until the drop is brought to rest. The weight of the oil drop is now balanced by the electrostatic force on the charge:

$$mg = Eq = \frac{V}{d}q \quad \Rightarrow \quad q = \frac{mgd}{V}$$

A value for the charge requires four measurements. The voltage, the separation of the plates and gravitational field strength are the easy part, measuring the mass of the oil drop is the tricky part. This is done by switching off the voltage supply and letting the oil drop fall. It's terminal velocity is given by:

$$v = \frac{2r^2 \rho g}{9\eta}$$

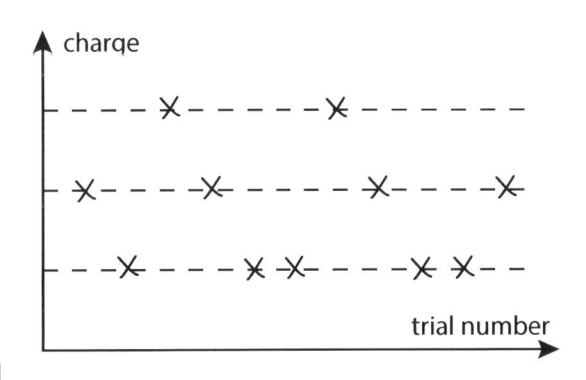

The formula contains the gravitational field strength, the density of the oil and the coefficient of viscosity. These are all known quantities. Measuring the terminal velocity gives the radius and hence the mass of the drop (knowing the density and assuming a spherical shape). An alternative is to estimate the radius using the microscope scale. His results are usually presented like the display opposite. It shows the results for 11 trials. Charges only lie on definite levels with nothing in between. Hence charge is quantised. Millikan published his final value in 1917 as $(1.592 \pm 0.002) \times 10^{-19}$C.

One of his students at the University of Chicago had measured the coefficient of viscosity. Years later, it was found to be too small. Had the student obtained the correct value, Millikan's result for the elementary charge would have been even better!

## Electrostatic Potential

We've reached that dreaded word again. Like gravitational potential (page 57), it's just a way of helping us work out the energy needed to move around in a field. This time it's the electric field produced by a charge 'Q'. We wish to calculate the energy required to move a small charge 'q' from 'A' to 'B'. Remember the recipe?

- Take the number for the start position 'A'
- Take the number for the finish position 'B'
- Calculate 'finish number – start number'
- Multiply by the charge moved 'q'
- That's the energy required

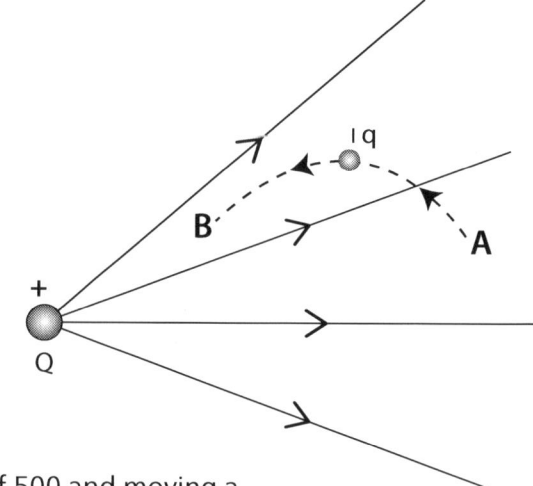

For example, a start number of 200, a finish number of 500 and moving a charge of 6 coulombs. The energy required is (500-200) × 6 = 1800 Joules. Does this look familiar? It's just 'Work Done = Vq' where 'V' is the potential **difference**.

To make the units consistent, the start and finish numbers have units of joules per coulomb (JC⁻¹). These numbers are called the electrostatic potentials at point 'A' and at point 'B'. Notice how the calculation only depends upon the start and finish positions. You can take any route in between. That's weird. The electrostatic field shares this feature with the gravitational field; the energy required does not depend upon the path. They are examples of conservative fields. (If the field wasn't conservative, you could go around in a closed loop and gain energy on each circuit).

The expression for the **electrostatic potential at a point due to a point charge 'Q'** is similar to the one for the gravitational potential due to a mass 'M':

$$V = \frac{1}{4\pi\varepsilon_o} \frac{Q}{r}$$

The large constant jumble (9 × 10⁹) appears again and sets the scale. A new feature is that the electrostatic potential can be negative or positive depending on the sign of the charge 'Q' producing the field.

**Examples** A distance of 40m from a +6µC charge: $V = \frac{1}{4\pi\varepsilon_o} \frac{Q}{r} = 9 \times 10^9 \times \frac{(+6 \times 10^{-6})}{40} = 1350 \, J\,C^{-1}$

A distance of 15m from a -8µC charge: $V = \frac{1}{4\pi\varepsilon_o} \frac{Q}{r} = 9 \times 10^9 \times \frac{(-8 \times 10^{-6})}{15} = -4800 \, J\,C^{-1}$

Electrostatic potential is a scalar, so if there's more than one source charge contributing to the field, just add them as numbers. Remember to take the signs into account; plus for positive charges, minus for negative charges. And the bottom line has an 'r', not an 'r²' as in the electric field strength.

Units: The unit for electrostatic potential is the joule per coulomb. Writing it this way reminds us that it is a step on the way to calculating energy. Its alternative name is your old enemy, the 'volt'. Using this word creates mystery and cranial discomfort, but we're stuck with it. However, you might cause confusion if you go into a shop and ask for a nine joules per coulomb battery!

# Electromagnetism

## Derivation of Electrostatic Potential

Here's a definition which works for **any** electrostatic field:

***the electrostatic potential at a point is the work done per unit charge by external forces in moving a positive test charge from infinity to that point.***

You often see it erroneously written without the 'per unit charge' bit. This can give you the wrong impression that potential is the same as the work done. If you drag a 1 Coulomb charge from infinity the numbers will be the same, but 6 volts isn't 6 joules; it's 6 joules per coulomb. Period. Now here's the derivation for the **special case** of the electrostatic potential due to the field of a **point charge** 'Q'.

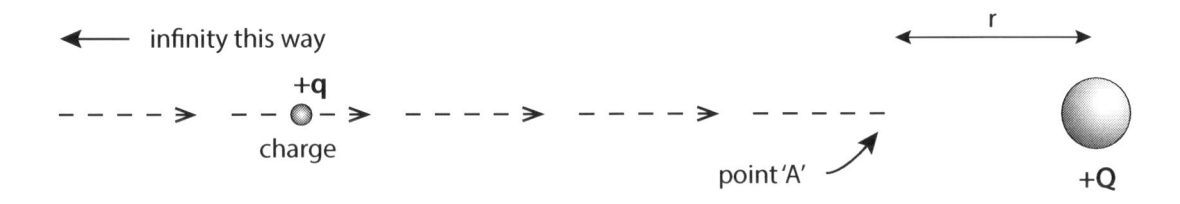

Let's translate the definition from words to mathematics. We have to use the integral form for the work done since the force on the charge 'q' isn't constant:

$$\text{Work Done} = \int F dx = \int_{\infty}^{r} F_{ext} dr$$

The diagram shows the field is created by a positive charge +Q. The charge being moved '+q', will be repelled, so the external force (that's from you) will be pointing inwards. This external force is in the opposite direction to the electric field: $F_{ext} = -F_{elec}$. This gives:

$$\text{Work Done} = \int_{\infty}^{r} F_{ext} dr = -\int_{\infty}^{r} F_{elec} dr = -\int_{\infty}^{r} \frac{1}{4\pi\varepsilon_o}\frac{qQ}{r^2} dr = -\frac{qQ}{4\pi\varepsilon_o}\int_{\infty}^{r}\frac{1}{r^2} dr$$

Now evaluate the integral:

$$\text{Work Done} = -\frac{qQ}{4\pi\varepsilon_o}\int_{\infty}^{r}\frac{1}{r^2}dr = -\frac{qQ}{4\pi\varepsilon_o}\left[-\frac{1}{r}\right]_{\infty}^{r} = \frac{qQ}{4\pi\varepsilon_o}\left[\frac{1}{r}-\frac{1}{\infty}\right] = \frac{1}{4\pi\varepsilon_o}\frac{Q}{r}q$$

This is the Work Done in joules, by you, in getting the system from an infinite distance apart (where there's no energy) to a distance 'r' apart where the system now has electrostatic potential energy. The above expression is the **electrostatic potential energy** of the system. We have one last thing to do to get the electrostatic potential; divide by the charge 'q' you pushed inwards (remember it's the Work Done *per unit charge*!). This gives:

$$V = \frac{1}{4\pi\varepsilon_o}\frac{Q}{r}$$

A charge +Q will give potentials which are positive and a charge –Q will give negative potentials.

**Example** Calculate the electrostatic potential at 'P'.

$$V_{+5\mu C} = \frac{1}{4\pi\varepsilon_o}\frac{Q}{r} = 9\times 10^9 \times \frac{(5\times 10^{-6})}{22} = 2045 \, J\,C^{-1} = 2045 \text{ volts}$$

$$V_{-8\mu C} = \frac{1}{4\pi\varepsilon_o}\frac{Q}{r} = 9\times 10^9 \times \frac{(-8\times 10^{-6})}{37} = -1946 \text{ volts}$$

Giving a potential at point 'P' of +99 volts.

169

## Infinity and Planet Earth

The expression for electrostatic potential, $V(r) = \frac{1}{4\pi\varepsilon_o}\frac{Q}{r}$, means that you have to go an infinite distance from 'Q' to reach zero potential. Zero potential is a reference point. It would be nice to be able to attach a wire to infinity and measure our potential differences with respect to it. But we can't. So we make do with the fact that it's potential **differences** which are important. All we need ask of our reference point is that it doesn't change electrically if we attach our wire to it. We've traded 'nothing' for 'neutral'. What we need is a reservoir big enough to act as a place to put electric charges and get them back, without measurably changing its own electrostatic potential. In practice we have to use planet Earth; it becomes our zero of potential. The earth symbol is shown on the parallel plates diagram below. Houses in the country sometimes have to provide their own earth system (known as a 'TT'). You dig a one metre deep hole in the ground, bury a copper rod in it with the top sticking out, and attach your earth cable from the rod to the earthing terminal on the consumer unit in the house.

## The Electrostatic Potential between Parallel Plates

This is another example of the use of the definition of electrostatic potential. In this case we don't need integration since the electric field is constant. My x-direction starts at the earthed plate (x = 0) and increases towards the positive plate. The charge 'q' is positive and you're moving it to the positive plate, so the external force 'F' needs to be applied in the same direction as my x-direction.

Connecting the bottom plate to earth, gives it a potential of zero (it's 'neutral'). Starting the trip from the bottom plate (x = 0) means we can write the work done by you as:

Work Done = Force × distance
$$= F\,x = qE\,x$$

Divide both sides by 'q' and recall that work done divided by charge is the potential difference:

$$V(x) = E\,x$$

The potential V(x) is proportional to the distance 'x' from the bottom plate. The dotted lines on the diagram show what this means in practice. These parallel lines (called equipotential lines) cut the electric field lines at 90° (compare page 162)

*Nerdy Note:* The lines of equal potential and the electric field lines cross each other at 90°. The electric field lines cannot force a charge to move across the surface. They can make it move away from the surface, but not across it. There is a more general relationship between the electric field strength and the electrostatic potential which works for any electric field pattern (not just parallel plates). We drag a small positive test charge 'q' from infinity towards a charge 'Q' which produces the electric field. Start from the vector dot product expression for the Work Done (it's like the page 169 derivation).

$$\text{Work Done} = \int \underline{F}_{ext} \bullet d\underline{x} = -\int qE\,dr = -q\int E\,dr \quad \Rightarrow \quad V = -\int E\,dr \quad \Rightarrow \quad \int E\,dr = -V$$

Differentiate both sides with respect to 'r': $E = -\frac{dV}{dr}$ (really a 'partial' derivative). In words, the electric field strength is the negative of the gradient of the potential. For a positive charge 'Q', the gradient of the electrostatic potential is negative (the potential goes from a positive value near the charge and decreases to zero at infinity; imagine the graph), so the minus sign makes the electric field positive.

# Electromagnetism

## Points of Balance

The electrostatic potential 'V' due to a positive charge has a positive sign (eg. +80volts at a particular point) and the electrostatic potential due to a negative charge has a negative sign (eg. -50volts). To calculate the potential at a point due to two charges, you use the Principle of Superposition. Electrostatic potential is a scalar so forget directions and just add them like ordinary numbers with signs. If both charges are positive, the sum of two positive numbers must be another positive number. If the two charges have opposite signs then there will be places where the result for the potential will be zero (eg. +70volts and -70volts giving a result of zero volts).

What about the electric field from two charges? You can get places where the electrostatic field (E) due to two charges will add-up to zero. In this case we are dealing with vectors, and you can get a result of zero by having two vectors of the same size but pointing in opposite directions (eg. 80N/C to the right and 80N/C to the left giving a result of zero Newtons per Coulomb). A point of zero electric field is a point of interest to us since it wouldn't accelerate a charged object.

Here is an example of a calculation in one dimension using the **electrostatic potentials** due to two charges of opposite sign (+8µC and -5µC which are 30cm apart).

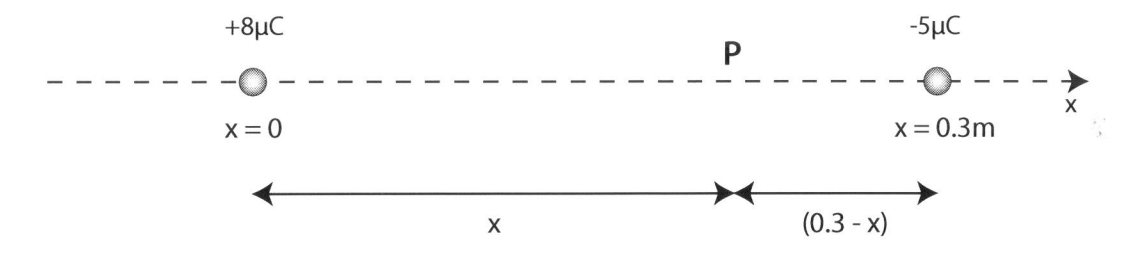

```
        +8µC                                      -5µC
                                     P
  ------ O ----------------------- O ------>
                                                         x
         x = 0                                x = 0.3m

         <-------------- x --------------><--(0.3 - x)-->
```

The point 'P' is where the potentials from each charge will be the same size but opposite in sign. The distances from each charge are as indicated.

Potential at 'P' due to the +8µC charge:     $V = \frac{1}{4\pi\varepsilon_o}\frac{Q}{r} \Rightarrow \frac{1}{4\pi\varepsilon_o}\frac{8\times 10^{-6}}{x}$

Potential at 'P' due to the -5µC charge:     $V = \frac{1}{4\pi\varepsilon_o}\frac{Q}{r} \Rightarrow \frac{1}{4\pi\varepsilon_o}\frac{-5\times 10^{-6}}{(0.3-x)}$

The total at 'P' should add up to zero:     $\frac{1}{4\pi\varepsilon_o}\frac{8\times 10^{-6}}{x} + \frac{1}{4\pi\varepsilon_o}\frac{-5\times 10^{-6}}{(0.3-x)} = 0$

At this stage of the algebra, you can usually cancel out the common terms (the $10^{-6}$ and the $4\pi\varepsilon_o$) to get:

$$\frac{8}{x} - \frac{5}{(0.3-x)} = 0 \Rightarrow \frac{8}{x} = \frac{5}{(0.3-x)} \Rightarrow 8(0.3-x) = 5x \Rightarrow x \approx 0.185m$$

If you input this value in the individual expressions for the potentials, you get +390kV from the +8µC charge and -390kV from the -5µC charge. The point 'P' is at zero electrostatic potential.

Here are some questions. Is this the only position with zero potential? You don't get a point of zero potential to the left of the +8µC charge. Why is this? Can you show that you get a point of zero potential to the *right* of the -5µC charge? See the diagram on the middle of the next page, then repeat the above method to show that it is at x = 0.8m. If we remember that the two charges are in 3-dimensional space, will there be an equipotential **surface** at zero potential? What shape would the zero equipotential surface be if the charges were the same size but opposite sign? (Answer: a flat plane out of the page at midpoint).

Now let's look for 'points of balance' of the **electrostatic field**, places where the electric field is zero. The simplest arrangement is with two charges. There are three possible combinations of two charges. These are shown below with the electric field directions for the individual charges drawn at three places (to the left 'A', in between 'B', and to the right 'C', of the pair of charges).

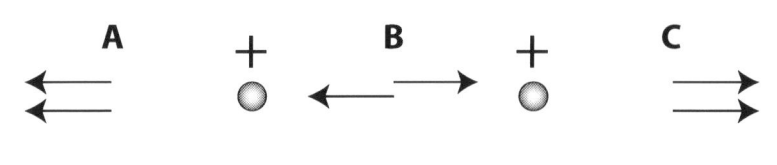

The top arrow in each pair is the field direction from the left hand electric charge, and the bottom one is that due to the right hand charge. The lengths of the arrow aren't significant; they just indicate where you might get the total electric field adding up to zero. We can see that you might get zero electric field strength in-between charges of the same sign, or outside of charges of the opposite sign. The details will depend upon the size of each charge. For charges of equal magnitude of the same sign, zero electric field must occur at the midpoint (by symmetry).

**Example**  Calculate the zero electric field position 'P' for opposite-sign charges in the diagram below. The magnitudes are the same as the previous potentials diagram (page 171).

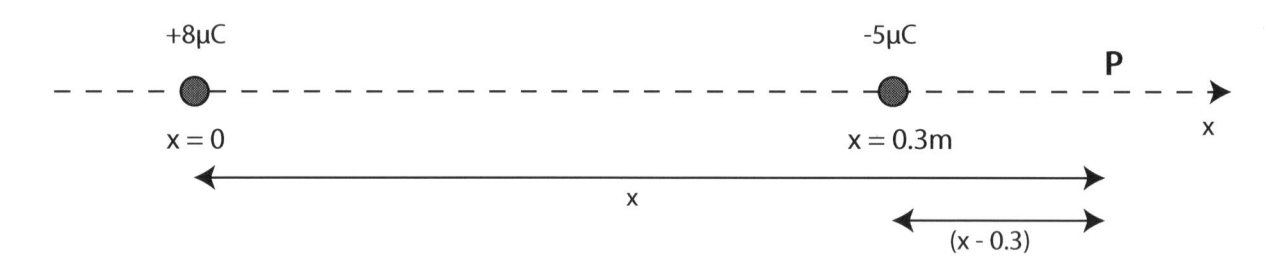

Electric field strength due to the +8µC charge: $E = \frac{1}{4\pi\varepsilon_o}\frac{Q}{r^2} \Rightarrow \frac{1}{4\pi\varepsilon_o}\frac{8\times 10^{-6}}{x^2}$ **to the right**

Electric field strength due to the -5µC charge: $E = \frac{1}{4\pi\varepsilon_o}\frac{Q}{r^2} \Rightarrow \frac{1}{4\pi\varepsilon_o}\frac{5\times 10^{-6}}{(x-0.3)^2}$ **to the left**

These should be equal in magnitude: $\frac{1}{4\pi\varepsilon_o}\frac{8\times 10^{-6}}{x^2} = \frac{1}{4\pi\varepsilon_o}\frac{5\times 10^{-6}}{(x-0.3)^2}$

As before, cancel the $10^{-6}$ and the $4\pi\varepsilon_o$ to get a quadratic equation $\left(x^2 - 1.6x + 0.24 = 0\right)$ with two solutions x = 1.432m and x = 0.168m. The first solution x = 1.432m, locates the point 'P' to the right of the righthand charge as expected, but what about the other solution at x = 0.168m? It sneaked in uninvited when we wrote down the equation which said 'these should be equal in size'. That covers both possibilities where they point in the same direction or point in opposite directions. The point x = 0.168m is in between the charges where the contributions are equal in size, but pointing in the same direction (to the right) so that they don't cancel. Another question. Why don't you get a point of zero electric field strength to the left of the left hand charge in this particular example (except at infinity)?

# Electromagnetism

## Equipotential Lines and Surfaces

As the name implies, all points on an equipotential surface are at the same potential. So the potential difference between any two points on the surface is zero. Overall, no work is done in going from one point on the surface to any other point on the surface. You can start and finish at the same point, going in a closed loop, with the same result.

As with gravity, the equipotential surfaces of a point electric charge are spheres. Two negative point charges will produce a diagram like the gravitational one on the bottom of page 60. Two positive charges would produce the same shape and make the numbers positive. Two point charges of the opposite sign placed a distance apart is called an electric dipole. The electrostatic potential at any point in the space around it is best shown in three dimensions. The diagram on the right is a 2 dimensional slice across the middle of it. The negative charge (about -11nC) has twice the charge of the positive one.

The units are Joules per Coulomb with a grid spacing of one metre. For example, moving a +2 coulomb charge from anywhere on the -12 volt surface to anywhere on the +4 volt surface requires 32 joules from external sources.

If you plot the values for the electrostatic potential up the way on a z-axis, instead of marking them on a 2-D diagram, the slice across the middle gives this wireframe diagram:

The net lines are not equipotential lines, they're for illustration. In real 3-D space, the equipotential surfaces are mostly egg shaped (imagine rotating the top diagram about a left-right horizontal axis through the charges). Taking a horizontal slice at, say, the $z = V = -12 JC^{-1}$ level, would reproduce that particular contour in the top diagram. The 32 joules example would go from inside the hole to part-way up the hill.

Having twice the charge, the negative charge has a bigger electrostatic potential well than the positive charge.

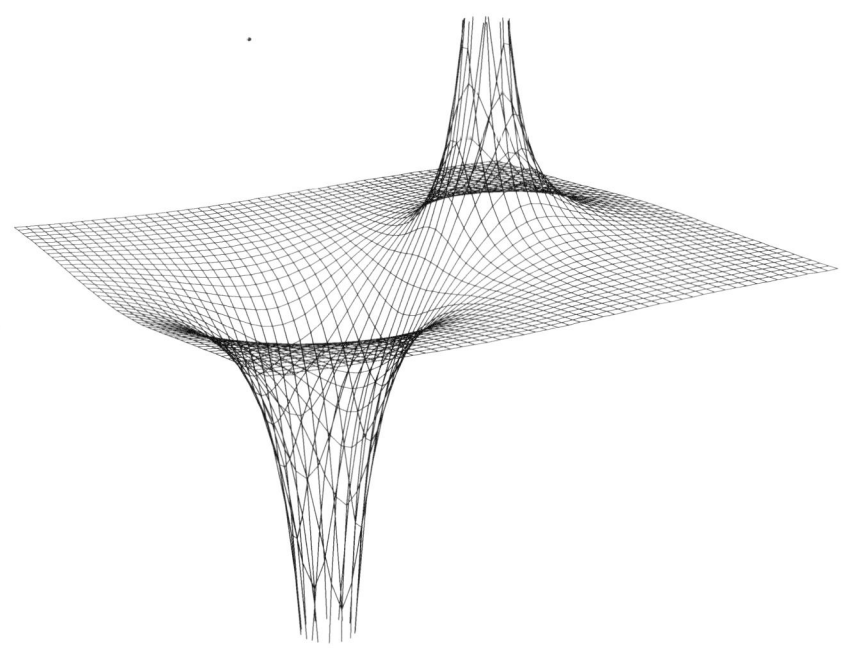

## Inside Conductors

The sources of the electric field (the charges) can move within a conductor. As we've seen, they redistribute themselves within the top two atomic layers of the surface of the conductor. This means that the conductor can be hollow or solid; the charges come to rest on the surface. For a conductor in the shape of a sphere, the electric field produced **outside** is identical to the field of a point charge at the centre. **Inside** the sphere, the electric field is zero. No electric field inside the sphere means that a test electric charge does no work (its got nothing to work against), so does not increase the system potential. The potential inside stays constant (equal to its surface value). Here are graphs of the electric field strength (left pair) and electrostatic potential (right pair) through the centres of 1m radius spheres for both positive and negative charges (±0.44nC). The units are metres, volts per metre and joules per coulomb.

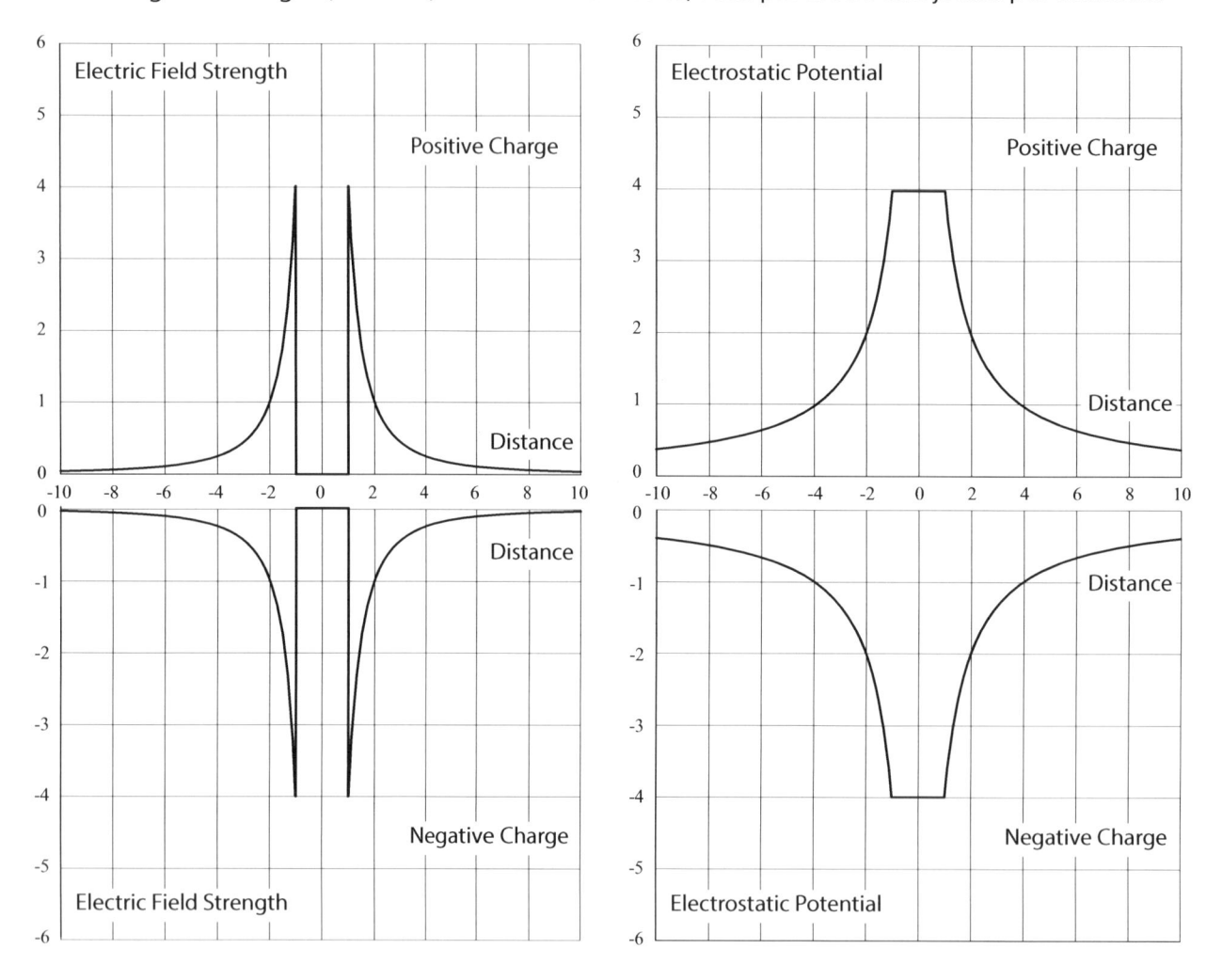

The reasoning on this goes back to Newton. Take a point 'P' inside a charged sphere (hollow or solid). Draw two cones opposite to each other with their tips joined at 'P'. On the diagram, the bigger cone cuts the surface over a bigger area 'A', and covers more charge. The smaller cone covers a smaller area of charge 'B', on the opposite surface. These areas are proportional to the square of the distance from 'P' (twice the distance, four times the area). The charge is evenly spread across the surface on a sphere, so twice the distance would be four times the area and contain four times the electric charge. The electric field strength at point 'P' gets contributions from the charge from both area 'A' and area 'B'. They cancel, since the greater charge at 'A' combined with its greater distance (remember it's inverse square) produces the same answer as that due to 'B'. The resulting electric field inside is zero. The maths is easier with a spherical shape, but this result also holds for any shape.

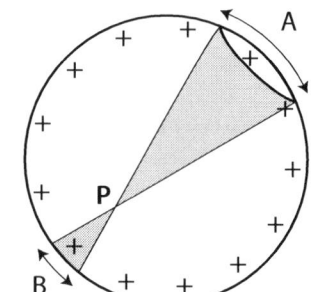

174

# Electromagnetism

## Rutherford Scattering (closest approach)

*'It is well known that the alpha and the beta particles suffer deflexions from their rectilinear paths by encounters with atoms of matter'*

These are the opening words of Rutherford's paper on the structure of the atom in the Philosophical Magazine of May 1911. Knowing that atoms were mostly empty space, his experiment was a way of discovering the size of the nucleus. In our analysis, we only consider the case where the alpha particle is aiming straight at a nucleus and recoils backwards. We make the assumption that the alpha particles went unimpeded until they met a nucleus. Initially, Rutherford assumed that the negative charges in the atom were spread out uniformly and would alter the speed of the alpha particles; this modifies the potential energy slightly. We also assume that the nucleus doesn't recoil. The real situation has a nucleus which is about fifty times heavier than the alpha particle so it will recoil a bit, but not much. Using a very thin gold foil means that the chance of a collision with another nucleus is small.

The alpha particle comes from 'infinity' with speed '$v$' aiming straight at a nucleus. It slows down to rest due to electrostatic repulsion at its distance of closest approach (usually given the symbol '$r$', but I'm using Rutherford's symbol '$b$'). The alpha particle then recoils back to infinity.

Rutherford used metals like gold and platinum for his target. My diagram shows a sodium nucleus containing 11 protons and 12 neutrons ($^{23}_{11}\text{Na}$) being targeted by an alpha particle containing 2 protons and 2 neutrons ($^{4}_{2}\text{He}$). We solve the problem using energy rather than forces. The kinetic energy of the alpha particle changes into potential energy. When the alpha particle is at its closest approach, all of its kinetic energy has been converted into the electrostatic potential energy of the system. The potential energy of the system (equal to the work done in assembling it) is: $E_{pot} = \frac{1}{4\pi\varepsilon_o}\frac{Qq}{r}$, where the charge on the alpha particle is '$q$' and the charge on the nucleus is '$Q$'. The alpha particle has charge $+2e$ and the nucleus has charge $+Ze$ where '$Z$' is the atomic number of the element and $e = 1.6 \times 10^{-19}$C.

Equating the kinetic and potential energies for a non-relativistic α particle gives: $\frac{1}{2}mv^2 = \frac{1}{4\pi\varepsilon_o}\frac{Qq}{b}$

**Example** An alpha particle with a speed of $5 \times 10^6$ m s$^{-1}$ aiming straight at the sodium nucleus.

Mass of alpha particle $m = 6.64 \times 10^{-27}$kg  Charge of alpha particle $q = 2 \times 1.6 \times 10^{-19}$C

Charge of sodium nucleus ($Z = 11$)  $Q = 11 \times 1.6 \times 10^{-19}$C

$$\frac{1}{2}mv^2 = \frac{1}{2} \times 6.64 \times 10^{-27} \times (5 \times 10^6)^2 = 8.3 \times 10^{-14} \text{ joules} = \frac{1}{4\pi\varepsilon_o}\frac{Qq}{b}$$

$$b = \frac{1}{4\pi\varepsilon_o}\frac{Qq}{8.3 \times 10^{-14}} = 9 \times 10^9 \frac{(11 \times 1.6 \times 10^{-19})(2 \times 1.6 \times 10^{-19})}{8.3 \times 10^{-14}} = 6.1 \times 10^{-14} \text{m}$$

The radius of the sodium nucleus is about $3.4 \times 10^{-15}$m (3.4fm), so our alpha particle got to within about ten diameters at its closest. The collision is elastic.

# Section 3.1b Magnetic Fields

Magnetism has a feel of mystery about it. Its existence had been known for a long time through rocks and compass needles, but it wasn't until the early 1800's that a systematic study was made of its properties. The break-through came in 1819, with Oersted's discovery of the magnetic field created by a current of electricity. Experiments by Biot and Savart put electromagnetism on a quantitative basis (describing it using magnetism numbers and relating its properties using equations). In 1820, Ampere showed that two current carrying parallel wires attracted each other; this led to the modern definition of our unit of current, appropriately called the amp.

What was lacking at that time, was a unified understanding of electricity, and of magnetism, which we now possess. Take an electric current; why should the current produced by a chemical 'voltaic' cell be the same as that produced by Faraday's moving coils or the same as the 'animal electricity' discovered by Galvani? We know they are the same, but they didn't. Why should magnetism from lumps of iron be identical to magnetism produced by currents? We know they are, but they didn't.

Unification of electricity and magnetism came with James Clerk Maxwell at Cambridge in 1873. The understanding of what it actually is, started in 1905 with Einstein. Magnetism is no longer a mystery. We now know it to be the relativistic effect of a moving electric charge. An observer moving along with an electric charge will not detect a magnetic field. If the observer moves with a different velocity from the charge, he will detect a magnetic field.

Electrostatics is the study of fixed source charges. The study of magnetism associated with steady currents is called magnetostatics. Additional effects occur with changing currents, and we will study this when we reach inductors. As with electrostatics, we restrict ourselves to the physics of magnetic fields in a vacuum. It's easier!

**James Clerk Maxwell with colour wheel**

## Making Magnetism Quantitative

Electric fields can be described qualitatively with words like 'weak' and 'strong'. We made it quantitative by considering the force on a test charge at a point in the field. The electric field strength was then defined as F = Eq. We wish to make the physics of magnetism quantitative. However, we cannot try the same technique as the electric field since you cannot get north poles on their own.

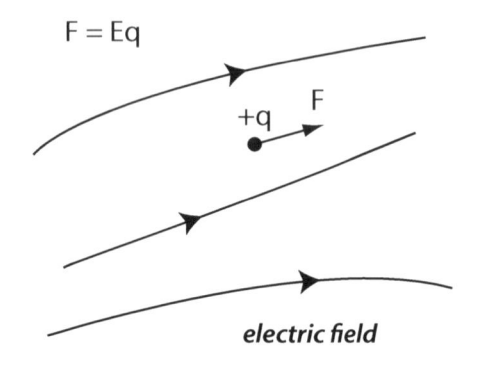

*electric field*      *magnetic field*

Two alternatives have been used. The first takes a small bar magnet (north at one end and south at the other, an arrangement called a magnetic dipole), places it in a magnetic field and measures the torque on it as it aligns itself with the field. We don't use that method. We use the second alternative, which has to do with currents.

# Electromagnetism

The symbol for the electric field strength is 'E'. For magnetic fields, we have a corresponding word and symbol. You would probably bet your last penny that it's called the magnetic field strength, and guess that the symbol is 'M'. Wrong! The symbol is 'B' and it's called the magnetic induction. It's also known as the magnetic flux density. When writing books and scientific papers, physicists use these terms, but in normal day-to-day discussions with colleagues, the turds just use 'magnetic field strength'!! To confuse things further, 'magnetic field strength' should properly be used for a quantity similar to magnetic induction, but not the same!! Yuck!

An electric field is produced by two types of charge, negative and positive. The rule is that an arrow on an electric field line comes out from a positive charge. A magnetic field is produced jointly by north and south poles. It is also a vector so we must distinguish whether the magnetic induction, 'B', points away from a north pole or a south pole. As before, you don't do an experiment to find the answer; it doesn't matter which one you choose. You make a choice, then stick with it. Arrows come out from a north pole and end on a south pole (though see page 182 for closed loop field lines!). The drawing shows the magnetic field line pattern of iron filings around a bar magnet.

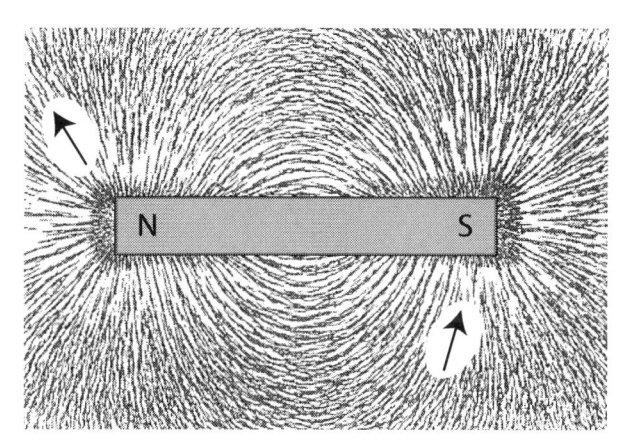

## Defining Magnetic Induction 'B'

Take a uniform magnetic field in a vacuum. This could be obtained between the poles of a horseshoe magnet as in the diagram below. Place a straight conducting wire AB, of length 'L' within the magnetic field, and at right angles to the magnetic field lines.

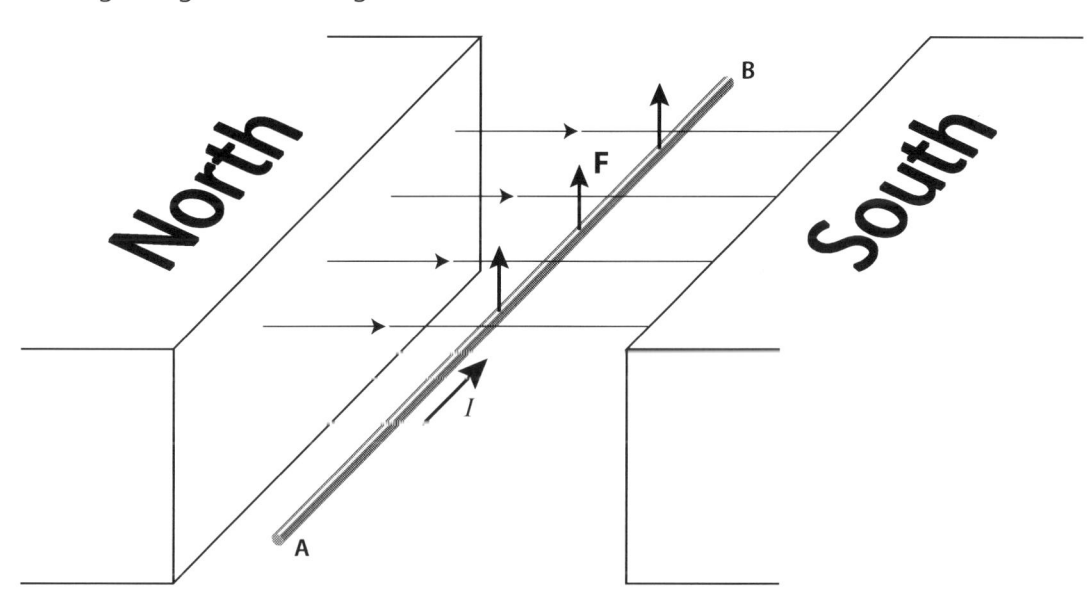

Pass a steady current through the wire and it will experience a force. Things like this give physics a bad name. The wire moves but there's no contact! With the magnets and current direction as shown, the wire gets pushed upwards. The magnitude of the force is given by this equation:

$$F = BIL\sin\theta$$

The angle 'θ' is the angle between the current direction and the magnetic field line direction (north to south). In the diagram above it is a right angle 90°. The formula is easy to remember; it has a boy's name in it! But, why an upwards push rather than downwards?

The direction of the force on the wire is a bit odd. It's neither the current direction nor the magnetic field line direction. Supernerds will smell a vector cross product, and they'll be correct. But, that's another story. There is a rule for working out the direction. The one I will give you is simple and straightforward to use; here it is:

You must use the **right hand**. Point your fingers as shown.

The direction of the current is **true electron flow** (the way negative electrons travel).

Point your first finger in the direction of the magnetic field lines (from north to south).

Point your second finger along the direction that the electrons travel (from the negative side to the positive side of a dc supply).

Your thumb gives the direction of the force on the wire.

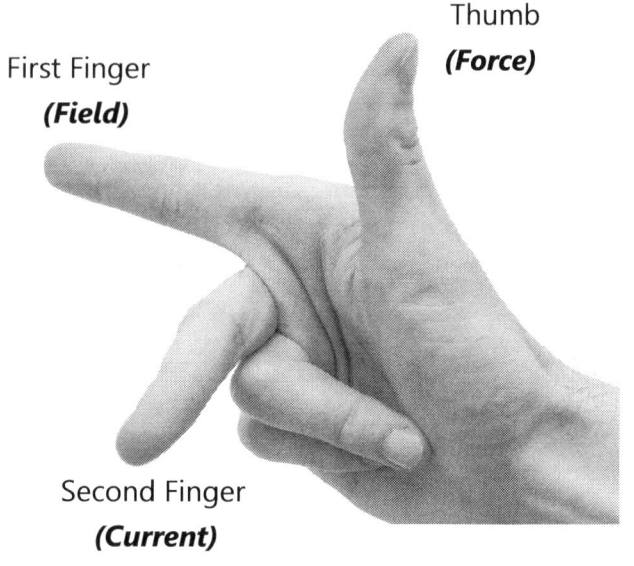

First Finger
*(Field)*

Thumb
*(Force)*

Second Finger
*(Current)*

That is the rule I suggest you use as a beginner. Note that the current doesn't have to be going through a wire. It could be a beam of electrons in the vacuum of an old fashioned television tube. Sometimes you get a question on a beam of protons (or alpha particles) which are positively charged. I always give my students a choice at this point. They can use the right hand rule above, then just take the opposite answer for the force, or, they can use their left hand. They usually choose the former.

The above system will **annoy some teachers** (with some justification); so here is a diversion into the shadow world of 'conventional current'.

**Other Systems**

1. Benjamin Franklin thought that positive charges flowed through wires, and scientists agreed with him for over a century, until they discovered the electron. His system is called 'conventional current'. Many books still use this system. Look for a circuit with a battery and arrows on the wires; their arrows will come out from the positive side. They will use the left hand with their conventional current to determine the direction of the force. Note that not all currents are due to the flow of electrons. You get positive ions moving through liquids in electrolysis, so it's not as daft as it looks.

2. Some teachers use different fingers for each quantity, and some hold their fingers differently. For example, holding the palm of the left hand flat and using the thumb for the current and the other four fingers for the magnetic field. The force is given by 'the way you would push'.

**Units for Magnetic Induction 'B'**

From the equation $F = BIL\sin\theta$, re-arrange to get: $B = \dfrac{F}{IL\sin\theta}$ $\Rightarrow$ $\dfrac{N}{Am}$ $\Rightarrow$ $NA^{-1}m^{-1}$

Converting the newton 'N' into its basic units (kg ms$^{-2}$), finally gives us: kg s$^{-2}$ A$^{-1}$.

The first version (NA$^{-1}$m$^{-1}$) is occasionally used, but nobody uses the one with the basic units. An international committee made up a unit and named it after the scientist, Nikola Tesla. The unit for the magnetic induction 'B' is the Tesla (T). That's another 'T' to add to the list (period, temperature, torque). A magnetic induction of 1 Tesla is quite big, so milli- and micro- subdivisions are often required. A magnetic induction of 1T will produce a force of 1N on a 1m length of wire with 1A of current flowing through it. But only if the wire and field are at right angles. Remember the sinθ. Line the wire up with the magnetic field lines and you get no force (see later with the electric motor).

# Electromagnetism

Here are some examples to give you the scale. Interstellar space is typically about B = 1nT. Over the UK, the Earth's magnetic field produces a magnetic induction of B ≈ 50µT. Magnetic Resonance Imaging (MRI) scanners used in hospitals produce fields of about 0.3T to 3T (This is a powerful field; in 2001 a patient was killed when a steel oxygen cylinder was attracted into the compartment). The superconducting magnets at the LHC at CERN have currents of 11000A (!!!) to produce fields of 8.6T. The strongest continuous magnetic field produced has B = 80T. Some neutron stars have magnetic fields with B ≈ $10^{10}$T and are called 'magnetars'. The most powerful permanent magnets (lumps of metal) are made from neodymium. The attraction of a neodymium-iron-boron magnet is so strong that when the magnets touch each other they may chip or cause a small bruise if your fingers are caught. If you have a heart pacemaker fitted, keep it under 0.5mT. And 16T will levitate a frog.

**Example 1** Calculate the force on a 35cm length of wire carrying a current of 4A at right angles to a uniform magnetic field of 0.18T.

$$F = BIL\sin\theta = 0.18 \times 4 \times 0.35 \times \sin 90° = 0.252\,\text{N}$$

The direction of the force on the wire is out of the page (right hand, first finger pointing to the right, second finger pointing to the top of the page, and the thumb should point out of the page).

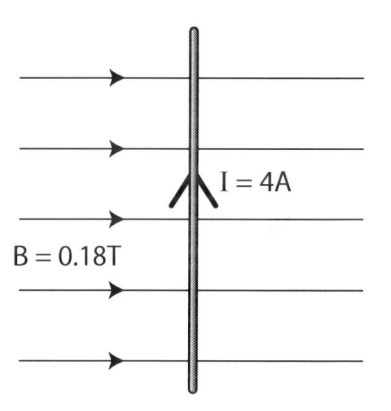

**Example 2** The force on a 20cm section of copper wire carrying a current of 0.75A in a magnetic field is vertically upwards. The diagram shows a cross-section through the wire (32 S.W.G.) with a diameter of 0.274mm and a density of 8920kg m$^{-3}$. Calculate the magnetic induction (B) of the field, if the weight of the wire is balanced by the upwards magnetic force on the wire ('magnetic levitation').

First, calculate the mass of the wire, then its weight:

$$m = \rho V = 8920 \times \pi r^2 L = 8920 \times \pi \left(\frac{2.74 \times 10^{-4}}{2}\right)^2 \times 0.2$$

$$\Rightarrow m = 1.05 \times 10^{-4}\,\text{kg} \quad \Rightarrow W = mg = 1.03 \times 10^{-3}\,\text{N}$$

Equate this to the magnetic force:

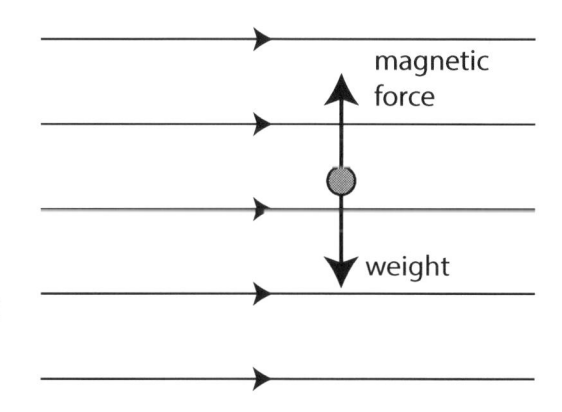

$$1.03 \times 10^{-3} = BIL\sin\theta = B \times 0.75 \times 0.2 \times \sin 90° = 0.15B \quad \Rightarrow B = 6.9 \times 10^{-3}\,\text{T}\ (=6.9\,\text{mT})$$

This is about 140 times the magnetic induction at the Earth's surface over the UK. The wire also heats-up due to the current. Can you show that the wire increases its temperature by a bit under 1°C each second? Its resistance is 0.057Ω and its specific heat capacity is 380J kg$^{-1}$ °C$^{-1}$.

## Measuring Magnetic Induction 'B' using a Balance

The force on a current carrying wire in a magnetic field can be measured using a balance (a weighing machine). We can determine the magnetic induction if the current and length of wire are known, or test the relationship between the current and the force produced (testing $F \propto L$ ).

The wire consists of three sections: two vertical lengths and one horizontal. For the current direction and magnetic poles as shown in the diagram, we can work out the directions of the forces on each section of wire. Using the right-hand rule, the force on the upright sections point horizontally towards each other, and so don't contribute to the reading on the balance. On the middle section, the force on the wire is upwards. That is, the magnetic field pushes the wire upwards. However, **the wire is fixed in position** above the balance, so rather than the wire moving upwards, the magnets and balance pan are forced downwards. This increases the reading on the balance. Here are some readings:

Current = 5amps
Length of middle section of wire = 4cm
Reading on balance (no current) = 658.2g
Reading on balance (current on) = 665.3g

The increase in the reading of the balance is $(665.3 - 658.2) = 7.1g = 0.0071 kg$. This is equivalent to a force of $W = mg = 0.0071 \times 9.8 = 0.0696 N$. Finally, use this with $F = BIL\sin\theta$ (the angle is 90°).

$$F = BIL\sin\theta \quad \Rightarrow \quad B = \frac{F}{IL\sin\theta} = \frac{0.0696}{5 \times 0.04} = 0.35 \text{ Tesla}$$

Look again at the diagram and you'll notice that the north and south poles are on the large faces (unlike the usual bar magnet where the poles are at each end). Why is this necessary?
Using the same apparatus to show that $F \propto L$ would give this table of readings and graph:

| Current (amps) | Reading on Balance (g) | Force (N) |
|---|---|---|
| 0 | 658.2 | 0 |
| 1 | 659.6 | 0.0137 |
| 2 | 661.0 | 0.0274 |
| 3 | 662.5 | 0.0421 |
| 4 | 663.9 | 0.0559 |
| 5 | 665.3 | 0.0696 |
| 6 | 666.7 | 0.0833 |
| 7 | 668.1 | 0.0970 |
| 8 | 669.6 | 0.1117 |

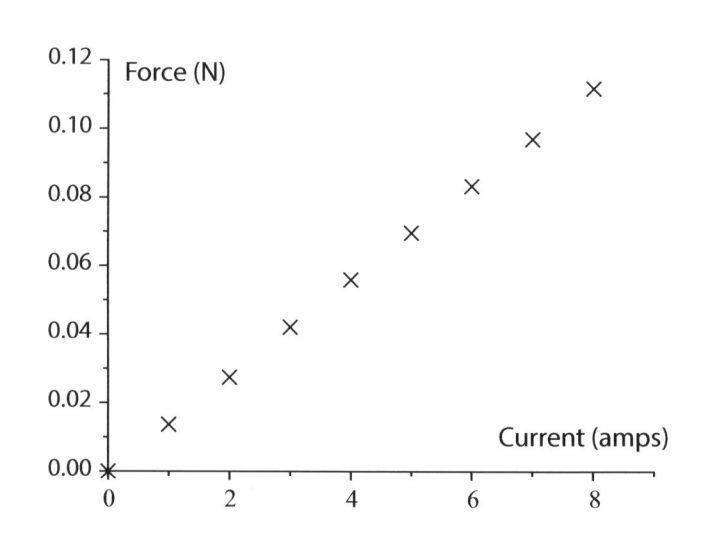

# Electromagnetism

## The Electric Motor

At its simplest, the electric motor consists of a rectangular loop of wire carrying a current in a magnetic field (mid page diagram). Each of the four sections of wire experiences a force. Forces are necessary, but not sufficient, to turn the loop of wire. To make it turn, the forces must produce a **torque** on the loop. Here is how two equal and opposite forces can produce a turning effect, or nothing at all:

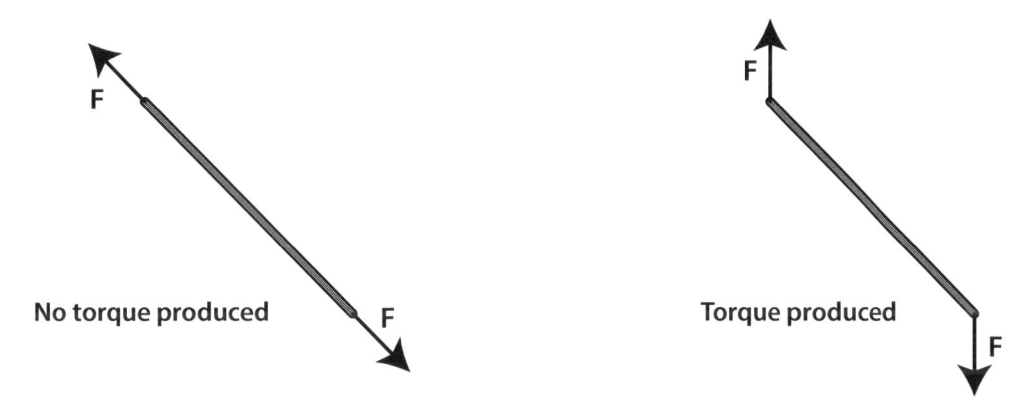

**No torque produced**

**Torque produced**

No turning effect is produced in the above left drawing since the two forces act along the same line. On the right-hand drawing, the two forces are still equal and opposite, but don't act along the same line (this is known as a 'couple').

The rectangular loop of wire in the electric motor consists of two pairs of sides. One of the pairs (the wires beside the spindle) produce forces but no torque. The other pair (usually the longest sides) produce forces which yield a torque. In the diagram opposite, the north pole of the magnetic field would be on the left and the south pole would be on the right. The current circulates in a clockwise direction. In the position shown, use your right-hand rule to check the directions of all four forces (it's good exercise for your joints).

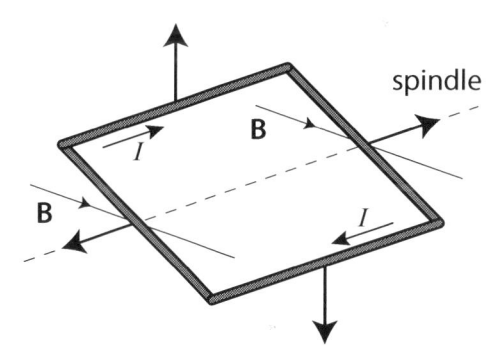

We now know which forces are involved. Notice that these 'up and down' forces always act 'up and down'. It doesn't matter which way the coil sits. The section of wire on the left side is always forced upwards and the right side is always forced downwards. The section of wire which had its current moving in one direction on one side of the spindle has to reverse its direction on the other side of the spindle. You must reverse the direction of the current when the coil reaches the vertical '12 o'clock 6 o'clock' position. A midge sitting on the wire would be alternately forced up and down every half turn. The coil will continue turning clockwise. Notice that the pair of forces on the short sides will also change direction, but still not contribute to the torque. As the coil turns, they try to squash and stretch the coil along its long axis.

Here is an end-on view of the rectangular loop. A small cross in the left-hand wire shows current going into the page, and a dot on the right-hand wire shows current coming out of the page. The force (F) on each side $F = BIL\sin\theta$ is constant since $\theta = 90°$ in all positions. It's the torque which changes.

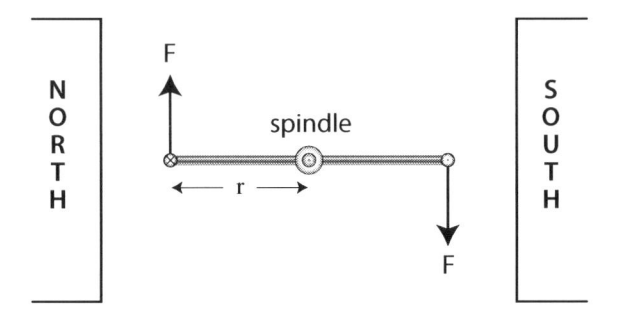

In the position shown, the 'r' and the 'F' are at right-angles, so the torque on each side is $T = rF$ (double to get the total from both sides). As the coil turns, the torque will reduce according to $T = rF\sin\phi$, where '$\phi$' is the angle between the outward pointing 'r' and the force 'F'. You could calculate the angular acceleration in the position shown if you know the moment of inertia of the loop.

## Creating a Magnetic Field

Magnets are commonly divided into two types: permanent magnets and electromagnets. Permanent magnets are lumps of material (often iron) which derive their magnetism from the fields of each atom making up the substance. In turn, each of these atoms has a magnetic field due to the electrons (most atoms give no magnetic field since the contributions from all the electrons cancel; iron is an exception). Ultimately, it's due to the movement of electric charges, the same as an electromagnet.

The simplest example of an electromagnet (diagram on right) is the magnetic field due to a straight current-carrying wire. Notice how the magnetic field lines don't come straight out from the wire, they are concentric circles. Magnetic field lines don't 'just come out of north poles'! (see page 114 for example of the sun). The magnitude of the magnetic induction 'B' depends upon the distance 'r' from the wire. Points of constant 'r' will have a magnetic induction of the same magnitude; hence the circles. The direction of 'B' points along the tangent to the circle and is shown by the arrows. The direction of the arrows is easy to remember; here's how.

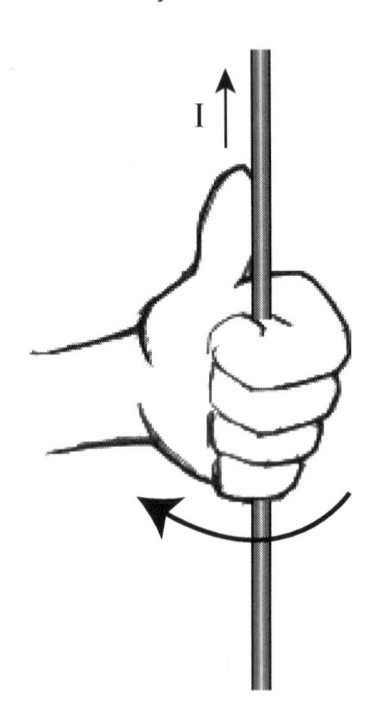

Take your **left** hand and hold it as shown. Point your thumb along the direction that the electrons travel in the wire (out from the negative end of the battery and into the positive end). Your other fingers curl around the direction of the magnetic induction 'B'.

The magnitude of the magnetic induction is calculated from this equation:

$$B = \frac{\mu_o I}{2\pi r}$$

The constant $\mu_o$ (pronounced 'mew nought') sets the scale and it's small. Its full name is the 'permeability of free space' and its value is exactly $4\pi \times 10^{-7}$. This will remind you of the constant we have for the electric field $\varepsilon_o$, the 'permittivity of free space'. You can blame the Victorians for the names; they thought that free space (ie. the vacuum) was a 'thing' with properties, and these were two of its properties. The more economical names, 'electric constant' and 'magnetic constant' are gradually replacing the old terms.

**Example** Calculate the magnetic induction 'B' at a distance of 18cm from a straight wire carrying a current of 2.5A.

$$B = \frac{\mu_o I}{2\pi r} = \frac{4\pi \times 10^{-7} \times 2.5}{2\pi \times 0.18} = 2.78 \times 10^{-6} \, \text{T}$$

**Units** for $\mu_o$ As usual, derive it from the defining equation: $B = \frac{\mu_o I}{2\pi r} \Rightarrow \mu_o = \frac{2\pi r B}{I} \Rightarrow \text{T m A}^{-1}$

Then decompose the tesla 'T' into its basic units of kg s$^{-2}$ A$^{-1}$, to give: kg m s$^{-2}$ A$^{-2}$ (notice this is N A$^{-2}$). When we come to inductors, we meet a unit called the Henry 'H' (don't laugh). Combined with the 'metre', it gives the most common unit for $\mu_o$, Henries per metre (H m$^{-1}$).

# Electromagnetism

## Parallel Wires.....the Definition of the Amp

In the diagram opposite, two parallel wires, P and Q, carry currents $I_1$ and $I_2$ flowing in the same direction. Both currents produce magnetic fields. Only the direction of the magnetic field from 'P' is shown.

We will use both the left-hand rule and the right-hand rule to show that the wires attract each other.

Firstly the left-hand rule. The magnetic field from the current in wire 'P' comes out of the page on its right and into the page on its left. Where it meets wire 'Q', it comes out of the page.

Now apply the right-hand rule. Wire 'Q' sits in the magnetic field created by wire 'P' and has a current $I_2$ flowing in it. Use the right-hand rule to work out the direction of the force. It's to the left.

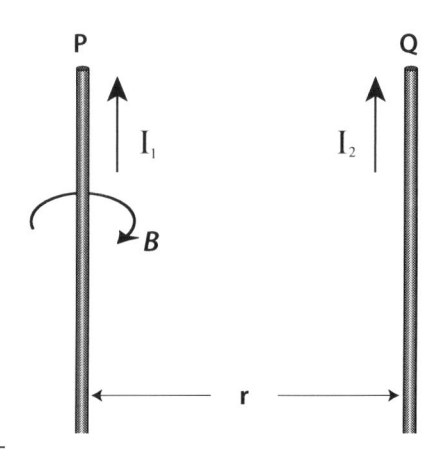

That was a qualitative description; here is the quantitative version. Wires 'P' and 'Q' are a distance 'r' apart. The magnetic induction due to wire 'P' at a distance 'r' is: $B = \dfrac{\mu_o I_1}{2\pi r}$. At wire 'Q', a magnetic induction 'B' with a current $I_2$ produces a force on the wire 'Q' of $F = BI_2 L \sin\theta$. The angle between the field and the current is 90°, so $\sin\theta = 1$, $F = BI_2 L$. The 'L' in the formula is the length of wire 'Q'. Now substitute for the magnetic induction 'B' to get:

$$F = BI_2 L \quad \Rightarrow \quad F = \left(\frac{\mu_o I_1}{2\pi r}\right) I_2 L = \frac{\mu_o I_1 I_2 L}{2\pi r}$$

This is the force on length 'L' of wire. We can calculate the 'force per unit length'. Our unit of length is the metre, so if our length of wire was 5 metres (L = 5), we would divide the force by five to get the force on just one metre of wire. In other words, divide the formula by 'L' to get the force on each metre of wire:

$$\frac{F}{L} = \frac{\mu_o I_1 I_2}{2\pi r} \quad \text{(force per unit length)}$$

This expression is used to **define the unit of current** (the ampere). The wires are placed one metre apart (making r = 1). Now for the clever bit. The top line contains a constant $\mu_o$ and the currents. There is a $2\pi$ on the bottom line, so why not set $\mu_o$ to be a multiple of $\pi$ and make the maths easy so the $\pi$'s cancel (no horrible numbers). We have the freedom to do this since we don't have a unit for current. Choose a suitable multiple of $\pi$ so that the amp is of a sensible size (choosing $\mu_o = 4\pi \times 10^{-7}$ does this). Putting in these values with currents of 1A gives:

$$\frac{F}{L} = \frac{\mu_o I_1 I_2}{2\pi r} = \frac{4\pi \times 10^{-7} \times 1 \times 1}{2\pi \times 1} = 2 \times 10^{-7} \, \text{N m}^{-1}$$

We now have the definition of the amp. Two parallel wires, one metre apart, with currents of 1 amp flowing in the **same direction**, will **attract** each other with a force of $2 \times 10^{-7}$ N on each metre of wire.

## Electromagnetism and the Speed of Light

During the first half of the 19th century, many scientists created the jigsaw pieces for the big puzzle called electromagnetism. James Clerk Maxwell fitted them together in 1873 in his theory of electromagnetism. This consists of four equations (called 'Maxwell's equations'), containing the electric and magnetic fields ('E' and 'B'), together with their sources (the electric charges 'Q', and currents 'I'). If you fiddle about with the mathematics a bit, they reveal a wave equation. In the position in the wave equation where the speed of the wave is supposed to be, Maxwell found the combination $\frac{1}{\sqrt{\varepsilon_o \mu_o}}$. Putting in the values gives:

$$\frac{1}{\sqrt{\varepsilon_o \mu_o}} = \frac{1}{\sqrt{8.85 \times 10^{-12} \times 4\pi \times 10^{-7}}} = \frac{1}{\sqrt{1.11 \times 10^{-17}}} = \frac{1}{3.33 \times 10^{-9}} = 3 \times 10^8 \, \text{m s}^{-1}$$

This is the speed of **light**! Maxwell had discovered that light rays come from a unification of electricity and magnetism (hence the name 'electromagnetic spectrum'). When you have an equation like this, which relates three quantities, knowing two of them fixes the value of the third. In this case, $\mu_o = 4\pi \times 10^{-7}$ is exact, and the value of the speed of light is defined to be exactly 299,792,458m s$^{-1}$, so the electric constant $\varepsilon_o$ is also exact (though irrational). This is why you don't do experiments to measure any of these quantities.

## Coil of Wire

A straight length of wire carrying a current produces a magnetic field around it. A decent amount of magnetism would be 0.1T. At a distance of 10cm from the wire, you would need a current of 50,000A going through it. So it may be useful to be able to switch on and off an electromagnet (unlike a lump of iron), but it would have very limited application unless we can produce stronger fields. Fortunately, there is a way; coil-up the wire!

A single straight wire carrying current will produce a magnetic field given by $B = \frac{\mu_o I}{2\pi r}$. A single turn loop of wire carrying a current will produce a magnetic field. At the centre of the circle of wire of radius 'R', the magnetic induction is very similar to the last expression, but without the π: $B = \frac{\mu_o I}{2R}$. Coiling it 'N' times makes the field 'N' times bigger: $B = \frac{\mu_o N I}{2R}$. By 'coiling it up', I mean squashing the coils against each other. You can also coil-up a wire so that it's pulled out, like the one below. The shape of the field produced is very similar to the field of a bar magnet. Use your left-hand grip rule to work out the direction of the current through the coil. Since the field lines come out of the left side, that must be the north end. The magnetic field inside the coil is almost uniform and is given by: $B = \mu_o n I$. This time, the 'n' isn't the number of turns; it's the number of **turns per metre** of length of coil (not length of wire, but length of coil as in holding a ruler along the top). The diagram shows the field of a loosely wound coil. You can see that the field inside is quite uniform. A uniform magnetic field is important since moving charges will experience a constant force in the field. We can now produce a uniform magnetic field with both permanent magnets and with an electromagnet. Producing a field of 0.1T could be achieved using a current of 80A with a coil of 1000 turns per metre (and probably melt it). (On the diagram, the current direction is 'in from the right' and 'out to the left').

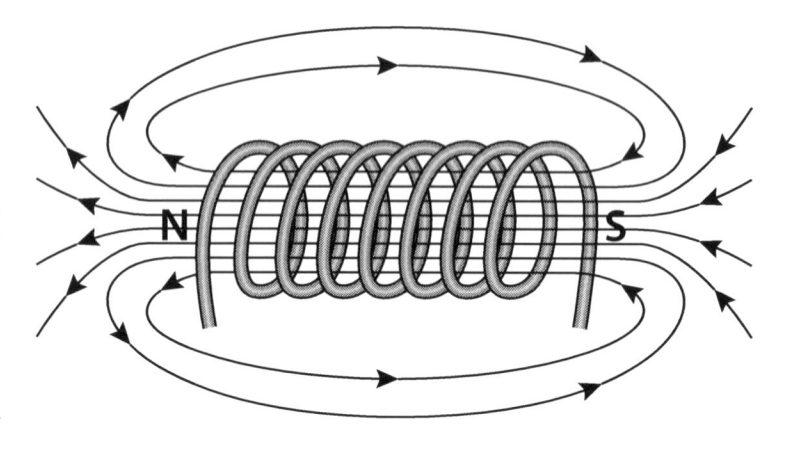

At CERN in Geneva the ATLAS experiment at the Large Hadron Collider uses a coil to produce a magnetic field. This is a superconducting design with a current of 7600A producing a field inside of 2T. The inner detector sits within this coil in a system of concentric cylinders. It records the passage of each subatomic particle using thousands of tiny reverse biased silicon diodes. The system of detectors gathers lots of data but will eventually suffer radiation damage through time.

# Electromagnetism

## The Hall Effect

There are occasions when even the best scientists get things wrong. Lord Kelvin famously asserted that human-powered flight was impossible, and in 1917 Rutherford insisted that no practical benefit would ensue from studying the nucleus. There was an error which the great James Clerk Maxwell made concerning magnetism, and which few people know about. It has to do with the force on a current carrying wire in a magnetic field. We now know it is the electric charges moving within the wire which experience the force; Maxwell thought it was the wire itself! At the time (late 1870's), this was controversial. In 1879, Edwin Hall devised and performed an experiment which would discriminate between the two theories and eventually refute Maxwell's idea. It's known as the 'Hall Effect' and has become important in the study of semiconductors and the measurement of the strength of magnetic fields.

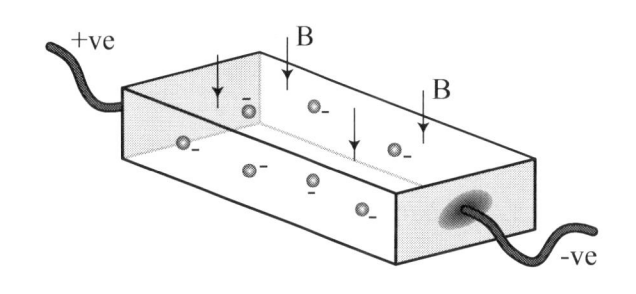

Start with a conductor in the shape of a cuboid (diagram on right). Attach a battery across one pair of faces (+ve to one face, -ve to the other). Apply a magnetic field 'B' across another pair of faces. The battery sets up a current which flows through the magnetic field from right to left. We know that there is a force $(qvB\sin\theta)$ on the charges at right angles to both the velocity of the charges and the magnetic field. It will push the charges towards one of the third pair of faces. This build-up of charge on one side would result in a potential difference across the third pair of faces. If a potential difference was detected, it was the charges moving and Maxwell would be wrong. Hall detected a voltage across the third pair of faces; now known as the Hall Voltage $V_H$.

Apply the right-hand rule to the electrons in the diagram. Your thumb should end up pointing towards the right-hand back face (the long, narrow one). The negative charge of the electrons would build-up on that face. Eventually, this build-up of charge would push back on any further charges trying to reach the face (it's a bit like a capacitor charging) and a **steady** Hall Voltage would exist.

We know it's electrons which move in conductors like copper, but what would happen if positive charges moved? Driven by the battery, they would have to come out from the positive end of the battery and go into the negative end. So we not only change the sign of the charges, we also change their direction. Using the right-hand rule, you find that they get pushed in the same direction as the electrons, towards the back right face. But this time, it's a build-up of positive charge. A voltmeter (across the third pair of faces) reading the Hall Voltage would have the opposite sign. Here is a view of both cases, looking down on the large top face with the magnetic field going into the page:

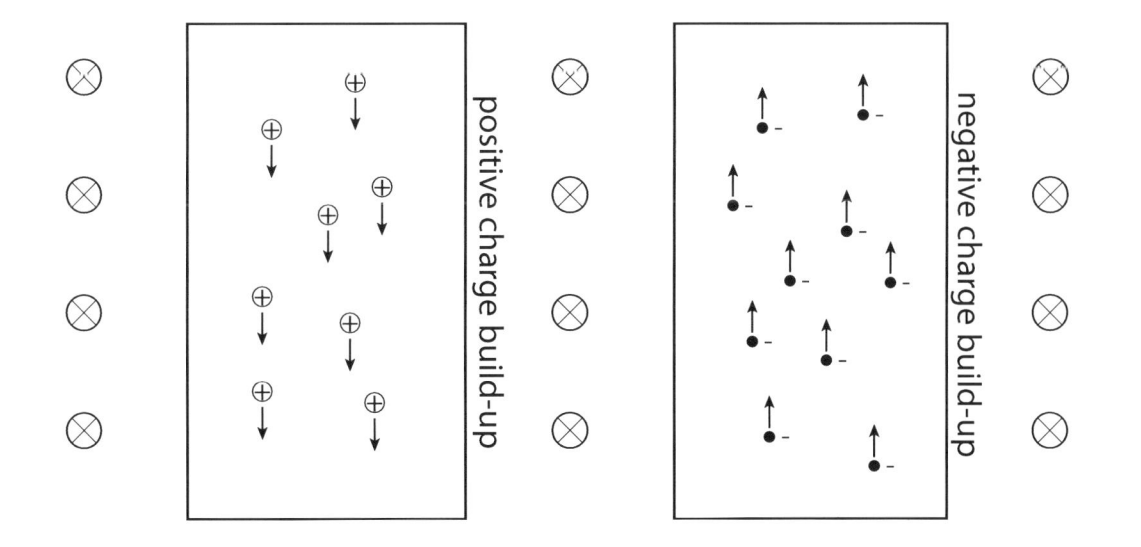

The **sign** of the Hall Voltage allows you to distinguish between negative charges flowing one way and positive charges flowing the other way. An ammeter can't tell the difference. It's used in the study of conduction in semiconductors where it can distinguish between the two main methods of conduction: conduction by electrons in n-type material and conduction by 'holes' in p-type material.

The **size** of the Hall Voltage is very small. A very large current of about 100A from the battery, passed through a centimeter-sized copper strip in a strong magnetic field of about 1Tesla, will only produce a Hall Voltage of the order of a microvolt. How could you make this bigger? The current and magnetic field are already large, so you couldn't increase them much more. There is one more variable in the mix and that is the number of charges per cubic metre in the material. With copper, there is one free electron per atom (it gives about $8 \times 10^{28}$ electrons per cubic meter). What we want is a material with a different 'charge density'. You would think that having more electrons per cubic metre would accumulate more charge on one of the faces and give a bigger Hall Voltage; but in fact it's the opposite.

Here's the reason. The Hall Voltage sets up an electric field $E_H = \dfrac{V_H}{d}$ across the third pair of faces.

When a steady Hall Voltage is achieved, no more electrons move across since the force against them due to the Hall electric field is balanced by the magnetic force on the moving charges:

$$F_{elec} = F_{mag} \quad \Rightarrow \quad qE_H = \left(\frac{qV_H}{d}\right) = qvB \quad \Rightarrow \quad E_H = vB$$

For a given current, the electrons in a material with lots of conduction electrons per cubic metre will move with a small speed 'v'. (Remember that the current is the amount of charge passing each second). Put a small speed in the last equation (like copper) and you only need a small Hall Voltage for balance.

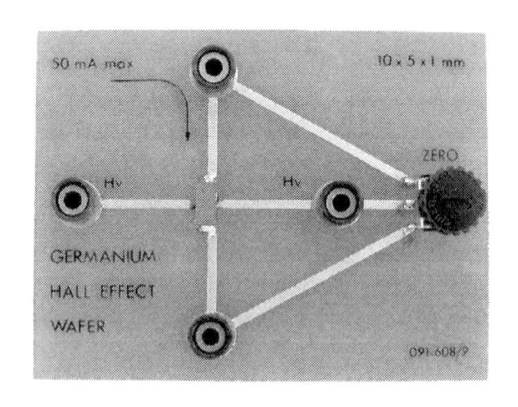

What we want is a material which is still a conductor but has fewer charges per cubic metre. At room temperature, pure semiconductors have too high a resistance but doped semiconductors are ideal. The charge density (good books call it the 'charge carrier concentration') is a lot less than copper and you can get Hall Voltages of tens of millivolts with modest magnetic fields and currents.

A Hall Probe uses the Hall Effect to measure magnetic induction 'B'. Basic Hall probes come mounted on a rod. It is wired to a box containing two pairs of 4mm sockets; one pair is connected to the battery to supply the current and the other pair to a voltmeter. Some models have a battery inside the box, with a switch, and just one pair of sockets for connection to a voltmeter. You also have a 'set zero' control, where you adjust the voltmeter reading to zero before you apply the magnetic field you wish to measure.

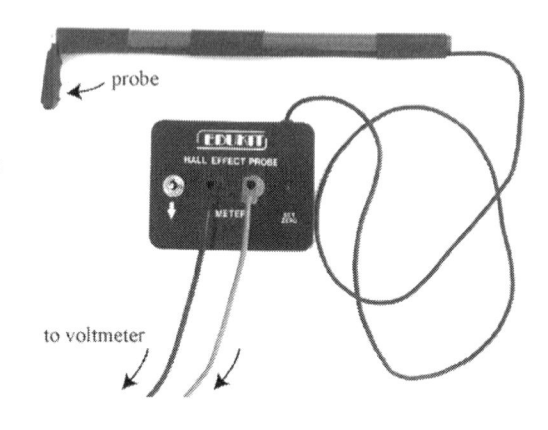

### The Quantum Hall Effect

The Hall Effect above only required an analysis in terms of classical electromagnetism. If you cool down the semiconductor to 1K (to reduce collisions between the electrons and the lattice atoms), apply a very large magnetic field (above 1T) and restrict the movement of the electrons (essentially into a 2D plane), you can observe quantum effects. The resistance to the motion of the electrons along the direction of the Hall Voltage reaches a plateau at exactly 25812.806 Ohms (it's equal to $h/e^2$); regardless of the material or its shape. Rather than the ohm, this could become a new standard of resistance. It's a bit on the high side (except for op amps) and the name isn't too catchy; the 'klitzing'.

# Electromagnetism

## Magnetic Materials

We're all familiar with magnets based on iron. As heavy lumps of metal, they attract steel cans and paperclips for amusement, but also drive electric motors and help generate electricity. The scientific effect goes under the name of ferromagnetism, from the Latin word *ferrum*, translated as *iron* or *sword*. To discover how it works, we need to drop into the world of the atom and its fundamental particles.

There are two sources of magnetism. We know about the first one; motion of an electric charge relative to an observer. This could be current flowing through a copper wire, or it could be an electron in orbit around the nucleus of an atom. The second source of magnetism is within the fundamental particles themselves. Particles like the electron, proton and muon, have their own magnetism whether they are moving or at rest. By 'magnetic' we mean that if you place a 'magnetic' material in a magnetic field, it will **do** something. In the case of an electron, it experiences a torque and has its spin axis realigned.

Here's the magnetic story of an atom:

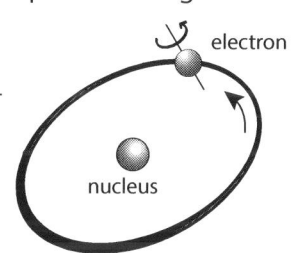

- Electrons move around the nucleus in orbits. This is magnetism due to moving charges and by itself produces a weak magnetic effect called *diamagnetism*. It's usually swamped by other magnetic effects, but if found on its own, a diamagnetic material will be repelled in an external magnetic field (think of a diamagnetic 'paperclip' being pushed away).

- The intrinsic magnetism of the electrons in orbit is contained within their spins. They can spin 'righthanded' or 'lefthanded'. The Pauli Exclusion Principle makes electrons pair-off together in orbital shells with opposite spins, cancelling their intrinsic magnetic effect. An atom with an unpaired electron will react in an external magnetic field due to the intrinsic magnetism of that electron. This is called *paramagnetism*. It's usually a weak effect. Applying an external magnetic field to a paramagnetic material will align the spins with the field and increase the overall field by about 0.01%. Paramagnetic materials are attracted in an external magnetic field (a paramagnetic 'paperclip' would be attracted).

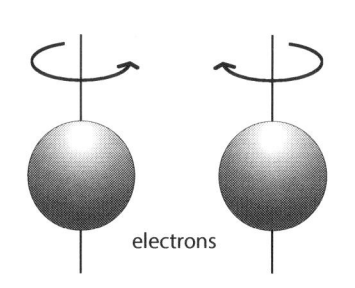

- Electron spins can be more complicated in some materials. A single unpaired electron will align its spin axis with an external magnetic field. But electrons also react to neighbouring unpaired electrons. You'd expect them to 'get together' magnetically and pair-off with opposite spins (think how two bar magnets stick together). But sometimes they don't. Like soppy pet cats, they seek out the lowest energy state, which happens to have the neighbouring spins aligned (diagram at right), together with a slight rearrangement of the atoms. Only a few atoms can pull-off this trick: Iron, nickel, cobalt and some rare earths. It's called *ferromagnetism*. This effect can be the dominant magnetic one in materials. In an external magnetic field, ferromagnetic materials feel an attractive force (a steel paperclip is attracted).

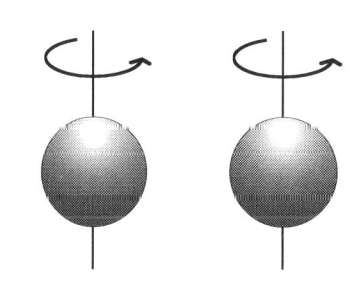

Of course, atoms are tiny. We only get everyday measureable effects when we take very large numbers of them. Each atom could have a large magnetic moment (as it's called) and if it was a scalar quantity we could have a lot of fun, but these magnetic moments are vectors with directions and in most materials we get cancellation. The fun begins when large numbers of atoms have their spins aligned.

A lump of iron contains small regions where the magnetic field directions of millions of individual atoms all point in the same direction. This adds up to give a powerful field within that volume. But there might be a neighbouring region where the magnetic field from the atoms lines up in another direction. These regions are known as domains (diagram on next page). Overall, the domain fields point in random directions and we have an unremarkable lump of iron. But now imagine all the domains with their magnetic fields aligned in the same direction!

187

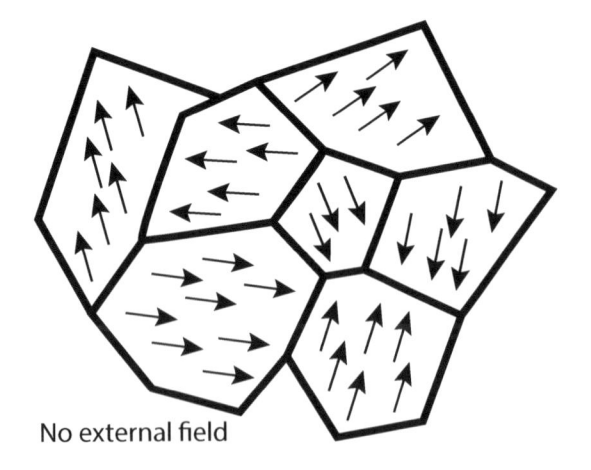

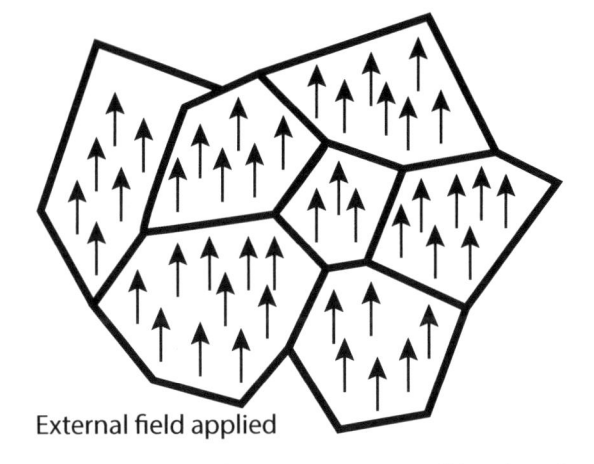

Start off with a sample of a ferromagnet which has a randomly aligned domain structure (like the above left diagram). Overall, it won't be a 'magnet' (position 'A' on the graph below right). Apply a uniform external magnetic field to the sample. The atoms in each domain will be forced to line-up with the external field. A sufficiently strong external field will result in the domain structure of the right hand diagram above (position 'B' on the graph). The 'y' axis on the graph plots the total magnetic field resulting from the external field plus the field due to the sample. Now reduce the applied external field to zero. The domain structure starts to reform but the domain boundaries grind against each other and get stuck. The domains can't get back to their original randomised directions (top left diagram), and the sample has become a 'magnet' (position 'C' on the graph). The graph is one quadrant of what's called the hysteresis curve.

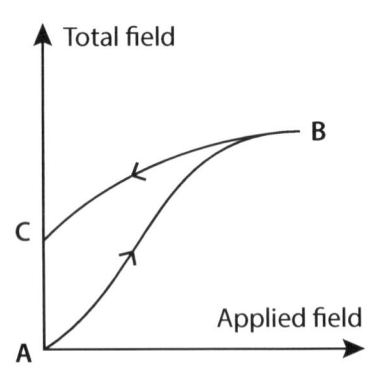

At room temperature, the magnetic field strength inside a domain is over 2 Tesla for pure iron (when all the spins are as aligned as they can be, the field strength inside is called the saturation magnetisation). The thermal energy of the atoms due to their vibrations is small and it doesn't disrupt the 'special trick' which allows neighbouring spins to be aligned. This is the plateau area on the graph on the left. As we increase the temperature of the iron, the atoms vibrate more, and the spin directions start to wander. Eventually, the thermal energy of vibration overcomes the 'special trick' mechanism and the spins revert to opposite pairs as in paramagnetism. Iron is ferromagnetic below that special temperature and paramagnetic above it. With iron, you need a temperature of at least 770°C for the process to work. It's called the Curie temperature $T_C$, named after Madame Curie's husband. For nickel the Curie temperature is 354°C, and for the rare earth's, neodymium is 320°C and gadolinium is only 19°C.

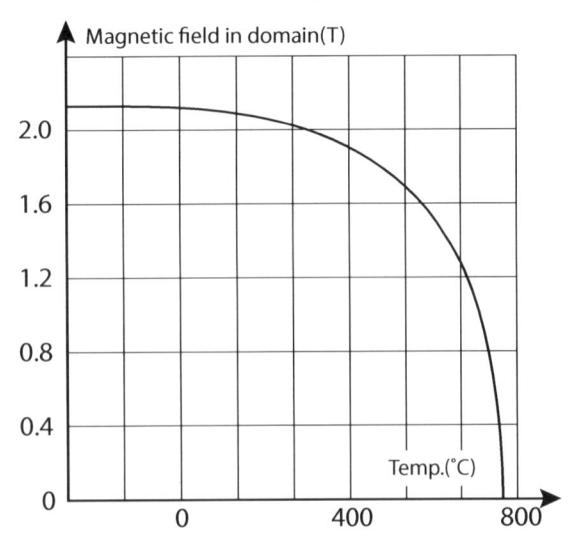

Aligning and realigning the domains of a ferromagnet will use energy and generate heat (investigate that 'hysteresis' curve). Some ferromagnets use very little energy over the apply field / release field cycle. These are called 'soft magnetic materials' and are useful in transformers where a mains AC supply changes the field at 50Hz. Transformers in the electricity supply industry handle huge amounts of energy and have to be as efficient as possible. Elaborate means are used to keep them cool. Other ferromagnets generate heat during a cycle but resist changes to their internal magnetism when external fields are applied. These are called 'hard magnetic materials' and are suitable for storage applications like magnetic tape, hard disc drives and swipe cards.

# Electromagnetism

## Section 3.2a Capacitors

Capacitors are one of the three basic building blocks in simple circuits (along with resistors and inductors). In Higher Physics, we covered the basic definition Q = CV, and drew graphs of charging and discharging in a series CR circuit. At Advanced Higher we make it more quantitative and introduce the 'time constant'.

The basic **charging circuit** is shown on the right. The voltage supply is direct current, so the capacitor will charge-up over a period of time before the circuit settles into a constant state. The 'time constant' gives us the timescale over which this temporary change takes place. Potential difference is a scalar, so at any instant the supply voltage $V_S$ (6volts in this case) is the simple sum of the pd across the resistor $V_R$ and the pd across the capacitor $V_C$.

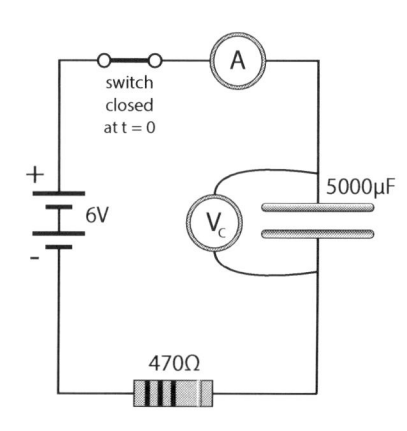

$$V_S = V_C + V_R = \frac{Q}{C} + IR$$

$$\frac{dV_S}{dt} = \frac{1}{C}\frac{dQ}{dt} + R\frac{dI}{dt}$$

$$0 = \frac{I}{C} + R\frac{dI}{dt}$$

$$0 = \frac{I}{CR} + \frac{dI}{dt}$$

$$I = I_o e^{-\frac{t}{CR}} \qquad I_o = \frac{V_S}{R}$$

At time zero, there is no charge on the capacitor and the only resistance to the flow of current '$I_o$' comes from the resistor 'R'. The combination 'CR' is called the time constant and is in units of seconds.

$$CR = \frac{Q}{V} \times \frac{V}{I} = \frac{Q}{I} = t$$

With the values from the above circuit, the time constant is: $CR = 5000 \times 10^{-6} \times 470 = 2.35s$. This time is shown by the dotted line on the graphs.
From the equation for the current, put $t = CR$:

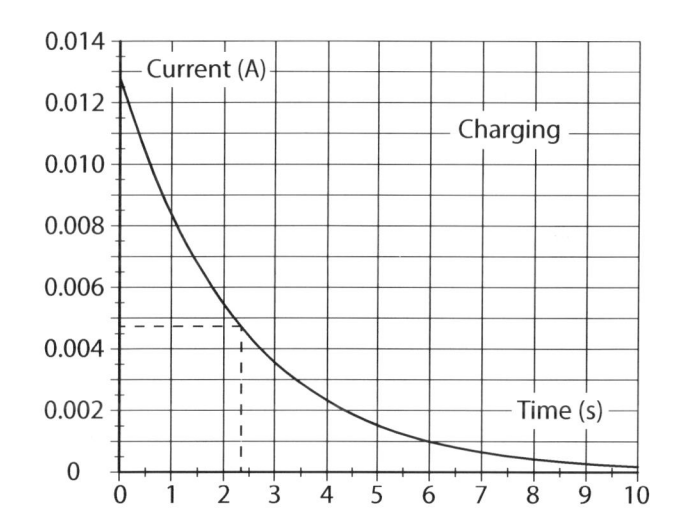

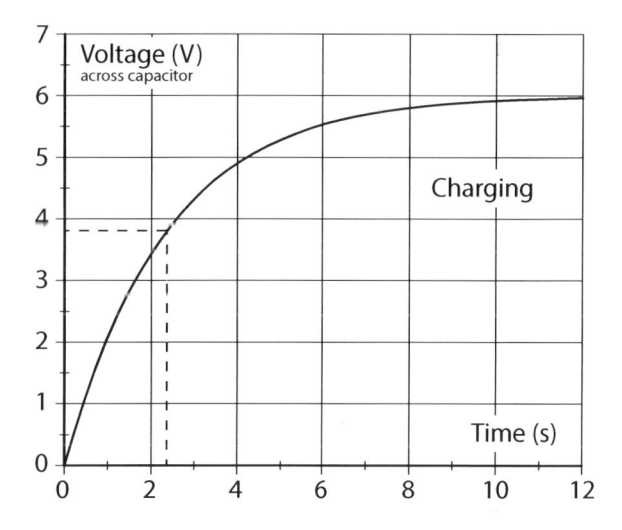

$$I = I_o e^{-\frac{t}{CR}} = I_o e^{-1} \Rightarrow \frac{I}{I_o} = e^{-1} = \frac{1}{2.718} = 0.368 \Rightarrow I = 0.368 I_o = 0.368 \times \frac{V_S}{R} = 0.0047 A$$

The voltage across the capacitor is given by:

$$V_C = V_S - V_R = V_S - IR = V_S - I_o R e^{-\frac{t}{CR}} = V_S - \frac{V_S}{R} R e^{-\frac{t}{CR}} = V_S(1 - e^{-\frac{t}{CR}})$$

After one time constant the voltage across the capacitor is: $6(1 - 0.368) = 3.8$ volts. See the graph above.

At that time, the voltage across the resistor is $V_R = V_S - V_C = 6 - 3.8 = 2.2$ volts. After a time of 2CR the factor is now $1/e^2 = 0.135$, the current will have dropped to 0.0017A, and the voltage across the capacitor risen to 5.12 volts. Can you show that it takes a time of 4.6CR for the capacitor pd to reach 99% of the supply voltage?

The circuit on the right is one typically used for **capacitor discharge**. The capacitor is charged with the switch at position $S_1$ (no resistor this time so it charges 'instantly'). The switch is then moved to position $S_2$ and the clock starts for discharge of the capacitor through the resistor. I've chosen smaller values for 'C' and 'R' this time. The previous charging circuit could have just about used a hand timer to record the data, but the time constant in this circuit is far too short and would require an interface and software.

The capacitor would be charged to a pd of 9volts by the battery, so this is the initial voltage $V_0$ of the capacitor at the start of the discharge. The discharge circuit is like the charging circuit without the chemical battery, so the maths is very similar:

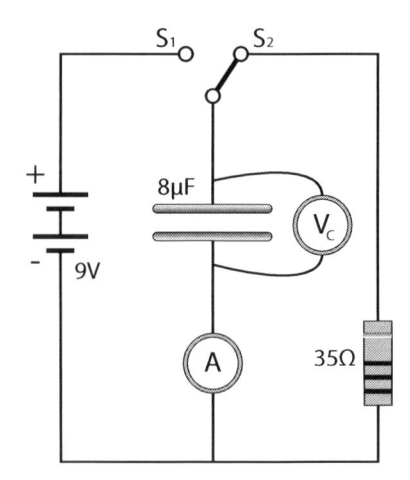

$$0 = V_C + V_R = \frac{Q}{C} + IR$$

$$0 = \frac{1}{C}\frac{dQ}{dt} + R\frac{dI}{dt}$$

$$0 = \frac{I}{C} + R\frac{dI}{dt}$$

$$0 = \frac{I}{CR} + \frac{dI}{dt}$$

$$I = I_o e^{-\frac{t}{CR}} \qquad I_o = \frac{V_0}{R}$$

This is the same as for the charging current with the same time constant. The values on the diagram give a time constant of $CR = 8 \times 10^{-6} \times 35 = 0.28$ms and an initial current of $9/35 = 0.257$A. The pd across the capacitor is the same magnitude but opposite polarity to the pd across the resistor. From the current we can derive an expression for the pd across the resistor.

$$I = I_o e^{-\frac{t}{CR}} = \frac{V_0}{R} e^{-\frac{t}{CR}}$$

$$V_R = IR = R \times \frac{V_0}{R} e^{-\frac{t}{CR}} = V_o e^{-\frac{t}{CR}}$$

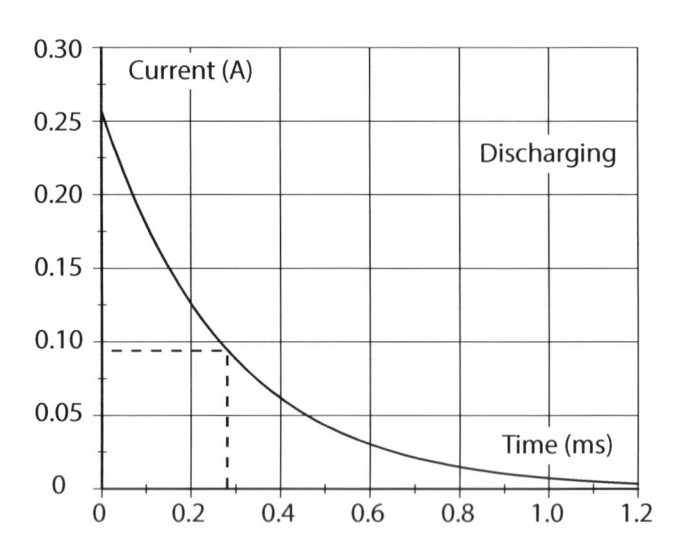

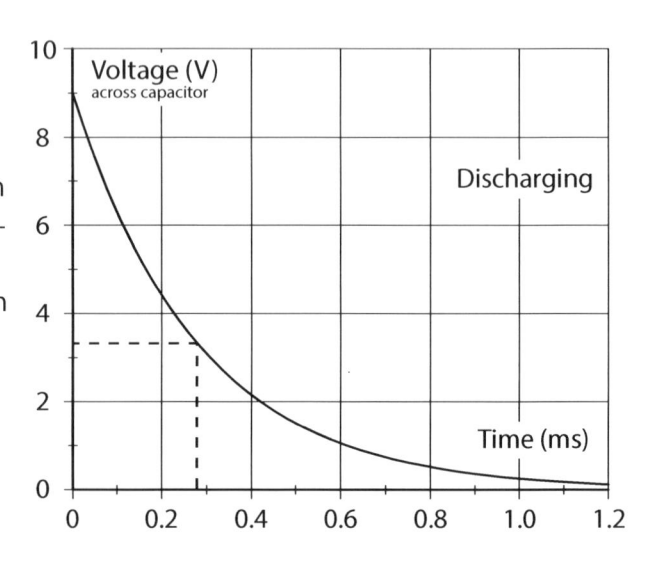

The pd across the capacitor is of the same shape and is drawn on the lower graph. We now understand the qualitative results from Higher Physics on the effect of increasing or decreasing the capacitance or resistance. The shapes of the graphs are exponentials and the charge/discharge time is controlled by the product capacitance times resistance.

# Electromagnetism

## Capacitors and A.C.

A resistor with current 'I' flowing through it will have a potential difference 'V' across it. The ratio of these two quantities V/I is a useful way of describing the behaviour of a resistor in a circuit. We can form the same ratio for capacitors, even though current doesn't flow 'through' them. It's commonly used to describe capacitors in A.C. circuits where it's known as the 'reactance' rather than the 'resistance'. The symbol is $X_C$ and is in units of ohms.

The circuit on the right shows a capacitor connected to an A.C. supply. The capacitor is the only other active component in the circuit and we assume a perfect ammeter, so the supply r.m.s. voltage equals the r.m.s. voltage across the capacitor. Both meters are set to measure A.C. values.

In A.C. circuits, the resistance of a resistor stays constant regardless of the supply frequency, the current or the voltage. For capacitors we will discover that the ratio V/I depends on the frequency 'f'. We model the supply voltage as a sinewave with peak voltage $V_o$:

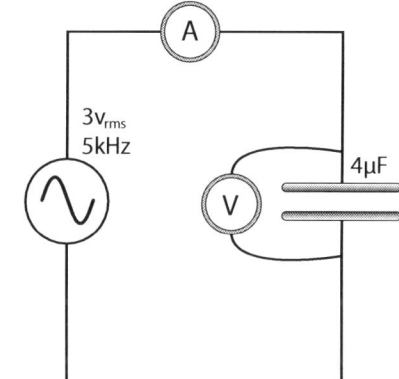

$$Q = CV$$

$$I = \frac{dQ}{dt} = \frac{dCV}{dt} = C\frac{dV}{dt} \qquad V = V_o \sin \omega t$$

$$I = C\frac{dV}{dt} = C\frac{d}{dt}(V_o \sin \omega t) = CV_o \frac{d}{dt}(\sin \omega t)$$

$$I = \omega C V_o \cos \omega t = I_o \cos \omega t$$

$$X_C = \frac{V_o}{I_o} = \frac{1}{\omega C} = \frac{1}{2\pi f C}$$

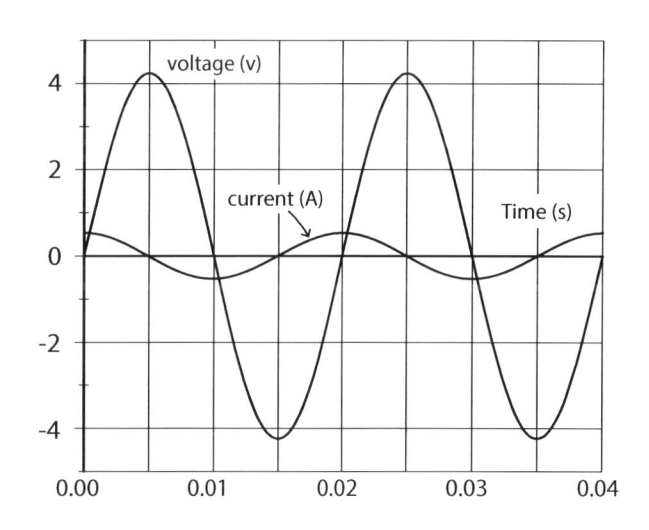

The frequency dependence is on the bottom line, so the higher the frequency the lower the reactance (when you see the word 'reactance', think of ohms). A low reactance means that a large alternating current will flow from a low voltage a.c. supply. The capacitance 'C' is also on the bottom line, so more farads means lower reactance. Plotting reactance against frequency is the smart thing to do. A plot of current against frequency *for constant voltage* would be a straight line through the origin.

The voltage/time and current/time graphs for the values in the top circuit are plotted above. Voltage follows a sine curve and current follows a cosine curve. This means they are out of step by 90°. The current reaches its peak first so is 90° ahead of the voltage. Compare with a resistor where current and voltage are in step. The peak voltage is $3\sqrt{2} = 4.24$ volts and the peak current is $\omega C V_o = 0.533\,A$.

**Example**  Calculate the capacitive reactance $X_C$ of a capacitor if a current of 0.03A r.m.s. flows in the circuit when it's connected to a supply of 12volts r.m.s.

$$X_C = \frac{V}{I} = \frac{12}{0.03} = 400\,\Omega$$

The current and the voltage are out of phase in a capacitor and this has implications when we consider circuits with several components. A mathematical device called a phasor is used to make the calculations simpler and we illustrate its use with a resistor and capacitor in series.

## Phasors

A phasor is a radius of a circle, labelled 'A' on the diagram at right. The length of it is equal to the peak value of the waveform. If it's a voltage waveform like $V = V_o \sin \omega t$, the radius equals $V_o$, and the 'y' on the diagram is the instantaneous value of the voltage. For a sinewave like this, the phasor moves around at a constant rate in the direction shown. The angular frequency 'ω' is related to the angle 'θ' in the usual way $\theta = \omega t$. The phasor diagram is a snapshot of an instant in time. The beauty of this approach is that you can draw two phasors on the same diagram and instantly see the phase relation between them. We use phasors to analyse the CR series circuit.

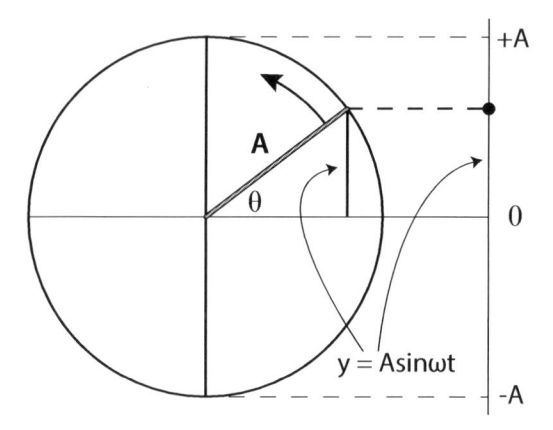

## CR Series Circuit

The current is the same at all points in a series circuit and provides a handy reference when studying the voltages across the circuit components. The supply is sinewave AC of peak voltage $V_S$ driving a current $I$. This current can be represented by a phasor rotating at the supply frequency 'f' (top diagram below). The voltages across the resistor and capacitor can be represented by phasors (lower diagram left). The voltage across the resistor is in phase with the current, but the voltage across the capacitor is 90° behind the current. These two diagrams are a snapshot at the same instant. The supply voltage $V_S$ is the sum of the two out of phase voltages $V_R$ and $V_C$. They are added using a right angled triangle (this can be proved using energy conservation).

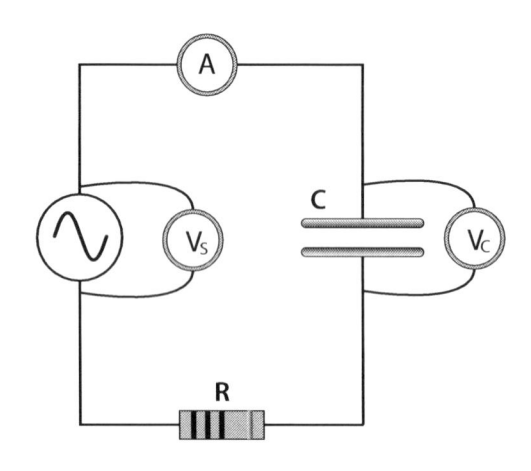

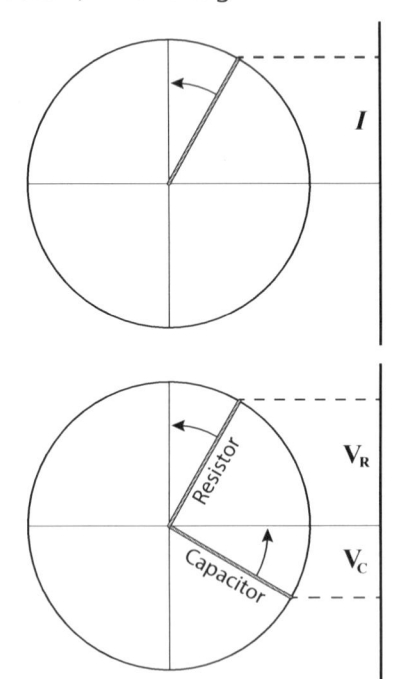

Using Pythagoras Theorem:

$$V_S^2 = V_R^2 + V_C^2$$

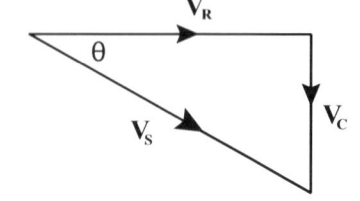

Now write each of these voltages as a product of a current times a 'resistance':

$$I^2 Z^2 = I^2 R^2 + I^2 X_C^2$$

The left hand side represents the overall circuit, so $Z = V_S / I$ is the 'resistance' of the whole circuit. But the word isn't 'resistance', it's 'impedance'. So we have three words for this thing measured in ohms: *resistance* for things which produce heat, *reactance* for things which limit the current but don't produce heat, and *impedance* for circuits which do both. Resistors have resistance, capacitors only have reactance; inductors can have both resistance and reactance. You'll come across different definitions, but this is the coolest. (Okay, for nerds: impedance can be expressed as a complex number, with resistance the real part and reactance the imaginary part).

Cancel the $I^2$'s in the above equation and substitute for the capacitive reactance:

$$I^2 Z^2 = I^2 R^2 + I^2 X_C^2 \quad \Rightarrow \quad Z^2 = R^2 + X_C^2 = R^2 + \frac{1}{\omega^2 C^2} \quad \Rightarrow \quad Z = \sqrt{R^2 + \left(\frac{1}{2\pi f C}\right)^2}$$

At a frequency of 0Hz (aka. D.C.), the circuit impedance is infinite (as it should be due to the capacitor). As the frequency increases, the circuit impedance drops to reach a constant R ohms. The voltages across

# Electromagnetism

the resistor and capacitor give us the ability to selectively reject low or high frequencies. Taking the output voltage as the voltage across the capacitor gives us a low pass filter ie. one which passes low frequencies and blocks high frequencies (graph below left). If you take the output across the resistor, you have a high pass filter; it passes high frequencies and blocks low frequencies (graph below right).

The graphs below are drawn for a CR series circuit with resistance 60ohms and capacitance 8μF. The vertical scale is the voltage ratio of output/input and the frequency scale is logarithmic (making what is a gentle slope look steeper than it is!)

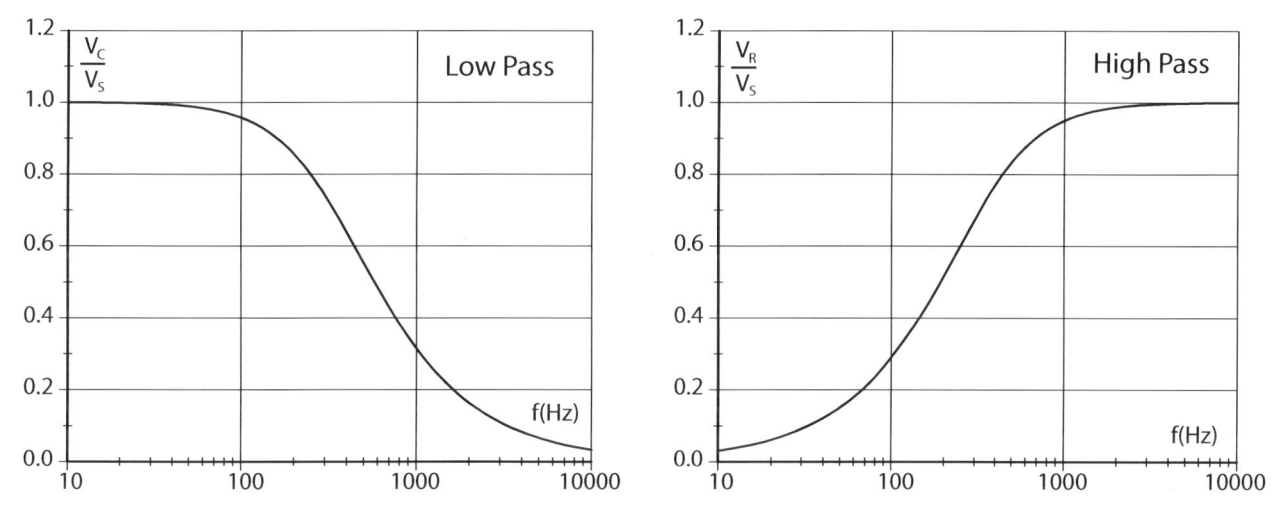

The slopes in these graphs are quite gentle. A steeper fall-off would be desirable in many applications.

## Section 3.2b Inductors

An 'experiment' which students remember for years and years is the one where they get a shock when a switch is opened in a circuit. Teachers are fond of the experiment, not just because of its 'impact', but because it's so simple, it's direct, and it always works as intended. Here's the circuit:

Volunteers are invited to hold a lead in each hand. The switch is closed then opened (opening it produces the interesting bit). The teacher starts off with a small coil with no core (where you don't feel anything), then in stages, goes to lots of turns with a core. The electric shock can be quite 'memorable'. Adopt a responsible attitude.

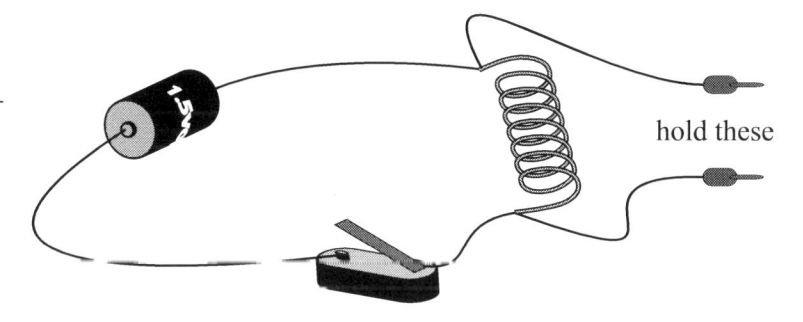

A more gentle introduction to the idea that 'there is something odd going on', is the circuit below.

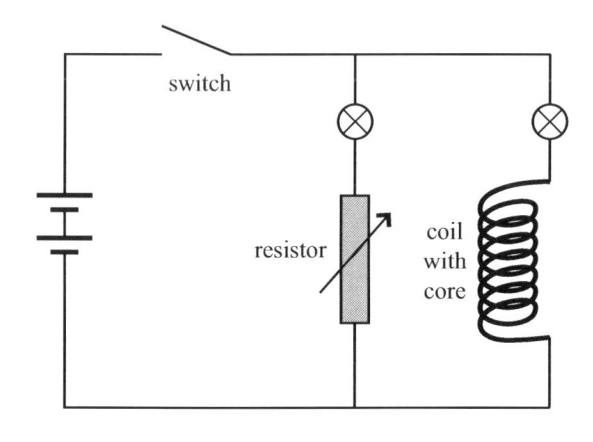

Start with a coil but no core. Close the switch and adjust the variable resistor until the two bulbs have the same brightness (so the resistor and coil have the same resistance). Open the switch. Put a core inside the coil. Close the switch and you should notice that the bulb beside the coil comes on about a second later than the other bulb. If it doesn't, go and fetch a bigger inductor (one with a low resistance). The effect indicates a slow build-up in the current in the inductor. It's as if the battery isn't the only emf in town. By comparison, the resistor reacts instantly and goes about the business of converting electrical energy into heat energy.

These odd effects produced by changing currents in coils were investigated during the first half of the 19th century by Michael Faraday. You've already met the transformer and used the relationship connecting the turns ratio with the voltage ratio. That's an example of a system with two separate circuits, the primary and the secondary circuits. A changing current (from an a.c. supply) in the primary circuit produces (a better word is 'induces') a current to flow in the secondary circuit.

Textbooks often describe it as producing a voltage in the secondary circuit (which drives the secondary current), but they don't use the word 'voltage'; they use the term 'emf'. There is a Law of Electromagnetism which states that the emf produced in the secondary circuit is proportional to the rate of change of current in the primary circuit: $emf_{(sec)} \propto \dfrac{dI_P}{dt}$. The constant of proportionality when using the two coils is called the 'mutual inductance'. An emf is not only produced in the secondary coil; the changing current in the primary coil produces an emf in its own coil! Once again, this emf is proportional to the rate of change of current: $emf_{(prim)} \propto \dfrac{dI_P}{dt}$. This time, the constant of proportionality is called the 'self inductance'. In this course, we don't study mutual inductance, only self inductance (with the signs of quantities, + and -, playing a big part).

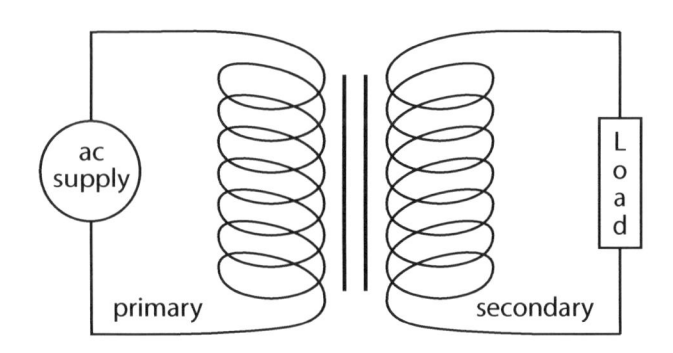

## The Definition of Inductance

From now on, we only consider self-inductance, the effect of a changing current in a coil producing an emf across its ends. At this point, it's traditional to divert off into what's called 'flux'. I'm not going to follow this route, and instead, continue to describe the effect as due to a changing current (rather than a rate of change of flux, which is the usual expression of Faraday's Law). A changing current through a coil produces a voltage across its ends. Expressed mathematically, this is:

$$E \propto -\dfrac{dI}{dt} \quad \Rightarrow \quad E = -L\dfrac{dI}{dt}$$

The 'E' is the emf in volts across the ends of the coil and you'll have noticed the minus sign. This tells you the polarity of the voltage. It is such that it opposes the change in current (hence the term 'back emf'). This is an important point and I'll return to it shortly. For the moment, let's concentrate on the 'L'. This is the self-inductance (or just simply the 'inductance') of the coil. Like all physical quantities, it has a unit. In the S.I. system, it is the Henry (H). We now have our definition:

*a rate of change of current of 1amp per second in a coil of inductance 1Henry*

*will produce an emf of 1volt across its ends*

**Example 1**   The current in a coil increases uniformly from 3A to 8A in a time of 0.12s. Calculate the emf induced across its ends if the coil has an inductance of 0.5H.

$$\dfrac{\Delta I}{\Delta t} = \dfrac{(8-3)}{0.12} = 41.\dot{6}\,\text{A s}^{-1} \quad \Rightarrow E = -L\dfrac{dI}{dt} = -0.5 \times 41.\dot{6} = -20.8\,\text{volts}$$

**Example 2**   At a certain instant, the back emf across a coil is 75volts. Calculate the rate of change of current if the coil had an inductance of 32mH.

$$E = -L\dfrac{dI}{dt} \quad \Rightarrow \quad -75 = -0.032 \times \dfrac{dI}{dt} \quad \Rightarrow \quad \dfrac{dI}{dt} = \dfrac{75}{0.032} = 2344\,\text{A s}^{-1}$$

# Electromagnetism

Suppose you wanted to increase the back emf (E). From the defining equation, you have two options, increase the 'L' or increase the rate of change of current. When you open a switch in a series circuit, the rate of change of current is extremely high; this is why you get a shock when opening the switch, but not when closing it (like the experiment on page 193). The other way of increasing the back emf is by increasing the inductance 'L' of the coil. The inductance just depends upon the geometry of the coil and the number of turns of wire. Placing a lump of soft-iron core down the middle of the coil will dramatically increase the inductance.

The inductance of a close-packed coil with no core (like the one on the right) is: $L = \mu_o n^2 lA$ where 'n' is the number of turns per metre of length, 'A' is the cross-sectional area of the coil (usually a disc shape) and the length of the coil is 'l'. The term 'lA' is the volume of the coil, and is in metres cubed. It is usually a small number for typical coils found in schools. With $\mu_o$ being small, the only hope of getting a reasonable inductance with an air core is the 'n' term (and being squared is useful). The 'n' in the formula is obtained by dividing by the number of turns by the length of the coil (not the length of the wire).

## Lenz's Law

To a student, this often feels like another one of these mystery areas in magnetism. Think of it this way; Faraday's Law gives the size of the induced emf across the ends of the coil and Lenz's Law tells you which end is positive and which is negative. There are more complicated and confusing ways of expressing Lenz's Law, but roughly speaking, it says that the induced emf will oppose the change in current. If the current is increasing, then the induced emf will try to stop it increasing. This is shown in the circuit diagram below left. If the current is decreasing, the induced emf will try to stop it decreasing. This is the circuit diagram below right. It's the Battle of the EMF's!

In the circuit diagrams below, look at the polarity of the battery and of the back emf across the coil. In the left diagram it's like two cells connected the 'wrong way around' (see how the positives are back to back). This is how the back emf resists the build-up of current. In the right circuit diagram it's like two cells connected the correct way (joined positive to negative). This is how the back emf tries to maintain the current.

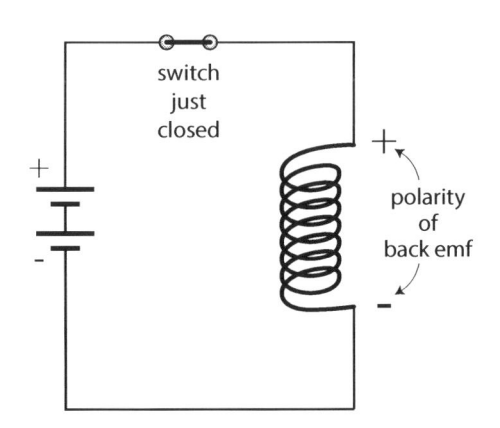

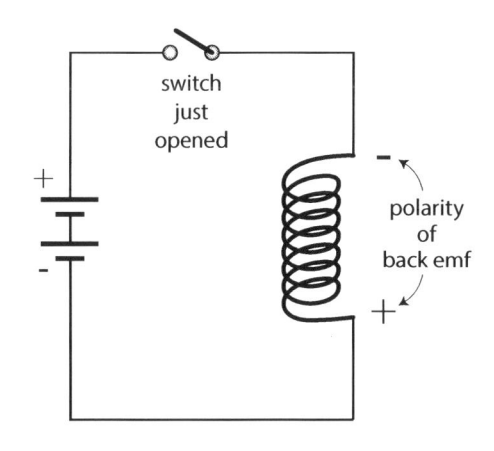

Consider what happens when you push a bar magnet towards a loop of wire. The loop feels a changing magnetic field and generates a current. This current makes its own magnetic field. Use the left-hand rule with the direction of the current in the loop as in the diagram. You should get the field lines coming out from the centre towards the left. Magnetic field lines come out from north poles, so magnetic north is to the left of the loop. This repels the north pole of the bar magnet. In this way, the current generated opposes the bar magnet (that's also Lenz's Law).

Lenz's Law is really an expression of conservation of energy. Consider what would happen if things were the opposite of Lenz's Law. Rather than being opposed, the bar magnet would be pulled in faster, generating a bigger current which would pull it in even faster etc. etc. On passing through to the other side, the real Lenz's Law would generate a magnetic field from the loop which would try to stop the bar magnet; whereas the 'opposite of Lenz's Law' would repel the bar magnet. What you'd have is a gun which shoots magnetic missiles! The Law of Conservation of Energy doesn't allow that to happen.

**Resistance, Capacitance and Inductance**

These are the properties of components where a voltage is compared to the current flowing through it, the charge stored by it and the rate of change of current within it. Resistors are devices which convert electrical energy into heat energy (heat is the tell-tale sign of resistance in a circuit). Capacitors are devices which store energy in an electric field. Inductors are devices which store energy in a magnetic field. Together, they make an orchestra of only three players; but one which is capable of playing many tunes.

**The Build-Up of Current through an Inductor**

If you switch on a circuit consisting only of a battery and resistances, the current reaches its steady value almost immediately. At switch-on, a circuit with an inductor will produce a back emf across the inductor and oppose the build-up of current. Large inductances can prevent the current from reaching a steady value for several seconds.

The circuit in the diagram on the right has a battery with an emf of 3volts driving current through a 2Ω resistor and a 0.25H inductor. Think of the circuit as being in two parts; a part which stores electrical energy (the sources of emf, that is, the battery and the back emf of the inductor), and a part which converts that electrical energy into heat (the resistor and possibly the resistance of the wire of the coil). You may recall a voltage rule for series circuits when you first encountered electricity: 'the sum of the voltages around the circuit equals the battery voltage'. Assuming no internal resistance in the emfs, our version is: 'the sum of the emf's equals the sum of the pd's around the circuit'. As an equation, this is:

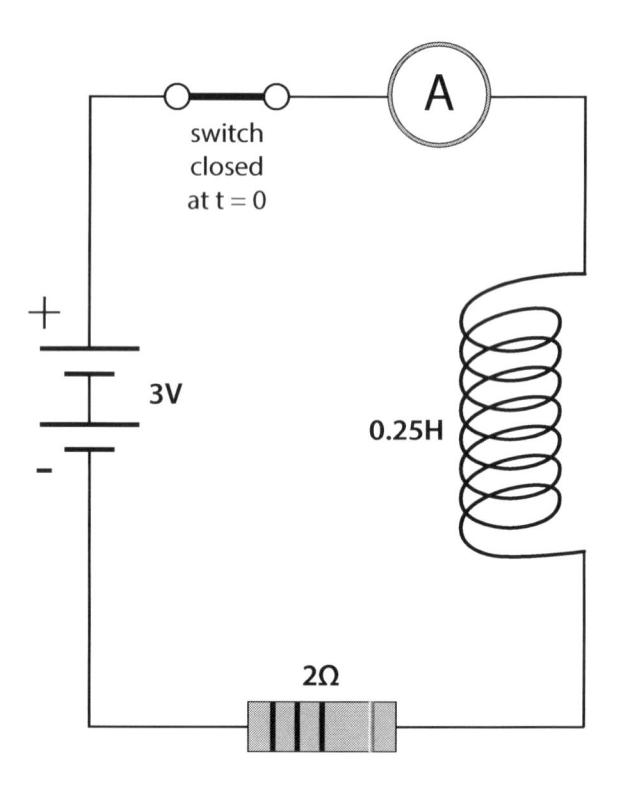

$$E_{batt} + E_{back\ emf} = IR \quad \Rightarrow \quad E_{batt} - L\frac{dI}{dt} = IR$$

The current '$I$' and the time '$t$' are the variables; the '$E_{batt}$', '$L$' and '$R$' are the constants. It's an example of a first order differential equation. The solution expresses the current as a function of time.

# Electromagnetism

Here is the result plotted graphically. It's often described in books as 'exponential growth', but obviously isn't since it tails off to a constant level.

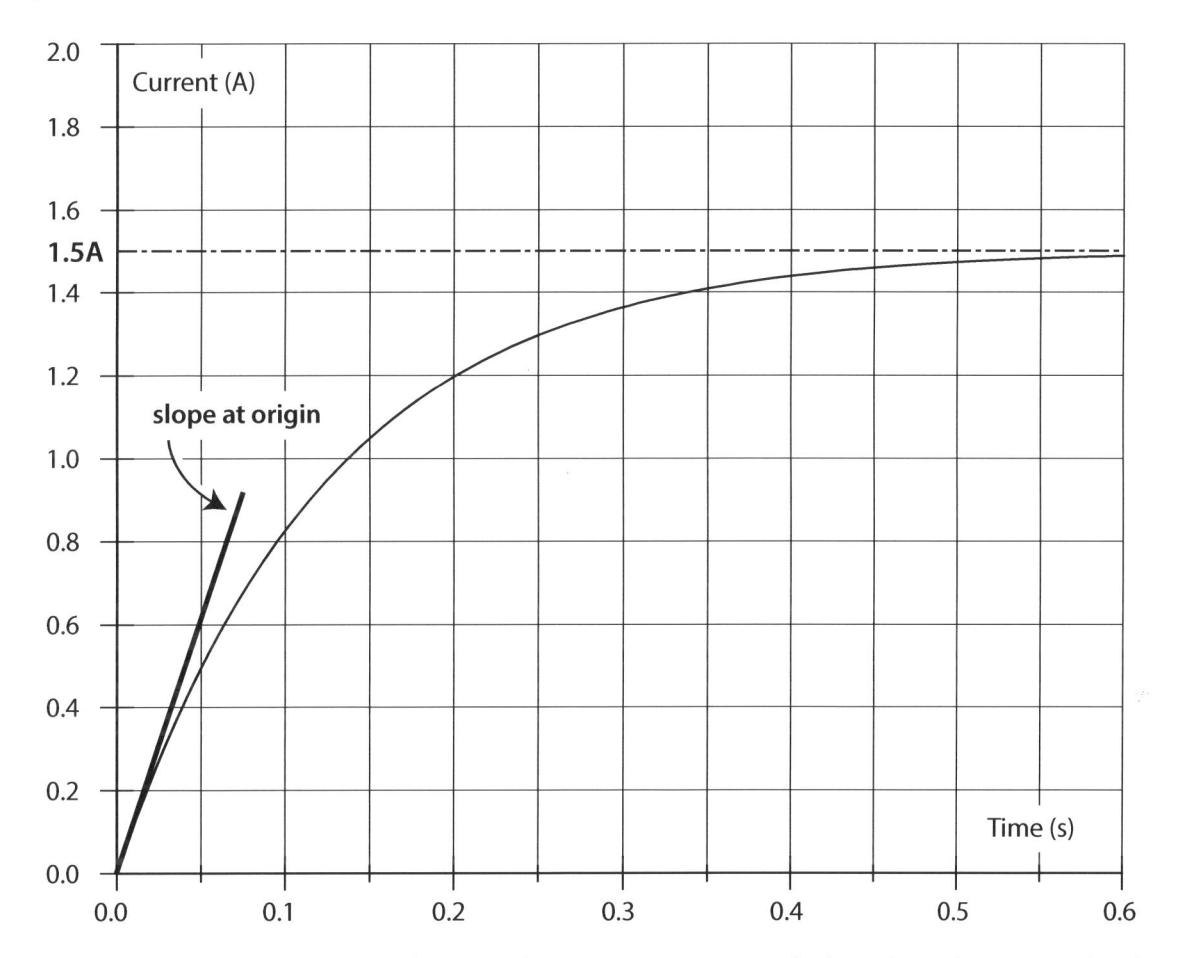

You can see the gradual build-up of current from zero to 1.5A. With the values chosen, it takes less than a second. If you removed the inductor, it would rise straight from zero to 1.5A. In addition to the final value of 1.5A (the dotted line), I've marked on the **gradient of the curve at the origin**. If you didn't know the value of the inductance, this gradient is used to measure it. Plotting the current against time means that the gradient is $\frac{dI}{dt}$. At the origin (time = 0), the current is zero, so this gives:

$$E_{batt} - L\frac{dI}{dt} = IR \quad \Rightarrow \quad E_{batt} - L \times \text{gradient at origin} = 0 \times R \quad \Rightarrow \quad \text{gradient at origin} = \frac{E_{batt}}{L}$$

With a 3volt battery and a 0.25H inductor, this gives a gradient of 12 amps per second (A s$^{-1}$). Your big problem is measuring the gradient at the origin from a graph. It's a favourite exam question and it's difficult to be accurate. Just place your ruler at the origin and swing it about a bit until it 'looks ok'!!

Predicting the value at which the current levels off (1.5A in the example) is easy. The gradient becomes zero so the basic circuit equation becomes:

$$E_{batt} - L\frac{dI}{dt} = IR \quad \Rightarrow \quad E_{batt} - L \times 0 = IR \quad \Rightarrow \quad I = \frac{E_{batt}}{R} \qquad \left(1.5 = \frac{3}{2}\right)$$

At values in between (eg. at a current of 1.2A), the equation is:

$$E_{batt} - L\frac{dI}{dt} = IR \quad \Rightarrow \quad 3 - 0.25 \times \frac{dI}{dt} = 1.2 \times 2 \quad \Rightarrow \quad \frac{dI}{dt} = 2.4 \text{A s}^{-1}$$

At this time, the back emf is: $-L\frac{dI}{dt} = -0.25 \times 2.4 = -0.6$ volts and the potential difference across the resistor is: $IR = 1.2 \times 2 = 2.4$ volts. In numbers, the equation becomes: (3.0 - 0.6 = 2.4 volts). The first order differential equation we've been using has a mathematical solution:

$$E_{batt} - L\frac{dI}{dt} = IR \qquad \text{solution is:} \quad I = \frac{E_{batt}}{R}\left(1 - e^{-\frac{R}{L}t}\right)$$

This is the equation of the curve on the graph on the previous page. It's a good exercise to try the solution in the equation and check that it works. If you have a graphics calculator, type in the solution using the data from the example above $I = 1.5(1 - e^{-8t})$ and evaluate the gradient at the origin. If you have access to Maths software like Autograph, type in the equation $y = \frac{a}{b}\left(1 - e^{-\frac{b}{c}x}\right)$ with constants a = 3, b = 2, c = 0.25 and vary the 'b' and 'c' values to show the effect of changing the inductance and resistance. This is it graphically:

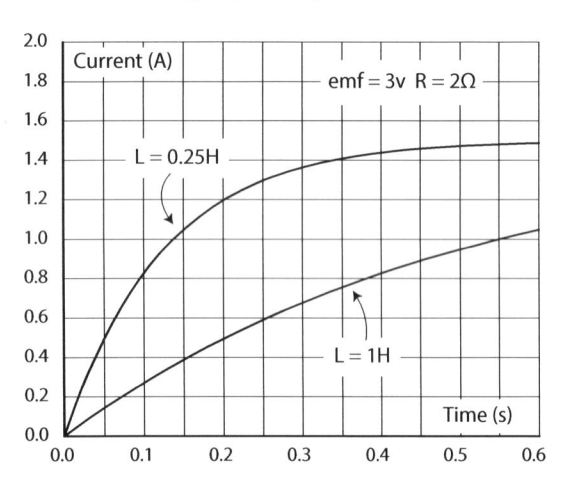

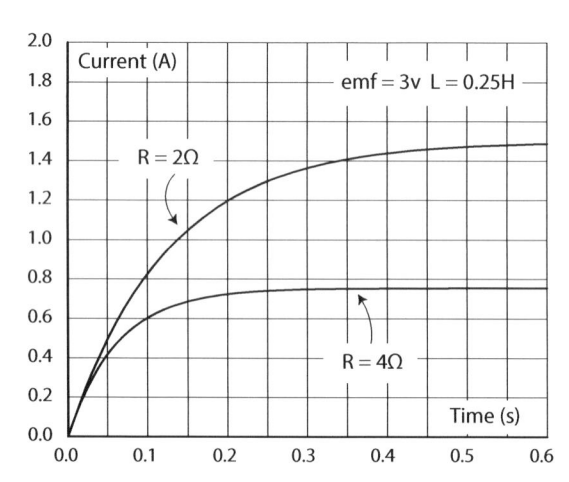

Make sure you can explain the different shapes, the gradients at the origin and the level-off currents.

## The Energy Stored in an Inductor

I'll tell you the answer first $\left(\frac{1}{2}LI^2\right)$ then show how to derive it. We already had the basic equation relating the voltages in the circuit. Our strategy is to multiply these voltages by the current to get the power, then bring in the time 't' to obtain the energy. Here goes:

$$E_{batt} - L\frac{dI}{dt} = IR \quad \Rightarrow \quad E_{batt}I - LI\frac{dI}{dt} = I^2 R \quad \Rightarrow \quad E_{batt}I = LI\frac{dI}{dt} + I^2 R$$

The left side of the last equation is the electrical power delivered by the battery and the right side shows where it goes. The last term on the right is the rate at which the resistor makes heat energy and the middle term is the rate at which energy is built up in the magnetic field of the inductor. We now bring in the time (t). The power changes with time so we have to use the integral form: ∫Pdt (instead of 'energy = Pt '). To calculate the energy stored by the inductor, just consider the middle term:

$$E = \int Pdt \quad \Rightarrow \quad \int_0^\infty LI\frac{dI}{dt}dt \quad \Rightarrow \quad \int_0^I LIdI = L\int_0^I IdI = L\left[\frac{1}{2}I^2\right]_0^I = \frac{1}{2}LI^2$$

This depends upon the current, and it implies 'no current, no energy stored'. It doesn't depend upon the time taken (unlike a resistor where the longer the time, the greater is the energy converted to heat).

**Example**     Calculate the energy stored in a 450mH inductor with a steady current of 1.8A.

$$E = \frac{1}{2}LI^2 = \frac{1}{2} \times 0.45 \times 1.8^2 = 0.729 \text{ joules}$$

# Electromagnetism

## The Decay of Current through an Inductor

Using the circuit on the right, the switch is set to position 'A' and sufficient time is allowed for the current to reach a steady value. The switch is then moved to position 'B'. A current flows as the energy stored in the magnetic field of the inductor is transferred to the resistor where it will appear as heat energy. The current starts high then decays to zero as the magnetic field collapses. We wish to plot a graph of current as a function of time. Our starting point is the equation we used before, but this time without the battery emf '$E_{batt}$':

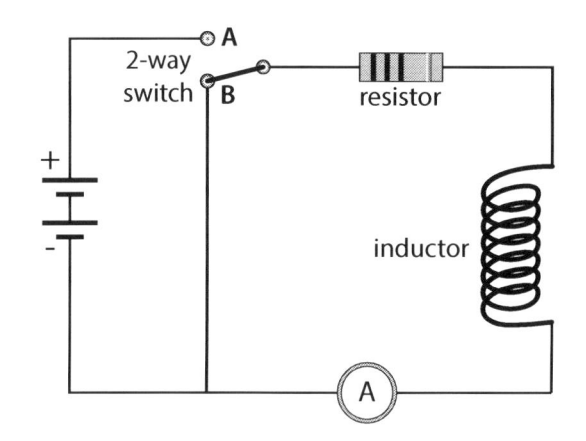

$$E_{batt} - L\frac{dI}{dt} = IR \quad \Rightarrow \quad 0 - L\frac{dI}{dt} = IR \quad \Rightarrow \quad L\frac{dI}{dt} + IR = 0$$

This is a simpler first order differential equation than the previous one. The solution is: $I = I_o e^{-\frac{R}{L}t}$ where $I_o$ is the initial current. It is the standard exponential decay curve, starting from value $I_o$ and approaching the time axis asymptotically. What is the value of the initial current? The answer is $I_o = \frac{E}{R}$.

You can't get this from the differential equation (it cancels out). It is the same value reached when the current was building-up with the switch at position 'A'. Here are typical decay curves showing the effect of changing the resistance and the inductance:

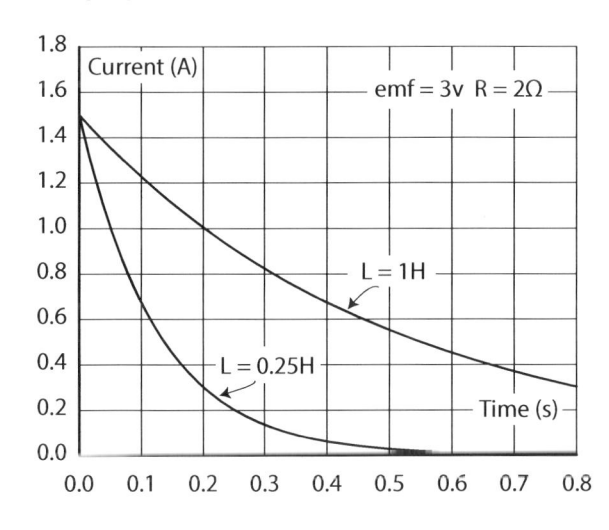

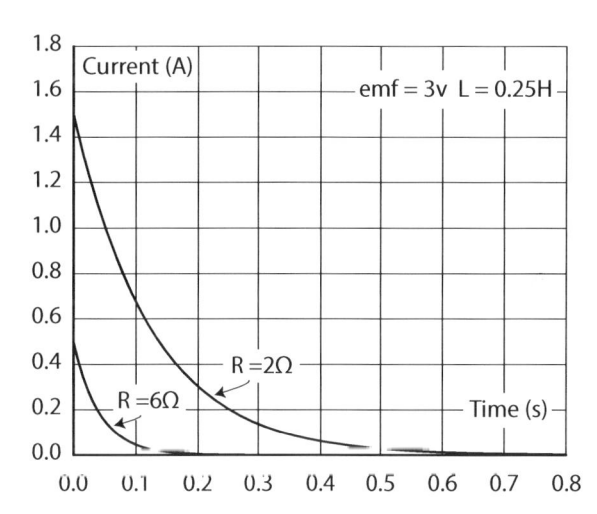

## Time Constants

Of the three components, (resistor, capacitor and inductor), the resistor reacts immediately to changes in potential difference across its ends. If a resistor is placed in series with a capacitor or inductor, the time taken can be controlled; faster or slower.

Inductor (build-up): $E_{batt} - L\frac{dI}{dt} = IR \quad \Rightarrow \quad I = \frac{E_{batt}}{R}\left(1 - e^{-\frac{R}{L}t}\right) \quad \Rightarrow \quad$ time constant $\frac{L}{R}$

..... to take a longer time, use larger 'L' and smaller 'R'.

Capacitor (charging): $E_{batt} = IR + \frac{Q}{C} \quad \Rightarrow \quad I = \frac{E_{batt}}{R}e^{-\frac{t}{CR}} \quad \Rightarrow \quad$ time constant $CR$

..... to take a longer time, use larger 'C' and larger 'R'.

# Inductors and A.C.

We've already noted that inductors produce a back emf when the current is changing. If the current changes more quickly, a bigger back emf is generated. When you increase the frequency of the supply, you change the current more quickly. So, at higher frequencies we would expect an inductor to produce a bigger back emf and 'react' more strongly against the supply. In effect, inductors don't 'like' high frequency supplies. Consider this circuit and graph:

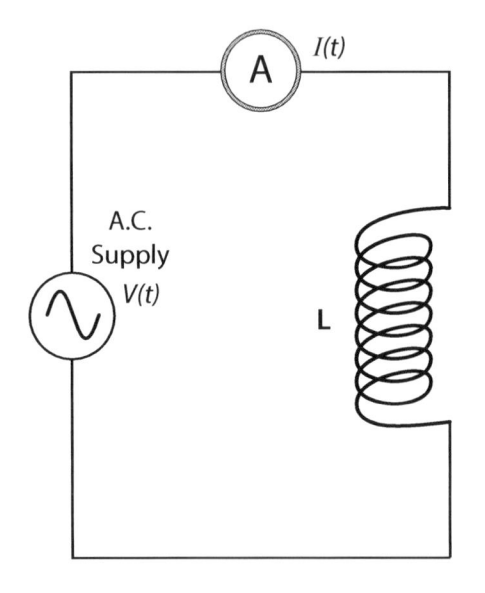

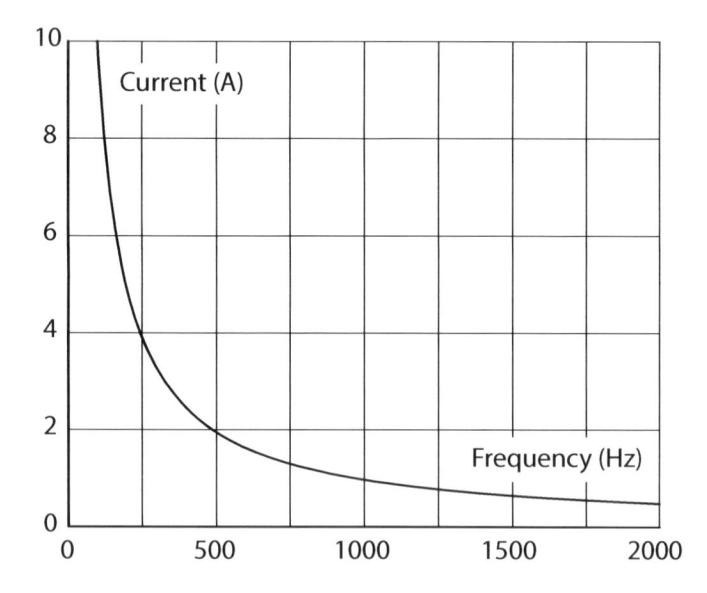

The graph shows how the current is 'choked off' at high frequencies. The data is for an ideal air filled solenoid with n = 1000 turns per metre, L = 0.2m and radius = 0.025m. The A.C. supply is 3V rms and the current readings are rms values (what you get on a digital meter display). The inductor is assumed to have no resistance and the supply has no internal resistance, so there is no limit on the current as the frequency decreases to zero (no changing current so no back emf).

The inductor is the second component we've met which displays frequency dependence. Like the capacitor, we can define a reactance for the inductor $X_L$ from the ratio of voltage to current. And like the capacitor, it's measured in ohms and is frequency dependent. Here's how to derive the reactance.

The circuit above has supply $V(t)$ driving a current $I(t)$. It's like the basic circuit on page 196 without the resistor 'R', so we start with the basic equation with R = 0. I've also used a sinewave for the supply voltage to be consistent with the derivation of capacitive reactance.

$$V(t) - L\frac{dI(t)}{dt} = 0 \quad \Rightarrow \quad V(t) = L\frac{dI(t)}{dt}$$

$$\int V(t)dt = L\int dI(t) \qquad V(t) = V_o \sin \omega t$$

$$I(t) = \frac{1}{L}\int V_o \sin \omega t \, dt \quad \Rightarrow \quad -\frac{V_o}{\omega L}\cos \omega t$$

$$I(t) = -I_o \cos \omega t \qquad \frac{V_o}{I_o} = X_L = \omega L$$

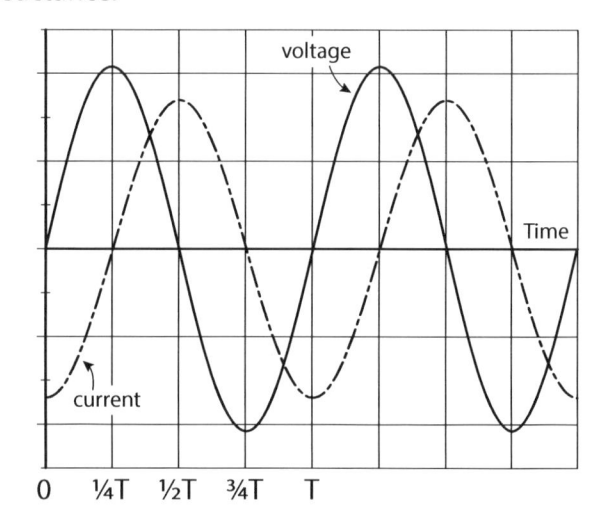

This is the inductive reactance $X_L$. It has the opposite frequency behaviour from the capacitor. This is nice. It wouldn't be much use if it was the same! The current follows a negative cosine dependence on the time. The above graph shows the current and

# Electromagnetism

voltage together. I've marked the time scale along the bottom using fractions of a period rather than numbers in seconds. The voltage reaches a peak at a time of ¼T whereas the current doesn't reach it until a time of ½T. Thus the voltage is 90° ahead of the current in an inductor. Note that this assumed no resistance 'R' in the circuit (neither as an outside resistor nor as resistance of the inductor coils). If there is resistance, the phase difference is less than 90°.

**Example:** Calculate the reactance of a 20mH inductance connected to a sinewave AC supply of frequency 300Hz.

$$X_L = \omega L = 2\pi f L = 2\pi \times 300 \times 0.02 = 37.7\Omega$$

## LCR Resonance Circuits

We now understand the behaviour of the three basic circuit components: resistor, capacitor and inductor. Resistors are indifferent to changes in frequency. Capacitors and inductors have the opposite dependence on frequency. With capacitors, it's easier to pass current at high frequencies. This is quite neat, since you can now design circuits to block out high frequency signals (use an inductor) or allow them to flow (use a capacitor). Put both an inductor and a capacitor in a series circuit and you can block both high and low frequency signals allowing a middle range to pass current. Put an inductor and a capacitor in parallel and you can pass both high and low frequency signals while blocking out a middle range. Below is the series circuit which passes a narrow range of middle frequencies.

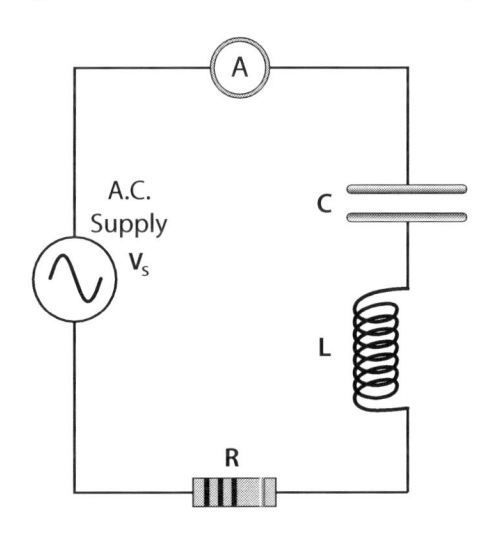

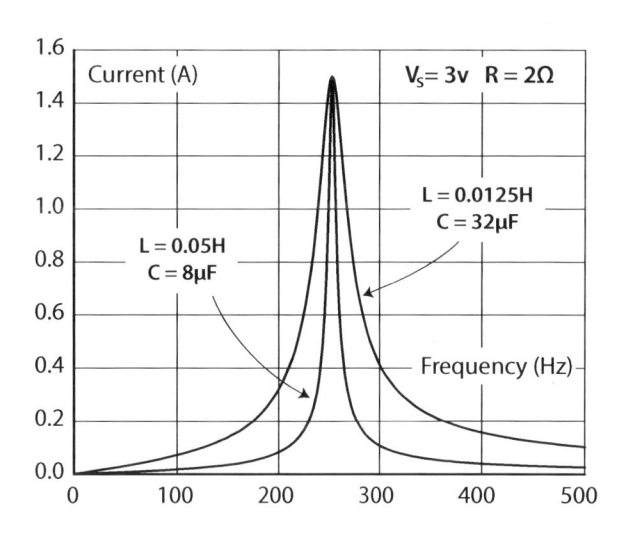

The analysis of the circuit is a bit beyond what we've covered so far. Phase comes into it with the current in all parts of the circuit being in step, but the voltages across the capacitor and inductor are 180° out of step. The area around the peak of the graph is the 'middle bit' I mentioned. At lower frequencies, the capacitor reduces the current, and at higher frequencies the inductor reduces the current. The frequency at the peak is called the resonance frequency and is given by $f_o = \dfrac{1}{2\pi\sqrt{LC}}$. The resistor in the circuit prevents a short circuit (I've chosen a 2Ω resistor with a supply of 3v rms, giving a limiting current of 1.5A). The resistance of the coils of the inductor (that's old fashioned resistance, not reactance) can be included in the 'R' value.

The expression for the resonance frequency contains the product LC. You could double the capacitance, half the inductance and still keep the resonance frequency constant. But you would change the sharpness of the peak. The graph above shows two combinations of capacitance and inductance which have the same product, and hence the same resonance frequency of 252Hz, but have a quite different effect upon the shape of the curve. This width is important in electrical tuning applications where you may need to tune in to a very narrow range of frequencies.

# Section 3.3 Electromagnetic Radiation

Nothing isn't the same as neutral. Neutral is the cancellation of two quantities of equal size but opposite sign. A vacuum is the kind of neutral which doesn't show-up in experiments. It appears like 'nothing' until you disturb it. Shaking an electric charge disturbs the vacuum. A ripple, where the cancellation is temporarily upset, travels through empty space at the speed of light. We call it an electromagnetic wave. Once it passes, the vacuum returns to neutrality.

James Clerk Maxwell was the first to discover the connection between electricity, magnetism and light rays. He took the equations based on Faraday's experiments plus the work of Ampere and Gauss, added his own contribution, and fiddled about with the maths. Out popped the speed of light.

As mentioned on page 184, the speed of light in a vacuum is related to the permeability and permittivity of free space through the relation $c^2 = \dfrac{1}{\varepsilon_o \mu_o}$. The permeability of free space $\mu_o$ has a value of $4\pi \times 10^{-7}$ and was chosen to have this value to make calculations simpler ($\pi$'s cancel out, useful if you didn't have a calculator back in 1860), and have a unit of current (the amp) of a sensible size. The speed of light was redefined in 1983 to have the exact value of 299,792,458 m/s. This means that the equation gives the permittivity of free space $\varepsilon_o$ a fixed value (it's an irrational number starting off 8.8541878.....× $10^{12}$ Fm$^{-1}$). All three quantities are fixed. We know the values exactly. We don't need to do an experiment to discover the answers.

Guess what. The syllabus calls for two experiments to measure the electric constant $\varepsilon_o$ and the magnetic constant $\mu_o$. Yes it does. So, without further ado, here are the two experiments.

### 'Measuring' the Permittivity of Free Space $\varepsilon_o$

You have to find an equation containing the permittivity of free space $\varepsilon_o$ and then measure all the other quantities in the equation. The standard experiment uses the circuit on the right. The capacitor isn't the usual disc or rolled-up little cylinder. Each plate is a square about 30cms on a side and consists of aluminium foil flattened over a rigid plastic sheet. The two identical plates are held apart by insulating spacers (several millimetres thick) at each corner. It looks just like the symbol for a capacitor and its capacitance is given by:

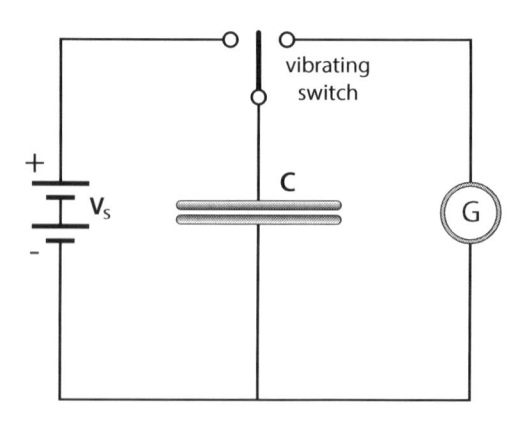

$$C = \dfrac{\varepsilon_o A}{d}$$

The area of overlap of the plates 'A' is 0.3m × 0.3m and the separation is 'd' (a few millimetres). We find the capacitance 'C' from the defining equation $Q = CV$. The circuit is a charge / discharge one without any resistor so the time constant is very short. The switch isn't the usual type of three-way switch. This one vibrates back and forwards between the charge (left contact) and the discharge (right contact) circuits at a frequency of 50Hz. Every 1/50$^{th}$ of a second the capacitor gets a charge 'Q' (the time constant is much less than this so the capacitor gets its full whack). And the next 1/50$^{th}$ of a second the capacitor gets discharged through the ammeter (again, the time constant is much smaller, ideal ammeters have no resistance, so it fully discharges). The charge $Q = It$ where '$I$' is the current on the ammeter.

$$Q = CV_S \quad \Rightarrow \quad Q = \dfrac{\varepsilon_o A}{d} V_S$$

$$Q = It \quad \Rightarrow \quad It = \dfrac{\varepsilon_o A}{d} V_S \quad \Rightarrow \quad \varepsilon_o = \dfrac{Itd}{AV_S}$$

# Electromagnetism

Before setting-up the experiment, you should do a quick calculation to get an idea of the sizes. We know the answer (remember?) and for 30cm×30cm plates 5mm apart you will get about 1.5μA current with a D.C. supply of 200volts. This means it's dangerous (near mains voltage with only a few mm separation), and that you need a good ammeter. The classic ammeter was a ballistic galvanometer (reach right in to the back of the cupboard and watch out for any dust on the box). That's why there's a 'G' in the circuit symbol. This thing doesn't have a calibrated scale; you have to do a separate experiment with a battery and a big resistance to get the same reading, then use Ohm's Law. It doesn't 'sample' readings like a digital meter and is slow to react to changes. That's why it's the right choice.

## 'Measuring' the Permeability of Free Space $\mu_o$

As before, we need an equation containing the permeability of free space and the ability to measure all the other quantities in the equation. This time it's the force on two current carrying wires as described on page 183. The apparatus is called a current balance, can be expensive, is rare in schools, and comes with variations. The diagram shows one version. Equal currents flow through the two parallel bars (supply not shown). The top bar is part of a rectangle whose weight is balanced using a small sliding weight on a rod. The currents flow through the parallel bars in opposite directions. The bottom bar is fixed, so the top bar is repelled upwards.

A light weight is placed on the top of the top bar sufficient to restore the reference marks to their previous position. The equation is:

$$\frac{F}{L} = \frac{\mu_o I_1 I_2}{2\pi r}$$

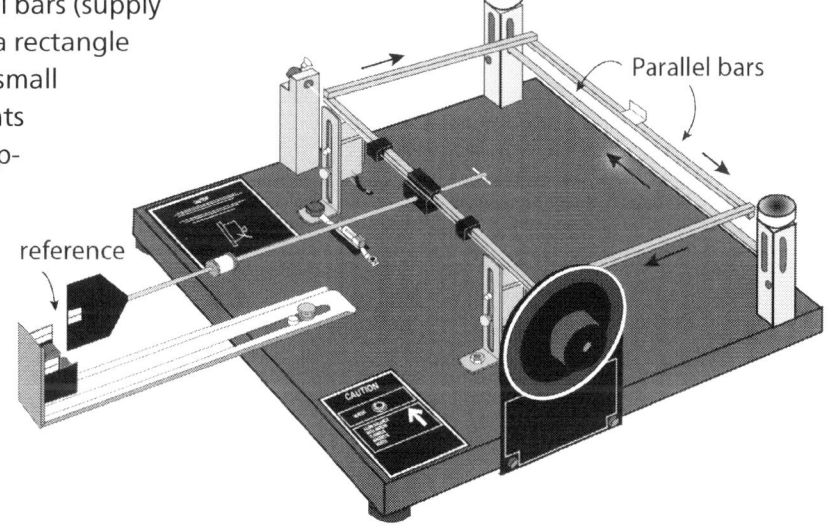

The currents $I_1$ and $I_2$ are the same magnitude, 'L' is the length of a bar, and 'r' is the separation of the parallel bars. The force 'F' equals the weight of the small mass on the top bar. It sounds simple but in practice there's a lot to it. As before, it's wise to do a calculation beforehand to get an idea of the sizes. You need quite a large current, in the range up to 10amps and the bars need to be about 1cm apart or less. The above apparatus uses two small reservoirs of warm gallium to pass a current into the rectangle with low friction. Clever. Hinges aren't used to balance the frame; this one is suspended using a wire under tension (the big dial is used to tighten and zero the reference marks). You even have to consider how the connections get from the D.C. supply to the pillars!

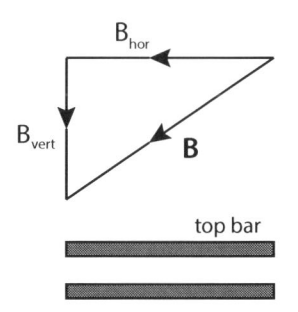

Then there's the Earth's magnetic field. This can alter your readings unless you're careful. The Earth's field ('B' on the diagram on the left) points at an angle to the ground. Split it into horizontal and vertical components as shown. If you point the parallel bars in the east-west direction, the horizontal component of the Earth's field will also be at right angles to the direction of the bars (and hence the current). Using your right hand rule, the force on the bar will either be straight up or straight down. This will mess-up your readings, so make sure and align the parallel bars along the north-south direction. The Earth's horizontal component over the UK is about 17μT. This would be the same value at the top bar due to the magnetic field of the bottom bar with a current to separation ratio ($I/r$) of 85. That's 0.85amps with the bars 1cm apart. Better to align them north-south!

# Index

## A
absolute magnitude of star  93
acceleration angular  18
acceleration centrifugal  18
acceleration centripetal  18
acceleration definition  6
acceleration tangential  18
aircraft  23
air wedge  144
ampere, definition of  183
amplitude addition of  107
angular acceleration  12, 18
angular acceleration measuring  16
angular displacement  11
angular frequency  124, 134
angular mom. conservation  44, 49
angular momentum  42
angular motion  10
angular velocity  11
antarctica  56
antinode  134
apparent brightness  94
apparent magnitude of star  93
arc second  148
Aristarchus of Samos  65
asteroid earth collision  56
Astronomical Unit  92
ATLAS experiment  184
aurora  115
   planetary  121

## B
back emf  194
balance  17
Balmer JJ  100
Barany Chair  17
beat frequency  136
Betelgeuse  149
Big Bang  85
Big Dipper  93
big G  51
big G experiment  52
Binary Pulsar  82
black-body  94, 97
Black Hole  84
Böhr Atom  100, 102
Böhr Einstein photograph  101
Boltzmann Ludwig  98
Bragg's Law  105
Brahe  66
Brewster angle  154

## C
can crusher  36
capacitor  189
   and A.C.  191
   capacitive reactance  191
   charging circuit  189
   CR series circuit  192
   discharge  190
   impedance terminology  192
   time constant  189
carbon-12  89
car on banked track  24
car on bend  20, 22
Carrington Event 1859  115
cavendish experiment  52
celtic park  56
centripetal acc at equator  21
centripetal acc derivation  20
centripetal force  21
   in magnetic field  118
Cerenkov Radiation  91
CHARA Array  149
charon satellite of pluto  68
choke  200
circular motion magnetic field  118
CNO cycle  89
coherence  138, 152
component of force aircraft  23
component of force con pend  26
Compton scattering  104
conductor field lines  162
conductor inside of  174
conductors and insulators  161
conical pendulum  26
conservation of ang momentum  49
   planets  67
constructive interference  138
conventional current  178
Copernicus  50, 65
corona  114
cosmic Dark Ages  86
cosmic microwave b/g  85, 112
cosmic neutrino background  86
cosmic rays GKZ cutoff  112
cosmic ray shower  111
Cosmic Rays introduction  111
Cosmic rays origin  113
Coulomb Charles experiment  156
Coulomb's Law  156
cross product  37
   angular momentum  44
   torque  43
CR series circuit  192
cupola  17
current balance  203
cyclotron  166
cylinder rolling down ramp  46

## D
Davisson / Germer Experiment  104
de Broglie eqn and uncertainty  108
de Broglie Louis  103
Delta particle  109, 112
deuterium  85
diamagnetism  187
diffraction  105, 148
double slit experiment  105, 146
Dubhe  93

## E
ear  17
earth and moon receeding  52
earth, magnetic field of  179, 203
earth mass of  68
earth's future  90
earth symbol  170
Eddington Sir Arthur  80, 149
Einstein and Newton  74
Einstein Ring  80
electric charge force on  156
electric constant  182
electric Fields  156
   definition of field strength  159
   lines  159
   parallel plates  162
   point charge  159
   zero points  172
electric motor  181
electromagnetic radiation  202
electromagnetic wave  152
electron volt  165
electrostatic potential  168
   energy  169
   parallel plates  170
   points of balance  171
elements, heavy, in stars  86
energy time uncert. relation  109
energy unit electron volt  165
equations of motion  6
   angular  13, 15
   derivation linear  7
equator  21
equinox  47
equipotential lines  173
equipotential surfaces gravity  60
escape velocity  63

## F
Fermi Enrico magnetic mirror  113
ferromagnetism  187
Feynman Richard  105
field gravitational  53
field lines as model  162
field lines rules for gravity  54
fluorescence, cosmic rays  112
Foucault pendulum  128
Fourier analysis  137
freefall  78
fringes  145
   diffraction effects  148
   double slit  147

## G
Galileo  50
Galileo telescope  65
Gamma Ray burst  87
Gamow George, tunnelling  110
General Relativity 1919 test  80
General Relativity introduction  78
geodesic  81
geometric path length  140
G experiment  52
GKZ cutoff  112
Gliese 710 star  76
Global Positioning System  84
God  89
G.P.Thomson Experiment  105
GRACE satellite  56
gravitation  50
gravitational field  53
   accuracy of mgh  60
   energy  57
   variation with height  55
gravitational mass  78

# Electromagnetism

gravitational potential  57
  derivation  58
gravitational potential well  61
gravitational redshift  82
gravitational wave obs.  150
gravity as a lens  80
gravity assist for satellite  70
gravity inverse square law  50
gravity mapping  56
G, universal constant  51
gyroscope  48

## H
Hall Effect  185
  quantum  186
Halloween event 2003  115
hamster wheel  26
Hanford interferometer  150
harmonics  137
Heisenberg Uncertainty eqn.  108
helium-4  85
helix  120
Hertzsprung-Russell diagram  95
higgs field  53
high pass filter  193
Hohmann transfer orbit  69
Hubble space telescope  48
hydrogen emission spectrum  100

## I
ibrox park  56
ice skater  45
impedance  192
Inductance, definition of  194
inductance of coil  195
inductive reactance  200
Inductor  193
  and A.C.  200
  back emf  194
  current build-up  196
  effect of L and R  198
  current decay  199
  energy stored  198
  mutual inductance  194
  time constant  199
inertial mass  78
inertial reference frame  74
inflation of early universe  85
Interference  97, 138, 151
  air wedge  144
  by Division of Amplitude  139, 142
  by Division of Wavefront  139, 146
  quantum  106
International Space Station  55, 71
invariant  75
inverse-square law of gravity  50
inverse square law test  157
iron-60 from supernovae  96

## J
Jonsson Claus electron interf.  106
Jupiter magnetic field  121

## K
Kelvin-Helmholtz mechanism  86
Kepler  50
  and Galileo  66
  as rebel  66
  Laws  67
kinematics  6
kinetic energy of rotation  27, 46
Kirchhoff  97
KOI-172.02 extrasolar planet  76

## L
Lagrange points  72
Laplace  64
  quotation  107
laser beam to moon  52
laser interferometry  150
LCD  155
LCR resonance  201
Leaning Tower of Pisa  78
Lenz's Law  195
light bending near sun  79
light polarised  152
lightsource  138
LIGO  150
Liquid Crystal Display  155
Livingston interferometer  150
longitudinal wave  151
low pass filter  193
luminosity  94
lunar laser ranging  51

## M
magnetic constant  182
magnetic field  116
  circular motion in  118
  coil of wire  184
  direction of force on mocing charge  116
  due to straight current-carrying wire  182
  equation for force on charged particle  116
  flux rope at sun  114
  force on a conductor  177
  introduction to  176
  iron filings around a bar magnet  177
  left hand rule  182
  Maxwell James Clerk  176
  parallel wires  183
  right hand rule  178
  solenoid  184
  vector components  118
magnetic induction  177
  measuring using balance  180
  units  178
magnitude of star  93
Malus Etienne-Louis  151
Mars magnetic field  121
mass gravitational  78
mass inertial  78
Maxwell James Clerk  152, 183
McDonald Observatory  51
Merak  93
mercury precession of orbit  81
Michell John  52
Michelson Albert  149
Millikan's oil drop experiment  167

moment of inertia  28
  example  34
  flat disc  30
  simple shapes  29
  table of shapes  34
  thin hoop  30
  thin rod  32
momentum angular  42
momentum position uncert.  108
moon  52
  journey to  62
  magnetic field  121
music  137

## N
neodymium magnet  179
nerdy notes  134
  current and charge  116
  electrostatic potential  170
  kinetic energy  49
  scalar and vector products  37
  wave equation  134
  wavetrain  143
neutrino  92
  detector  91
  oscillations  92
  sun  88, 91
Newton, field inside sphere  174
Newton's First Law  18
Newton's rings  145
Nicholson John  101
node  136
normal reaction at equator  21
normal reaction banked track  24
nuclear reactions in sun  88

## O
'Oh-my-God' particle  111
oil drop experiment  167
optical path difference  140
optical path length  140
Orion constellation  149
oscillator  98

## P
parallel plates  163
parallel wires exp.  183
paramagnetism  187
parsec  92
particle accelerator  165
particle lifetime  109
path length  140
path, quantum  107
pendulum  127
  Foucault  128
  torsional  53
permeability of free space  182, 202
  experiment to 'measure'  203
permittivity of free space  157, 202
  experiment to 'measure'  202
petrol stain  143
phasor  126
  capacitor voltage  192
Photoelectric Effect  99
  Einstein  99
  Millikan's graph  100

205

photon beam to moon  52
photon neutrality test  157
photosphere of sun  87, 113
Pierre Auger Observatory  112
pion  111
Planck's constant  99
plane of vibration  152
planetary magnetism  121
planetary motion  65
pluto mass of  68
polarisation examples  155
polarisation of light  151, 152
polaroid sheet  153
potential well  61
precession of the equinoxes  47
precession, orbit of mercury  81
Priestley Joseph  156
primary cosmic rays  111
Principle of Equivalence  78
Principle of Relativity  75
Principle of Superposition  134
Principle of Uncertainty  107
probability  106
protogalaxy  86
PSR J0737-3039  82
pulley wheel  40
pulsar  82

## Q
quantum entanglement  110
quantum Hall Effect  186
quantum interference  105
Quantum of Solace  149
quantum path  107
quantum physics  97
quantum tunnelling  110

## R
radians  10
radiant emittance  94
rainbow  155
Rayleigh Lord  97
reactance, capacitive  191
reactance, inductive  200
redshift gravitational  82
reference frame  74
reflection phase change  141
reflector on moon  51
refractive index  140
relativistic energy  76
relativistic mass as pop culture  76
resonance circuit  201
resonance frequency  201
right hand rule  116
rigid body  27
rolling cylinder  46
rotational dynamics  27
rotation axis  49
Rutherford scattering  101
 closest approach calculation  175
Rydberg constant  102

## S
saddle point, gravitational  62
Sagan Carl  70
satellite control  48

satellite, energy of  71
satellite motion above earth  69
saturn aurora  121
Schwarzschild radius  84
secondary cosmic rays  111
self inductance  194
semi-circular canals  17
simple harmonic motion  122
 angular frequency  124
 damped  130
 energy  129
 equation of motion  123
 function of position  126
 graphs  124
 restoring force  122
 weight on spring  128
sirius  76
skater  45
slingshot of satellite  70
SN-1006 supernova  96
SN1987A supernova  91
Snell's Law  154
soap bubble  143
SOHO satellite position  72
solar neutrinos  91
solar wind  113
 disruption on Earth  115
spacetime  74
spacetime curved  79
spacetime interval  75
Special Relativity introduction  73
speed of light and e/m theory  183
star brightness  92
star diameter measurement  149
star lifecycle  95
stars, earliest  86
star size and mass  95
Star Trek  95
stationary wave  134
Stefan-Boltzmann Law  94
Stefan Jozef  98
stellar interferometry  148
stellar nuclear reactions  87
stellar physics  85
Stokes George  141
Sudbury Neutrino Observatory  91
sun as red giant  90
sun event horizon  64
sun irradiance on earth  90
sun, mass of  68
sun rotation and age  89
sunspot cycle  114
sunspots  113
sun, temperature  113
supernova  96
superposition principle of  134
synchrotron  166

## T
tangential acceleration  18
Tau Ceti  94
tension in pulley  40
tension, string whirling cork  25
Tesla Nicola  179
Tesla, unit  178

thin film  142
Thomson JJ, x-ray scattering  100
time dilation in muons  111
Tonomura Akira electron interference  106
torque  36
 and moment of inertia  38
 frictional  38
 of electric motor  181
torsional pendulum  53
torsion balance  156
transformer  194
travelling wave  131
 direction of  133
 equation  132
tunnelling  110
turntable  12
twin paradox  76

## U
ultraviolet catastrophe  98
uncertainty principle  107
universal constant of gravitation  51
universe big bang  85
universe expansion z parameter  86
Ursa Major  93

## V
vacuum of space  50, 152
vega  149
velocity  7
venus  121
 magnetic field  121
 phases  65
vestibular system  17
vibration generator  134
Voyager 2 future path  70
Voyager probes  70

## W
wave equation  134
wavetrain  138, 151
whirling cork  22
 vertical  25
Wien Displacement Law  98
wing force of aircraft  23
Wolf-359  95
work done in electric and magnetic fields  120
work function  99
world lines  80

## Y
Young Thomas  97, 146
yoyo de-spin  48

Printed in Great Britain
by Amazon